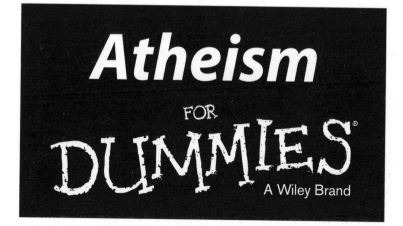

Atheism
FOR
DUMMIES
A Wiley Brand

by Dale McGowan, PhD

FOR
DUMMIES
A Wiley Brand

Atheism For Dummies®

Published by
John Wiley & Sons Canada, Ltd.
6045 Freemont Blvd.
Mississauga, ON L5R 4J3
www.wiley.com

About the Author

Dale McGowan, PhD, conducted orchestras, earned a doctorate in music composition, and spent 15 years as a college professor before chucking it all to become a writer.

Editor and co-author of *Parenting Beyond Belief* ("A compelling read"— *Newsweek*) and *Raising Freethinkers,* the two top-selling books for nonreligious parents, Dale also offers secular parenting workshops in cities across North America and writes a popular blog for nonreligious parents called "The Meming of Life" (www.parentingbeyondbelief.com\\blog).

Dale edited the historical anthology *Voices of Unbelief: Documents by Atheists and Agnostics,* and reviewers have called his satirical novel *Calling Bernadette's Bluff* "an undoubted triumph of satire" and "a riot."

He was named 2008 Harvard Humanist of the Year for his work in nonreligious parenting. In addition to writing and speaking, he is the founding executive director of Foundation Beyond Belief, a nonprofit charitable foundation focusing and encouraging humanist generosity and compassion.

Dale lives near Atlanta with his wife and three kids. To learn more or to contact Dale, visit DaleMcGowan.com.

Dedication

This book is dedicated to my parents, Dave and Carol McGowan, who raised me to be curious about the real world and never told me there was a thought I couldn't think.

To my kids, Connor, Erin, and Delaney, to whom I return the favor.

And to Becca, the perfect partner for a great adventure.

Author's Acknowledgments

Thanks first of all to the great and friendly atheist Hemant Mehta, the first person to think I'd be a good person to write this book. I'm deeply indebted to Ed Buckner and Amanda Metskas, two giants of the freethought world who took the time to read this book while it was in progress and whose rod and staff guided me when I went astray.

Greta Christina and Jennifer Michael Hecht are the two great writers and thinkers on whose work I've drawn more than any others for this project.

Immense thanks to the staff and interns at Foundation Beyond Belief who kept things humming while I wrote: Airan Wright, Brittany Shoots-Reinhard, Claire Vinyard, Kelly Wright, Walker Bristol, Joshua Brose, Cathleen O'Grady, Andrew Geary, Sam Shore, Sarah Hamilton, Kate Donovan, Chana Messinger, Corey Glasscock, Lauren Lane . . . and special praise for the dynamic duo of Noelle George and AJ Chalom.

A hat tip to my blog readers at The Meming of Life who helped plumb the depths of several big questions.

Many thanks to the professional and supportive team at John Wiley & Sons, Inc., especially Anam Ahmed and Chad Sievers, and my splendid agent Dr. Uwe Stender.

Finally, all thanks and love to my wife, Becca, who also read and improved every page, and our three spectacular kids, Connor, Erin, and Delaney. You make it all worthwhile.

Publisher's Acknowledgments

We're proud of this book; please send us your comments through our online registration form located at `http://dummies.custhelp.com`. For other comments, please contact our Customer Care Department within the United States at 877-762-2974, outside the United States at 317-572-3993, or fax 317-572-4002.

Some of the people who helped bring this book to market include the following:

Acquisitions and Editorial

Associate Acquisitions Editor: Anam Ahmed

Production Editor: Lindsay Humphreys

Project Editor: Chad R. Sievers

Copy Editor: Chad R. Sievers

Editorial Assistant: Kathy Deady

Cartoons: Rich Tennant (`www.the5thwave.com`)

Cover photo: © Kasiam / iStock

Composition Services

Senior Project Coordinator: Kristie Rees

Layout and Graphics: Jennifer Creasey, Joyce Haughey

Proofreaders: Susan Moritz, Wordsmith Editorial

Indexer: Ty Koontz

John Wiley & Sons Canada, Ltd.

    Deborah Barton, Vice President and Director of Operations

    Jennifer Smith, Vice-President and Publisher, Professional Development

    Alison Maclean, Managing Editor

Publishing and Editorial for Consumer Dummies

    Kathleen Nebenhaus, Vice President and Executive Publisher

    David Palmer, Associate Publisher

    Kristin Ferguson-Wagstaffe, Product Development Director

Publishing for Technology Dummies

    Andy Cummings, Vice President and Publisher

Composition Services

    Debbie Stailey, Director of Composition Services

Contents at a Glance

Table of Contents

Introduction

A friend who heard I was writing *Atheism For Dummies* said it would be the skinniest book on the shelf. "Just one sentence long," he said. "'Atheists are people who don't believe in God.'"

I replied by suggesting a book on the Grand Canyon: "The Grand Canyon is a big hole in Arizona." Of course that sentence would miss most of what's really worth knowing about the Grand Canyon — its geology and geography, how it came to be, its wildlife and formations, and its significance among other formations on the planet.

Likewise, a book on atheism that stops at the definition of the word would miss what's really interesting about the startling idea that (despite what your mother and your hunches may tell you) God doesn't actually exist. It'd be just as incomplete as saying, "Religious people believe in God," and leaving it at that. There's a bit more to say.

People who've entertained the possibility that God doesn't exist, and sometimes even said it out loud, make up a seldom-explored thread of human history that intersects with the biggest questions in human life:

- How did everything get here?
- What is the meaning and purpose of life?
- How can you (and more importantly, that guy over there) be a good and moral person?
- What happens when you die?
- Seriously, is somebody steering this thing?

The idea that an unseen power created and runs the universe is surely as old as the human mind. From the first time one *Homo habilis* saw his neighbor fall down and never get up again, the curious human neo-cortex would have demanded an explanation. Lacking any good way of figuring out what happened, that same neo-cortex would have provided an answer that *seemed* true.

But every guess in human history that "seemed right" has almost certainly been doubted by somebody in the room. When the guess is "God," and the doubt rises to the level of strong conviction, you have yourself an atheist.

Atheist. If that word makes you flinch, you're not alone. People are conditioned to flinch at certain words. When my son came home in seventh grade and said, "You know what? I think I'm a communist," I nearly flinched down a flight of stairs. He'd learned about systems of government, you see, and the one where everybody shared what they had sounded good to him. But I grew up in the 1970s, and before I could actually *learn* anything about communism, I'd heard it hissed so many times that I couldn't think about it at all. All I could do was flinch.

The same is true of atheism; however, it's much less flinch-worthy than you may think. And one purpose of this book is to bring that flinch down to a mild tic.

About This Book

This is a book about atheism written by an atheist. I'm also an agnostic and a humanist, which makes more sense when you finish Chapter 2. *If you finish* Chapter 2, I should say, because this book is written for dipping and diving. Skip Chapter 2 completely if you want.

This book isn't the first one about atheism written by an atheist, but it's different from most. It's an overview, an intro for people who are interested in finding out more about the topic. It does include some of the reasons atheists are atheists, but it's not written to convince you to become one. If that's what you're after, other books can serve you better. And though it includes some of the complaints atheists have about religion — because hey, that's part of the picture — it's not a broadside against religious belief either. In fact, I spend a good deal of ink talking about the good things religion has to offer and the things believers and nonbelievers have in common. Chapters 17 and 18 are bursting with that sort of thing, which is one of the likely surprises for readers of *Atheism For Dummies*.

Although a lot of atheists spend a lot of time (and rightly so) fighting against the bad things religion does, just as many of atheists are interested in co-existing with religion and religious people. And sometimes the same person goes back and forth, depending on the issue. If the idea of atheism freaks you out a bit, my hope is that this book can help you relax. Atheists are mostly perfectly normal folks, and everyone will be better off if they're less fearful of each other.

On a personal note: You'll see a lot of personal notes in this book. It's one of the most striking differences between *Atheism For Dummies* and, say, *Catholicism For Dummies*. There's no atheist Vatican, no catechism, no scripture, so I can't point to a central, defining authority to tell you who atheists are or what they believe. I end up relying on surveys, on the reports of organizations, on research, on histories, on anecdotal evidence from the thousands of atheists and humanists I've met during my years in the freethought movement, and on my own personal experience as an atheist and humanist. (To keep myself honest, Dr. Ed Buckner, one of the true giants of the American freethought movement, is the book's technical editor to catch my errors. If any got through, blame Ed.)

The lack of an atheist Vatican is a good thing. Just as not all Catholics believe what the Vatican defines as "Catholic belief," so any central atheist authority would instantly fail to represent the true diversity of belief among those who claim one of the many labels under that great big umbrella.

So as you flip through this book, instead of a single grand procession through history, you can see religious disbelief as it really is — a collection of millions of individual voices, millions of separate stories, millions of individual human beings asking questions, questioning answers, and finally arriving at the conclusion that God, for better and worse, is all in our heads.

Finally, no one should expect a complete reckoning of the wonderful world of atheism. It's not possible, it's not desirable, and it's not the purpose of this book. Instead, I try to stick to the things that are most interesting and relevant to the past and present of atheism, then give you tips for finding out more if you want to.

Conventions Used in This Book

I use the following conventions throughout the text to make things consistent and easy to understand:

- ✔ All Web addresses appear in `monofont`. However, I don't give a lot of URLs. There's nothing as tedious as copying out a long web address from a book. So I often give an organization name, for example, and let you search for it online.

- ✔ New terms appear in *italics* and are closely followed by an easy-to-understand definition.

- ✔ Though a lot of nonbelievers capitalize Atheist and Humanist, many others don't. For reasons I explain in Chapter 2, I'm with the lower-casers. I follow the convention of capitalizing the names of religions, and I capitalize God when used as a proper name ("she believes in God"), just like I capitalize Steve ("she believes in Steve"). But when it's a generic god or gods ("they worship a big blue god"), no cap. I plan to be pretty inconsistent on this one.

- ✔ **Bold** is used to highlight the action parts of numbered steps and to emphasize keywords.

In addition, let me warn you that atheists are a wordy bunch. We tend to read and write and talk a lot. And the analyzing, oh the analyzing. As a result, we have countless words and terms and labels, including some with microscopic differences between them (or none). If I can spare you from a term in this book, I do. If two words have important differences in meaning, I let you know. If they're basically synonyms, I may use them interchangeably, just to irritate atheists who know the tiny differences and care too much. I even plan to irritate myself in this way.

You may also notice that I almost never make an absolute claim about atheists — or theists, for that matter. (See? I said "almost never." Get used to that.) You may see a lot of qualifiers like

- ✔ "Atheists *tend* to . . ."
- ✔ "Atheists *usually* . . ."
- ✔ "*Most* atheists . . ."

Aside from not believing in God, not many things can be positively said about all nonbelievers.

What You're Not to Read

Don't feel like you have to read every word to get something out of this book. I've made it modular, so you can flip to any part of the book and start reading at any heading without needing to have read anything up to that point.

Sidebars are interesting but nonessential, as is anything marked with the "Technical Stuff" icon. You can skip them at will. If anything makes your eyes glaze over, I'm sorry, and you can skip it.

Everything else is golden.

Foolish Assumptions

From the start, I assume a certain ideal reader. Here are the assumptions that I make about you:

- ✔ You're probably not an atheist yourself and don't know much about the subject, but you're curious and would like to learn more.

- ✔ If you identify as atheist, agnostic, or secular humanist, I bet you can come away from this book knowing and appreciating more about the history and underpinnings of our worldview. If you can stand being relegated to the nosebleed seats for this performance, I promise to occasionally aim the KissCam at you or shoot a T-shirt your way.

- ✔ You're not actually a dummy. In fact, one of the best assumptions made by the publishers of the *For Dummies* series is that its readers aren't dummies in general, just uninformed about a particular subject. So although I've tried to keep the tone light and the details brief, I assume you can chew on some serious ideas and handle a few unfamiliar terms.

How This Book Is Organized

This book is divided into five parts. Each introduces you to an important dimension of atheism.

Part 1: Understanding What Atheism Is

The first part is all about the nuts and bolts of atheism: the labels (and labels, and labels) that go along with it, a few other key terms, how someone can be both an atheist and an agnostic, and what atheists actually believe, and don't believe, and why.

Part 11: Following Atheism through the Ages

Part II takes a reckless ride through the long, fascinating history of the idea that (despite persistent rumors to the contrary) there aren't any gods, from ancient China and India to 21st century Britain and America.

Part 111: Reading the Great Works of Atheism

Part III goes back to Square One and retraces the steps of atheism through the ages, this time using important written works in every era as stepping stones. If you're looking for additions to your reading list, you can find them in this part.

Part 1V: Living a Full Life without Belief in God

This part walks you through what it's actually like being an atheist, including what atheists think about meaning, ethics, and death. Here I discuss how many nonbelievers are in the world today and why their influence is growing. I also discuss how the nonreligious get some of the benefits of the church without the detriments — and without the actual church.

Part V: The Part of Tens

Every *Dummies* book has a Part of Tens — lists with (about) ten fun and interesting things each that relate to the main topic. I cover surprising things about atheists, some famous nonbelievers you didn't know are nonbelievers, and ways you can explore atheism.

Icons Used in This Book

You can notice these small icons in the margins that map important points in this book. Here are the icons I use:

This icon identifies a few of the most important atheists, agnostics, and humanists in freethought history.

This icon signals a bit of information that's especially important to remember.

This icon points you to a bit of advice that can help in thinking about a difficult issue.

This one warns about common misconceptions. If you want to avoid jumping to conclusions, pay special attention to these.

This icon appears next to information that you may find interesting but won't kill you to skip.

Where to Go from Here

Now you have the very basic flavor of this book. If you go straight into Chapter 1, you can get a more detailed synopsis of the whole book. If you're a dip-and-diver, Chapter 1 can help you figure out where to go next. You can also check the table of contents or index, find a topic that interests you, and start reading.

Or you can read straight through. Any way works just fine, as long as you remember to skip anything that loses your interest. However you read it, by the end you'll know whether you want to explore further.

Part I

Understanding What Atheism Is

"Something in your nontheist section."

In this part . . .

This part is all about the nuts and bolts of atheism: the labels that go along with it, some key terms, how someone can be both an atheist and an agnostic, and what atheists actually believe, don't believe, and why.

Chapter 1

Meeting Atheism

· ·

· ·

The idea that no God exists is a startling one. Most people grow up hearing that the existence of God is a settled question and that nothing else can explain this complex, astonishing world.

But through the centuries, some people have always doubted the God conclusion — and some have even come to the firm conviction that humans created God, not the other way around.

Of course saying such a thing out loud tends to cause a lot of sputtering and fainting from people who disagree, not to mention the occasional smell of something burning. So you can safely assume that most of those who disbelieved the religions and gods of their times kept mum about it.

Fortunately, a lot of nonbelievers spoke up anyway, and they keep doing so today; otherwise this book wouldn't exist, and you'd be looking at your palms. People would talk. But the book does exist, and this chapter gives you a flying overview of what to expect as you leaf through it.

Getting a Grip on Atheism

Atheism is a big umbrella. It covers anyone who doesn't believe in a supernatural god or gods. But under that umbrella are many shades and grades of disbelief and many people with different ways of approaching and expressing it.

Atheists become atheists for many different reasons, and it rarely has anything to do with unanswered prayers or major life calamities. In fact, such a major trauma drives people *into* belief at least as often as it drives them out of it.

The chapters in Part I provide some of the basic definitions and descriptions that can help you make sense as you read the rest of the book.

Seeing the many forms and faces of religious disbelief

There are about as many ways to disbelieve as there are ways to believe — different degrees, different emphases, and different expressions.

Here are some examples:

- *Antitheists* (atheists who actively oppose religion and work toward a world without it)
- *Accommodationists* (atheists who emphasize the common ground between the religious and nonreligious rather than the differences)
- *Agnostics* (people who emphasize their uncertainty about the question of God's existence and often claim that it's unknowable)
- *Humanists* (people who focus on how to live a good human life in a natural universe)
- *Religious atheists* (including many Buddhists, Hindus, Unitarians, and Jains who keep their religious identities and philosophies without bothering any gods)
- *Freethinkers* (people who form their opinions about the universe without the undue influence of religious authority)
- *Unaffiliated* or *"None"* (they're not religious, but generally not interested in any label at all, thank you very much)

Even some religious opinions (like Deism and pantheism) exist that are so far removed from any traditional conception of God that many people include them under the atheist umbrella. And a single nonbeliever can, and often does, claim several of these labels at once. They emphasize different things, but most aren't mutually exclusive. Check out Chapter 2 to nicely complicate your idea of what an atheist is.

Examining what nonbelievers believe and don't believe — and why

I learned about history from historians and history teachers. I learned about religion by listening to believers and reading their scriptures directly. But most of what people know about atheism they learned from people who aren't atheists and don't especially like or even understand them.

That's a recipe for misinformation if ever there was one.

I went to church for 25 years for various reasons, including family and job, and was every bit as much of an atheist as I am now. Doing so was a big part of my own religious education. But over and over, I heard myself described from the pulpit in ways that made me sad and upset. Being an atheist, I was apparently a very nasty and selfish guy, not all that smart, and bad to the core. I heard that I didn't care about others and couldn't be trusted, and that I'd come to my beliefs by hardening my heart, by serving false gods, by not wanting to acknowledge God's power over me.

One Sunday I sat through a sermon in which the Christians in the room who were married to nonbelievers — that included my wife, by the way — were urged to leave their marriages (2 Corinthians 6:14). That's when I stopped going entirely.

If you want to find out more about a religious perspective, I am a poor choice for a guide. You'd be better seeking someone out from that perspective. But if you want to know what atheism is actually about, may I humbly suggest an actual atheist for a guide. I happen to be available, so read on!

In Chapter 3, I spend some time describing what atheists actually believe and debunking some common myths about them. Most atheists take ethics very seriously, for example, and find life deeply meaningful and inspiring. We're not mad at God — at least no madder than the Pope is at Chaac, the Mayan god of rain — and though some atheists arrive at their disbelief after something bad happened to them, that's not the most common path.

Most atheists come to their conclusions after really working on it for a while, then becoming convinced by things like these:

- ✔ Realizing that religious answers are just a bit too convenient
- ✔ Comparing religions and reading their scriptures
- ✔ Examining the classic arguments for belief
- ✔ Solving the *complexity problem* (the idea that the universe is just too complex to have come about without a designer) and (really) understanding evolution
- ✔ Noticing the steady retreat of religious answers
- ✔ Grasping the size and age of the universe, as well as the implications
- ✔ Noticing that the universe is just as an informed person would expect it to be without a God

There's much more, of course, and Chapter 3 is one of the places to find it.

Seeing the Progression of Atheism

A lot of people think that atheism is a recent idea. But religious disbelief actually has a long and fascinating history, and the chapters in Part II take you on a quick ride through it. Just as a student of Christianity would want to know about a few rather significant things that happened 2,000 years ago, someone who wants a better understanding of atheism likewise needs to know what atheism has been up to for the past 30 centuries or so. These sections provide a quick overview.

In the distant past and in different cultures

People tend to think of certain times and places as completely uniform in their beliefs. India is full to the brim with Hindus. The Greeks all worshipped the gods of Olympus. Everyone in Medieval Europe was Christian. Right?

A closer look shows all of these claims to be misleading. Just as political "red states" (Republicans) and "blue states" (Democrats) in the United States are really all various shades of purple, every place and time in human history includes a lot of different beliefs — including atheism.

That's not to say all points of view have the same chance to speak into the cultural microphone. Religion in general and the majority religion in particular tend to call the shots and write the histories, especially prior to the late 18th century. Add to that the fact that atheism (or blasphemy) has often been punishable by imprisonment or death, and you can see why atheists in certain times and places tend to *whisper*.

Ancient and medieval eras

But the voices are there, including some in the distant past and in cultures both in and out of Europe. In the chapters in Part II of this book, you can meet

- Atheists in ancient China, where atheism was a welcome part of the conversation among philosophers
- Atheists in ancient and medieval India, including religions with completely godless branches
- Atheists in ancient Greece, where they were seldom welcome
- Religious skeptics in early Islam who called Muhammad a liar
- A hero in 13th century Icelandic legend who said, "It is folly to believe in gods" — then lived happily ever after anyway
- Three 14th century French villagers whose disbelief was ferreted out by a shocked bishop during the Inquisition

The thread of atheism in the ancient and medieval world is a story that very few people know. Even *atheists* are usually in the dark about this part of their history. Read Chapters 4 and 5, and then share them with an atheist you love.

The Enlightenment

By the early 18th century, disbelief was gathering serious steam in Europe. Secret documents challenging religious belief had been circulating for 50 years, just steps ahead of the censors. French parishioners going through the papers of their Catholic priest who died in 1729 found copies of a book, written by the priest for them, telling how much he detested and disbelieved the religion he'd taught them for 40 years.

By the end of the century, philosophers in France, Germany, and England were openly challenging religious power and ideas and establishing modern concepts of human rights and individual liberty. It all culminated, for better and worse, in the French Revolution, when a brief flirtation with an atheist state was followed by the Cult of the Supreme Being and the Reign of Terror — at which point atheism went back underground for a bit. (For more on this, refer to Chapter 6.)

The 19th century

The idea that God didn't really exist never completely went away, even when someone like Napoleon shut it down for a while. It was always bubbling under the surface and occasionally shooting out sideways through someone who just couldn't stand to keep it quiet.

The poet Percy Shelley proved to be one such person, getting himself kicked out of Oxford in 1811 for expressing an atheist opinion. Then the early feminists of England and the United States made it plenty clear that they considered religion to be a stumbling block in the way of women's rights.

Science really put the wind in the sails of atheism in the 19th century. By paying close attention to the natural world, Darwin turned himself from a minister in training to an agnostic and solved the complexity problem that prevented so many people from letting go of God. As the biologist Richard Dawkins once said, atheism might have been possible before Darwin, but Darwin made it possible to be an "intellectually fulfilled atheist." But a flurry of activity after Darwin's death tried to hide his loss of faith, including some selective slicing and dicing of his autobiography and a false deathbed conversion story dreamt up by a British evangelist with little respect for the Ninth Commandment.

In Darwin's wake, a golden age of freethought opened up in the United States and the United Kingdom. It's all laid out for your enjoyment in Chapter 7.

The 20th century

Atheism also doesn't guarantee good behavior any more than religion does, and "Absolute power corrupts absolutely" becomes a tragically apt phrase in the 20th century. There are plenty of examples of corruption and immorality in positions of unchecked power, both by atheists (such as Mao Zedong in China, Joseph Stalin in the USSR, and Pol Pot in Cambodia) and theists (such as Adolf Hitler in Germany, Francisco Franco in Spain, and Idi Amin in Uganda).

But there's also good news, including the growth of humanism as a movement and court victories for the separation of church and state — something that benefits both the church and the state.

The 20th century also saw one of the most fascinating developments in the history of religion as two God-optional religions formed and flourished: Unitarian Universalism and Humanistic Judaism. Chapter 8 gives you more information.

Atheism today

A movement called The New Atheism was born the moment religion flew planes into buildings on September 11, 2001. Though atheists had been around for centuries, the horror and clarity of that moment, and the very clear part played by religion, was the last straw and a call to action for countless nonreligious people. A powerful, unapologetic new form of atheism grew up in response to that moment, including countless books and blogs calling for an end to the free pass from criticism that religion has traditionally enjoyed.

A huge upsurge in atheist thought, identity, organization, and action followed the initial wave. Driven by the young medium of the Internet, the freethought movement did in ten years what many other social movements take generations to achieve.

A quieter, more humanistic, but no less passionate form of disbelief rose up in the wake of the New Atheists — one that makes an effort to discern between benign and malignant expressions of religion, seeks common ground between the religious and the nonreligious, and focuses on building humanist community and defining a positive vision for the future. These two sides of contemporary atheism spend a lot of time kvetching at each other over the best way forward. Though it does break a little china, kvetching can be a good way of sorting good ideas from bad.

Chapter 9 brings you a hopelessly incomplete but hopefully tantalizing snapshot of the big, messy, complicated wonder of atheism today.

Examining Atheism in the Written Word

The history of atheism is the history of an idea. To understand that history, you have to look primarily at the written word — books, letters, diaries, pamphlets, and more recently, blogs. The chapters in Part III take a survey of the great written works expressing and exploring the idea that gods don't exist, including

- A telling two-sentence fragment from an ancient Greek play

- An ancient Indian *sutra* that suggests religion is a human invention and the authors of the sacred Vedas are "buffoons" and "knaves"

- An ancient Chinese philosopher who explains why "heaven" can't have a mind

- An Islamic doubter who calls Muhammad "fraudulent" and dismantles the idea of prophecy

- A secret, anonymous 17th-century book of skeptical writings from the past and suggests that every great philosopher has been an atheist

- A Catholic priest writing a secret book filled with his atheist opinions

- One of the most beloved authors in American history calling Christianity "bad, bloody, merciless, money-grabbing, and predatory"

- The 19th century speeches of "The Great Agnostic"

- Hilarious satires and other humor that skewers the sacred

- The fake scripture of a delicious parody religion

- Manifestos of humanism

- Powerful denunciations of religious belief in the 21st century

- A humanist chaplain's description of how a billion people are good without God

- A "faitheist" who doesn't believe in God but seeks common ground with the religious

With all those diverse voices of unbelief, you just may see something worth picking up yourself.

Understanding What Atheism Means in Everyday Life

After a person is an atheist, her question about whether God exists is replaced by questions about the best ways to live her life without God following her around, solving her problems, and giving her a place to put her feet after she is dead.

In other words, the question is how to be an everyday atheist.

The chapters in Part IV of this book are all about regular folks who don't believe in God, including

- How many there are and where they live
- Why such simple things as the numbers and locations of atheists are really tricky to figure out
- The most interesting corners of the disbelieving world (*cough* Québec)
- How atheism plays out in political identity
- Why young adults of today are a lot less religious than any other generation was when *they* were young adults
- Why (some) atheists are (sometimes) so angry
- What September 11, 2001 did to modern atheism
- Different kinds of nonbelievers
- Gender and ethnicity in the movement
- Atheist issues in other countries

That's all in Chapter 14, one of my favorites.

Then there's the nagging question of whether a person can possibly be good without belief in God — the focus of Chapter 15. The answer is *yes,* which should be a relief to everyone because nonbelief is growing rapidly and possibly even coming to a next-door neighbor near you. This chapter also defines morality, shows how it actually works, and helps everyone relax about it.

Chapter 16 is all about how the world looks with no gods blocking the view. Conventional wisdom has it that the loss of faith is followed by a plunge into an abyss of despair, after which the new atheist climbs out of the abyss and starts hurting puppies.

I can report that "freedom and relief" is a much more common description of the post-religious life than "despair and puppy smooshing." And there's also a common feeling of overwhelming responsibility and accountability after you realize that it really, truly is just humanity here, and that people could all use a hug once in a while. Or a nice, smoky, single-malt scotch.

Then there's

- The setting aside of Bronze Age ideas about virtues, vices, and honest doubt
- The updating of cultural views on sex and gender
- The challenge of accepting death as a reality — not a yummy one, sure, but part of the package, and something that can actually make life much more precious
- The fact that a universe this wonderful happened naturally (which isn't the same as happening by chance, as you'll see) is much more amazing than if an intelligence designed it
- The question of whether an atheist can be spiritual, which depends on your definition of spiritual
- The opportunity to grasp the real implications of evolution
- The slightly scary but ultimately invigorating freedom to decide for yourself what life is all about

One of the most pressing questions for the nonreligious is how to interact with and respond to the religious world around them. Chapter 17 explores the many issues around that, including

- Choosing battles and knowing the rules
- Grappling with church-state issues
- Living in the closet, and coming out
- Choosing how to interact with religious friends and relatives on religious issues
- Getting religiously literate
- Taking a seat at the cultural table

Chapter 18 looks at the many ways nonreligious people are finding to achieve the benefits that religious communities enjoy without the supernatural beliefs. It starts by understanding the real reasons people go to church — not my opinions, you understand, but actual research on the topic — then follows up with

- Creating community
- Celebrating life's landmarks
- Counseling and support without religion
- Doing good together

Getting personal: Why I'm an atheist

Atheists come to their conclusions for a lot of different reasons. Here is a brief look at mine.

My own path to atheism was smoother than some. I didn't have a painful break with religion, and I was certainly never "mad at God." I figured if he did exist, he was probably exasperated at the way most religions described him — petty and egotistical, and more than a little inconsistent. And if he was real, I thought he was likely to be a better sport than that. But I wondered, from a very early age, if he actually existed, or if humans had made him up.

Our family went to church, but I was never pushed to declare any particular beliefs. I also had a ravenous curiosity about the world. Everything about it fascinated and amazed me. My parents encouraged my curiosity as much as they could, and they gave me space to think and explore. One of the things I explored was whether any god or gods exist. How could I not? It's the most interesting question in the world! If there's a supernatural being that created and controls everything, that's astonishing. If the universe developed and runs without such a being, *that's* astonishing. I just wanted to know what was actually true. In short, I treated the question of God as a real question.

I explored the question in every way I could think of. I went to church for 25 years, asked believers why they believe this and not that, and read scriptures from every religion I could lay my hands on. And I thought about it, a lot.

I also studied the sciences, a lot. Eventually I came to see them both as expressions of the human mind's need to know. Leaving a lot of blanks in the human head about how the world worked didn't feel safe for most of human history. People needed to fill those blanks in with something so they could at least cultivate the illusion that they were in control of things — or at least someone powerful and good was in control. Science is asking many of the same questions about the world, but by controlling human biases, it has a much better chance of getting the right answers.

I've left our most of the details, of course; Chapter 3 fills in the rest. But that's my basic story. I'm an atheist because I felt the question of God was wonderful enough to deserve an honest answer.

Chapter 2

Unweaving the Rainbow of Disbelief

. . . .

In This Chapter

▶ Understanding basic terms and labels associated with atheism

▶ Sliding along the scale of belief and disbelief

▶ Getting comfortable with doubt

▶ Feeling the humanist pulse of atheism

. . . .

For as long as religious claims have been made, some people have surely been standing in the back of the room, hands in pockets, declining to buy into those claims. And the ways and degrees and reasons they disbelieve, not to mention the things they actually do believe, are fascinating and varied. This chapter introduces the characters who populate that world — including the atheist, the agnostic, the freethinker, the skeptic, the humanist, and more — and shows how one person can be, and often is, several of those characters at once.

Here you also discover how to think of religious belief not as an on-off switch, but as a sliding scale, see what a difference a capital letter can make, and begin to explore the rich landscape of humanism, the life philosophy that flows from the decision to set supernatural beliefs aside.

Tomato, Tomahto? The Wonderful, Maddening World of Atheist Labels

Labels can be helpful. A good, clear label can guide me to the right off-ramp or keep me from shampooing my steak. Likewise, labels can provide a quick and useful shorthand for understanding what a person does, or who she is, or even what he believes is true about the world.

However, labels can also be unhelpful, especially if they cause you to make assumptions about a person that aren't true. You may have heard the word "atheist" used as a shocked accusation (accompanied by a theatrical gasp). I sure have. As a result, you may have a hard time seeing that word and similar labels in a more neutral, descriptive way. The fact that you picked up this book is a good sign that you're up to the challenge.

The following sections explain a bit more about what labels mean when discussing atheism. I discuss in general what atheism is, explain different types of atheists, and examine the capitalization question.

Defining atheism: Implicit versus explicit

A quote from an 1861 speech by the pioneering feminist and atheist Ernestine Rose shows how many atheists think of atheism. Rose said, "It is an interesting and demonstrable fact, that all children are Atheists, and were religion not inculcated into their minds they would remain so." In other words, people who set religious belief aside are returning to a state that is natural for humans — atheism.

Although technically true, I've come to see this conception of atheism as a bit misleading. If you define *atheism* as simply "the absence of belief in God," a newborn baby (not to mention a pastrami sandwich) qualifies as an atheist because it lacks belief in God. But I'm inclined to see the difference between my atheism at birth and my atheism now as a pretty important one. These two terms define that difference perfectly:

- ✔ **Implicit atheism:** An *implicit atheist* is one who doesn't believe in any gods but hasn't consciously rejected such belief.

- ✔ **Explicit atheism:** An *explicit atheist* is one who has consciously chosen to disbelieve — who has, to put it plainly, an actual opinion on the matter.

Whenever I talk about atheism in this book, I am referring to explicit atheism — not the implicit atheism of babies and deli sandwiches.

Other abstract labels exist — implicit negative, explicit negative, weak versus strong, soft versus hard, and so on — and they range from mildly interesting to redundant to silly. You don't need to know what they all mean to understand what atheism is. For my sake as much as yours, I will skip those and turn to labels that matter more in the next section.

Coming to terms: A quick look at labels

Ask a religious person to identify his or her belief and you're unlikely to hear, "Who me? I'm a Theist!" It's accurate, but it says too little. They might say, "I'm a Christian," "I'm a Lutheran," or even "I'm a Missouri Synod Lutheran," and all three could be true at once. The same goes with Jewish, Jewish Orthodox, and Lubavitcher Hasidim. Several labels can easily apply to one person, each emphasizing a different aspect of belief or a different degree of detail.

Identifying some of the more common labels

The same is true of atheism. A few of the most common and useful descriptive terms in and around atheism are

- **Atheist:** A person who's of the opinion that no supernatural god or gods exist.

- **Agnostic:** One who doesn't claim to know whether a god or gods exist, and often also thinks that it's unknowable.

- **Freethinker:** A person who holds opinions based on independent reasoning without the undue influence of authority, doctrine, or tradition.

- **Skeptic:** Someone who withholds judgment until sufficient evidence is available.

- **Humanist:** A person who believes that concerns in this world and this life are of primary importance. Sometimes used as a synonym for *secular humanist,* though not always. Someone can believe in God and heaven, for example, but still feel this life should be our main focus.

- **Secular humanist:** A humanist who also asserts disbelief in the existence of a supernatural god.

I for one am all of these things, as this imaginary conversation demonstrates:

Q: *Do you think God exists?*

Me: *No, I'm an atheist.*

Q: *But are you absolutely certain?*

Me: *Of course not. I'm an agnostic.*

Q: *And do you believe as you do because some authority told you to?*

Me: *No, I'm a freethinker.*

Q: *And if there's no God, don't you think it's important for us to take care of each other?*

Me: *Of course. I'm a humanist.*

You get the idea.

One of the most important takeaways here is that most of these aren't mutually exclusive. You can be an atheist and a secular humanist, for example, and most people who are one are also the other.

Viewing how some secondary labels are used

Some secondary labels also allow atheists to describe other aspects of their belief system, like the way they choose to interact with religion. Are you an atheist who believes religion poisons everything and should therefore not just be declined but actively opposed? You're an *antitheist*. An atheist who seeks common ground with religious believers despite differences? That's an *accommodationist* — or, if you want to be snarky, a *faitheist*.

There's also the big picture: how to describe all of these labels in a single, big-bucket, global term. Some like the word *naturalist*, meaning a person with no supernatural views. This really appeals to me in one way, but *naturalist* instantly brings to mind David Attenborough in a safari hat, whispering and pointing at a rare blue-footed booby. Other people prefer *secularist*, though this technically has the narrower meaning of an advocate for the separation of religion from public and political life.

The word *bright* was coined in 2003 as a positive collective term for all people with a naturalistic worldview. Just as "gay" was intended as a positive substitute for "homosexual," so "bright" was offered as a less baggage-laden substitute for "atheist." But the word was quickly laden with baggage of its own as many commentators howled at the suggestion that if nonbelievers are "bright," believers are therefore "not so bright." Even the uncompromising atheist Christopher Hitchens said the word made him cringe.

Don't think for a minute that this is a complete list . . . and hey, you're welcome for that. But as long and often silly as the list can seem, the name game is an admirable attempt by those who have set religion aside to clearly state what they consider to be important and true. As with any label, the most important thing to remember is that every individual has the right to choose his or her own label — or none at all.

Answering the capital question: Is it Atheist or atheist?

Capitalizing a word really changes the effect. Note the difference between god and God, for example. And why on Earth am *I* capitalized and *you* aren't?

Language style guides usually indicate that the words "atheist" and "atheism" aren't capitalized. Some atheists feel that the capital letter (Atheist, Humanist) commands respect and puts these worldviews on par with religion. Others find capitalizing these terms off-putting for exactly that reason, as if the capital letter suggests a set of dogmas and doctrines, a creed that must be adhered to. For many people who are recent immigrants from the more dogmatic religions, dogmas and doctrines just aren't appealing.

The word "freethinker" is especially interesting in this way — the only word I know that, when capitalized, can easily become its opposite, developing rigid dogmas of its own. I can't tell you how many times I've heard a fellow atheist insist in a huff that someone isn't a real Freethinker because he or she has come to a different conclusion. That's the upper case F talking.

One of the nice features of genuine freethought (lower case) is that you can decide what you think is best, I can do the same, and then you and I can talk about it. As you've probably guessed, I'm a big fan of the lower case. A lot of the worst nonsense in human history has resulted from Capitalized Things and the mindset that accompanies them. I prefer to underline our humble origins and our tiny place in the scheme of things by keeping the capitals to a minimum. You are free, of course, to read with a fine tip marker and change Every Last One (unless this is a library book).

Believing and Disbelieving by Degrees

Thinking of religious belief as a kind of on-off switch is common. Either you have it or you don't. But the reality is much more interesting — more of a dimmer switch, if you will. (Which end of the belief spectrum is dim and which is bright is the subject of perpetual debate.)

The following section helps bring this analogy to life, showing the many degrees and shades of color in the rainbow of disbelief.

Roberts's rule: "We are both atheists"

It's important not to slap a worldview label on someone against his or her will. If you want to really annoy an atheist, for example, tell her you know she really does believe in God, *deep down*.

Likewise, if you thought this section's heading implied that all religious believers are really atheists *deep down* — well, you can relax. It's much less annoying and more useful than that.

Like most thought-provoking ideas, this one was surely around for centuries before it was crystallized in a concise and memorable way. In this case, the crystallizer wasn't a famous philosopher or bestselling author but regular guy Stephen F. Roberts, a database designer in Virginia. In 1995, Stephen began signing his online posts with the following tagline:

> I contend we are both atheists. I just believe in one fewer god than you do. When you understand why you dismiss all the other possible gods, you will understand why I dismiss yours.

The passage originated in an online debate he'd had around that time. When a Christian in the discussion asked why Stephen ignored the evidence for the Christian God, he asked in turn why the Christian chose to ignore the evidence for Shiva, Zeus, or any of the other possible gods. He used this quote to point out that believers in any given god are in fact atheistic toward all other possible gods — that they have declined to believe in the existence of those gods in very much the same way Stephen has. Stephen, though, has simply gone one god further.

Russell's labels: Why most atheists are agnostics and vice versa

British philosopher Bertrand Russell (1872–1970) expressed an idea that is both simple and striking: He felt that all opinions, without exception, should be held *conditionally* (capable of being changed), not *dogmatically* (etched in stone). When people feel the evidence for a claim is strong, they can be confident in the claim, consider it true, and act accordingly, but they should always keep their minds open to new evidence or further thinking that might change their opinions.

The idea is quite simple, but people seldom think this way. Russell thought life would be much better if they did. Imagine how different life would be if every statement of opinion ended with the words, "Of course, I might be wrong." Discussing even the most delicate subjects without coming to blows would be possible. Just imagine:

Theist: "I feel very strongly that God exists. Of course, I might be wrong."

Atheist: "I feel just as strongly that he doesn't. I might be wrong as well."

Suddenly, a real conversation becomes possible. Both sides can offer forceful, passionate arguments, and the admission that some degree of doubt always exists allows each to better hear what the other has to say.

Of course Russell couldn't simply wish this solution on the world, and once in a while, the conflict between his understanding of how opinions should be held and the way other people understood it created a real problem. When he traveled to a foreign country, for example, he was always asked by officials (as was the convention at the time) what his religion was. He never knew quite what to say. Russell was of the strong opinion that God didn't exist, and he admitted (as he did with all his opinions) that he might be wrong about that. In other words, he fit comfortably in two categories that most people think are mutually exclusive: atheist and agnostic.

Russell was well aware of the popular misconceptions that atheists are entirely certain and that agnostics are precisely in the middle, and he knew that other philosophers shared his understanding. So when speaking to philosophers, as he often did, Russell always described himself as agnostic, because as he put it, "I do not think that there is a conclusive argument by which one can prove that there is not a God," and philosophers would understand what he meant.

But he also wanted to give an accurate impression to everyday people. If he described himself as agnostic to a general audience, he knew they'd think he was smack in the middle between belief and disbelief, shrugging his shoulders, when in fact he leaned heavily in the direction of disbelief. If he was going to call himself agnostic about the Christian god, he once said, he should really also call himself an agnostic toward Zeus, Apollo, and the rest of the Greek gods as well. He didn't think they existed either, but he certainly couldn't prove it. Proof of Zeus could come to light tomorrow afternoon. But it's so incredibly unlikely that most people would find it strange to say they were agnostic toward the existence of Zeus.

Russell's position on the God of the Bible is exactly the same as most people's position on Zeus. Because most people consider themselves fully atheistic toward Zeus and friends, Russell would call himself an atheist when addressing a general audience.

In 1958, Russell hit on a useful analogy to explain this position even more clearly. He asked his readers to imagine their reaction if he said he believed that a tiny bone china teapot is in orbit around the Sun between Earth and Mars — one too tiny to be seen even by our most powerful telescopes. Would you be obligated to believe the teapot exists just because you could not disprove it? Of course not. Nobody thinks the existence of such a thing is likely enough to be taken into account in practice, Russell said. And he considered the Christian God just as unlikely as the teapot.

To understand Russell's meaning, take a moment to prove conclusively that no such teapot exists or that Zeus and the rest of the gods of ancient Greece don't exist. (Be sure to show your work.) Russell said doing so is impossible. I certainly can't do it.

Yet even though such certain proof can't be found, acting and living as if they don't exist seems reasonable. Russell felt very much the same about the God of the Judeo-Christian Bible. Agnostics today who share his position often call themselves "teapot agnostics" in tribute to that evasive little piece of china.

Agnostic underlines the uncertainty; *atheist* underlines the opinion that one conclusion is much more nearly certain than the other. ***Note:*** Russell opts to capitalize Atheist and Agnostic.

Dawkins's degrees: The seven-point belief scale

Biologist Richard Dawkins (b. 1941) was renowned as a popularizer of science for more than 25 years before turning his attention to advocating atheism and critiquing religion. Since that change of focus, Dawkins's direct, forthright approach has made him the ultimate atheist in the popular mind.

Even though most atheists agree that God's nonexistence can never be stated with absolute certainty, most people who know of Dawkins assume that he, surely, claims to be certain that God doesn't exist. In fact, he doesn't say that, and never has, and almost certainly never would.

Science doesn't work like that, he explains — and despite earnest claims to the contrary, "the existence of God is a scientific hypothesis like any other." Science is about increasing or decreasing confidence in a hypothesis, not switching between complete doubt and complete certainty.

In his book *The God Delusion,* Dawkins created what he called a seven-point belief scale between the extremes of certainty in religious belief. A "1" on the scale indicates certainty that God exists. Someone who scores a "1" says that no new information can ever change their opinion. On the other end of the scale is the person who claims to be certain that God does *not* exist, and that no new information can ever change their opinion. That person scores a "7." These are the dogmatic thinkers Bertrand Russell warned about in the previous section.

Someone who scores a "2" believes God is very probable and lives his or her life as if he does exist, but stops short of claiming absolute certainty. A "6" indicates a strong probability that God does not exist, but stops short of absolute certainty.

Russell would surely have called himself a "6" — and he's not the only one. Dawkins also calls himself a "6" on the scale. In a 2012 interview with the Archbishop of Canterbury and philosopher Anthony Kenny, Dawkins was asked why he doesn't call himself an agnostic if he says he isn't completely sure. When he said that he does in fact consider himself an agnostic, there was a shocked gasp from the audience, not to mention the worldwide press the following day. The world's most famous atheist had admitted he was actually an agnostic!

Of course saying he "admitted" to being an agnostic was as silly as saying a Christian "admitted" he is actually a Lutheran. Dawkins was laying claim to two entirely compatible labels. But unlike Russell, he made the statement in front of an audience that was unlikely to know that the labels are compatible.

Emphasizing Doubt: Agnostics Aren't Sure (and Neither Are You)

In a world of loud, confident positions, few are as misunderstood as the humble agnostic. Just as atheism means "without god belief," *agnosticism* adds that same "a" to the Greek word for knowledge *(gnosis)* to mean "without knowledge." An agnostic is someone who doesn't know something, or (more usefully) someone who chooses to emphasize his or her lack of certain knowledge. In most cases it refers to a person who emphasizes a lack of knowledge about the existence of God. But as Bertrand Russell pointed out, an agnostic is rarely just in the shrugging middle. (For more information on Russell, refer to the previous section, "Russell's labels: Why most atheists are agnostics and vice versa.")

According to Richard Dawkins's seven-point belief scale (check out the earlier section, "Dawkins's degrees: The seven-point belief scale" for more information), people may vary in their opinions, but most, including Dawkins himself, fall between the extremes of certainty that God exists and certainty that he doesn't. If any degree of doubt qualifies a person for the label, most believers and nonbelievers alike are technically agnostics. They may have strong opinions, but they don't claim to know for sure.

Just like the word atheism, agnosticism breaks down into a blizzard of sublevels, the two most interesting being weak and strong.

- A *weak agnostic* position says, "I don't know if a god exists, but there might be enough evidence one way or another at some point."

- A *strong agnostic* says God's existence is both unknown and unknowable. Or, as one of my favorite bumper stickers puts it: MILITANT AGNOSTIC — I don't know and you don't either.

The following section traces the origin of the word agnostic and shows that the idea itself was around long before there was a word for it.

Though religious doubt had been around for millennia, the word *agnosticism* itself wasn't coined until 1869 when the English biologist Thomas Henry Huxley created it as a label for his own beliefs. Huxley felt that atheism implied certainty, and though he was very confident God didn't exist, he didn't want to imply he was 100 percent sure. But he was also nowhere near being a religious believer.

After puzzling over the problem for some time, Huxley came up with the word *agnostic* — Greek for "not knowing" — to describe his position. He quickly learned that he was not alone, because countless writers and thinkers in England and beyond quickly adopted the term themselves.

Agnostics before agnosticism

Agnosticism was around long before there was a word for it. The ancient Greek philosopher Protagoras of Abdera wrote, "Concerning the gods, I have no means of knowing whether they exist or not or of what sort they may be" — a sentence that could easily have come from Thomas Henry Huxley himself. And a generation before Huxley's birth, pioneering feminist Frances Wright said, "With respect to myself, my efforts have been strenuously directed to ascertain what I know, to understand, what can be known, and to increase my knowledge as far as possible" instead of bothering ourselves with unknowable things like whether God exists.

In each of the hundred generations between Protagoras and Wright, countless other people, well known and unknown, shared Huxley's position before a term existed to capture it.

Discovering Humanism: The Thousand Steps That Follow

Atheism is a huge statement about the biggest question of all — whether a supernatural God exists. Though atheism itself answers this one question and goes no further, the implications of that answer are enormous. The idea of God answers questions and solves problems. That's what it was created for — to fill in the gaps in human knowledge and to provide comfort in the face of the admittedly serious problems of human existence.

When you remove the God solution, the problems themselves remain. So what's the best way to respond to a world in which there is no God? The answer for many atheists is *humanism,* the thousand steps that follow the conclusion that God doesn't exist. Humanism is a worldview that focuses care, compassion, and a sense of wonder on this world and this life instead of focusing on a God and an imagined afterlife.

Looking at the world in a different way

A world without a God is very different from a world with one, but basic human needs, hopes, fears, and aspirations remain very much the same. People still seek pleasure and avoid pain. They still need to understand what it means to be good and to be motivated toward ethical behavior. They still fear death, and they still seek meaning and purpose.

An unseen but accessible deity who is all-powerful and all-good solves these problems pretty neatly. Want to know how to behave? No problem — he's written a book (though if actual morality is what you're after, I'd skip the first few hundred pages). Afraid to die? No worries — God cancelled death. Need a purpose? Serve God and do his will.

Humanism is an ongoing attempt to address these same needs using reason and compassion instead of religious tradition, church authority, or holy scriptures. It's a different way of looking at the world, one that offers both challenges and opportunities.

Coming to terms with terms: Humanist or secular humanist?

In the mid-19th century, a British agnostic named George Holyoake coined the term *secular humanist* to more clearly distinguish humanists who don't believe in a deity from those who do. (Holyoake was interestingly also the last person in England to be convicted of blasphemy, in 1842.)

So what term should you use when referring to a humanist? In the years since Holyoake, the presumption of religious belief reversed itself. *Humanist* without a modifier now implies a secular humanist, and religious humanists are the ones who must add the modifier (religious) to be clear. As with the word "atheist," sometimes the letter H in Humanism is capitalized, and sometimes it's not.

Getting to know the Renaissance humanists

The first humanists were not always atheists but included many religious believers living in the Renaissance era. Like modern secular humanists, these religious humanists felt that human concern should focus on this world and this life, not on the supernatural or the afterlife, and that human reason could and should guide our ethics and decision making. Their work was inspired and informed in part by discoveries of ancient Greek and Roman philosophical works extolling a similar approach.

The Renaissance humanists urged social and educational reforms including a greater emphasis on literacy, critical thinking, tolerance, and informed engagement in civic life. It was a crucial step toward the scientific revolution and the Enlightenment, helping Western thought to find its way out of the reliance on scripture and authority that held sway on the continent for over a thousand years.

Renaissance humanists included the poet Petrarch (1304–1374) and monk, scholar, and satirist Desiderius Erasmus (1466–1536).

FAMOUS FREETHINKER

Setting God aside: The implications

In her brilliantly funny and personal one-woman show *Letting Go of God,* comedian Julia Sweeney describes her process of letting go of Catholic religious belief to become an atheist. In a way both humorous and deeply touching, Sweeney describes the implications of a world without God, one by one, and responds at every point with the essence of humanism — the urgent desire to understand the world, to support each other, and to put human compassion and justice in place of a divine illusion.

One of the most extraordinary parts of the monologue describes her first encounter with the idea of a world without God. "I'm embarrassed to report that I initially felt dizzy," she says. "I actually had the thought, 'Well, how does the Earth stay up in the sky? You mean we're just hurtling through space? That's so vulnerable!' I wanted to run out and catch the earth as it fell out of space into my hands." Then she remembers that gravity and angular momentum do the trick without divine intervention.

She wonders why we are ethical, realizing at last that we evolved a moral sense in order to live in community with each other. She thinks about innocent people in prison who are praying to no one for help, and then shouts out, "We gotta do something to get those people out of jail!"

Finally she confronts the most difficult reality of all: that we really do die, and that everyone she loved who has died is really gone. It also hits her that Hitler didn't face any ultimate justice or punishment. Her reaction is deeply humanistic: "We better make sure that doesn't happen again."

Slowly she begins to see the whole world differently. "I had to rethink what I thought about everything," she says. "It's like I had to go change the wallpaper of my mind."

Seeing the humanist heart of atheism

Atheism is often described (even by some atheists) as being too much about thinking and not enough about feeling. Many atheists would rightly counter that there's a good reason for this — that emotional need is what gets people into religion in the first place, and that intellect and reason help them get out and stay out.

REMEMBER

True enough. But eventually people find themselves confronting those human needs again, many of which are expressed in emotional terms. And that's where humanism, "the heart of atheism," comes in. When an atheist works to alleviate poverty or support human rights, or helps a friend or neighbor, he or she might be motivated by atheism, by the conviction that there's no God to do these things for people. But the compassionate actions themselves are best described as an expression of that person's humanism.

Forcing a Square Peg into a Round Hole: The Unpigeonholeables

No discussion of religious belief and disbelief is really complete without recognizing the galling presence of people who've thought so carefully about their labels that they decline to sit in any of the black-and-white categories the world has prepared for them. Religious believers and atheists alike are quick to claim the best of them as their own and to shunt the worst of them to the other side. But they aren't traditional believers in any creed, and they aren't strictly atheists either. I call them the Unpigeonholeables.

Not surprisingly, some of the deepest and most complex thinkers of every generation have fallen into these categories outside of categories. That's what thinking can do to a person. Even within each of the labels in this section, you can find a lot of qualifiers like "Pantheists *most often* . . . " and "Deists *generally* . . . " and "Religious atheists *usually* . . . " Even in their exile from the broad categories, these folks are hard to pin down.

Believing in a different kind of creator: Deists

Deism was first described in the 1620s and for two centuries was the philosopher's worldview of choice. Deists generally believe in the existence of a supernatural creator, but that's as far as the parallels to traditional religion go. They tend to believe that this creator-god set the universe in motion but hasn't clocked in since. He doesn't answer prayers, and most believe he doesn't reward or punish behavior. In fact, given the heaping helping of pain, bad manners, and bum luck in the world, many deists think he/she/it doesn't even know humans are here at all.

Deists have no central creed or authoritative scripture, and they tend to believe that human reason and observation of the natural world are the best ways to understand that world, to see evidence of an intelligent creator, and to work out how to behave.

This may be confusing at first, but it really does make sense. You can criticize *Star Wars* and still be a movie fan. Likewise, you can criticize Christianity and still believe in a creator god — just a very different kind.

Though deism as a label fell into decline in the early 19th century, it helped give rise to a number of liberal religious movements. According to a 2005 Baylor University study, when you scratch the surface, about a third of religious believers in the United States hold beliefs that are closer to deism than anything else. That means they really have as much if not more in common with nonbelievers than with believers in a traditional, prayer-answering, behavior-watching God.

Many Founding Fathers were deists

Although some people claim that all the Founding Fathers of the United States were Christians, many, in fact, were deists. Because Thomas Jefferson said in his personal correspondence that the Gospels were built on "a groundwork of vulgar ignorance, of things impossible, of superstitions, fanaticisms, and fabrications," called the Book of Revelation "merely the ravings of a maniac," and said "The day will come when the mystical generation of Jesus, by the Supreme Being as his father, in the womb of a virgin, will be classed with the fable of the generation of Minerva in the brain of Jupiter," he was often assumed to have been an atheist. But no — Jefferson was a deist.

Thomas Paine called the Bible "trash" and "[a] collection of lies and contradictions." But he wasn't an atheist; Paine was also a deist. And even though Benjamin Franklin said, "Lighthouses are more helpful than churches" and called Christian dogma "unintelligible," he also said, "I never doubted . . . the existence of the Deity."

Seeing nature as God: Pantheists

Pantheism, which means "all-God," is the view that the universe and God are one and the same. Any reverence or worship is directed not to a god in human form, or in any form at all, but to the whole of the cosmos, and spirituality is centered not on a traditional deity but on nature.

Daniel C. Dennett, a prominent atheist philosopher, said, "Is something sacred? Yes, say I with Nietzsche. I could not pray to it, but I can stand in affirmation of its magnificence. This world is sacred." Though I doubt Dennett would call himself a pantheist, his quote touches on this nontraditional worldview, one that found itself a name in the late 17th century.

As with agnosticism and other labels, the practice predated the term by thousands of years. Many thinkers in ancient Greece, China, and India expressed conceptions of God that today is called *pantheistic*. Christian church leaders considered pantheism heretical during the medieval period, and then it was revived and gained its name in the run-up to the Enlightenment.

Being religious without a god: Religious atheists

Though she doesn't believe any gods exist, Ursula Goodenough sounded awfully religious when she said, "I profess my Faith. For me, the existence of all this complexity and awareness and intent and beauty, and my ability to apprehend it, serves as the ultimate meaning and the ultimate value. The continuation of life reaches around, grabs its own tail, and forms a sacred circle that requires no further justification, no Creator."

She would agree — in fact, she calls herself a *religious naturalist,* and many who share her exact views call themselves *religious atheists.* This name drives some atheists completely nuts. Others find it an inspired solution to a real problem.

No matter what your perspective, the idea of religious atheism is probably a head-spinner at first. If I say "religion," the odds are pretty good that "God" is one of the first related words to pop into your head. Religion and God have been joined at the hip from the beginning. So it's a good bet that when you saw the heading "Religious Atheists," you did a bit of a snort-take.

On the other hand, maybe the Albert Einstein "Is-He-Or-Isn't-He" game in the sidebar has you prepared for anything.

In fact, a person can be an atheist who also considers him or herself religious. Just keep God out of it and you're good to go. Entirely nontheistic branches of Hinduism and Buddhism have existed for thousands of years, and the Jain religion is completely gods-free.

Pantheism through the ages

Though the philosopher Baruch Spinoza held strongly pantheistic views, it was an especially popular worldview for poets and other romantics of the 18th and 19th centuries, including Walt Whitman, Ralph Waldo Emerson, Henry David Thoreau, and William Wordsworth. Like all good unorthodoxies, pantheism drew a sound papal spanking, this one from Pius IX's 1864 *Syllabus of Errors.* In fact, "pantheism" had the distinction of being the very first word in the document — a résumé-brightener for any heresy.

In more recent times, Albert Einstein often made statements that suggest a kind of pantheistic belief: "I believe in Spinoza's God, who reveals himself in the harmony of all that exists, not in a God who concerns himself with the fate and the doings of mankind," for example, and "I do not believe in a personal God . . . If something is in me which can be called religious, then it is the unbounded admiration for the structure of the world so far as our science can reveal it." Yet Einstein disclaimed pantheism as a label in another letter, saying, "I don't think I can call myself a pantheist." And despite his use of the word "God" (for example, "God doesn't play dice with the universe"), he also made it clear that he didn't believe in the existence of any kind of traditional, personal God.

As for atheism, Einstein was adamant in rejecting what he saw as a declaration of certainty that God doesn't exist, and especially rejected "fanatical atheists" who combat religious belief.

In the end, though claimed by all sides (for obvious reasons), and despite an ongoing flirtation with pantheism, Einstein preferred what he called an "attitude of humility," saying, "You may call me an agnostic."

Well okay then.

Religion has always included much more than the worship of a deity. Community, spirituality, the search for meaning, ethics, rights of passage, mutual support, a chance to have a good sing, the experience of beauty and wonder — all these have been part and parcel of the institution of religion.

Though they have usually been framed in theistic terms, not one of these elements relies on the idea of a deity. Some even feel that God gets in the way of the fullest expression of human spirituality, an idea captured in science writer Chet Raymo's book *When God is Gone, Everything is Holy.*

So even as they dismiss the idea of God, many atheists express a desire to partake of these very real benefits of religious community in a God-optional or even fully God-less way. Some have built entire movements and denominations to make it happen. They are the religious atheists. The following are three examples of religious atheist denominations or movements.

Concentrating on ethics: The Ethical Culture movement

The Ethical Culture movement, one such experiment in God-optional religion, was founded in New York by professor and social reformer Felix Adler. Adler had been trained as a rabbi, but his first sermon, given to his father's congregation in 1873, quickly became his last when he laid out a future for Judaism without once mentioning God.

Four years later, Adler created the Society for Ethical Culture, giving a series a Sunday lectures on ethical issues and forming a mutually supportive community of religious (but God-optional) humanists. The movement gradually spread to include more than 25 Ethical Societies across the United States, all emphasizing "deed before creed" — that what we do is more important than what we believe. Many members of Ethical Culture are theists; many are atheists. All are religious.

Focusing on human values: Unitarian Universalists

The 1961 merger of Unitarianism and Universalism, the two most liberal Christian denominations at the time, created a new creedless denomination with the cumbersome eleven-syllable name of Unitarian Universalism. UUs (as they are mercifully called) gather not around shared belief in a deity or the authority of a sacred text but around seven principles emphasizing such human values as justice, dignity, equity, and compassion. Some UUs are theistic believers of one kind or another, while those who self-identify as humanists, atheists, and agnostics are religious without God. Refer to Chapter 8 for more discussion.

Converging around Jewish culture: Humanistic Judaism

In 1963, just two years after the birth of Unitarian Universalism, Rabbi Sherwin Wine announced to his congregation in Windsor, Ontario that he hadn't believed in God's existence for quite some time.

"It is beneath my dignity to say things that I do not believe," Wine said, then invited those who wished to do so to follow him in creating a nontheistic Jewish congregation. Eight families did so.

Wine developed a new humanistic liturgy that reflected Jewish culture, identity, and history while teaching humanist ethics, all without reference to God. It was the birth of Humanistic Judaism, a nontheistic religious movement that now has more than 40,000 members and is recognized as one of the five main branches of Judaism. Chapter 8 has more discussion about Humanistic Judaism.

Moving beyond labels: The rise of the Nones

One of the most important and interesting labels refers to people who, when asked for their religion, simply reply, "None." The *Nones* represent a much larger, more diverse, and faster growing population than any single label I discuss in this chapter. Some Nones also claim one or more of the specific labels of unbelief, but many simply want nothing to do with labels of any kind.

Even in the highly religious United States, those claiming no religion grew from 8 to 20 percent of the population between 1990 and 2012, far outnumbering the combined total of all non-Christian religions in the country. And that percentage increases dramatically as age decreases, with fully 1 in 3 Americans ages 18 to 22 claiming no religious identity — far more than any previous generation when they were the same age. Nones in several European countries are well ahead of the US curve, including more than 50 percent of the population of the United Kingdom and more than 70 percent in several Scandinavian countries. (For more number-crunching on the Nones, refer to Chapter 14.)

So when you hear media stories about the Rise of the Nones, know that it isn't a horror story set in a convent. It's one of the most fascinating and important social trends currently underway.

Chapter 3

Recognizing What Atheists Do and Don't Believe — and Why

In This Chapter

▶ Separating the real reasons atheists are atheists from some common misconceptions

▶ Finding out what atheists actually believe

▶ Reconciling science and religion — or not

*I*f you want to know the beliefs of a particular religion, you can start with that religion's scriptures. But scriptures written long ago aren't likely to match up too well with beliefs that are held today. Few 21st century Jews or Christians think that women are the property of their husbands or that slavery is a good thing, even though their scriptures are still trumpeting those Bronze Age ideas.

Atheists avoid this problem by not having a central scripture. That doesn't mean they have no beliefs or values, just that their beliefs and values aren't codified in an unchanging document. Atheists also have no central authority, no Vatican or High Council to decide and transmit any approved set of beliefs.

The best way to find out what people believe, whether religious or nonreligious, is to ask them. And because those beliefs can vary from person to person, the more people you ask, the better your understanding will be.

This chapter explores what atheists tend to believe, and just as important, what they *don't* believe — the myths and misconceptions about atheists that find their way into people's heads through forwarded e-mails and the occasional sermon. But first I spend some time explaining *why* atheists are atheists — what it is that leads them to walk away from religious answers.

Throughout the chapter, I offer not just my own opinions, but also the general consensus of atheists, humanists, and other freethinkers whenever possible.

Understanding Why Atheists Don't Believe in God

Not all atheists follow the same route to their disbelief. That's partly because they don't all start in the same place. For example, the path varies depending on whether a person is raised

- ✔ In a religious family that discourages or punishes the questioning of religious ideas
- ✔ In a religious family that *encourages* questioning, even of religious ideas
- ✔ In a secular family that's tolerant of religion and encourages religious literacy
- ✔ In a secular family that's hostile to all religion
- ✔ In a family that's just indifferent to religious questions

Then there's geography, family history, a person's own inclinations — each of these has a profound effect on the way a person encounters and questions religious assumptions. These sections list a few of the most common reasons atheists give for coming to their conclusion that God doesn't exist.

Crossing from the will to believe to "the will to find out"

Ask an atheist why he or she doesn't believe in God, and you'll usually hear that the evidence just doesn't hold up. I agree with that. But there's another piece of the puzzle that isn't talked about enough — *What makes it possible for a person to ask the questions in the first place?*

That question may sound strange. Anyone can ask whether God exists, of course. But most people don't ask that question in any serious way. People are presented with God as a fact from the time they're very young, told that life and love and the sun and stars are gifts from God, and that good people accept these things without question. So why would you question, especially when it comes with the best of intentions from someone who loves you?

Selected myths about why atheists are atheists

A few of the reasons people *think* atheists are atheists:

✔ **"You're mad at God."** Try though I may, being mad at something that I don't think exists is pretty difficult. I'm about as mad at God as I am at Paul Bunyan's blue ox.

✔ **"You don't want to be answerable to God. You want to be free to sin."** I suppose this is possible, but it would be a pretty bad idea — a bit like flooring the accelerator because I don't want to be answerable to the police car behind me. If God is real and his rules are as advertised, he will indeed catch up with me, and a life of not answering to him will be followed closely by an eternity of answering to him in a big and smoky way. So once again, not wanting to be answerable to God doesn't make a lick of sense as a reason to stop believing he exists.

✔ **"You just haven't found the right church."** Most atheists go through a period of searching to see if they missed anything. In fact, I pretty much *assumed* I'd missed something, because it looked like everyone around me believed in God. (That wasn't true — it almost never is — but I didn't know that yet.) So over the course of 25 years, I attended churches in nine denominations, listening carefully and asking questions everywhere I went. It's a common story among atheists — and the more I saw, the clearer my conclusions became. Besides, if God exists, I can't believe his case is so tenuous that you have to be in a particular building, or framed in a particular set of teachings, to figure that out.

✔ **"You haven't tried hard enough to believe."** Like anyone, I'd much prefer to have my death cancelled and to have a source of ultimate goodness and justice to appeal to in times of trouble. But the form of the objection is actually telling. It's true that I never tried hard to believe — instead, I tried hard to find out what was true, something the philosopher Bertrand Russell addresses later in this chapter. My desire to know has always been stronger than my desire to believe any particular answer. If I want to know the truth, trying hard to get a *particular* answer is the surest way to fail.

✔ **"Something bad happened to you, and you blame God."** I'm sure some atheists' position is based on a traumatic event, but this is much less common than one based on a long period of reflection and questioning. On the contrary, it's much more common to hear of a traumatic event causing a person to *seek* religious consolation than to run away from it.

Speaking for myself, I asked the question because I thought it was the most interesting one anyone could ask. If there's a God — then *oh my God, there is a God! There's a supreme being who created everything and cares for us!* It affects everything. If on the other hand there's no God — then *oh my God, there is no God! There's no supreme being. We're really on our own!* It affects everything.

Either answer is startling and fascinating. Either one is acceptable. I just want to know which one's true.

I was really lucky to be able to ask the question at all. Like many of my friends who are now atheists, I attended church regularly with my family when I was young. But I was never given the message that questioning is a bad thing. On the contrary, curiosity and education were both valued in our home, and I was allowed to chase ideas wherever they led.

Just as importantly, I felt personally safe and secure. Religion is often an understandable response to feeling alone, afraid, or unsafe. Depending on a person's circumstances, being alive and vulnerable in an uncertain world can be terrifying. But fear and insecurity were never a big part of my upbringing. I had enough to eat and a loving home. My education allowed me to take control of my life. I don't recall ever being threatened with hell. Not everyone with these lucky conditions becomes an atheist, of course, but those conditions are helpful in allowing a person to relax and open up, to ask the questions with a mind both clear and unafraid. In short, these conditions allowed me to doubt. In the end, they allowed me to *decide.*

Religious texts in many traditions warn about doubt — and for good reason. After a person begins to treat one of the Big Questions as a real question, not as the set-up for a preferred answer, many of the old questions that were so easily deflected in the past begin to appear in a new light. The philosopher Bertrand Russell called this the difference between the will to believe and the will to find out, which he says is the exact opposite.

Many children go through this same change in their questions about Santa Claus. At first they believe without hesitation. But at some point, questions start to nag at the back of their minds: *How do the reindeer fly? How does Santa get around the world in one night? How does he get into my house if we have no chimney and the alarm is set?* For a while, the child's strong preference is to continue believing, so the most transparently silly answers from Mom and Dad ("The reindeer eat magic corn!") are eagerly accepted at first. Tellingly, a child at this stage rarely asks directly if Santa is real because she doesn't really want to know yet. Her will to believe is stronger than her will to find out.

As the child grows and learns more about the world, the answers become less satisfying, and the urge to know the truth starts to overtake the will to believe. That's when the direct question comes at last: *Is Santa real?*

By offering a universe that cares for everyone after all, and by cancelling death, the idea of a loving God solves many of the deepest human problems. When it comes to God, the will to believe can be so overwhelming that most people never cross the threshold into the will to actually find out. Whatever doubts they have are easily shooed away by the religious equivalents of magic corn.

Those who are able to cross that threshold find that they're able to revisit the many questions they had shooed away so easily while their will to believe was strongest — questions about good and evil, meaning and purpose, life and death — and to see them in a whole new light. Many end up coming to the conclusion that the God hypothesis just doesn't fare well in that light, and that it's much more likely that humanity lives in a natural universe without gods.

Getting a handle on confirmation bias

Many people who eventually identify as atheists notice early on that religion is a perfect fit for the deepest human hopes and fears. Suspiciously perfect, you might say.

Confirmation bias is the human tendency to see things the way you prefer, and it's the single biggest obstacle to getting at the truth in any area of life. It leads people to notice and accept evidence that seems to support their beliefs while ignoring evidence that contradicts it.

It's funny how consistently my kids are the most amazing performers in the talent show, for example, or the most gifted athletes on the field. Of course I tend to notice the things that confirm my opinion (the jump shot or high note that's successful) and forget the ones that contradict it (the jump shot or high note that's missed). That's why I'm a terrible choice to judge their talent shows or referee their games — confirmation bias impairs my judgment, tilting me in the direction of the conclusion I'd prefer — that my kids are the best.

Likewise, any person who wins eternal life if a certain religious idea is true is a terrible judge of whether it is *actually* true.

The satirist H. L. Mencken said he respected someone's opinion on his own religion no more or less than his opinion that his wife was beautiful and his children were smart. No one can be trusted to be an objective judge when one particular answer showers him or her with glory.

That's one of the central problems many people notice when they first begin to look closely at religion — that the claims and conclusions of the faith so often play to the preferences of the faithful in a really big way.

The 19th-century agnostic feminist Susan B. Anthony said she distrusted people who claimed to know what God wanted, because it always seemed to line up really well with their own wishes. My thoughts exactly. If someone says he can cancel my death (which is one of my least favorite things, by the way) in exchange for my signature, I'm strongly inclined to reach for that clipboard. But if I'm more eager to see the world as it is than see it as I'd like it to be, it's important for me to be very skeptical of claims that fit my preferences like a glove. That doesn't mean I reject the claims outright, just that I need to ask some probing questions and follow the answers wherever they lead.

Asking new questions

After the old questions are reassessed, entirely new questions pop up. Some of these new questions may never have occurred to the person while deep in belief. A few examples include:

- ✔ How do I determine my own values, and how can I best live them out?
- ✔ If God didn't create the world, how did everything get here?
- ✔ What's the basis for human morality?
- ✔ What else have I taken for granted that isn't true?
- ✔ Because God isn't providing ultimate justice, how can humanity create a just world?
- ✔ What does it mean to truly die?
- ✔ Why did it take me so long to figure out what now seems obvious?

The answers to these new questions can speed the process of shedding religious assumptions. Some of them can make a person a little dizzy. But new atheists commonly describe an intoxicating mix of freedom, maturity, and deep responsibility that results from asking such questions without worrying about what Jesus or the minister may think. (For more on the commonly described sense of freedom, flip to Chapter 16.)

Comparing religions

One of the most common "Aha!" moments for atheists is their first exposure to a religion that's not the one in which they were raised — not a two-dimension snapshot of another religion, but the real deal. Meeting a fully developed system of thought with its own gods, its own stories, and its own claims — one that deeply contradicts their own religion and is held to be absolutely true by millions of people and absolutely false by everyone else — is an eye-opening moment. And many of those people come to the conclusion that both systems are simply ancient attempts to explain the world and comfort human fears before there were better ways of doing so.

I loved Greek and Roman mythology as a child; I knew every god and every myth by heart. In second grade, when it was time to do a project, everyone rolled their eyes as little Dale, dressed like Apollo, held up his helpful chart of the 12 gods of Olympus and their major fields. But the biggest lesson I got from those gods was that something could be earnestly believed by a whole civilization, and then discarded as obviously false by pretty much everyone a few generations later.

Then I had the related "Aha!" moment: If I'd been born in a different place, family, or time, I would have almost certainly been a faithfully observant believer in the religion of that place, family, or time. Many atheists cite that realization as yet another big step toward complete unbelief.

Reading the Bible

Science fiction writer Isaac Asimov calls the Bible "the most potent force for atheism ever conceived" — and many atheists agree. I read the book straight through at 14, and it was a big part of making an informed decision.

I'm more than willing to agree that the Bible has some really magnificent passages. I've never found a more eloquent tribute to love than the one in Paul's first letter to the Corinthians. That's why it was read at my wedding, and if you're married, probably at yours, too. The 23rd Psalm is unsurpassed for its poetic expression of peace and acceptance in the face of death. And the Sermon on the Mount distills the best ethical principles of Christianity into what has been rightly called the moral essence of the faith.

But most people are only familiar with that carefully handpicked sampler of inspiring passages from the Bible. For each and every inspirational passage that finds its way into pulpits and needlepoint pillows, half a dozen immoral horrors stay pretty well hidden. When you decide to read the book on your own, without a filter, a very different picture emerges.

I won't bore you with a long list of these atrocities. I can't say it's important to get away from filters and cherry picking, then just pick cherries from the other side of the tree. I will have to offer a few of them, just so you believe me about the sour fruit on the other side of that tree. But if you want to assess my claim that the Bible includes some very bad stuff, there's no better way to do so than reading the Bible.

Wait wait, come back! I'm not suggesting you read the whole thing. You certainly can if you want, but for now, just start with two books: Genesis and Matthew. Religious scholar Stephen Prothero estimates that 80 percent of the religious references you'll hear in American culture — from political speeches to figures of speech to Christmas carols — get their start in one of those two books.

Genesis will take you three hours of reading, Matthew even less. And (here's the small bowl of sour cherries I promised) before you reach your first bathroom break in the middle of Genesis, you'll encounter the stories of two fathers and their children. Both fathers behave with astonishing cruelty toward their kids, and — here's the thing — both are immediately praised and rewarded by God. Worse that that, God even *ordered* one of those cruel acts.

Now I don't hold such stories against God, by the way. Even if he exists, I always picture him smacking his ineffable Forehead in disbelief at the way he's portrayed. But I do hold it against the Bible and those who wrote it. And as I continued slogging through the Old Testament, that work of the human imagination has the poor Guy first instructing his people not to kill, then directly ordering them to kill neighboring peoples by the tens of thousands, including every child and infant.

"It says *what*?!" asks God. (See, even *he* knows the book mostly from needlepoint pillows.)

In Matthew, I found the story of a mortal woman impregnated by a god just as fascinating and compelling as when I'd read it in the Greek myth of Danaë and Perseus. And for all the beauty and moral poetry in the rest of the Gospel, Matthew is where Jesus introduces the world to hell, speaking with some satisfaction about the eternal "wailing and gnashing of teeth" by those individuals who don't follow his teachings.

I heard in Sunday school that the New Testament was intended to cancel out the Old. But read it yourself and see that Jesus puts that idea firmly to rest in Matthew 5:17–18: "Do not think I have come to abolish the Old Law. [That's the Old Testament.] I come not to abolish but to fulfill it. And until Heaven and Earth pass away, not one jot or one tittle of the Old Law shall pass away."

So all the commands to kill homosexuals, disobedient children, and nonbelievers, and to enslave and kill the people of neighboring countries — until Heaven and Earth pass away, it's all still in force.

Okay, enough sour cherries. Perhaps you can see why reading the Bible (or the Qur'an, which fares no better, or whatever the home team's scripture may be) is an important part of the process for many people who come to doubt, or completely reject, the religious claims around them.

Reading the Bible didn't make me an atheist, but it took that book off the list of possible reasons to believe. It was an essential step, though by no means the final one.

Admitting the weakness of the arguments and evidence

After someone begins to doubt aloud, he quickly encounters the arguments for God's existence, whether from a peer on the playground, a parent, or a Sunday school teacher. If the person's will to believe is stronger than his will to find out, the arguments will do their job, tucking the questioner back into his comfortable belief.

On the other hand, if the will to find out is stronger, the questioner is often surprised by the astonishing weakness of the arguments. I certainly was. I had been convinced that my doubts *had* to be wrong. It was impossible for so many billions of people to be mistaken! I had to have missed something big.

I wasn't surprised that the playground arguments were weak — *The Bible is true because the Bible says so, you have to believe or you'll go to hell,* and so on. But I thought that the more I probed and questioned, the more challenging the arguments would become. Instead, they didn't rise too far above the playground level: *I feel it in my heart, it isn't that kind of question,* and so on.

The most common kind of evidence I heard was the "I feel it in my heart" variety — the direct experience of God. Though most people take this for granted now, this approach is actually a pretty recent one for talking about faith. Direct experience only replaced the formal arguments for God's existence when those arguments started falling apart. (More on that in a few paragraphs.) Believers may speak of a feeling of transcendence, a near-death experience, a random act of kindness, or the sensed presence of God as a reason for believing. These feelings are beautiful and genuine, and I've had several of them myself — feelings of profound connection, of transcendence, and of overwhelming love and peace. I'm pretty sure we're talking about the same things. The question is whether they originate with a God or in the natural, human heart and mind.

If I heard from a very young age that every good feeling I have originated with God, then I'd see every good feeling as proof of God's existence. And if I heard from a young age that faeries cause rain, I'd see every spring shower as proof of faeries. Confirmation bias was at work again, so the evidence of experience failed to convince me.

Finally I reached the highest level — the ministers and theologians — fully expecting more challenging answers. Instead, more than one minister gave me the weakest reply of all — I should abandon my doubts and take a "leap of faith." When I spoke to theologians, I learned that many had quietly defined God right out of existence. One friend who is a Catholic theologian said the idea of "God" is really just "a response one gives to mystery," the name people call that which is unknown or unknowable. Another theologian friend — yes, I have several — told me in writing that the idea of an individual soul surviving death is "an elementary-schoolish belief that is no longer widely held."

Because modern theology was quietly putting "God" in quotation marks, I turned to the classics of theology to check out the arguments there. Most are variations on three ideas:

> ✔ **The ontological argument:** God is the greatest being conceivable. It's greater to exist than not exist. Therefore God exists. This argument is kind of stunning in its silliness, don't you think? It says God must exist because of the human definition of God. Yet people were so caught up in the will to believe that it held everyone's attention for centuries.

✔ **The cosmological argument:** Everything that exists must have a cause. At the beginning of the "chain of causation" must be a First Cause, that was not itself caused; that's God. This argument has some attraction, until you realize that it cancels itself out. Everything needs a cause, and God provides that cause. So what caused God? Simply contradict the opening statement by declaring he *doesn't* need a cause, then pretend that something has been solved. Yet again, this strange argument holds human attention for many centuries.

✔ **The teleological argument:** The universe is so complex and purposeful that it must have been designed by an intelligence. That's God. Now there's a problem worth thinking about, a genuine challenge that can't be dismissed out of hand. It's the kind of head-scratcher I'd hoped for when I started thinking about God. I'm not at all surprised that so many people find the seeming design or "purpose" in the universe convincing, especially when the alternative seems (incorrectly) to be blind assembly by random chance.

If I were born just two centuries ago, I'm pretty sure I'd have been a believer of some sort — perhaps a Deist. The reason would have been the seeming design and complexity of the universe. Though "God did it" has some serious problems of its own (check the second bullet, "cosmological argument"), no better explanation had yet been advanced at that point.

That changed, suddenly and decisively, in 1859.

Solving the complexity problem

Have you ever wondered why evolution in particular is such a hot-button issue in the culture war? I wondered that for years. Sure, it contradicts the creation story in Genesis, but so do a lot of other modern discoveries. Why does this one in particular inspire so much heat? The answer is found in the problem of complexity, especially the complexity of life on Earth — a problem that evolution solves very well.

Evolution by natural selection doesn't just uproot one branch of religious belief. Challenging the idea that humans are special and separate from animals uproots the whole tree, mills it into lumber, and builds a very nice house out of it. And not a house of God, let me tell you.

Still, most people don't decide what to believe by looking at abstractions like these. Darwin or no, the complexity of the universe, and especially of life on Earth, seems to make a designer a sure thing for most people. "I may not know what this God looks like or thinks or wants," they say, "but come *on!* I can't believe that this tree, or that moose, or the human body . . . I can't believe these things just knitted themselves together by random chance!"

You know what? They're right. If there's anything less likely than a supernatural God, it's the idea that all of this happened by random chance. Somebody once compared that idea to a whirlwind passing through a junkyard and assembling a 747.

For most of human history, those were the two apparent choices, God or random chance. Given those choices, I'm not surprised most people opted to believe in a designer. But in 1859, British naturalist Charles Darwin published the theory of evolution by natural selection. Suddenly people had *three* choices — and Darwin's theory, properly understood, finally provides a credible fit for the evidence.

Understanding evolution

An intelligence doesn't guide evolution; evolution also isn't a process of random choice. In a nutshell, here's how it works:

- All organisms include differences among individuals — bigger or smaller hands or feet or eyes, a tendency to react a certain way to loud noises, different coloration, and so on.

- Some of these differences don't matter. Some have a negative effect, making it harder to survive or to have as many babies. But some differences are actually helpful. They make it a little easier for the individual to live longer or have more babies.

- If the difference — say a slightly longer beak — gives even a tiny advantage, the lucky organism will have slightly more offspring and pass the same feature to them. The advantage will have been naturally selected. It's not magic, just math.

- The kids will tend to have the same long beak, passing it on to their own slightly greater number of kids, and so on. And if one of them has an even longer beak, the selective process continues. Eventually, if the longer beak keeps giving an advantage, it becomes the norm.

- Fast-forward millions of years, and millions of selected traits produce the incredible diversity and complexity of life.

The variation is random, but the selection is anything *but* random.

Keeping God in the process?

Many religious believers have tried to reconcile evolution and religion, saying God uses evolution to create, but honestly, there's really not much for him to do. Natural selection works just fine without a guiding hand. In fact, after a person understands the theory, it's clear that it works *inevitably* without that guiding hand. Thomas Henry Huxley captured this idea when he hit his forehead and said, after first reading Darwin's theory, "How extremely stupid not to have thought of that!"

Defining "theory"

Even though the scientific community now accepts evolution as fact, it's still called a theory. So is the theory of gravity, which doesn't mean there's much doubt about what will happen when you step off your roof.

In science, *theory* simply means an explanation. Some theories are weak and don't survive close examination, like *geocentricity* (that says the Earth is at the center of the universe) and *phrenology* (a person's personality is reflected in the shape of his head). Other theories survive that close examination — like *heliocentricity* (the sun is at the center of the solar system) and evolution by natural selection.

But weak or strong, they're all called theories.

Not all scientists in the 1860s felt the same. They weren't sure for some time whether such a process could really account for *all* the variations people see. So for 70 years after Darwin's theory was published, they did what scientists do — they squabbled and argued and challenged the details. Not until the 1930s and 1940s did a "synthesis" of genetics and biology solve the legitimate problems that had kept many scientists from accepting the idea up to that point. But after that powerful synthesis happened, an overwhelming majority of the scientific community accepted the theory.

Despite claims to the contrary by those driven by their own confirmation bias, evolution by natural selection is now as solidly established as the orbit of the Earth around the sun.

Accepting a better solution

Evolution uprooted the tree of traditional religion in several ways. But perhaps the strongest blow was to the argument from design. For thousands of years, everyone from theologians to the person in the street found the complexity of life to be the strongest argument for the existence of God. Now a powerful, simple, natural explanation was available, one that presented fewer problems than an uncreated Creator.

In *The Blind Watchmaker*, Richard Dawkins described the importance of evolution to atheism. Before Darwin, an atheist may have said, "God's a poor explanation for complex biology, but I don't have a better one." That's a pretty unsatisfying position to be in. But Darwin's theory made it possible to be what Dawkins called "an intellectually fulfilled atheist." The single most compelling reason to believe in God could finally be set aside with confidence.

Noticing the steady retreat of religious answers

Religions haven't been shy about offering explanations for the universe — how Earth was formed and how old it is, what causes weather, how humans and animals are related, how life on Earth came to include such incredible variety, why bad things happen, and what happens after death, to name a few. The original purpose of religion was to provide these answers before other methods were available.

Science has answered many of these questions — not all, but quite a lot. And in every case, a natural explanation has replaced a supernatural one.

If scriptural claims are valid, it seems that scientific inquiry should be constantly confirming those claims. Instead, they're found to be incorrect, one after another, and there's a steady retreat of supernatural explanations into the remaining gaps in human knowledge — an approach sometimes called "the God of the gaps."

Getting humble about humanness

Christianity was the religion I was born into the middle of, so Christian ideas were naturally some of the first I wrestled with, Jacob-like. And one of the defining Christian ideas is that humans are special, created separate from animals and endowed with immortal souls. Now that science has determined this isn't the case — that humans are in fact animals, and that they share common ancestors with other animals living today — the very idea of the soul and human specialness deserves another look. And when people take that look, many find that the central narrative of Christianity no longer works.

Astrology took a similar blow when it lost one of its central, foundational principles — that Earth is in the center of the universe — about 600 years ago. But that hasn't hurt horoscope sales too much.

Humans weren't here from the beginning — in fact, *Homo sapiens* have only been on the planet for less than one tenth of one percent (0.1 percent) of its history. (More on that in the next section.) If other animals are without souls, God must have chosen a moment in evolutionary history when humans were "human enough" to merit souls. Because evolution happens by achingly tiny steps, no single moment happened when humans crossed a line from "prehuman" into "fully human." Among other problems, such a sudden transition would result in a generation of children who are ensouled but whose parents aren't — a very weird prospect, I'd say.

Go the other way, declaring that yes, animals also have souls, and I'll have to follow that down the tree of life, ensouling bacteria and my front lawn at the same time. A lovely idea in its way, but it does challenge the very heart of the Christian narrative.

No matter how you spin it, the idea that I have a soul and my dog doesn't have one is an enormous problem, one that many find fatal to the idea of the soul and salvation.

It is important to note that not everyone finds evolution and Judeo-Christian belief incompatible. I'm glad they find that possible. I (and most atheists) don't quite see how they manage it, but it's nice to have their support for evolution education.

Coming (really, really) late to the party

One discovery that deals an especially strong blow to the idea that humans are at the center of creation is how very recently humanity has arrived on the scene. The following example puts the human animal in humbling perspective.

Spread your arms out to your sides, like a plane. Your wingspan is a timeline. Your left fingertip represents the time of the first single-celled life on Earth, and your right fingertip is right this minute. Between the two is 3.7 billion years of time, the history of life on Earth. At what point in that span would you say the dinosaurs enter the picture? And what about humans?

When I was young, I'd have put the dinosaurs somewhere around my left shoulder, and then people somewhere in the middle of my chest. Then I spent some time with Carl Sagan, one of the great popularizers of science, and learned that I was off by . . . well, kind of a lot.

From your left fingertip, all the way up your arm, past your left shoulder, across your chest, and past your right shoulder, life on Earth is nothing but bacteria. By the time you reach your right wrist, the most impressive form of life on Earth, the king of the beasts, is the worm. In the middle of your right palm you finally get your dinosaurs, and they're extinct by your last finger joint.

Run your eyes along that history again so far. All that history, all that life, and still no appearance by the Main Attraction, the species for whom everything is supposedly made — humankind.

So when *do* humans finally show up at the party? Well, it's more than fashionably late. *Homo sapiens* fits in one small fingernail clipping.

Realizing that the human species has only arrived on the scene in the last *one tenth of one percent* of the history of life on Earth . . . well, it's a humbling earthquake of perspective, one of several that seriously cracked the foundations of traditional religion.

Grasping the size of the universe

In the first millennium BCE (1000 BCE to 1 BCE), when most of the major religions were born and most scriptures got themselves written down, Earth was believed to be the center of a really small universe, one that could fit inside what now is known to be the orbit of the moon. You can easily see why humanity was pretty cosmically important when the stage was that small.

Fast forward about 2,500 years, and science now recognizes the sun as one of about 200 billion stars in the Milky Way galaxy, which is one of 100 billion galaxies in the universe. To take a single step into that immense scale, drop a penny on the ground, and call it the sun. At this scale, the nearest star — the very nearest one — would be another penny 350 miles away. And it goes from there, trillions of times over. Earth is a speck in space and a blink in time. That makes it pretty unlikely that humans would be the central concern of the creator of all that, but people can still be the central concern of each other. All of humanity is in the same itty bitty boat.

It's not surprising that religions born prior to the Scientific Revolution put humanity at the center of creation and at the core of God's concern. The universe as humans understood it then made it possible to do so. Making such a claim with a straight face today is much more difficult, and many people find it impossible.

Seeing that the universe is just as you would expect it to be without a God

Some religious answers to challenging questions about God are worth considering carefully. Others require some Olympic-quality back bending. If the judges place no limit on the amount of back bending allowed, reality can indeed be made to conform to the God opinion. But to meet the world honestly, I'd rather conform my opinions to reality.

One of the best ways to do this is by applying a principle called Occam's Razor. When deciding between two possibilities, the one that requires the fewest assumptions — the least back bending — tends to be the right answer. An all-powerful, all-good God can be made to fit into this universe, explaining away evil and catastrophe and death and uncertainty like a game of cosmological Twister — *Left hand blue! Right foot red!* — or a person can notice, at long last, that the universe is just as one would expect it to be if no supernatural God is at the wheel.

I can like the fact or I can dislike it, or some combination of the two. But as soon as I decided to disregard my preferences and instead to discover reality as honestly as I could, there was little left to do. I was an atheist.

The next step was deciding what that meant and what to do with it.

Knowing What Most Atheists Actually Do Believe

A lot more is worth knowing about the atheist point of view than the fact that atheists don't believe in God. Many other beliefs and values tend to come along with that disbelief. These sections look at a few of the more important ones.

Seeing the natural universe as all there is — and enough

After a talk in Northern Ireland in which writer and gay icon Quentin Crisp described himself as an atheist, a woman stood and said, "Yes, but is it the God of the Catholics or the God of the Protestants in whom you don't believe?"

It's a funny story, but it also reflects the general feeling many believers have that atheists must be rejecting just one *particular* concept of God. Often people assume that I don't believe in the "old man with the white beard," so a religious friend will rush to assure me that she doesn't believe in that God either. It's a well-meaning attempt to find common ground, but it misses the mark. I do share an awful lot with my religious friends — see Chapter 16 — but I promise we're not going to find any of that common ground under the feet (or hooves, or wheels, or swirling pink vapor, or imperceptible, immaterial spirit) of *any* kind of God.

Most atheists believe that this natural, physical, material universe is all there is. That doesn't mean everything has been explored, understood, or even perceived. But if we as atheists ever could explore to the far reaches of that universe, and into every plane of existence there is, I think our explorations would continue to find a natural, physical, material universe.

No good reason exists to believe a supernatural realm of any kind exists — no gods, ghosts, or spirits of any sort. I may be wrong about that, and that wouldn't bother me a bit. As a matter of fact, it would be entirely awesome.

But right now, everything that's been suggested as evidence of a supernatural realm has a better, more likely natural explanation. And that's the position of most other atheists as well. They aren't just disbelieving in a particular idea of God, but in the whole idea of gods. And disbelief in all other supernatural entities and realms tends to be part of the package.

Some atheists wish God did exist. Though I could do without some of his advertised qualities, an all-powerful, entirely good God would solve a lot of real problems. But I'm fully satisfied with the universe however it is, with or without God, and I feel privileged to be awake in it, if only for a moment or two. More astonishing wonder and meaning and sheer delight exists in this natural universe than I can wrap my mind and arms around in a single lifetime. Oh, but I plan to wear myself out trying.

I bang on about this at some length in Chapter 16, but for now, let me just say that most atheists share my feeling that this natural universe is not only all there is, but it's also more than enough.

Accepting that this is our one and only life

Aside from some Eastern atheistic religions that include a belief in reincarnation, like Jainism and some departments of Buddhism, you can safely say that atheism includes the opinion that this life is your one and only. Religious believers often recoil in horror at the thought, saying it's an unbearable idea that drains life of all meaning.

I've never understood that. Why would added time add meaning, even if that additional time is infinite? If I live to be 80 instead of 40, is my life automatically more meaningful? Most people would probably agree it's not. How about 200 years, or 500? Ten thousand? These changes in quantity don't seem to budge the meaning meter at all. No matter how long you live, right up to eternity, the basic question remains in place. (In fact, the novel and movie *Tuck Everlasting* does a great job making the opposite claim — that immortality actually *robs* life of its meaning.)

That life ends, and ends for good, should give what time you do have an extraordinary preciousness. If this moment is only one of an endless parade of moments, *that* seems less special to me. But knowing that this moment is part of a limited life, one with no do-overs, can lend a whole new depth, intensity, and meaning to that moment.

And you're spending this precious moment reading my book? *Seriously?* Go outside, plant a tree, hug your kids, dance naked in the rain! (Just kidding, keep reading.)

Valuing ethical behavior

Most religious believers want to live in a world in which people behave ethically. Funny thing . . . so do most atheists. An ethical society is simply safer, less scary, easier, more satisfying to live in, and simply better, whether or not a person believes in God. That's the kind of place I want my kids to live in. You know, heck with them — it's the kind of place *I* want to live in.

Be careful not to confuse atheism with *moral nihilism* — the idea that nothing is inherently right or wrong. In fact, when it comes to defining right and wrong behavior, studies show an amazing amount of agreement on the most basic ethical ideas, even among people with wildly different religious and political beliefs. They may put stronger emphasis in one area or another, and there are certainly some areas of disagreement. But that's up in the branches. Down at the roots of moral understanding, most atheists and theists agree that they want to live in a world where people treat each other fairly and don't harm one another.

After everyone recognizes this shared desire, we can all talk about how to make it a reality.

Taking responsibility for ourselves and each other

The transition from religious belief to unbelief often packs a one-two punch. Many people who've been through the transition often describe an initial sense of freedom and relief, something I describe further in Chapter 16. But then many talk about an enormous feeling of responsibility for themselves and for others.

Believing in God solves an awful lot of problems — or feels like it does. If I give my problems over to God and encourage others to do the same, it can feel like I've done something productive, moved toward a solution. But "putting it in God's hands" often keeps a person from *actually* doing something to improve the situation.

After a person sets religious belief aside, a huge feeling of responsibility often sets in. Life has no divine safety net and no escape clause into the next life. If humans want a better world, they have no one but themselves to turn to. This idea strikes me, and many other atheists, with the overwhelming desire to do it right — to work for human rights, justice, peace, and equality in this, our one and only life.

Asserting that God is actually "that kind of question"

I clearly remember a sentence from my childhood, one that Sunday school teachers and playground peers alike offered up whenever I got to poking around at God: "It's not that kind of question."

I never understood what they meant. Did they mean the most interesting question of all — "Is there a God?" — can't even really be asked? Why would that be? I asked anyway. And after some time, I began to figure out productive ways to ask the question.

Suppose you make an unusual claim, like, "A hundred purple ponies are on the dark side of the moon, galloping in patterns that control our destinies." I won't run out and start building a rocket to check it out. I'd say, "What in the world makes you think that?" If you tell me you saw it in a dream, or that an ancient prophet predicted it . . . heck, I wouldn't even leave my chair.

If people are telling me a God does exist, I don't need to go looking for God; I just need to know why they think there is one. Then I can decide whether their reasons are convincing to me. Suddenly God is "that kind of question."

Religious claims are claims of fact, claims that impact this natural world. That's why atheist scientist Richard Dawkins and Catholic theologian Scott Hahn agree that a universe with a God would be a very different one from a universe without one, and that the presence or absence of a God is indeed a scientific question, even though everyone haven't all agreed on the answer yet. (I should note that not all scientists or theologians agree with this claim. See "Answering the Question: Is Science Incompatible with Belief in God?" at the end of this chapter.)

Addressing the negative consequences of religious belief

Religious belief has inspired a lot of beautiful works of art and music as well as acts of profound generosity and selflessness. Can I get an "Amen!" from the congregation? I thought so.

But if a religious belief inspires bigotry and hatred and violence, it would be immoral to look the other way just because that belief is religious. Amen?

In addition to the good things that religious ideas and people have done, they have done a great deal of harm as well, including

- ✔ The use of biblical arguments to extend slavery in the 19th century and delay women's rights in the 20th
- ✔ Perpetual violence in the Middle East, fueled in large part by conflicting Jewish and Islamic religious claims to the land
- ✔ The ongoing opposition to equal rights for gays and lesbians — which are almost exclusively framed in religious terms
- ✔ Catholic opposition to reasonable contraception, which has worsened calamities of overpopulation and HIV/AIDS in the developing world
- ✔ The terrorist attacks of September 11, 2001, which relied on selected Islamic texts to inspire self-sacrifice and hatred of "infidels"

That's a greatly abbreviated list, as I'm sure you know. Atheists believe that any idea that inspires such harm must be challenged, and should certainly not be protected from criticism just because it's a religious idea.

Discovering meaning and purpose

When someone hears that I am an atheist, a meaning-and-purpose question is never far behind — something like, "But how do you get out of bed in the morning?", or the closely related question, "So you think you are just a collection of molecules?"

As Adam Lee, one of my favorite atheist bloggers, puts it, I'm not "just" any of those things, any more than a house is "just bricks" or a book is "just words." It takes both a special arrangement and an infusion of purpose to make those things. The same is true of me. I am responsible for making sure I'm not "just" a collection of molecules, not even "just" an organism, but one whose brief time on Earth is full of meaning and purpose.

We all ought to get out of bed in grateful surprise every single morning, giggling with amazement at our luck to be conscious things, to be inside that tiny window of existence between two infinities of nonexistence. Most mornings I fail to wake up that way, and boo on me for that. But when I do, it's partly because I have scads of meaning and purpose in my life.

Many believers think meaning and purpose has to come from God, and that the goal in human life is to discover his purpose for me and run with it. That's fine, I suppose — but I'm here to tell you it's entirely possible to find your own meaning.

Doing so isn't always easy. Much like your need for a pancreas, you never even know you have the need for meaning and purpose until it begins to fail — which mine did, in no uncertain terms, when I graduated from college. For the first time in my life, I had no idea what was next. I had no idea which way to go professionally. All of my romantic relationships had ended in flames and the waiting room was empty. I felt like a photocopy of a photocopy of a hollow log that wonders what the point is. It was my first genuine core-shaking crisis of meaning and purpose, and it lasted for years. It was really unsettling.

I did a lot of thinking and talking to friends during that time. Some of them had found meaning in a particular career. One had joined the Peace Corps and was pursuing a meaningful life through service to others. It all sounded great, but none of it seemed quite right for me.

Eventually it hit me: I wanted a family. That was it. Just thinking about that idea lit up my personal meaning-meter like nothing else had. A few years later, I married my favorite person, and we are raising three incredible kids together. Talk about waking up every morning in grateful surprise! Meaning and purpose, once a crisis for me, is pancreatic again.

Family won't feed the bulldog for everyone, of course, and it shouldn't. Even for me, family isn't the only source of meaning and purpose. Putting all of one's meaning eggs in a single basket has never been a good idea. My work has also been an important source of purpose, one that has ebbed and flowed for years as I've found my way forward, as it does for so many people.

Meaning and purpose isn't an all-or-nothing commodity. It goes up, and it falls down. It swings around wildly, trying to find its bearings. I don't believe there is, or should be, one universal "meaning of life," God-based or otherwise, no one thing that keeps our needles pinned. Neither do I believe we make our own meaning from total scratch. I *discovered* what was fulfilling for me. I felt in the pit of my stomach when I was on a hollowing path, then registered a shock of recognition when I veered onto another that filled me up.

Those who've defined their own meaning and purpose in life tend to say that the process made it much more worthwhile than something received from the outside. I agree; I wouldn't have it any other way myself.

Realizing that a universe without God can be even more wonderful and inspiring

Far from being grey and joyless, the natural universe that science is gradually discovering is packed with more wonder and inspiration than it's possible to absorb in a lifetime. A list of my favorite wonders would include the following:

✔ Every atom in your body has existed since the beginning of time and will continue to exist until the universe ends.

✔ The human mind is a way for the universe to become aware of itself.

✔ The iron in your blood was created in the final moments of the collapse of a dying star.

✔ You're standing on a ball spinning at 900 miles an hour.

✔ A complete blueprint to build you exists in every cell of your body.

✔ A thought or memory makes a physical path in your brain. When you see another person experiencing pain or joy, the same pathway in your brain "lights up" as if you had the experience yourself.

✔ When you speed up, time slows down.

✔ You entered the world through another person's body.

✔ You're literally related to all life on Earth, from apes to amoebas to trees and whales.

Everyone really ought to be paralyzed with wonder and amazement all the time. And the fact that it all happens without a designer, and that it's even possible to figure out *how* it happens, is more amazing still.

Setting Aside Misconceptions: Things That Few (If Any) Atheists Believe

Many common misconceptions exist regarding what atheists believe. In this section, I address some of those misconceptions to continue bringing the atheist perspective into clearer focus.

That there is no right and wrong

One of the most common misconceptions about atheists is that they're unable (or unwilling) to distinguish between right and wrong actions. Most atheists have even heard that disbelieving in God is a license for murder. Atheists tend to blink in surprise at this idea. Moral development supports their surprise by showing that most believers and nonbelievers tend to have the same basic moral understanding, as one researcher put it, "whether they are of one religion, another religion, or no religion at all."

There is something greater than myself

Being an atheist is a big part of living a meaningful life, and there's no supernatural required.

I can see why it would bother someone to feel that there's nothing greater than him or herself, no bigger picture, nothing larger to connect to. When I was a kid, I sometimes pictured God being depressed by that. But it's never been a problem for me, even though I've never been convinced God was that greater thing.

When I got married, I was immediately part of something greater than myself. When I had

kids, that "something" got larger. That feeling you get when you sing in a choir, or in a stadium at a concert, or play in a band (as I often did as a kid), or play on a sports team (which I, uh, never did) — all are experiences that put a person in touch with something greater than him or herself. I'm part of a neighborhood, a community, a nation. Each connects me to other people, creating something larger than the sum of its parts.

Morality is about how people treat each other. That's why the single most sensible moral idea, one that appears in every religious and philosophical system in the world, is "treat others as you would like to be treated." If I don't do this — if my natural empathy fails, and I go around doing harm or treating people unfairly, who will hold me accountable? *People,* that's who. My life will be made much more difficult, and rightly so, by the society in which I live.

When someone tells me that only belief in God prevents people from committing acts of violence, I always wonder — does he really think his *own* belief in God is the only thing that keeps *him* from strangling me on the spot? If we were arguing over God's existence, this is about the time I stop trying to convince him and slowly back away.

Actually, I think better of him than he does of himself. I don't think for a minute that too many believers are kept in line only by the idea that they're being watched by a supernatural being. That can help someone who needs constant babysitting, I guess, but behaving well also makes rational sense. Check out Chapter 15 where I discuss this topic in greater depth.

Avoiding punishment is just one reason everyone tends to behave more often than not — and it's one of the lowest reasons at that. But it nicely parallels the religious idea that people behave well to please God and avoid his wrath. In fact, people also behave well to please *each other* and to avoid *each other's* wrath.

But what all sides tend to miss in this conversation is the simple, demonstrable fact that most people behave morally most of the time, regardless of their religious perspectives. Think about the billions of decent, nonviolent human interactions that occur every day. Yes, there are plenty of moral transgressions as well, but it's objectively true that a basic, shared moral sense is evident most of the time. Almost everyone seems to agree on what's right and what's wrong more often than not — and that includes atheists.

That life arose and evolved by chance

If atheists believed that life arose and evolved by random chance, they'd deserve to be laughed out the door. It simply isn't credible. But anyone who believes such a thing — *or* who believes there's a conscious designer behind the curtain — hasn't caught up with the best of human knowledge.

The evidence points overwhelming to a third option I describe earlier in this chapter — evolution by natural selection. The word "selection" gives away the fact that a *non-random* process is going on, one that naturally favors certain variations over others. Life is thought to have arisen through a process called *abiogenesis,* through which simple inorganic materials, responding to a few physical principles, combined to create the basic building blocks of single-celled organisms. Add a couple billion years of natural selection, stirring constantly, let cool, and you get the variation we see around us. (For even more detail, flip to the earlier section, "Solving the complexity problem.")

So it bears repeating — atheists think life is pretty amazing and complex, but they don't believe it happened by chance *or* by intentional design.

That all religion is the same

Some atheists are guilty of putting all religion into the same category. I know a few of these folks myself. One very good reason not to treat all religion all the same is that . . . it's not all the same.

But most atheists I know have spent enough time around people of different perspectives to know that there's a massive difference between a snake-handling Pentecostal and a liberal Quaker, not to mention between the Reverend Fred Phelps (whose church pickets funerals with signs reading God Hates Fags) and the Dalai Lama.

Enormous differences even exist within one denomination. A progressive Catholic differs from a conservative Catholic on almost every major political and social issue. These differences matter, and atheists — at least those who pay attention — can and should recognize them instead of painting all religion with a broad brush. Progressive religious believers have much more in common with the nonreligious than they do with fundamentalists, and it's better to work together against genuinely poisonous beliefs than to push progressive religious believers aside just because we differ on God.

That religion has made no positive contributions

Some atheists also feel that religion has made no positive contributions to the world. Even Bertrand Russell, a pretty levelheaded guy on most days, credits religion only with establishing the calendar, saying he can't think of any other contributions.

Most atheists, even those who feel religion is a bad influence overall, can usually think of a bit more than the calendar:

- ✔ Many great artists and composers are inspired by their belief. Johann Sebastian Bach, for example, wrote SDG *(Soli Deo Gloria,* "For the Glory of God alone") at the end of each of his compositions.
- ✔ Catholic monks preserved the works of antiquity throughout the Middle Ages as an act of religious devotion.
- ✔ Quaker activists have been at the forefront of every movement for peace and human rights in the past 200 years.
- ✔ Hinduism and Jainism have developed principles of nonviolence that have led to the peaceful resolution of countless conflicts, large and small.
- ✔ Christian church communities worldwide have developed enviable cultures of charitable giving and service to the poor.

Of course, this list is abbreviated, but you get the idea.

Many atheists would raise an objection here, saying these things shouldn't be credited to religion but to human beings who happened to be religious, and who simply framed their creativity and their values in religious terms. But others feel that religion at its best can indeed serve as a motivator and as inspiration for great things — even though it's not the only worldview that motivates and inspires.

Answering the Question: Is Science Incompatible with Belief in God?

If I ask whether science and religion are compatible, I'm committing a kind of category error. It isn't even like comparing apples and oranges — it's more like apples and math.

Any given religion is a collection of claims, values, and practices. You can think of it as answers to the problem of being human. Science is a method for asking questions. To put it simply, religion is a collection of answers, and science is a way of asking questions. The scientific method results in a body of knowledge, all subject to revision, but the knowledge itself isn't science.

Here's a better way to frame the question: Is the scientific method compatible with the religious method of learning about the world? Now it's apples and apples. If we're talking about traditional revealed religion, which takes the word of prophets and scriptures as final, the answer is clearly no. You can either declare a revelation infallible or pursue science, but you can't do both. At the heart of science is the refusal to accept any information as final, infallible, unchangeable. It's the polar opposite of the religious concept of revealed sacred truth. So the two methods are deeply incompatible.

In 1997, biologist Stephen Jay Gould suggested that science and religion can be thought of as "non-overlapping magisteria," each with its own domain of authority. Science is about the *what* and *how* of the universe, he said, while religion is king in the area of meaning and morality. Everything would be fine, he said, if they'd just stay out of each others' sandboxes.

This idea is nice, and many atheists and agnostics agree with Gould. But others think the idea that science and religion can be separated in this way has several fatal problems. Religion makes factual "what and how" claims all the time, for example, and science has begun to say quite a bit about morality. So in the end, many atheists (and many religious believers as well) feel that Gould's nice idea solves nothing. (I get into more detail in Chapter 8.)

Does this mean you can't be a religious person and a scientific one? Apparently not, because there are many religious scientists and science-minded religionists alive today. It works in part because many religious expressions in the last century or two have gotten far away from the idea of divine revelation. They see scriptures as a source of inspiration written by other human beings, fallible folks like themselves. After a person gets to that point, reason can be applied to the ideas in scriptures. They can be challenged and even discarded as need be: *Slavery? No thanks. Love your neighbor? Super, let's keep that one. Six-day creation? Clearly not true — let's call it a metaphor.* And on it goes.

So yes, science and religion can snuggle comfortably and honestly in the same brain — but only if the methods of gaining knowledge can be brought into reasonable agreement. Some people find that possible, and some don't.

Part II
Following Atheism through the Ages

The 5th Wave   By Rich Tennant

"I believe in the dance."

In this part . . .

This part takes a reckless ride through the long, fascinating history of the idea that (despite persistent rumors to the contrary) there aren't any gods, from ancient China and India to 21st-century Britain and the United States.

Along the way, you can find atheists and agnostics in the most unexpected places. They're present not just among Greek philosophers and Renaissance scholars, but also in a tiny French village during the Inquisition, in the middle of medieval Islam, and in the heartland of America.

Chapter 4

Finding Atheism in the Ancient World

● ●

● ●

*T*hough the history of religious doubt is probably as long as the history of religious belief, doubt leaves fewer footprints. The first evidence of supernatural belief appeared as early as 130,000 years ago in ritualized burials by Neanderthals. But the guy rolling his eyes in the back pew didn't leave any clues about his opinions.

Unbelief begins to show itself more clearly after prehistory gives way to recorded history, flicking the ears of each and every supernatural belief the human mind creates.

I start by describing how people in modern times have figured out what the ancients believed or didn't believe — a trickier proposition than you may think. After that, I make a sweeping survey of the ancient world, discovering individual doubters and outright nonbelievers in cultures from Greece to India to China, and even in the shadow of the Temple of Jerusalem.

Uncovering What the Ancients Believed (Or Didn't)

Finding evidence of religious unbelief in the ancient world isn't always easy, but that doesn't mean it isn't there. The challenge is figuring out how to determine what people thousands of years ago believed or questioned.

Disbelief tends to disappear from history for several reasons. Most of what people know today about the past depends on written records passed down hand-to-hand over thousands of years and hundreds of generations. This process isn't ideal, but it's the only one available — and religious unbelief is among the least likely ideas to have made it through.

To determine whether disbelief existed thousands of years ago, consider what it takes for an idea to get from an ancient mind to yours today.

1. **Someone had to write it down.**

   Most ideas are already out of the game at this point because most never left the heads of the people who thought them. No matter how brilliant an idea was, if it wasn't written down, it wasn't likely to have reached future generations.

2. **The written document had to survive, one way or another, for more than 2,000 years.**

   In order to reach modern times, it must be the case that no person or thing destroyed the document — not just in its own time, but also in every year, decade, and century that followed. Surviving over time is quite a challenge because most documents were on things like papyrus, paper, or parchment. Preserving those documents isn't easy because the Earth's oxygen-rich atmosphere likes to set such things on fire, not to mention a hundred other unhelpful conditions. (Even the original US Declaration of Independence, which after a mere two centuries now lives in a titanium condo full of argon gas, isn't doing too well.)

   So even the things that were lucky enough to be written down in ancient times are now mostly gone. One of the greatest ancient scholars, Didymus of Alexandria, earned the priceless nickname "Bronze Butt" for sitting long enough to write more than 3,000 books — of which zero survived. One literary historian in the fifth century compiled 1,430 quotations from the greatest authors of the ancient world — 1,115 of which are from works that are now lost. And the revolutionary ideas of Democritus, one of the greatest thinkers of all time, survive only in glowing references by other writers.

3. **People in every generation naturally tend to preserve and recopy the ideas that they agree with most.**

   Because religious unbelief has usually been a minority opinion, and a deeply disliked one at that, it's surprising that *any* hint of ancient atheism found its way to readers today.

On the other hand, sometimes the reviled status of atheism has actually helped pass down the idea. If an idea's disturbing enough to the mainstream, writers in a given time often spend reams of paper and gallons of ink recording just how wrongheaded it is. In the process, they provide strong indirect evidence that the idea existed in the first place. And because their own writing represents mainstream opinion, it's carefully preserved and passed on — and the disturbing opinion rides the critic's coattails down the centuries.

A lot of the evidence I present for ancient atheism in the following sections, though not all, is of this indirect kind.

Leaping Forward: The Axial Age

Something amazing must have been in the water between about 800 and 200 BCE. A number of different world cultures, including China, India, Persia, and Greece, gave rise to whole new ways of thinking about the world. Humanity seemed to take a giant step from a focus on survival to a more conscious, questioning, planful, and searching approach to life.

The period has been called the Axial Age because the world seemed to pivot on a mental axis and continue in a whole new direction. In the span of a few centuries, new philosophies and religions popped up like daisies, including:

- ✔ Confucianism and Taoism in China
- ✔ Judaism in Judea
- ✔ Buddhism and Jainism in India
- ✔ Several key schools of philosophy in Greece

And kicking and wailing in each and every one of those maternity wards, right alongside these infant faiths and philosophies, was newborn baby atheism.

Noting that atheism was present in the Axial Age doesn't mean that no one doubted the existence of gods *before* that time. As I mention in the previous section, religious doubt has surely been hanging around as long as religious faith. But this period was the first time atheist thought pulled itself together into a coherent recorded philosophy. And the fact that it happened at just about the same historical moment in far-flung cultures is yet another reason the Axial Age is well worth exploring.

So why does all this thinking, questioning, and moral concern kick into gear at the same time in several cultures? Some sociologists note that many of these cultures were in a period of intense and bloody conflict during that time. In each case, a more unified nation eventually emerged from a collection of smaller states. Even as life headed toward greater stability, the memory of chaos and vulnerability was fresh. The new ethical systems were naturally concerned with how human beings should live together to prevent the madness from happening again. They immediately pushed back against the aggression that nearly consumed them.

So it really isn't a coincidence that so many Axial Age cultures turned most hungrily to religions or philosophies that emphasized peace and nonviolence (Jainism and Buddhism) or ethics and social order (Confucianism). And though theistic religions like Judaism usually get the biggest shout-out in the

Axial Age, each of the three peaceful, ethical systems I just named is completely atheistic.

Inferring Unbelief in Ancient Judea

Few documents have had as easy and secure a ride through history as the Judeo-Christian Bible. And wedged in among the praising and smiting in the Book of Psalms is some ironclad evidence that atheism existed in ancient Judea. It's Psalm 14:1: "The fool says in his heart, 'There is no God.'" The psalmist doesn't sugar-coat his opinion of these unbelievers: "They are corrupt, their deeds are vile; there is no one who does good . . . They devour my people as though eating bread . . . [and] frustrate the plans of the poor." Maybe just a passing thought? Hardly. The whole thing is repeated, almost word for word, in Psalm 53.

Far from being a tiny presence on the fringes, evidence suggests that religious doubt had something of a heyday in Judea in the centuries after the Psalms were written. In her seminal book *Doubt: A History,* historian Jennifer Michael Hecht notes that a good number of Jews in the region came to identify with Greek culture and to doubt Jehovah's existence so strongly that in the second century BCE, they supported the rededication of the Temple in Jerusalem to *Zeus.* That's not because they suddenly believed in the gods of Olympus, but because they appreciated their own cultural identity as part of the sprawling Greek Seleucid Empire. (The ancient Judean equivalent of Fox News must have had a collective stroke.)

Secular Jewish identity runs alongside religious Judaism right through the centuries, finally becoming official in the 20th century when Humanistic Judaism was named one of the five recognized branches of the faith. (Refer to Chapter 8 for a complete discussion of Humanistic Judaism.)

Finding Unbelief in Ancient China

China has always been one of the most receptive cultures on Earth for atheism. In fact, nontheistic ideas have been front and center in Chinese philosophy and national government for at least as long as records have been kept.

Even religion in China often does just fine without gods, including some forms of Buddhism and Taoism, while Confucianism — a secular philosophy focused on reason and natural ethics rather than gods — has easily been the greatest influence on Chinese thought for more than 2,500 years.

Because godlessness has been an accepted part of the Chinese cultural conversation for so long, a clearer picture of atheist ideas emerges from Chinese history than it does from most other cultures. Best of all, instead of bringing nontheistic ideas down to modern readers solely through the critics, the Chinese culture preserved them in their original written form.

In the following sections, I introduce a few of the concepts and thinkers that have made China one of the richest sources of nontheistic thought.

Understanding the concept of t'ien (heaven . . . but not quite)

Chinese philosophers spent a great deal of time and thought on the concept of *t'ien*, which translates loosely as "heaven." But *t'ien* has no connection to the traditional Western idea of a place for human souls to commune with a deity after death. Instead, *t'ien* means, "that which causes the world to be as it is."

Philosophers in China who considered a deity to be the cause of everything used *t'ien* to denote that deity, whereas philosophers who saw only natural causes at work, whether or not they fully understood those causes, used the same word to mean comprehensible natural laws. Whatever it is that makes the world as it is, that's *t'ien*.

Two of the most famous nontheistic philosophers in ancient China were Xun Zi (312–230 BCE) and Mencius (372–289 BCE). They disagreed on human nature:

- ✔ Xun Zi felt that humans are basically bad, but improvable by education and discipline
- ✔ Mencius felt humans are basically good, but are led astray by the influence of society

They did agree that *t'ien* had nothing to do with a conscious god, seeing it instead as predictable, natural laws at work.

Xun Zi returned to the idea of *t'ien* over and over in his work, making arguments that sound like something an atheist blogger could have written today:

> Pray all you want — heaven can't hear you. It's not going to stop the winter because you are cold, and it's not going to make the Earth smaller because you don't want to walk so far. You pray for rain and it rains, but your prayer has nothing to do with it. Sometimes you don't pray for rain and it rains anyway. What do you say then? If you act wisely, good things tend to happen. Act like a fool and bad things tend to happen. Don't thank or curse heaven — it's just the natural result of your own actions. If you want to have a better life, educate yourself and think carefully about the consequences of your actions.

That's a very humanistic approach to life.

Getting to the roots of Confucianism

If the chaotic collision of ideas was their idea of a good time, Mencius and Xun Zi picked an especially good era in which to be born, right in the middle of a period called the *Hundred Schools of Thought*. It was a kind of Golden Age for Chinese philosophy, with countless new and different ideas contending for the hearts and minds of the Chinese.

As with several cultures during this time (see "Leaping Forward: The Axial Age" earlier in this chapter), this battlefield of ideas coincided with a lot of literal violence — in this case, the military clashes that would eventually turn China from countless tiny states into seven big warring states and finally into a unified nation.

People enduring a period of incredible chaos and uncertainty are thirsty for order and compassion and a system of ethics that describes a reasonable path back to civilized behavior. So perhaps it's not surprising that Confucianism, a system of thought that stresses exactly those qualities, emerged as the clear winner in the war of ideas, forming the backbone of Chinese culture and thinking for more than two millennia.

Confucianism is a secular system of philosophy and ethics, an approach to life that encourages self-improvement and the cultivation of virtue, including altruism and compassionate action to help others achieve a better life. And it does it all without appealing to gods for help.

Confucius is credited with coining the earliest version of the Golden Rule: "What you do not wish for yourself, do not do to others." You may also recognize it as one of countless variations of that ethical principle found in cultures around the world.

Whether Confucianism is a philosophy or a religion is a source of perpetual and mostly pointless debate. You can call it either one. But even if you consider it a religion, it is (like Jainism and some forms of Buddhism) a nontheistic one.

Visiting ancient India: 320 million gods and none at all

Say "religion" and "India" and most people will immediately think of Hinduism, and maybe even picture Shiva, the god most likely to win a tickle fight. But although 80 percent of Indians identify as Hindu, the last thing you should associate with this fascinating corner of the globe is any kind of religious uniformity. India is hands down the most religiously diverse region of its size on Earth and has been for millennia. Included in this tapestry of various beliefs is a thriving atheist tradition at least as old and honorable as the atheist voices of China.

India has been the birthplace of an impressive number of religious traditions and identities. Buddhism, Hinduism, Sikhism, and Jainism all started out in India and continue to have a huge presence, but India is also home to:

- ✔ 125 million Muslims
- ✔ 25 million Christians
- ✔ 60 million people who specifically identify as nonreligious

I focus on the three most prominent ancient Indian religions in these sections to show that each has included a healthy presence of nontheistic belief.

Doubting like a Hindu

Hinduism, which is the largest religion in India, is unlike any other religion on Earth. Most religions have a starting point, a founder who hears voices, or claims to have found gold tablets, then spreads the word. Inevitably, the religion splits into two or ten or a hundred sects over disagreements in doctrine or practice. But Hinduism goes the other direction, bringing a wide variety of ancient Indian religious traditions together under a single name.

Hindus (or even Indians) didn't coin the term "Hindu." Arabs to the west of the Sindhu (now Indus) River used the term for all the various foreign peoples on the other side of the Sindhu. Like "barbarian" or "gentile," the word "Hindu" started life as one of those words that's usually accompanied by a vague, hand-waving gesture at "those people over there." And Hindu wasn't even a religious category at first, which also helps explain much of the diversity it ends up containing.

Unlike the early Christian church, which held conclaves in its early centuries to decide on an orthodox core of beliefs, the many religious groups under the Hindu umbrella didn't lose their different traditions and beliefs. Individual freedom of belief is a given, and the idea of blasphemy or heresy is pretty much unheard of. A Hindu may believe in one god or other divine being, or many gods — up to 320 million by one count — or no gods at all.

So you can see why a lot of effort throughout Hindu history has been devoted to describing and cataloguing the many branches and colors and shades of Hinduism. One big division is between those schools of thought that accept the authority of the ancient Veda scriptures (known as *āstika* schools) and those that don't (*nāstika* schools). It's not as strange as it sounds, really; even Christian denominations vary a lot in the emphasis they place on the

Bible's authority — although Hinduism is radically different in Christianity because both the āstika and nāstika sides include some completely godless branches.

Samkhya, the oldest of the six main schools of Hinduism, entirely rejected the idea of gods, whereas followers of the Cārvāka system of thought were busily writing critiques of theistic belief 2,500 years before atheism hit the *New York Times* Bestseller list. "Do not perform religious acts," said one text from the third century BCE. "There is no heaven, no final liberation, nor any soul in another world . . . While life remains, let a man live happily; nothing is beyond death."

Around the same time, the *Purva Mimamsa* school laid out a more agnostic philosophy, saying the evidence for gods was insufficient, and that even if they do exist, humans can get along just fine without them. (Some scholars actually describe Mimamsa as more of an *apatheistic* branch — they don't care whether gods exist or not. Either way, they figure, there are more important things to think and talk about.)

Laughing at gods with Buddha

Buddhism was even more specifically atheistic at its start than Hinduism. Many scholars trace Buddhist atheism right to the horse's mouth, Gautama Buddha, who clearly rejected the idea of a creator god and was described as laughing uproariously when his followers said (as followers often will) that he himself was a god. Some forms of Buddhism do include reference to super-human beings, or *devas,* but these have neither the powers nor the other résumé items typical of gods.

Buddhist teaching often includes the specific caution that theistic beliefs and the desires that accompany them can get in the way of achieving *nirvana,* the total freedom from suffering that is the goal of Buddhist practice. Instead, like several other Indian and Chinese philosophies, Buddhism emphasizes the relationship between what people do and what effect that has on the universe — summed up (and ridiculously oversimplified) in the Western phrase, "What goes around comes around."

Doing no harm with the Jains

I saved my favorite for last. Jainism, an atheistic religion founded around the same time as Confucianism, gets my vote for Best Religion on the Planet. Based on pacifism and nonviolence toward all living things, Jainism was around centuries before Samkhya. Jains reject the idea of supernatural beings, including a creator god, and have written some of the most direct criticisms of supernatural belief and defenses of atheism ever produced. (See Chapter 5 for one of my favorite passages.)

One symbol's fall from grace: The swastika

The Jain religion uses several symbols to represent key concepts in its belief system. A kind of keyhole shape represents the three realms of the universe; three dots in a line represent the "triple gems" of right vision, right conduct, and right knowledge; and an extended palm symbolizes nonviolence toward all living things.

There's a fourth symbol that you may be familiar with: the swastika. Now almost universally seen as the ultimate symbol of hatred and evil, the swastika has the opposite meaning in the Jain religion, representing peace and the perpetual, cyclical nature of the universe. The very name *swastika* means "to be good" or "to be your best self."

In one of the bitterest ironies in the history of symbols, the violent warrior culture of Nazi Germany adopted this symbol of peace and goodness in 1920 to connect themselves to "proto-Aryans," the original European people to whom Indians are closely tied. But in pursuing an idea of racial purity, they couldn't exactly connect themselves to non-whites, so they borrowed the symbol of the Jains, but oddly claimed that *Norwegians* were the closest to true Aryans.

Jains continue to use the swastika in its original meaning today.

Once the dominant religion in southern India, Jains are now a fairly small minority in the country — about 6 million out of 1.2 billion people, or one-half of one percent of the population. Despite their numbers, Jains have had an outsized influence on Indian life in areas including ethics, literacy, and law. Such ethical concepts as *ahisma* (nonviolence) and *karma* (action that decides one's fate) are traced to Jain origins, and the oldest libraries and much of the most influential literature in India are Jain in origin.

Whispering doubts in Ancient Greece and Rome

Greece and Rome were hotbeds for ancient philosophy. *Ethics* (which deals in the difference between right and wrong, good and evil), meaning and purpose, the nature of existence, beauty, logic, politics — all these and more were fodder for thinkers in both cultures. But the voice of unorthodox religion, not to mention any hint of atheism, wasn't welcomed and was even punished in Greece and Rome.

The label *atheos* (meaning "godless one") was tossed at just about anyone who held a religiously unorthodox opinion during this period — even at those who actually did believe in gods. Socrates was no atheist, for example, but his suggestion that the gods of Athens weren't the right ones was enough to put the hemlock in his hand. (Granted, his insistence on publicly embarrassing those in power may also have had *something* to do with it.)

Socrates was by no means the first Greek to cast doubt on the religion of his time. Pre-Socratic philosophers explained the world in terms of natural laws that made things run without the need for divine intervention, an idea the powers-to-be considered deeply subversive. Democritus — often called the father of modern science for his idea that the universe is made of atoms — saw belief in gods as nothing more than a fearful response to the unknown. After we understand the natural causes for all we observe, he said, we'll transcend that fear and have no further need of gods. He became a mentor to some other god-doubting philosophers, including Theodorus and Diagoras, both of whom I discuss later in this chapter.

Even a perfectly mainstream opinion had little chance of making it through the shredder of history (for more on that shredder, see "Uncovering What the Ancients Believed (or Didn't)," earlier in this chapter). The fact that any *whiff* of atheism, the least orthodox opinion of all, made it all the way from the ancient Greco-Roman world to the present is frankly astonishing. But enough whispers confirm that a lively thread of religious doubt, up to and including complete atheism, was present and accounted for there at the roots of Western civilization.

Meeting the "first atheists" — Diagoras and Theodorus

Diagoras of Melos is almost certainly the most famous atheist in fifth century BCE Greece. He's often dubbed "the first atheist" — news that would have surprised the earliest Jain and Buddhist atheists if they hadn't already been dead by centuries.

Diagoras didn't write much about his atheism, but plenty of others on hand recorded his frequent jabs at the religious beliefs of his time. When a ship carrying Diagoras encountered a terrible storm, the crew shouted aloud that the gods were angry at them for giving passage to a godless man — leading Diagoras to wonder aloud if each of the other ships fighting the storm had its own Diagoras aboard.

When Athens slaughtered the inhabitants of his home island of Melos, one of the most vulnerable settlements in the Aegean Sea — for no other purpose than to prove their military power to Sparta — Diagoras publicly cited the lack of divine retribution against Athens' immoral act as proof that no gods existed. The leaders of Athens responded by throwing him into a cell. Only a sizeable ransom by his teacher and fellow disbeliever Democritus saved Diagoras from execution.

After such a close call, you'd think Diagoras would lie low. But not long after his release, he was described chopping up a wooden statue of Hercules and throwing it in his cooking fire. "Cooking my turnips will be his thirteenth labor!" he laughed to his horrified onlookers. When he revealed the secret rituals of the Greek Eleusinian mystery religion — thereby taking a bit of the air out of the "mystery" part — the Athenian authorities decided to be rid of him at last. They announced a reward — one piece of silver for his death or two for his capture.

Diagoras fled to Corinth, where he lived out his life and died, to everyone's surprise, in bed.

It's in his book *On the Gods* that Diagoras's atheism came through most clearly. Though the book was still around 500 years later to impress Diogenes Laertes, a biographer of philosophers, with its compelling arguments, the book finally vanished in the historical sinkhole of the early Middle Ages.

Theodorus, known as "The Atheist" of Cyrene — whose name ironically means "gift of the gods" — was another Greek philosopher who went beyond challenging the gods of the moment into complete unbelief in the existence of any such beings. The goal of human life is to seek joy and avoid grief, he said, and joy is found most readily in knowledge, while grief stems primarily from ignorance — including time wasted worrying about the whims of cranky, inscrutable deities.

One of the strongest influences on Theodorus was Epicurus, one of the most important philosophers of all time. Though he wasn't an atheist, I have to mention him here for his efforts to get any gods there might be out of the way of human happiness. If there are gods, he said, they have nothing to do with humans. As a result, we don't have to fear them and can get on with the business of being happy.

Epicurus was also responsible for one of the most thought-provoking statements about God ever made: the Epicurean Paradox. God is said to be all-powerful and all-good — but Epicurus says he can't be both. Here's why:

✔ Is God willing to prevent evil, but not able? Then he's not all-powerful.

✔ Is he able, but not willing? Then he's not all-good.

✔ Is he both able and willing? Then why is there evil?

✔ Is he neither able nor willing? Then why call him God?

For a brief moment, humanism stretched its wings.

Meeting the "first agnostic"— Protagoras of Abdera

It's a discovery story to rival Hollywood. While hauling a load of wood through the streets of Abdera, Protagoras supposedly crossed paths with Democritus, a celebrated philosopher who also lived in Abdera. Democritus noticed that the pieces of wood in Protagoras's load had been fitted together with such incredible skill and ingenuity that he figured Protagoras must have been a genius. He invited him to live and study philosophy in his home. They shared a deep affinity as thinkers, including the powerful idea that the gods were most likely bunk. And the rest is history — and philosophy.

Protagoras was best known for saying "Man is the measure of all things," an idea that stirred up plenty of outrage in his and subsequent generations. If everything should be assessed in terms of humanity, huff the huffers, then the gods are no longer at the center of people's concerns. Well exactly — and that's humanism stretching its wings again.

According to later historians, Protagoras's outspoken agnostic writings and speeches finally drove the Athenian leaders to do what they do best — sentence the dissenter to death. Fortunately they weren't especially good at carrying *out* those sentences, and Protagoras escaped, though the storm he encountered at sea took his life.

Some accounts have the Athenians rounding up all of Protagoras's books and burning them in the central agora. If true, they didn't do a very good job of that either: Over a century later, the agnostic writings of Protagoras were still being read and discussed. (I describe a fragment of one such work in Chapter 10.)

Guessing why people invented gods — Euhemerus

One of the most interesting job descriptions in ancient Greece belonged to the court mythographer, whose job included gathering stories of the gods and demigods and bringing them to life in narratives, poems, sculptures, paintings, and other artistic media. A bit of cultural anthropology was in the mix, too, because mythographers traveled into the hinterlands to gather these tales and brought them back to the court.

Euhemerus was a mythographer for the court of Cassander, King of Macedonia, about a hundred years after Protagoras. As you may imagine, his work gave him plenty of time to think about the gods, and he developed the earliest known explanation of how belief in gods actually began. Zeus, Apollo, Athena, Poseidon, Hermes, and all the rest of the Greek pantheon of gods were originally historical kings and heroes, he said. They were worshipped in their lifetimes, as kings and heroes tend to be. After they died, these cults of hero worship naturally took on supernatural dimensions, and boom! — you have the gods of Olympus.

"Euhemerism" came to describe any attempt to explain supernatural beliefs in natural terms. Even the early Christian fathers did it, including Clement of Alexandria, who patiently explained to a pagan believer that his gods were once just men like himself.

It's fun, and not too hard, to imagine the very next sentence out of the pagan's mouth.

Changing everything: Lucretius and On the Nature of Things

If you're going to give the world just one book, it may as well change everything. De rerum natura (On the Nature of Things), the sole surviving work by the Roman poet and philosopher Lucretius, was arguably just that kind of book. Written in the first century BCE, it was an epic poem intended to keep the ideas of Epicurus alive, especially the importance of freeing the human mind from the fear of gods and death.

> Nature does all things spontaneously, Lucretius said, without the "meddling of gods." The universe is made of atoms moving through space, colliding, connecting, and splitting apart again, making all that we see. There's no guiding intelligence and no master plan. Unhappiness comes mostly from worrying about the gods. Death is the end, and it constitutes total peace, with no "frowning ministers of hate in hell" waiting to torment selected souls.

Lucretius didn't deny the existence of gods outright; he simple said that if they did exist, they were so blissed out that they didn't bother with things like universe creation or rewarding and punishing human behavior.

With the help of a fortunate Catholic obsession — see Chapter 6 for more on that — De rerum survived all the way to 1417, when a book hunter in a monastery in Italy discovered the very last crumbling copy. Recopied and disseminated throughout Europe, many of the great thinkers of the following centuries credited the book with revolutionizing the way they saw the world. Many historians today believe it had a profound impact in jump-starting the Scientific Revolution, the Enlightenment, and even the whole modern world.

Not a bad life's work.

Naming names: Sextus Empiricus and Cicero

Most of the names of atheists and agnostics in the Greco-Roman world, especially those who didn't write (or had their works destroyed), would have been lost forever if not for a couple of well-placed mentions by other writers. In an essay called "On the Nature of the Gods," Roman philosopher and orator Cicero (106–43 BCE) listed several Greek atheists and agnostics who were still spoken of in shocked whispers during his time, including Protagoras, Diagoras, and Theodorus.

More than 200 years later, in his essay "On the Gods" — apparently they didn't put much creative effort into their titles — Greco-Roman philosopher Sextus Empiricus listed five Greeks who he said were the most prominent atheists of their time, including Protagoras, Diagoras, Theodorus, and Euhemerus.

If not for these two prominent listings of ancient atheists, the 21st century might never have heard of these courageous and intelligent people. I wonder how many more were born, lived, doubted, and died in this period of wondering and questioning, but didn't have a Cicero or Sextus to record their thoughts.

But enough of their roll call — what do Sextus and Cicero themselves think about gods?

Like many Skeptic philosophers of the time, Sextus suspended judgment, believing that to be the surest route to peace of mind, his ultimate goal. But Cicero, in the same essay in which he named those names, slipped his own wonderings in: "Do the gods exist or do they not?" he asks. "It is difficult, you will say, to deny that they exist. I would agree, if we were arguing the matter in a public assembly, but in a private discussion of this kind it is perfectly easy to do so . . . I confess that many doubts arise to perplex me about this, so that at times I wonder whether they exist at all."

Chapter 5

Going Medieval

*P*ick up almost any collection of atheist and agnostic writing through the ages and you'll get the impression that religious doubt takes a thousand-year holiday between the fall of Rome (fifth century) and the Renaissance (15th century). True, finding atheists in the Middle Ages isn't easy, especially in Europe, where the Christian church was as much a political force as a religious one. Any challenge to orthodoxy during that time wasn't just considered blasphemy but was also a kind of political treason that often separated heads from bodies.

But just as in every other place and time, unorthodox opinions including atheism were definitely present in the Middle Ages. You just have to know where to look.

A good place to start is outside of Europe, where (as I describe in Chapter 4) more than one advanced civilization already had a well-developed tradition of atheist thought that continued to thrive while European atheism went mostly silent.

This chapter checks in on India and China, two of the best such examples, to see how atheist thought developed through the Middle Ages. I also visit the Islamic Golden Age, during which the Arab world zooms past napping Europe in science, literature, medicine, the arts, and philosophy. This astonishing period in Arab history includes an explosion of secular ideas, complete with the rejection of belief in Allah and criticisms of Muhammad that would make an ayatollah faint.

Iceland also gets a nod, as the hero of a 13th-century saga turns Psalm 14 upside down, declaring that it's belief in gods, not disbelief in them, that makes a person foolish.

Finally I visit the Inquisition, a 600-year effort to ferret out heretics that once in a while turned up an actual atheist instead.

Continuing to Doubt in Medieval India

The common idea that India is an intensely theistic country is probably a result of *polytheism* (the worship of multiple gods). In the West, from the Sistine Chapel to Christ of the Ozarks, you can see depictions of the one God, or of his helpfully tangible son. Polytheists have an awful lot of gods to honor, so seeing hundreds or even thousands of gods and demigods colorfully carved and displayed in every nook and cranny of the Indian subcontinent is common. The result is the strong perception that everyone and everything in India is connected to god belief.

But as I describe in Chapter 4, atheist and agnostic schools of thought coexisted with theistic ones throughout India's history, not just as a fringe philosophy, but right at the heart — sometimes even the head — of each major religion. That certainly continued throughout the Middle Ages.

The Middle Ages was a great time to be an atheist in India. Atheist philosophy was a full partner in the conversation, and nontheistic schools even came to dominate the country for much of this period. As a result, Sanskrit — the main language for religious texts in India — ended up with a larger collection of atheist literature than any other ancient language, with the possible exception of Chinese.

The following sections explore the surprisingly strong role of atheism in medieval India.

Putting atheist Hinduism front and center

Even after accepting the idea of an atheist Hindu, many people still picture a small, tolerated group on the sketchy outskirts of a great religion. But the branches of Hinduism that rejected gods or declared them irrelevant were among the leading Hindu schools of thought for centuries.

The nontheistic Samkhya school, which I introduce in Chapter 4, grew to become one of the primary expressions of Hinduism in early medieval times.

When atheism led the Hindu world

In the 14th century, the hugely influential Hindu guru and philosopher Madhvacharya wrote *Sarvadarshansamgraha,* a book that attempted to name and describe all the various schools of thought that had accumulated under the Hindu name. One indication of the strength of Hindu atheism at the time was the very first chapter of the book — appropriately entitled "Atheism" — which presented not just a passive description, but also a strong argument in favor of doing away with belief in gods.

Samkhya Hindus weren't completely naturalistic in their beliefs. They saw the universe as having two realms — nature and spirit — but argued that there was really no place for an *Ishvara* (god) in their system, so they left it out.

Samkhya dominated Hindu philosophy for a good 600 years before starting to decline in the tenth century.

The agnostic Mimamsa school, which also began in ancient times, was still going strong in the Middle Ages. Like Samkhya, this school believed in an unseen spirit realm but had no positions available for actual gods. Instead, the spirit of the universe was fueled by *karma,* the acts of human beings.

Calling out "foolish men" — Jinasena

By the ninth century, the atheistic Jain religion had been going strong for 1,500 years, and a Jain teacher named Jinasena wrote *Mahapurana,* an important Jain text that remains to this day one of the most complete descriptions of Jain tradition and belief. And smack in the middle is one of the boldest defenses of atheism ever written.

"Some foolish men declare that Creator made the world," said Jinasena. "The doctrine that the world was created is ill-advised, and should be rejected. If god created the world, where was he before creation? . . . How can an immaterial god create that which is material? . . . If god created the world by an act of will, without any raw material, then it is just his will and nothing else, and who will believe this silly stuff?"

He went on at some length, anticipating many ideas of the Enlightenment a good 900 years before that period's opening bell: "If he created out of love for living things . . . why did he not make creation wholly blissful, free from misfortune? Thus the doctrine that the world was created by god makes no sense at all."

Sweeping Out the Superstitions in China

China has a funny habit of turning atheists into gods. Atheist philosophy in China during the medieval period was dedicated in part to restoring these figures to the status of important, but human, teachers:

- ✔ **Gautama Buddha:** He warned that supernatural beliefs — including the idea of gods — can create a serious obstacle to achieving *nirvana,* the total freedom from suffering. His followers were so impressed with his renunciation of gods that within a few generations they venerated him as a god. (Sigh.)

- ✔ **Laozi:** The philosopher Laozi founded Taoism around the same time that Buddhism and Confucianism started — the sixth century BCE, that stunning period I describe in Chapter 4. Laozi denied that any conception of a deity can be valid and warned against superstition — then upon his death, his followers revered him as a manifestation of the deity Daode Tianzun, the Grand Pure One. (Double sigh.)

- ✔ **Confucius:** Though deeply revered, Confucius has mostly managed to avoid being turned into a god. But that didn't prevent his practical, secular philosophy from gathering plenty of supernatural and superstitious elements, like burrs on its trousers, as it hiked forward into the Middle Ages.

To stay alive and relevant from one generation to the next, any system of thought needs a constant inflow of new ideas and lively discussion. Confucianism didn't get that kind of active attention in the early Middle Ages. After a few centuries with no one minding the store, it began to seriously lose its mojo. By the ninth century, superstitious elements from Chinese folk religion had strangled the rational, secular life out of Confucianism, just as they had done with Buddhism and Taoism long before.

Fortunately at this point Neo-Confucianism was born, a philosophical movement to restore Confucianism to the rational, secular philosophy Confucius intended. Job One was cleansing it of supernatural and mystical ideas.

Chang Tsai (1020–1077), one of the most important Neo-Confucian thinkers, wrote a book called *Challenging the Unenlightened* to spell out his vision for restoring Confucianism as a system of reasoned ethics and self-improvement. I think he'd be pleased with the result: Since then, a mostly rational, mostly secular Confucianism has formed the heart of Chinese thought and ethics, straight down to the present.

Tapping into the key themes of Confucianism

Confucianism centers on honesty and reason as the guiding principles of human life. Important themes include the following:

The Five Constants – individual virtues important for ethical living — are

✔ **Humaneness:** Being selfless toward others

✔ **Justice:** Showing the desire to be fair

✔ **Etiquette:** Observing rites and rituals of everyday life

✔ **Knowledge:** Acquiring a truthful understanding of the world

✔ **Integrity:** Acting in a way consistent with one's own values

Trash-Talking in Medieval Islam

Now step four centuries back to 622 CE and about three squares to the west into what is now Saudi Arabia. Muhammad was busily founding Islam, a religion that quickly became the mortar for a new empire. Just as a unified China emerged from countless tiny states a millennium earlier, Muhammad used Islam to knit the many tribes of the Arabian Peninsula into a political unit that immediately began conquering its way both eastward and westward.

By 750, after a century of violence and political uncertainty, one of the biggest empires in history sprawled over 5 million square miles from Spain through northern Africa and the Middle East, clear to the doorstep of India — all under the banner of Islam. These sections take a closer look at Islam and one of the most important "golden ages" in human history — one that included the small but vocal presence of religious doubt.

Kindling the Islamic Golden Age

As the new Islamic empire grew, it encountered and absorbed several thriving cultures, including Egypt and Syria. Both had been part of the extended Greek empire at one time, and both had kept the legacy of ancient Greek thought alive and carefully preserved in great libraries through the centuries.

Although an allergy to all things "pagan" had Christian Europe holding the works of ancient Greece at arm's length like a moldy sock, Arab scientists and philosophers began translating those same texts into Arabic. Picking up where the Greeks left off, Arab culture made rapid advances in optics, physics, astronomy, medicine, philosophy, and the arts, igniting a period known as the Islamic Golden Age.

It's called an *Islamic* Golden Age because the empire was unified under that religion, but Islam itself deserved little credit for the new flowering of learning. The Umayyad *caliphs* (Islamic clergy) shared Europe's allergy to Greek ideas and vigorously opposed the translations out of concern that they might seriously challenge the house religion.

And right they were. Eager to dip into the well of Greek knowledge, scholars and translators made an end-run around the caliphs, enlisting the support of wealthy businessmen to fund the translations, and the Golden Age happened anyway. A vibrant culture of intellectual inquiry was born. And unlike much later Islamic history, the chorus included voices challenging the religious party line, up to and including the integrity of the prophet Muhammad and the very existence of Allah himself.

Not many voices were singing those particular tunes, to be sure, but enough to get the attention of modern scholars — as well as some furious theologians in their own day.

Things began to really take off around 750 CE when a new caliphate took the reins of the empire — the Abbasids of Persia. Theirs was a more open and intellectual government than the Umayyad caliphate had been. They preferred sayings like, "The ink of a scholar is more holy than the blood of a martyr" over the less education-friendly platitudes of Muhammad. The Persians had been in touch with Greek ideas for centuries, after all, so the Abbasids quickly relaxed restrictions on the scholars' work. They brought the translation of Greek works out of the shadows, and the Golden Age was fully underway.

Railing theologians: "Against the Unbelievers"

Even though the new caliphate opened up to Greek ideas about the area of a triangle and the nature of the stars and such, they still weren't eager to tolerate full-throated challenges to Islam. As a result, virtually no texts from the agnostics and atheists of this period have survived.

Fortunately, just as in Judea and elsewhere, the outraged cries of their critics nicely confirmed their presence anyway. In fact, such cries were so common in this period that almost every major Islamic theologian of the time seemed to have written a treatise called, "Against the Unbelievers." There's no better testimony to the healthy supply of unbelievers, or *zendiqs,* than treatises addressed directly to them.

You can easily trip on the terminology here. Not all zendiqs are atheists. Just as in ancient Greece, it was common in medieval Islam for everyone whose beliefs were unorthodox to be called "unbelievers," and modern scholars know that *heretics* — people who believed in an unorthodox creed — were among the intended targets of these treatises. But scholars also agree that heretics weren't the only targets, because the theologians often wrote two separate, distinct arguments: one addressed to heretics, the other to outright unbelievers. One such work begins with a long proof that the world did in fact have a Creator — an argument generally intended for atheists rather than heretics.

Railing back: Unbelievers say "Muhammad was a liar"

Standing up in the middle of the ninth century Islamic Empire and calling Muhammad a liar took a stainless steel spine. But Abu al-Hasan Ahmad ibn Yahya ibn Ishaq al-Rawāndī — yes, *that* Abu al-Hasan Ahmad ibn Yahya ibn Ishaq al-Rawāndī — did just that.

Being a former Islamic theologian himself, al-Rawāndī knew what he was talking about, anticipating every argument of the theologians with a devastating counterargument. And he didn't mince words. Not only did he call Muhammad a liar, but he also said the miracles of Moses and Jesus (both of whom are also revered in Islam) were nothing more than "fraudulent tricks." Allah acts like "a wrathful, murderous enemy," he said, adding that he probably couldn't even add two and four. The Qur'an itself is described as "the speech of an unwise being" that contains "contradictions, errors and absurdities."

It's no surprise then that al-Rawāndī's written works — including his most famous, *The Book of the Emerald* — have vanished, except for a few fragments quoted by his hyperventilating critics. But his impact was still long-lasting; more than 200 years after al-Rawāndī's death, the Persian theologian al-Shirazi was still spilling gallons of ink arguing against al-Rawāndī's suggestion that truth can be discovered through human reason without the need for prophecy or revelation.

Being called a zendiq in medieval Islam was generally a death sentence, but some people still managed to have fun with it. No one had a better time than Abu Nuwas, a Persian poet who delighted in shocking polite society by writing about everything Islam forbids, from masturbation to drunkenness to homosexuality. A story was told of an *imam* (Islamic cleric) who began to read from the Qur'an in the mosque. When the imam got to the line, "Oh, you infidels!", Abu Nuwas shouted out, "Here I am!"

That did it. An angry mob dragged him to the authorities. They assumed he was a heretical follower of Manichaeism, a rival religion of the time. They gave him the standard test, ordering him to spit on a portrait of the prophet Mani, founder of Manichaeism. They knew he wouldn't be able to do it if he was a follower of Mani. *I'll do you one better,* he thought, then stuck his finger down his throat and vomited on the portrait.

Confused, the magistrates released him, never considering the possibility that he found Mani and Muhammad equally silly. Even if they had, an atheist was considered less threatening than a heretic. (I make that same point again later in this chapter in the "Giving Europe the Third Degree" section.)

Freezing Out the Gods in Iceland

If you want a peek at the soul of a culture, look at their legends — the stories they tell about themselves. For Iceland, that means the Sagas of Icelanders.

The first Sagas were written in the 13th century, at the tail end of a period wracked by violence and political uncertainty — you may be sensing a pattern here — and describe life in Iceland just after the Norse explorers settled it.

Hrafnkell's Saga tells of a warrior chief, Hrafnkell, who worships Freyr, the Norse god of lovely things such as wealth, sunshine, and sex. Hrafnkell gives Freyr his best offerings and constant devotion, even building a grand temple to the god. Despite all this devotion, Hrafnkell is attacked by an enemy, his temple burned, and he and his people enslaved.

"It is folly to believe in gods," he says, vowing never to perform another sacrifice. Stories of lost faith in hard times are easy to come by, and you can usually count on the hero to experience a sudden epiphany that leads him back to the fold before the closing credits. But Hrafnkell's Saga takes an unexpected turn: He escapes slavery, spares the life of his captor in exchange for freedom, and lives his life in peace and contentment *without* gods.

The most famous contributor to the Icelandic Sagas was the wonderfully named Snorri Sturleson. In addition to leading the nation's parliament and writing history, Snorri — like Euhemerus in Chapter 4 — was a *mythographer,* a gatherer of myths and beliefs. And interestingly, Snorri came to precisely the same conclusion as Euhemerus about the origin of god belief: Human warrior chiefs and kings were venerated in life, then venerated in death, then gradually became venerated as gods. The more contact a person has with human mythmaking, the more he or she seems to see the man behind the curtain.

The spirit of Hrafnkell in Iceland today

It's no surprise that Hrafnkell remains among the most beloved and widely read of the Sagas of Icelanders among Icelanders today. Though most are nominally Lutheran, fully 60 percent of Icelandic respondents in a 2011 poll said religion is unimportant in their daily lives, making Iceland one of the least religious countries on Earth.

Giving Europe the Third Degree: The Inquisitions

If the door-to-atheist opinion was open just a crack in ancient Greece and Rome, it slammed shut completely in 381 CE. That's the year Roman emperor Theodosius took a break from overseeing the collapse of the empire to ban all religious opinions other than his own, which was Nicene Christianity.

The Christian church fathers spent the early medieval period sorting out what constituted the church's official doctrine, banning this or that departure from the party line. For seven hundred years, it seemed to work because *heresy* (beliefs or practices that differ from those official sanctioned by the church) went fairly quiet. But by the mid-12th century, new movements within Christianity began finding adherents — and all hell broke loose.

The Inquisition was a long campaign by the Roman Catholic Church to eliminate unorthodox beliefs and practices in Europe by use of interrogation, torture, and even execution. It continued on and off for more than 600 years with the purpose of securing Catholic religious and political control over the continent.

This section introduces in greater depth what the Inquisition did through the stories of three otherwise unknown villagers in 14th-century southern France, as well as the man who interrogated them for unorthodox thinking.

Eyeing the Inquisition's main focus

The Inquisition's main concern wasn't nonbelievers. Nobody cared too much about the occasional French peasant muttering to himself about God being pretend. The idea was to root out fellow Christians who are forming sects that differed from the orthodox norm — differing sometimes (like many denominations today) in seemingly tiny ways. But the Catholic powers at the time perceived any organized movement to be a threat, so the Inquisitions ground on, generation after generation, casting a wide net to pull in heretics and give them a choice: Conform, or pay a terrible price.

The usual procedure follows instructions in Deuteronomy 17:

If a man or woman living among you . . . has worshiped other gods . . . and this has been brought to your attention, then you must investigate it thoroughly. If it is true . . . on the testimony of two or three witnesses, a person is to be put to death.

So the Inquisitor generally began by finding two or three witnesses against someone suspected of heresy before interrogating the actual suspect.

Meeting Jacques Fournier, Inquisitor

After an uneventful childhood in late 13th-century France, Jacques Fournier first became a monk, then a bishop in the local Catholic diocese. In 1317, he moved on to the Big Dance as an Inquisitor for the Catholic Church.

Fournier was ordered to begin local interrogations to smoke out adherents of Catharism, a sect that believed the good, spiritual God had an evil, physical counterpart, Rex Mundi, and that Rex, not God, created the world. That would answer the question of why evil exists — and there was an overabundance of evil in the 14th century — but it tinkered too much with the rest of theology to be acceptable to the Church.

Though the Catholic Church claimed it was all about theological differences, the Cathar habit of loudly pointing out the corrupt behavior of Catholic clergy surely had something to do with the attention the Cathars received. The Catholic Church did its level best to kill off every last Cathar in a 45-year crusade during the previous century, and for a generation or two it seemed to have worked. But reports of Cathar activity in southern France surfaced again by 1317, and Fournier was tasked with bringing the heretics in his region to the Pope's justice.

Fournier wasn't the only Inquisitor at the time, but he took the unusual step of having his interrogations transcribed in exquisite detail. Those transcripts make him pretty useful for my purposes, because while Fournier trawled around for Cathar heretics, once in a while he caught . . . an actual atheist.

Of 578 people interrogated by Fournier, five were executed. Most of the rest, including those I introduce in the next sections, were either imprisoned or forced to wear a double yellow cross, a mark of shame, for the rest of their lives.

Fournier's efforts were rewarded a few years later when he was first appointed cardinal, then elected Pope Benedict XII.

Finding unbelievers among the heretics

Jacques Fournier was probably surprised when his interrogations turned up an actual unbeliever rather than a heretic, but it did happen, more than once. And here's where it gets personal. These stories aren't of philosophers putting forward a challenging opinion in the marketplace of ideas, but everyday folks whose friends and family often reported them to the authorities for honest expressions of doubt. I introduce you to three such doubters, villagers in southern France in the early 14th century who were caught in the net of the Inquisition.

Aude of Merviel

In 1318, two years into his new post as Inquisitor, Fournier interrogated a woman named Aude of the village of Merviel. Aude had come to doubt *transubstantiation,* the Catholic doctrine that says the bread and wine of the Eucharist change into the literal body and blood of Christ (though human senses don't perceive the change). This doubt apparently led her further into disbelief, until she cried out to her husband, "Sir, how is it possible that I cannot believe in our Lord!" He swore and threatened her, then ordered her to confess to the priest.

The following week, Aude told her aunt the same thing and pled for help: "Aunt, what might I do to believe in God, and to believe that the body of Christ is really on the altar?" Brought in as a witness against Aude, the aunt testified about what she said to Aude in reply, which boiled down to *Try harder to believe — and don't infect others with your foul ideas!*

Imagining Aude's anguish is painful as she spilled her honest doubts in front of her husband, her aunt, and finally the Inquisitor, meeting nothing but fear and anger at every turn. In the end, she was sentenced to wear a double yellow cross on her back for the remainder of her life.

Guillemette of Ornolac

Guillemette of Ornolac ended up in the Inquisitor's chair because she told others — seemingly everyone she knew — that she doubted the existence of the soul. Called before the Bishop, one friend of hers described a conversation the two of them had the year before.

When the friend had told Guillemette that she was afraid for her own soul because she sinned so often, Guillemette replied, "The soul? You idiot! The soul is nothing more than blood." The friend told the Inquisitor that she told Guillemette to never say such a thing, to which Guillemette supposedly replied that she'd say it in front of anyone she liked, adding, "And what would happen to me if I did?"

Bishop Fournier called in another neighbor, who described a conversation in which Guillemette expounded on her reasoning a bit. When she cut off the head of a goose, the goose lived until the blood was gone, so she reasoned that what people call "soul" — the essence of life — is nothing more than blood.

Finally Fournier called in Guillemette. Under Fournier's questioning, she confessed not only to her idea that the soul is blood, but also to the opinion that death is final. When Fournier asked, "Did someone teach this to you?" — this is the greatest concern, of course, the spread of unapproved ideas — Guillemette said something wonderful: "No. I thought it over and believed it by myself."

She assured Fournier at last that her folly was in the past, and that she had returned to fully orthodox beliefs. When he asked what caused the change, she answered with unbearable honesty: "I heard tell that My Lord the Bishop wanted to carry out an investigation against me about it. I was afraid of My Lord Bishop because of that, and I changed my opinion after that time."

Like Audi, she was sentenced to wear a double yellow cross on her back for the rest of her life.

Raimond de l'Aire

The most colorful of Fournier's suspects was Raimond de l'Aire, a villager who seemed like Diagoras reborn (see Chapter 4). Witnesses described Raimond saying that God never made the world, that the world had always existed, that the resurrection was a myth, that the Eucharist was nothing more than bread and wine, that the rituals of the priests meant nothing, and that he gave to the poor not for his soul but so that others would see him as a good man.

At one point he apparently told a friend that Christ was created not through divine intervention, but "just through screwing, like everybody else" — then struck the heel of one hand against the other repeatedly to underline the point.

The witness assured Fournier that he told Raimond he was speaking evil and deserved to be killed. Whether he actually was killed isn't recorded.

Chapter 6

Enlightening Strikes

The 18th century saw one of the most important eras in intellectual history. Referred to as the *Enlightenment,* this period included the boldest challenges to religion ever mounted. It was also the first time people stood up and called *themselves* atheists.

But the Enlightenment didn't spring from the ground fully formed. First Europe went through a long and sometimes painful process of waking from its thousand-year nap. This chapter looks at the rediscovery of the doubters of ancient Greece and Rome and the important contribution of science in its cradle before plunging into the heady world of Enlightenment ideas, where everything, up to and including God, was ripe for challenge.

Transmitting the Classics

No culture contributed more to Western civilization than classical Greece. The contributions are so familiar — philosophy, medicine, ethics, government, astronomy, mathematics, art, dance, and drama — that I won't bother to list them.

But it wasn't a straight line from downtown Athens to the 21st century. As the Roman Empire declined and fell in the fifth century, it took knowledge of the Greek language along with it. The whole system of Roman education was abandoned, and with it any interest in books, much less those in unknown languages. The most important Greek texts lay untranslated and unread for centuries. Even worse, early medieval scribes started recycling old books, scraping off the old texts and writing prayers and shopping lists in their place.

If not for a couple of unlikely middlemen — the Islamic world and the Catholic Church — Europe may have lost this incredible heritage, and the foundation of modern atheism, for good and all. The Scientific Revolution and the Enlightenment, both crucial for later atheist thought, may not have happened at all if the following two hadn't kept Greek thought alive during Europe's long nap.

Bringing the Greeks back to Europe: The Arab scholars

The winding road that Greek learning took back to Europe started in eighth-century Baghdad as the Islamic Golden Age was just getting started. To be precise, the rediscovered Greek texts *were* the start of the Islamic Golden Age. And as I note in Chapter 5, Islam didn't really deserve the credit for this golden age — it was Arab scholars who saw the value of these texts and translated them into Arabic *despite* the opposition of the Islamic caliphs. As a result, the scholars brought the brilliant, innovative thoughts of ancient Greece from a nearly dead language into a living one. It hardly mattered what language it was — blood was running through the veins of Greek philosophy and science once again, and the scholars of Baghdad hungrily absorbed, applied, and expanded on them, fueling a golden age of philosophy and discovery three centuries long.

During this time, the Islamic Empire pushed into Sicily and Spain, bringing the culture with them, including those translated Greek texts. Spain became a thriving center of Islamic learning, and ancient Greek learning was right at the heart of things.

For about 600 years, Christian Europe and Islamic Spain did an interesting dance called the *Reconquista*. They'd kill each other for a while, then intermarry and exchange scholars for a few generations before returning to the killing. During the exchanges, Greek ideas and texts began to find their way into the rest of Europe. By the time the Arabs were pushed off the peninsula for good, the seeds of the continent's reawakening were planted.

Saving atheism: Catholicism's ironic role

While Europe was plunging into illiteracy after the fall of Rome, several Catholic orders went the other way, making literacy an absolute requirement for their monks. The rules for one monastic order specified that every new candidate was given 20 Psalms to read. If he couldn't read them, he would receive tutoring three times a day until he could.

Benedictine monks had a required reading time each day. If a monk wasn't reading during this time, he'd be loudly rebuked, and if necessary, thwacked. Superiors often read books aloud, sometimes also adding commentary. If a monk expressed an opinion about a passage, *thwack.* If he questioned the superior's commentary, *thwack!* Reading was for passive learning, not for the development of the intellect — and certainly not for debate.

This environment was pretty much the opposite of the atmosphere in ancient Greek schools of philosophy, which encouraged curiosity and contradiction as an important element of learning. But passive reading is still better than no reading at all. One interesting consequence of all the required reading in the monasteries was that books fell apart more quickly than they do in libraries where they sit quietly on the shelves. As a result, the same religious orders that required the reading started to require constant recopying as well. In the larger monasteries, well-lit rooms called *scriptoria* were filled with as many as 20 scribes scribbling in silence throughout the daylight hours, preserving ancient words and ideas even as the books that held them crumbled. Whole monastic libraries were copied and recopied straight through the Middle Ages. That's how the few surviving works of ancient Greece that were left in Europe after the fall of Rome were eventually delivered into the hands of the early Renaissance.

In addition to Aristotle, these ragged survivors included *De rerum natura* by Lucretius, which was the first and most complete book to imagine a universe without belief in gods — and to very much prefer it. The last surviving copy reached and fueled the Renaissance and the Enlightenment, inspiring the courage to challenge and doubt the very existence of God, thanks in part to the literate values and steady, dutiful hands of Catholic monks. (I wax poetic about that astonishing book in Chapter 11.)

Getting a (Bad) Name: Athée

The word "atheist" existed in ancient Greece as *atheos.* Today the word refers to somebody who doesn't believe in any gods, but the Greeks used it to signify anyone who rejected the gods of a given place and time. With rare exceptions (like Diagoras; see Chapter 4), the people who were called *atheos* were assumed to believe in *some* gods, but they didn't root for the home team.

The term reappears in mid-16th century France as *athée,* but it still wasn't quite the same meaning as today. It was an epithet, first of all — an accusation, not something anyone used to describe himself. And the accused was said to deny the Biblical God. Whether that person also denied Vishnu, Buddha, and the rest was trivial at that time and place. Denying the God of Abraham was shocking enough.

Not until the late 18th-century Enlightenment did any European start calling *himself* an atheist. Even then, the term still focused only on the God of the Bible.

Not until the 20th century did atheists begin to clearly make the universal point: "I believe there are no gods of any kind, shape, or description. I disbelieve not just in your god, but in all gods named and unnamed. Barring new and compelling evidence, I reject the very idea. Have a nice day."

Discovering a Whole New Way to Think: The Scientific Revolution

Copernicus's theory of the sun-centered solar system was published in 1543, though the author wasn't around when it hit the shelves, having wisely died a few weeks earlier. Even though few people read it and even fewer believed it at the time, this moment is as handy as any for calling the start of the Scientific Revolution.

You need to bear in mind that this revolution wasn't really about particular theories. It was about defining a powerful new way to think about the universe. By trying to control biases and establish objective frames of reference, this new way of asking questions and questioning answers revolutionized not just the sciences but humanity's view of itself and its place in the scheme of things.

Though it wasn't intended to address questions of God, this pursuit of objectivity was a big step in making the atheist point of view possible. As long as everyone was thinking inside a religious system built on unquestionable assumptions — among them the assumption that Scriptures are true because they say they're true — it's pretty hard to find the exit. By establishing objectivity as a goal worth striving for and showing just how amazing the results can be when you give it a try, the Scientific Revolution laid the groundwork for the Enlightenment's challenges to religious thought and just about everything that came afterward.

The Enlightenment and the Renaissance were two of the biggest developments in Western history. But compared to the Scientific Revolution, they're pebbles dropped into the human pond, and the Scientific Revolution is a Jack Black cannonball.

The following sections look at some of the events in the Scientific Revolution that proved important for later developments in atheism. Without these key moments, atheism would have remained in the starting gate, munching its hay. But with these crucial changes of perspective, atheism was out of the gates and around the first turn.

Copernicus knocks the Earth off-center; Galileo backs him up: The first humbling

It's easy for a person today to forget what a mental and emotional earthquake Copernicus eventually wrought by suggesting the Earth wasn't the center of the universe after all. All the problems explaining planetary motion went away if the sun was at the center and Earth was just another planet. But bigger problems quickly rushed in to replace them, including the need for people to eat a massive, steaming slice of humble pie, realizing they weren't apparently as important in the scheme of things as they thought.

Hearing Copernicus's theory had to be incredibly disorienting at the time. To the human mind, Earth had been not just central but stationery — see Psalm 93 if you doubt that. The universe had whirled around Earth, then overnight, Earth became part of the dance, unstuck in the fabric of space. I imagine people gazing up at the night sky and suddenly losing their balance, and possibly their dinner as well. (As a side note, after the Earth wasn't the center of the cosmos, the whole pretext for astrology vanished overnight — though news of this development has yet to reach about 100 million Americans.)

Copernicus explained the motion of the planets much better than Ptolemy's old system of orbital curlicues and planetary whirligigs. But 95 percent of his book was math with not much direct observational evidence to speak of. That made it easier for those people who wanted to keep denying that the Earth had been demoted from the Big Chair to do so. Historians estimate that for a half-century after publication, only about 15 astronomers in all Europe really accepted the idea. Others dismissed it out of hand — including the hierarchy of the Catholic Church. What sense did it make for God's children, the center of his concern, to not be in the center of his creation?

Good question.

In the early 1600s, Galileo brought the evidence home when he observed the phases of Venus and the moons of Jupiter through his improved telescopes and published his findings and his support for Copernicus. The Inquisition declared his conclusions unacceptable, as if declaring something unacceptable was the same as disproving it.

Galileo was arrested and tried for heresy. In exchange for sparing his life, he took it all back. (Some say he then took back the taking back, under his breath — but I'll leave that one for the mythmakers.) He spent his remaining nine years of life under house arrest for getting the universe right.

As late as 1820, the Catholic Church still referred to the idea that the Earth revolved around the sun as "just a hypothesis." But Galileo's books were removed from the Index of Forbidden Books in 1835, and Pope John Paul II vindicated Galileo . . . in 1992. (Mustn't rush these things.)

Neither Copernicus nor Galileo was an atheist, and decentering Earth by no means disproved God. But it was the first of several serious humblings for the human species. After the Earth was removed from center stage, it was easier for people to consider that religion had gotten a few other things wrong as well.

Reconciling science and religion (or not) — Whiston's New Theory of the Earth

In the 21st century, trying to reconcile a literal reading of the Book of Genesis with modern science requires a serious misconception of the state of human knowledge. A little dishonesty doesn't hurt either. But in 1696, science was still stretching its legs, and geology was a babe in arms.

So when an English theologian named William Whiston tried to reconcile the Genesis account with what little was known scientifically about the Earth in 1696, that attempt wasn't quite as dubious as the "intelligent design" game would be in later centuries. Whiston's *New Theory of the Earth* was a noble first attempt to make the two systems play nice. Whiston described the how and when of the world's creation, the Great Flood, and even the origin of Earth's atmosphere (which he thought may have come from a passing comet — a really interesting hypothesis).

He came from the same tradition as Archbishop James Ussher, who a couple of generations earlier used the generations and ages given in the Bible to come up with an exact date of Creation: October 23, 4004 BCE. Ussher is often ridiculed for that today, which I think is really unfair. He was trying to apply a kind of scientific rigor to the task, using the limited data available at the time.

Ussher and Whiston both deserve credit for a good 17th century try. Unlike their modern counterparts, they weren't making themselves willfully blind to science. There just wasn't much science to see yet.

Stirring the Pot: The Clandestine Manuscripts

Though atheist thought had been up and running for centuries in places like China and India, European atheism (aside from a few peeps in ancient Greece) didn't even start clearing its throat until the mid-1600s. At that time, anonymous books challenging the existence of God started to appear. Minor nobles and major thinkers of the time started to secretly pass them to each other. Blasphemy was still extremely illegal, and saying God didn't exist was as blasphemous as you could get.

The books were known as *clandestina,* or secret manuscripts. First came an anthology that pulled together some of the ancient Greek writings that challenged religious belief. Books with original arguments that added the perspective gained since the Scientific Revolution quickly followed. Then small pamphlets making individual arguments against belief in God began appearing across the continent — more than 200 in all.

With the sudden appearance of all of these secret documents, people started (secretly) talking and thinking about the existence of God in ways that were completely unthinkable a few generations earlier. They certainly didn't evict God from Europe's intellectual life — even the Enlightenment only posted a first eviction notice, maybe turned off a few utilities. But the anonymous clandestina marked the first time early modern Europe seriously considered the possibility that the divine apartment had never been occupied to begin with. (For more on secret and forbidden documents in atheist history, see Chapter 10.)

Singing the War Song of an Atheist Priest

In the last years of the 17th century, as Europe continued its slow recovery from 140 years of religious war, a young man named Jean Meslier became a Catholic priest — even though he didn't believe in God. He did so because his parents wanted him to, and because he felt he could do more to help people in need from inside the church than outside.

During the course of 40 years as a priest, Meslier's atheism and his contempt for all religion deepened. He felt that the Catholic Church made people subservient in his parish, that believing and saying things that weren't true was unworthy, and that more misery and fear flows from religious belief than comfort and inspiration. But he felt trapped in his job, unable to be honest about his views for fear of arrest and execution.

So Meslier did his priestly duties every day — serving the poor and sick, giving homilies, burying the dead, and performing baptisms and funerals. By night he then returned to his room and worked on his magnum opus: the first book-length work in Europe written from an explicitly atheist perspective with an author's name on it. And what a name it was — a priest in the Holy Catholic Church.

He wrote it for his parishioners, then left it for them to find upon his death. It remains one of the most astonishing, provocative, and moving works in the history of atheism. (For much more on Meslier's testament, turn to Chapter 11.)

Thinking Dangerous Thoughts: The Enlightenment Philosophers

Like a lot of social and intellectual movements, the Age of Enlightenment was halfway done before anyone really thought of it as a movement. Important thinkers like Spinoza (refer to Chapter 11), Bayle (check out Chapter 15), and Voltaire (see the next section) laid the groundwork for an explosion of challenging new questions and ideas. The magnifying glass that had been turned on the natural world throughout the 17th century was turned on human society in the 18th — and what it saw wasn't pretty. Unearned wealth and power were concentrated in the hands of a few, while the majority languished in equally unearned poverty and powerlessness. The Catholic Church held vast amounts of land and treasure, had several kings in its pocket, and exerted an oversized influence on what people could say, think, and aspire to.

Talk across Europe and in the American colonies turned to radical ideas like basic human rights, individual liberty, tolerance, and equality. In addition to kings and aristocracies, the greatest impediment to progress in these areas was the overwhelming influence of the church.

There are countless contributors to this new age of "dangerous" thinking, but a few well-placed thinkers can give you the flavor of the times. The following sections introduce those thinkers and their thoughts.

Crushing infamous things with Voltaire

The philosopher Voltaire (1694–1778) wasn't an atheist, but a *Deist,* meaning he believed in a good but mostly non-intervening, non-communicating God. No prayers heard, no wrath dispensed. (Given the knowledge available at the time, I'd probably have been a Deist too.) Deists think the superstitions and rituals created by organized religion only get in the way of understanding.

They believe reason is the only valid way to understand God and his creation, not tradition or revelation, and that tradition and revelation are therefore to be challenged and thrown out whenever possible.

Voltaire spent a lot of effort badmouthing the atheists of his time. He said the idea of God is so important that "If God did not exist, it would be necessary to invent Him." But because he challenged traditional religion, he was constantly accused of being an atheist anyway, something that irritated him to no end. Like it or not, his smart and articulate challenges laid the foundation for atheist thought in the Enlightenment and beyond.

Like others of his time, Voltaire saw the Church as the greatest stumbling block to progress. One of his favorite expressions was *"Écrasez l'infâme!,"* which means *Crush the infamous thing!* — specifically the Church and its clergy. Superstition was his enemy, and reason was his highest cause: "Superstition sets the whole world in flames," he said, "and philosophy quenches them." No philosopher did more to lay the foundation of the Enlightenment — and to fan the flames of the French Revolution that ended it — than Voltaire.

Daring to know: Kant's "Sapere aude!"

The Prussian philosopher Immanuel Kant (1724–1804) was a Deist who felt belief in God was "necessary from the practical point of view." And like Voltaire, Kant saw natural reason as the best way to understand the world, and he saw organized religion, ritual, and superstition as obstacles to knowledge and progress.

Kant was especially hostile to the idea that "pleasing God" was the way to moral rightness. He felt doing so was actually a huge distraction from focusing on actual, useful, sensible moral principles. (Modern research agrees with him; see Chapter 15.)

One of Kant's biggest contributions to the Enlightenment was an essay he wrote near the end of the period called "What is Enlightenment?" He said the lack of enlightenment came from people's inability to think for themselves — not because they lacked intelligence, but because they lacked courage. People have developed a reliance on others, especially the Church, to tell them what to think. "Enlightenment is man's release from his self-imposed immaturity," he said, in an attempt for humanity to find the courage to think for itself.

Kant said that *Sapere aude!* (Dare to know!) should be the motto of the Enlightenment. And the first step in finding that daring is rejecting the terrible idea that dogmas should be accepted without question.

Kant believed strongly that handing doctrines or beliefs from one generation to the next with firm instructions not to change or question them "prevent[s] all further enlightenment of mankind forever." If they're valid and worthwhile, ideas will be reaffirmed in each generation. If they're false or unworthy, humanity can throw them out. Even within a single lifetime, Kant said, humanity must be willing to think freely and to criticize all ideas, including religious ones, so that only the best remain. *That's* enlightenment. And when immaturity prevents such progress, Kant said, religion "is the most pernicious and dishonorable variety of all."

Not all of Kant is this clear, by the way. He had a reputation for being hard to read, using 35 words when three would do — and German words at that. But "What is Enlightenment?" is a terrific, powerful piece, clear as a bell, and hugely influential.

Meeting of minds in coffeehouses and salons

Living in the Age of Enlightenment didn't mean you had a license to blurt out your every thought in public. Plenty of ideas were still radical enough to get a person thrown in the Bastille or the Tower of London in the middle of the 18th century. Blasphemy, for example, was still illegal just about everywhere.

The definition of blasphemy was fuzzy enough to make anyone think twice before saying something off-center. France didn't abolish its blasphemy laws until 1791. England was still merrily prosecuting for it into the 1840s. Discussing the shortcomings of the king was no wiser in the 18th century than it had been in the tenth.

So where were those with radical or even revolutionary ideas to go? In London and Oxford, they went to the coffeehouses; in France, to the *salons*.

- The English coffeehouse culture of the 18th century offered a safe space for discussions of all kinds, including Enlightenment staples such as liberty, the natural rights of man, social progress, and religious doubt — up to and including atheism.

- In France, wealthy intellectuals and socialites held *salons* in their homes to have lively conversation. The hosts invited the most interesting and provocative thinkers in town to these salons, and the best such events, like the twice-weekly meetings hosted by Baron d'Holbach, gathered great thinkers to present and develop great ideas. (D'Holbach was also famous for serving legendary spreads of food and wine, but I'm sure they came mostly for the conversation.) Whole social and intellectual movements were set in motion in the *salons* of Paris, and most historians credit the well-fed *salon* of d'Holbach with laying the foundation of the French Revolution.

A lot of the regular visitors to d'Holbach's *salon* were prominent atheists, including Denis Diderot (see the next section). D'Holbach was an atheist and published several scathingly anti-religious books, including the hugely influential *System of Nature* (see Chapter 11). But he did so under a false name, which made it possible for him to die of natural causes.

Getting explicit in Paris: The incredible Encyclopédie

Think for a minute about the task Enlightenment thinkers had set for themselves. They wanted to strip the superstition out of human life and replace it with reason. That's like trying to take the marinade out of a steak that's been soaking for 5,000 years. Religion and superstition permeated humanity's knowledge, habits, and even humanity's understanding of itself.

The atheist philosopher Denis Diderot (1713–1784) saw the persistence of religion and superstition as a big problem in realizing the ideals of the Enlightenment. In order to "change the way people think," he set about the incredible task of creating a comprehensive reference book that would reframe all human knowledge in reasonable, rational terms, leaving religion and superstition on the cutting room floor.

He called it simply the *Encyclopédie* — 35 volumes with more than 75,000 articles by nearly a hundred contributors. (One contributor, Louis de Jaucourt, wrote more than 17,000 articles totaling nearly 5 million words.)

Though it's not on my bookshelf and probably isn't on yours either, the *Encyclopédie* had an enormous influence on many of the books that *are* on those shelves, including some of the first arguments against slavery and in favor of basic human rights and freedoms. The set sold more than 25,000 copies. It laid some of the foundations for the French and American Revolutions.

Most important of all was the concept itself — the stunning idea of changing the lens through which humanity had come to see itself and the world.

Challenging the Powers That Be: The French Revolution

All the talk about challenging tradition and authority found a receptive audience in late 18th-century France. The poor were kept poor with huge taxes, while Louis XVI and his nobles — supported by those very same taxes — paraded their wealth and privilege to ridiculous extremes. And standing at the head of the privilege parade was the First Estate — the clergy of the Catholic Church.

In addition to propping up the monarchy with the divine right of kings, the Church was the single largest landowner in France. So a lot of the taxes paid by tenant farmers went straight into the coffers of the Church, as did their tithes. So when the philosophers began filling the heads of the lower and middle classes with ideas about their natural rights to freedom and equality, little effort was required to connect the dots.

The French Revolution wasn't just a revolt against political power — it was also a revolt against the power and ideas of the Catholic Church. The following sections touch on events in the Revolution that directly related to challenging the Church and religion itself.

Dechristianizing France

A process known as the *dechristianizing* of France began very shortly after the Revolution itself. The goal was to destroy not only the undue power and privilege of the Catholic Church in France but to replace religion with new practices and beliefs based in human reason. Over the course of several years:

✔ All church land was confiscated.

✔ The Church's power to tax was revoked.

✔ Priests lost all special privileges and became state employees without allegiance to the Pope. Those who didn't consent to the change were subject to deportation or death.

✔ Angered by the former Church policies, mobs massacred hundreds of priests and nuns. Thousands of other priests and nuns were forced to marry.

✔ Crosses, statues, plaques, icons, and other religious symbols were removed from buildings and monuments throughout the country. Most churches were closed, destroyed, or converted to secular uses.

✔ The religiously based calendar was replaced with a new one with natural rather than supernatural names for the months. Instead of saints' feast days, each day celebrated a given animal, plant, mineral, or tool.

✔ A Cult of Reason was created in place of Christianity (refer to the next section for more information).

✔ Divorce was legalized, and all birth and death records became the property and purview of the state.

✔ Streets and towns with religious names were given secular names. Saint-Denis became Franciade, for example, and Saint-Amand-Montrond became Libreval.

Like the crackdown against the Mexican Catholic Church in the 1920s (refer to Chapter 8), the dechristianizing of France had more to do with power and privilege than with beliefs. And like many such rebellions, both included actions that most historians now agree were excessive and punitive — not to mention a contradiction of the principles of liberty, tolerance, and freedom they claimed to espouse. Napoleon reversed the process in 1801, and the Church regained most of its lost status and privileges.

Creating a Cult of Reason

The Cult of Reason was an attempt to organize a civic religion without gods to replace Christianity during the French Revolution. Centered on humanity rather than divinity, the goal of the cult was the perfection of mankind through the pursuit of truth and freedom.

Like most radical social experiments, it was interesting and more than a little weird. Christian rituals were replaced with secular ones, which sometimes worked really well and sometimes . . . just didn't. Reason was semi-personified as a being to be celebrated. Cathedrals were reconsecrated to Reason, and elaborate ceremonies were created to refocus attention away from religious ideas and toward the advancement and perfection of the human race.

One of the leaders of the cult was Joseph Fouché, a military commander who (among other things) ordered that all cemeteries would have only one inscription on the gates: "Death is an eternal sleep." A new national holiday called the Festival of Reason was briefly instituted.

Some atheists today may think of this kind of secular takeover of the culture as a dream come true. But I think most atheists see this cultural bulldozer for what it is — a violation of the rights and freedoms we cherish most. You can't complain about the church telling people there's only one way to think, then turn around and tell people there's only one way to think. If you're going to build a revolution around values like freedom and tolerance, you probably ought to exhibit them.

Back to the future: The Cult of the Supreme Being

The Cult of Reason lasted only about 18 months before the new dictator Robespierre denounced it, sent its leaders to the guillotine, and replaced it with a new official religion of the French Republic: the Cult of the Supreme Being. The Festival of the Supreme Being replaced the Festival of Reason in every city across France. Robespierre presided over the massive event in Paris. An enormous artificial mountain was built for the occasion. It must have been quite a show.

Just as the reason cult had replaced Catholicism, this new cult replaced a focus on reason with a belief in a living Creator God and the immortality of the human soul. Reason was now considered only a means to the ultimate end — public virtue. Like Voltaire and Kant before him, Robespierre said that belief in God was necessary for moral behavior and virtue — a "constant reminder of justice" that was essential to a civil society.

After Robespierre established his new religion to promote and maintain virtue, he turned his attention back to his Reign of Terror, in which 40,000 people were executed.

Checking In on the US Founding Fathers

Many Christian commentators today claim that the United States is a Christian nation. The Founding Fathers would probably be shocked by this notion because they were plenty clear that it wasn't anything of the sort. They'd seen what happened to Europe when religions insisted on their way — 150 years of continuous war. Mother England herself had gone through a century of rolling heads as the Crown passed from Catholic to Protestant to Catholic to Protestant to Catholic to Protestant in little more than a century. You can see why there'd be very little interest in establishing a state religion in any way, shape, or form.

When it came to religious identity, the founders themselves were quite a mixed bag. Among the signers of the US Constitution, for example, were

- 28 Anglicans
- 8 Presbyterians
- 7 Congregationalists
- 6 geese a-laying
- 2 Dutch Reformed
- 2 Catholics

✔ 2 Methodists

✔ 2 Lutherans

Then it gets even more mixed. Thomas Paine was a non-Christian Deist, Franklin was a Christian Deist, and historian Gregg Frazer classifies Washington, Jefferson, and Madison as "theistic rationalists."

Maybe it wasn't an interfaith summit, but it was a pretty diverse bunch religiously. So it makes sense that they founded a country where the freedom of religion was guaranteed, up front, in the first amendment of the Bill of Rights. That means it wasn't a Christian nation, but a nation in which citizens would be absolutely free to believe as they wished.

The Constitution contains only one reference to religion — and that was a specific ban on any religious requirement to hold office. God gets not a single mention in the whole Constitution. It's the first time a nation was founded entirely on a social contract between humans without pretending God had signed off on it.

This doesn't make the document atheistic, and it doesn't make the founders atheists. It just establishes a secular government, one that's entirely neutral on questions of religion.

American citizens of all persuasions should be grateful that the founders didn't push their own beliefs on the country. People today may all imagine their own worldview would come out the winner, but given the variety of the Founders' actual beliefs, it would have been like Forrest Gump's box of chocolates — you never know what you're gonna get. It's much better that they left the decisions to each individual.

Getting the message: The Treaty of Tripoli (1797)

The Treaty of Tripoli between the United States and the Ottoman Empire was intended to end the boarding of US vessels by Barbary pirates. It's mostly known today for one intriguing passage that says "the Government of the United States of America is not, in any sense, founded on the Christian religion". The purpose was to assure the Islamic Ottomans that no religious ideology would rear its head to annul any of the elements of the treaty.

Whether that reassurance helped isn't known — the treaty fell apart five years later. But it stands today as one of the clearest early indications of the founders' intent regarding religion and government. The people of the United States were then and are today predominantly religious. And thanks to a government that isn't "in any sense" founded on any one religion, they're free to pursue their belief (or disbelief) as they wish. It's one of the most indelible remaining fingerprints of the Age of Enlightenment.

Chapter 7

Opening a Golden Age of Freethought

*T*hink of the history of human ideas as a kind of wrestling match between head and heart, thinking and feeling, reason and faith. A surge of religiosity followed the heyday of reason in ancient Greece and Rome after the collapse of the Roman Empire and into the Middle Ages. The Renaissance sparked a . . . well, a *Renaissance* of reason that carried straight through the American and French Revolutions.

As the 19th century began, the pendulum swung back, as the art, literature, and even philosophy of the early 19th century returned to an emphasis on feeling over thinking, including a resurgence in religious fervor. But before the century ended, a golden age of freethought bloomed in the United States and Europe, driven in part by such scientific discoveries as Darwin's theory of evolution. By the end of the century, Friedrich Nietzsche declared that "God is dead" — then wondered how humanity would deal with the "shadow" of God, the lingering belief that was guaranteed to remain long after it stopped making sense.

Even as Nietzsche asked what was next, a "Great Agnostic" traveled the United States describing a world without gods, and a social reformer in New York founded a religion that's not about gods. This chapter traces the progress of the idea of atheism through one of its most formative centuries.

Killing God: Atheist Philosophers Do the Crime, a Pantheist Writes the Eulogy

Despite that heading, atheist philosophers didn't really kill God. (He was like that when we got here, I *swear.*) And though philosophy has been pounding away at religious assumptions for centuries now, science ended up putting those assumptions on life support.

An atheist philosopher, Friedrich Nietzsche (1844–1900), finally took the pulse of God and declared an end to the whole idea. When he said God was dead, it wasn't the jubilant *whoop!* most people think it was. On the contrary, he captured the despair many poets and writers expressed during this time of slipping religious faith:

> God is dead. God remains dead. And we have killed him. How shall we comfort ourselves, the murderers of all murderers? What was holiest and mightiest of all that the world has yet owned has bled to death under our knives: who will wipe this blood off us? . . . Is not the greatness of this deed too great for us? Must we ourselves not become gods simply to appear worthy of it?

Ignore that last part about turning ourselves into gods — that's just Nietzsche being Nietzsche. Don't try this at home.

Thomas Hardy finished what Nietzsche started by laying Jehovah to rest in a poem titled, appropriately enough, *God's Funeral.* A traditional Anglican believer for most of his life, Hardy eventually lost his Christian belief, adopting instead a kind of pantheistic view of the universe (see Chapter 2). And like Nietzsche, Hardy didn't express the feeling of freedom and elation that some others did, especially in later centuries. For Hardy, the loss was too fresh. It was a kind of bereavement.

The poem describes a solemn procession across a half-lit plain, carrying a dead figure. At first it "seemed manlike," then changes form, becoming a cloud, then seeming to sprout enormous wings, capturing the changes in people's concept of God as they struggle to make it work. As the procession slowly passes, Hardy remembers the history of this "man-projected Figure" — first jealous and fierce (Old Testament), then just and blessed (New Testament). Needing solace, humanity deceived itself as long as it could, he says, until reality made it too hard to believe at all.

In the middle is a wonderful bit of empathy for those individuals who continue to believe. Incredulous believers are chasing after the funeral procession in angry denial, calling it a mockery and a lie, shouting, "Still he lives to us!" Hardy doesn't call them fools: "I sympathized / And though struck speechless, I did not forget / That what was mourned for, I, too, long had prized."

I love it when someone without belief shows a little empathy for the believer. Search online for Hardy's poem. You should easily be able to find it.

Freethinking with Early Feminists

Almost every traditional religion puts women in an inferior or even degraded role compared to men. Nearly all bar women from serving as clergy. Women were (and often still are) held responsible for humanity's fall from grace in the Old Testament, told to stay silent and submissive in church in the New Testament, and relegated to a servant's role in the Qur'an. Hinduism instructs wives to worship their husbands as gods, even if said husbands lack a single good quality and sleep around. Even Jainism, my personal favorite (see Chapter 4), has one of its two main sects calling women "intrinsically harmful" and saying they can't achieve nirvana without first being reborn a man.

Aw, Jainism . . . *really?*

It does make sense that religions born more than 2,000 years ago would pick up the norms and values of their time. But when their scriptures carried bad ideas forward through the centuries along with the good, refusing all edits, until they collided with modern Enlightenment ideas like equality — that's when they needed a change. And change was exactly what the first wave of feminists in the 19th century demanded.

Outraged by the role religion had played in keeping women in submission, many feminist leaders of this early movement identified as atheists and agnostics. Those early feminist leaders include the following:

- **Frances Wright:** When not visiting Thomas Jefferson or other movers and shakers of her time, agnostic feminist Frances Wright (1795–1852) traveled the United States giving public lectures in favor of women's rights and the abolition of slavery. And she directly — *very* directly — condemned religion as the main problem in both areas. Doing so took incredible courage, in part because Wright was the first woman to speak publicly to an audience of both men and women in the United States, the first to publicly suggest that women should be equal to men, and the first to openly criticize religion. In a situation of multiple firsts, most people (myself included) would have been walking on eggshells, but not Wright. Her reward was to be assailed by clergy and press alike as "the great Red Harlot of Infidelity" and the "Whore of Babylon." After many of her own lectures, she had to flee through the back door to avoid being pummeled by the crowd.

✔ **Ernestine Rose:** Rose (1810–1892) followed on Wright's heels, using the same medium (public speaking) on the same topics (women's rights and slavery) with the same primary target (religion) and the same result (outrage, name-calling, and threats of violence). She was elected president of the National Women's Rights Convention in 1854, but not before several members tried to boot her from the platform because of her atheism. Susan B. Anthony, an agnostic herself, insisted that "every religion — or none — should have an equal right on the platform." The following year, one newspaper said Rose, being "a female Atheist," is "a thousand times below a prostitute."

✔ **Elizabeth Cady Stanton:** Stanton (1815–1902), an atheist, also supported abolition and women's rights. Like Wright and Rose, she shocked many of those fighting with her when she insisted, loudly and often, that "the Bible and the church have been the greatest stumbling blocks in the way of woman's emancipation." Stanton and Susan B. Anthony co-authored the 19th Amendment to the US Constitution — "The right of citizens of the United States to vote shall not be denied or abridged by the United States or by any State on account of sex" — which became law 18 years after Stanton's death.

Bracing for the Collision of Religion and Science

The long collision of religion and science that started in the 15th century picked up speed in the 19th century. No other century in human history contained quite so enormous a change in the way humans saw themselves. When the century opened its doors in 1801, there wasn't much reason for anyone to doubt Archbishop James Ussher, who 200 years earlier had used the Bible's chronology to put the creation of the world in mid-autumn of 4004 BCE. Certainly no theory in 1801 competed with the Genesis account of the special and separate creation of humankind.

How much older and wiser the world was less than a century later after a couple of new scientific discoveries humbled humanity and shook up humanity's assumptions about God.

Aging the Earth: The second humbling

Copernicus first pulled the rug out from under the ego of humanity in the 15th century by yanking the Earth out of the center of the universe. So the Earth wasn't at the universal belly button, but at least humanity still straddled the full span of time, right? Humanity was there at the beginning (okay, day six) and humanity is still here 6,000 years later, counting down to the

Rapture. But a *second humbling* was soon to come as the age of the Earth multiplied nearly a thousand times over.

No sooner had the century begun than the birthday of the Earth started sliding backward in time, pushed by the new sciences of geology and paleontology. In the 1830s, the work of geologist Charles Lyell called Noah's flood into question. The evidence after opening the Earth's crust pointed to gradual change over vast amounts of time — not a sudden flood.

As the window of history expanded from 6,000 years to 96 million and beyond, new questions emerged about the age of humankind. Have humans been here all these millions of years — or is *humanity's* birthday somewhere along the way?

Doing away with Noah's flood wasn't fatal to religious belief, of course. It was just one story among many, after all. A metaphor, one might say. Believers who accepted the new data maintained that God's stage had simply expanded, making the story of creation all the grander for it. As the 20th century began, that stage grew to an estimated two billion years — well on the way to the current estimate of 4.54 billion.

By itself, the work of Lyell and other geologists of the 19th century didn't directly challenge the importance of humans in the scheme of things. It did, however, provide a crucial ingredient — a vast landscape of time — for the next and biggest humbling.

Dethroning the human species: The third humbling

In the painful process of humbling humanity's self-image, no shock was more jarring than the one Charles Darwin administered in 1859 by saying that all life on Earth is related by descent, including humans.

The idea itself wasn't new with Darwin. As far back as the pre-Socratics in ancient Greece, people considered the possibility that all living things were related — not to mention anyone who ever looked a baboon in the face. Charles's own grandfather Erasmus Darwin suggested that all warm-blooded animals may have descended from a single ancient organism. And 15 years before Charles Darwin's *On the Origin of Species* was published, an anonymous book titled *Vestiges of the Natural History of Creation* appeared making the very same case — not thoroughly or well, but still the same basic claim.

So although evolution wasn't a new concept in 1859, Darwin's explanation of *natural selection* — the *way* evolution works — was new. The convincing and meticulous details in the *Origin* moved evolution from interesting notion to compelling scientific theory — at which point humanity's self-image was in for a bruising.

The idea that you and I were specially created in the image of the Creator of the Universe and given dominion over the world and all that's in it — that idea was now gone. After Darwin, you and I are trousered apes. Pretty impressive ones, but still, it's a serious pay cut.

Some people greeted the news by trying to stretch traditional religion to accommodate the theory, saying God started things going, then used evolution to create the diversity of life. It's a nice effort, but one that requires a major misunderstanding of natural selection. (Check out Chapter 3 for a fuller explanation of natural selection and evolution.) Other people took the simplest route, declaring evolution to be untrue because it contradicted Scripture. Done and done.

Even the scientific community didn't instantly embrace the idea by any means. Like all good theories, evolution withstood a withering crossfire of challenge in the following generations. For a while, it actually looked like the theory would fade away, partially or entirely. Not until the 1930s did advances in genetics boost evolution over the bar, solving the remaining problems and securing the solid consensus of biologists. Evolution had become a scientific fact as well established as the Earth's orbit of the Sun — another one that was hard to believe at first, but is nonetheless true.

Nowhere did the crisis of faith play out more dramatically in the wake of Darwin's theory than in his own time and place — England of the late 19th century Victorian era.

Doubting like a Victorian: The Crisis of Faith

Most people think of Victorian England as socially uptight and sexually repressed. And though the stories of covering piano legs (excuse me, piano *limbs*) in frilly trousers isn't true, they did set a high water mark for both prudery and its eternal sidekick — kinky sexual experimentation.

But the era was much more complex and interesting than high collars, stuffy manners, and even hidden fetishes can capture alone. An incredible surge of scientific discovery and debate turned the world and humanity's self-concept on its head — especially Darwin's theory of evolution.

The result was something called the "Crisis of Faith," a rapid spread of religious doubt in the late 19th century. As people learned and discussed the implications of new scientific discoveries, they threw the assumptions of Christianity into serious question throughout Europe. Genesis was the first to go, followed by pretty much everything else that had been held both true and unquestionable just a generation before.

The forceful challenge of religious ideas was suddenly in the open air. Philosophers, poets, artists, and scientists explored the idea of a world without God and nature without an inherent moral system. Some, like Thomas Huxley and the poet Algernon Swinburne, tucked in to this new world with giddy excitement. Others wrote dirges about the loss of faith, such as the poets Thomas Hardy and Matthew Arnold (see the earlier section, "Killing God: Atheist Philosophers Do the Crime, a Pantheist Writes the Eulogy.")

Religion and science, which had a testy enough relationship going into the Victorian era, mostly owned up to irreconcilable differences by the end and parted ways. And for all the screaming and thrown dishes, religion and science both walked into the 20th century without a noticeable limp. That's not to say they weren't changed — science had a new vision and an enormous new set of questions, whereas Christianity (in Europe at least) was less about making claims based on a literal reading of its ancient books and more about using religious stories to motivate social justice and the alleviation of suffering in this world. Britain ended up with a generally wiser, less literal, more positive form of Christian belief than some other countries I could name.

No greater testimony to the civilized outcome of a tumultuous period existed than the burial of Charles Darwin, the man who midwifed so much of the controversy, in Westminster Abbey in 1882. Of course, the Reverend Frederick Farrar, Canon of Westminster, assured the mourners that Darwin's theory was entirely compatible with belief in God. (I'll have to agree to disagree on that, Reverend. Check out Chapter 3.)

Debating Darwin's theory: Huxley-Wilberforce

Most people familiar with the current cultural debate over evolution may think Darwin would relish raising a hackle or three. But they don't know Darwin. The man whose theory overturned the most cherished assumptions of the human race was actually a conflict-avoider of the first rank. He was painfully shy, for one thing, and conflict irritated the chronic health problems that plagued him all his life.

He was especially disinterested in religious arguments. He had been there and done that as a youth, and he just didn't feel that they shed much light on the scientific questions that really interested him. He also had to consider his wife Emma's Christian faith. The implications of her husband's work pained her at times, and he in turn was pained by her pain. It was all just too much.

So after publishing *On the Origin of Species,* Charles retreated to his home to study orchids. The pitched debate was left to friends, such as biologist Thomas Henry Huxley, who loved a good rumble as much as Darwin hated it. Huxley eventually came to be called "Darwin's Bulldog" for his steadfast defense of the theory (and for his jowly face, I think, which you may now search for online).

Though Huxley spent the rest of his career promoting and explaining evolution, one event captured the whole fracas better than any other.

Just seven months had passed since *On the Origin of Species* turned the world inside out. Scientists and philosophers from across Britain had gathered at Oxford University to hear how the theory was setting Europe ablaze with debate and controversy. Both supporters and opponents of the theory of evolution were present, including

- **Thomas Henry Huxley:** He had been publishing articles and giving lectures in support of evolution steadily since the book was published the previous year.
- **Bishop Samuel "Soapy Sam" Wilberforce:** He was so nicknamed for the slippery evasiveness of his arguments and had recently published a 17,000-word review against Darwin's theory.
- **Richard Owen:** A scientist variously described as "distinguished," "odious," "brilliant," "hateful," and "sadistic," Owen published anonymous attacks on Darwin and coached Wilberforce before the event. (Search online for Owen's face, and prepare for nightmares.)
- **Joseph Dalton Hooker:** Hooker was a botanist, supporter, and close friend of Darwin.
- **Robert FitzRoy:** He was a highly religious captain of the five-year voyage of the HMS *Beagle* on which Darwin first began to formulate his theory. He was present by accident, scheduled to present a paper on weather forecasting that (thanks to the chaos described shortly) was never given.

Darwin himself wasn't present, of course. Orchids.

No one knows exactly what was said in the meeting, but by most accounts it was a terrific show. The discussion was civil enough with several good points made all around. Opponents of the theory voiced concerns about what would later be called social Darwinism, the misapplication of Darwin's theory to justify brutality and cruelty in human society.

At some point, though, the discussion escalated, as these things tend to do. Bishop Wilberforce rose and asked Huxley whether it was on his grandmother's side or his grandfather's side that he claimed descent from an ape. Huxley said that given a choice between a miserable ape for an ancestor or a man who used his great gifts to introduce ridicule into an important scientific discussion and to obscure the truth, "I unhesitatingly affirm my preference for the ape!"

Oh, that did it. Arguments broke out around the room. One account had Captain FitzRoy suddenly thrusting a Bible aloft over the din, telling those assembled, "Here is the truth! Believe God rather than man!" The crowd shouted at him, and he was abruptly escorted from the building. The room erupted into a frenzy of shouts and scooting chairs as all hell broke loose.

Of course another account said there was no shouting, that it ended very jovially, and that they all went to dinner together. But where's the fun in that?

Coining agnosticism

Though religious doubt had been around for millennia, the word *agnosticism* itself wasn't coined until 1869 when none other than Thomas Henry Huxley created it as a label for his own beliefs. Huxley felt that atheism implied certainty, and though he was very confident God didn't exist, he didn't want to imply that he was 100 percent sure. But he was also nowhere near being a religious believer.

The more he thought about it, he said, the less sure he was about the right label for his beliefs. After puzzling over the problem for some time, Huxley decided that uncertainty was the defining feature of his belief and coined the word *agnostic* — Greek for "not knowing" — to describe his position. (For more on agnosticism, see Chapter 2.)

As it turns out, he wasn't alone. "To my great satisfaction," he said, "the term took." You can say that again. Countless writers and thinkers in England and beyond quickly adopted the term themselves, and it remains an important description for many people today.

Mixing signals: The Vatican warns against "the unrestrained freedom of thought"

The Catholic Church often came in for criticism regarding its attitude toward advances in science, and it was often deserved. But to give credit where it's due, the Vatican was ahead of the curve in seeing the implications of human evolution for traditional belief in the 19th century. Allowing people to chase those implications wherever they led, however, was another matter.

"All faithful Christians are forbidden to defend as the legitimate conclusions of science those opinions which are known to be contrary to the doctrine of faith," said one pronouncement of the First Vatican Council, held ten years after *On the Origin of Species* was published. "Furthermore, they are absolutely bound to hold them to be errors which wear the deceptive appearance of truth." The more something appeared to be true, the more strongly it must be rejected if it contradicts Church doctrine.

So what was the official Catholic position on evolution? For more than a century, that wasn't clear. In 1860, a council of German bishops said, "Our first parents were formed immediately by God . . . to assert that this human being . . . emerged finally from the spontaneous continuous change of imperfect nature to the more perfect, is clearly opposed to Sacred Scripture and to the Faith." A prominent Jesuit newspaper that was considered a mouthpiece of Vatican opinion took an aggressive anti-evolution position for decades.

But it turned out that Catholic theologians were busy throughout this period engineering ways to make evolution and special creation work together, even explaining at what point in evolutionary history God might have inserted the soul. The Vatican Council said that "God, the source and end of all things, can be known with certainty from the consideration of created things, by the natural power of human reason." And *On the Origin of Species* was never added to the Index of Forbidden Books. So . . . green light?

The time was confusing for reasonable Catholics who were trying to figure out what to make of Darwin without getting on the wrong side of the Pope. Finally, in 1893, Pope Leo XIII made a statement that clarifies . . . well, he made a statement:

- Scientific theory is unstable and ever-changing.

- The Bible isn't always to be taken literally.

- Catholic scholars shouldn't "depart from the literal and obvious sense" of the Bible, except "where reason or necessity requires."

- People must beware of "thirst for novelty and the unrestrained freedom of thought" running rampant in this age.

- Theologians and scientists should stay out of each others' areas of expertise (an idea echoed a century later by biologist Stephen Jay Gould — see Chapter 8)

In 1950, Pope Pius XII opened the door a crack, saying evolution is "a legitimate matter of inquiry" on which "Catholics are free to form their own opinions." But "they should do so cautiously," he said, respecting "the Church's right to define matters touching on Revelation." They may not, however, consider the possibility that the soul itself evolved.

Call that the *restrained* freedom of thought.

Nearly half a century later, Pope John Paul II called evolution "more than a hypothesis," saying that independent studies arriving at the same conclusion are "a significant argument in favor of the theory." Once again, the Catholic Church reaffirmed that the soul can't have evolved. On this the Pope and I agree.

Let me take a moment to offer a salute. Though the process is slow, self-contradicting, convoluted, and unclear, the Catholic Church goes further than many religions and denominations in recognizing that evolution can't simply be tossed out the window. If they could just avoid saying, "Think all you want, so long as you don't end up with different conclusions," I'd be really impressed.

Challenging the Religious Monopoly in Politics

The requirements to hold public office vary from country to country and even state to state in the United States — be a certain age, live in the place you'll represent, and so on. It's unusual for almost any country today to require someone holding a political office to profess a particular religious belief. Even theocracies like Iran and Utah have a few members of religious minorities in their legislatures. (You think I'm kidding about Utah, but the Utah State Legislature has about the same percentage of non-Mormons as the Iranian Consultative Assembly has non-Muslims. That's just interesting.)

In countries founded since the 18th-century Enlightenment, protection from religious requirements is generally written into law. Here's a clause from the US Constitution:

> [All public officials] shall be bound by Oath or Affirmation, to support this Constitution; but no religious test shall ever be required as a qualification to any office or public trust under the United States.

It even includes the right to affirm rather than swear a religious oath — a nice touch. As the following sections explain, the United States was a full century ahead of the British on that one. But seven US states still have constitutions barring atheists from holding public office — not just in the 19th century, but in 2012. (Refer to Chapter 14 for more on that.)

Whether or not a religious test exists in the United States, religious disbelief has long been a de facto obstacle to holding public office there. In the United Kingdom, a different obstacle was in place until the late 19th century — a requirement to swear an oath to God and the Sovereign in order to be seated in Parliament. These sections introduce Charles Bradlaugh, the first member of Parliament to challenge that requirement and Robert Ingersoll, whose promising political career in the United States was set aside — fortunately for an even more promising career as a public speaker.

Denying unbelief a seat at the table: The Bradlaugh Affair

Imagine being elected to the British Parliament, only to be told you can't take your seat because of your beliefs. That's what happened to Charles Bradlaugh (1833–1891), a journalist, political activist, and prominent atheist.

On his first day of work as a newly elected Member of Parliament for Northampton, Bradlaugh was asked to take an oath of allegiance to the Queen in the name of God. He couldn't do that in good conscience, because he only believed one of them existed. So Bradlaugh claimed the right to *affirm* his loyalty rather than swearing a religious oath. Request denied, said the ruling Conservatives.

Fine, said Bradlaugh, I'll take the religious oath as a matter of form. Request denied, said the Conservatives again. That wouldn't be *sincere*. Bradlaugh attempted to take his seat anyway, a scuffle ensued, and he was briefly imprisoned in Big Ben before being released to go home.

The public outcry was immediate and fierce, especially from Northampton, the people who voted him in. (Most of them, it should be noted, were religious Christians themselves who elected Bradlaugh because he was the best person for the job and didn't like Parliament nullifying their votes.) But his seat was declared vacant and a by-election called — which Bradlaugh won easily. His candidacy was invalidated, and another election was called — which Bradlaugh won easily. Four times over six years, Bradlaugh won re-election and wasn't seated. He gradually won several prominent voices to his side, including former Prime Minister William Gladstone and the playwright George Bernard Shaw. In 1886, the Conservatives relented. Bradlaugh was finally allowed to affirm the oath, even though the existing law still technically forbade it.

In 1888, Bradlaugh led a successful effort to pass a new Oaths Act to permit affirmation as an alternative to the religious pledge — finally catching up the United Kingdom with the constitutional guarantee Americans have enjoyed since 1789. (The gloating so seldom flows in that direction, I just couldn't help myself.)

Bradlaugh continued his secular activism throughout 11 years in Parliament. And though his rejection of religion was unique in the Parliament of 1880, more than 100 nontheistic members of Parliament make up the All-Party Parliamentary Humanist Group in 2012.

Waxing eloquent in unbelief: Robert Green Ingersoll

Aside from canned campaign addresses by politicians, which other people usually write so the politician can deliver on a TelePrompTer, the whole idea of public speeches is unfamiliar today. But in the 19th century, before television and the Internet began to pile unfiltered opinion neck-high in every home, the average person looking for commentary on the issues of the day, or just some thoughtful entertainment, could attend a lecture by a traveling orator. Mark Twain, Charles Dickens, and Sojourner Truth were among the speakers traveling the United States and United Kingdom on lecture circuits in this era. But one orator in particular was guaranteed to draw and hold the attention of a standing-room-only crowd for up to two hours straight — Colonel Robert Green Ingersoll, "The Great Agnostic."

Ingersoll was a former Illinois state attorney general who was famous for his humor, his knowledge — he was allegedly able to recite entire Shakespeare plays verbatim — his courage, his decency, and his generosity. But his religious and political views made him unelectable to actual public office. Well, they would have, anyway, if his views had been known. After he served as attorney general, the Illinois Republican Party urged him to run for governor but wanted him to hide his agnosticism. He thought it would be unethical to conceal information from the public and refused. Good man.

But leaving politics didn't mean people wouldn't come out to listen to him speak — and that's just what they did, by the thousands, hearing Ingersoll on subjects from education to politics to women's rights to religion. And far from being a hindrance, his outspoken and eloquent critiques of religion were mostly responsible for his enormous popularity.

Creating a Religion without God: Felix Adler's Ethical Culture

When Rabbi Samuel Adler sent his son Felix to Germany in 1870 to continue his rabbinical studies, he forgot to tell him not to talk to any neo-Kantians. But Felix did just that, absorbing two ideas that would shape the course of his life:

- ✔ That the existence of God can't be proven or disproven
- ✔ That morality has nothing to do with religious belief

He returned to New York at age 23, knowing he wouldn't be a rabbi but still carrying all the passions that first drove him to consider that profession — a love of humanity, a deep interest in ethics, and a desire to help others find meaning and purpose in community. A teaching position at Cornell gave him the freedom to think about and eventually act on a revolutionary idea — a religion based not on beliefs, but on values and ethics, one that united all of humanity in moral social action. He began a series of weekly Sunday lectures, and in 1877, created the Society of Ethical Culture based on "deed, not creed" — on actions instead of statements of belief.

The society quickly became much more than a lecture series, applying Adler's ideas to compassionate action in the community. It created a visiting nurse service to provide healthcare for the indigent of New York and worked to improve conditions in the tenements of the city. The society also opened the first free kindergarten in the United States, as well as the Fieldston School, with a curriculum built around courses in ethics and moral philosophy, as well as active community service.

That first Ethical Culture Society is still very much there, a thriving community on Central Park West in Manhattan, and is still making tremendous contributions to the city and beyond. And the movement has spread to more than 30 Ethical Societies in cities across the United States.

I have a very warm place in my heart for Ethical Culture, and I'd love nothing more than to see an Ethical Culture Society in every city. Like Thomas Jefferson taking scissors to the New Testament (see Chapter 11), Ethical Culture keeps the good parts of religious community and leaves the outworn, outdated, and outgrown parts behind.

Chapter 8

Growing Up in the Tumultuous 20th Century

In This Chapter

▶ Getting corrupted by absolute power

▶ Midwifing modern humanism

▶ Experimenting with creedless religion

▶ Reconciling science and religion…or not

*T*he 20th century was an era of colliding "isms," from the arts (surrealism, expressionism, and minimalism) to politics (Fascism, Communism, and Zionism) to philosophy (existentialism, relativism, and post-modernism).

Atheism is no exception, playing a much larger role in politics and culture in the 20th century. And like any "ism" released into the wild, the results are mixed. As Ethical Culture demonstrates (refer to Chapter 7), it was no more difficult to behave ethically without belief in God than with it, but atheism also doesn't guarantee good behavior any more than religion does. "Absolute power corrupts absolutely" applies no matter what a person's worldview is, and the 20th century includes tragic examples of corruption and immorality in positions of unchecked power, both by atheists (such as Mao Zedong in China, Joseph Stalin in the USSR, and Pol Pot in Cambodia) and theists (such as Adolf Hitler in Germany, Francisco Franco in Spain, and Idi Amin Dada in Uganda).

The century also had some good news. An atheist committed to nonvio-lence led a newly independent nation, and atheists and theists alike worked together to build a global infrastructure of peace and to improve the human condition.

This chapter explores the highs and lows (and even some of the middles) of atheism in the 20th century, from the violent and immoral suppression of religion by Stalin to the courageous support of human rights, equality, and religious freedom by pioneering atheists and humanists including Corliss Lamont and Goparaju Ramachandra Rao (more commonly known as Gora).

Clashing at the National Levels: Atheism and Religion

Governments telling individuals what they can and can't believe is a bad idea, a violation of human rights so fundamental that the United Nations includes "freedom of thought, conscience, and religion" in the 1948 Universal Declaration of Human Rights (see the nearby sidebar for more information).

But several governments in the 20th century responded to centuries of religious domination by forcing atheism in its place, entirely missing the lessons of history. These sections look at some atheists who abused power at the national level.

Encountering violence and intolerance in the Soviet Union

Like many revolutions, the October Revolution that created the Soviet Union in 1917 swept a new group into power whose first order of business was to destroy any hint of the previous one. Everything to do with the old Russia was suddenly, and simply, bad.

Religion was high on the list of what the Bolsheviks considered bad influences from the past. The new Soviet Union was officially atheistic, and religion was targeted for complete elimination. "Religion is the opium of the people," said Vladimir Lenin, and is used by the cultural elites to exploit and stupefy the people. "This saying of Marx is the cornerstone of the entire ideology of Marxism about religion."

Declaring the right to freedom of belief worldwide

In 1948, after some of the worst decades ever for human rights, the United Nations established a Universal Declaration of Human Rights. Article 18 is a simple and clear declaration of the right to believe and think freely:

Everyone has the right to freedom of thought, conscience, and religion; this right includes freedom to change his religion or belief, and freedom, either alone or in community with others and in public or private, to manifest his religion or belief in teaching, practice, worship and observance.

By using the phrase "religion or belief," the UN makes it clear that this freedom includes all worldviews, not just religious ones.

Missing Marx's meaning: The "opium of the people"

Marx's statement that religion is "the opium of the people" is often misunderstood as a simple condemnation of religion. In fact, he said something much more interesting and complex.

"Religion is the sigh of the oppressed creature, the heart of a heartless world, and the soul of soulless conditions," he wrote. "It is the opium of the people." Medicinal opium was a common pain reliever during the 19th century. As long as the human condition included so much suffering, people would retreat into religion to blunt that pain. That was his point. He didn't think that retreat into numbness was a good thing, but his call wasn't to strip people of their medicine; rather, to end the suffering that made that medicine necessary in the first place.

Marx was unfortunately dead by this time — otherwise I picture him smacking Lenin silly, because Lenin had almost completely missed Marx's point about the "opium of the people" (check out the nearby sidebar). A few years later, Stalin put the antireligious drive into brutal high gear, confiscating religious property, harassing the faithful, and teaching official atheism in state schools. In one four-year period, more than 1,200 bishops and priests of the Russian Orthodox Church were rounded up and executed as enemies of the state.

Provoking the Cristero Rebellion in Mexico

Most people in the global North think of the global South as 100 percent religious. Although Christianity does have a strong hold on the South, including Catholicism in the former colonies of Spain and Portugal, a healthy presence of doubt actually exists there as well, and it sometimes reaches the open air — or even into the halls of power.

Just as in other places and times, the presence of the Catholic Church in Mexico was as much political as religious, and resentment about its power and influence started to boil over in the early 20th century, especially concerning progress in human rights and individual social freedoms. In 1917, after nearly a decade of civil war, Mexico ratified a new Constitution. It was an impressive one for human rights, including mandatory and free education, free speech, individual religious freedom, and clear rights for the accused.

But those in power wanted to curtail the huge political influence of the Catholic Church, which had found its way into nearly every aspect of Mexican life. The new Constitution included a massive backlash against the Church. Education was now to be completely secular in public *and* private schools. The Church had no official legal status in the country anymore, and the government seized all church property. Priests couldn't own property or hold public office. Worship services were to be held only in church buildings, and the government was now in control of the number and location of priests throughout the country.

The harsher of these restrictions were largely ignored until 1924, when an atheist named Plutarco Calles was elected president of Mexico. Under his leadership, the government enforced the restrictions and created strong penalties. Priests wearing their clerical garb in public were fined 500 pesos (more than $4,000 today). Any priest criticizing the government received up to five years behind bars. Church property was seized, all monasteries, convents, and religious schools closed, and all foreign priests deported. Chihuahua enacted a law allowing just one priest for the whole state, which is a little bigger than Great Britain. By 1934, the number of priests in Mexico had been reduced from 4,500 to 334, and more than half of the Mexican states had no priest at all.

Understanding Hitler's beliefs

Nobody wants Hitler on his team, which makes sense. If there's anything most people today can agree on, it's that Adolf Hitler represents the worst kind of human being. So ever since he breathed his last stinking breath, the battle's been on to "prove" that his beliefs lined up with the other side, Christians calling him an atheist, and atheists calling him a Christian.

His inconsistent statements don't help matters. Early in his career, he praised Christianity at every opportunity and identified with it directly. "I believe that I am acting in accordance with the will of the Almighty Creator: by defending myself against the Jew, I am fighting for the work of the Lord," he wrote in *Mein Kampf*. "My feelings as a Christian point me to my Lord and Savior as a fighter," he said in a speech in Munich. Many historians argue that he was just using religious imagery and identity to appeal to a religious country, using the long, sad history of Christian anti-Semitism to stir the hatred that boiled below the surface. Such an interpretation is plausible as well. And some sources had him raging against the Christian church as "weak" in the final months of his life.

Of course criticizing the church isn't the same as being an atheist, and no statement of religious unbelief has ever surfaced from Hitler. On the contrary, he associated atheism with the communist enemies of Germany and wanted it wiped from the face of the Earth. "We have therefore undertaken the fight against the atheistic movement," he says in a speech in 1933, "[and] we have stamped it out." Still, amazingly, the myth persists that Hitler was himself an atheist.

But Christians can take heart in one thing — even though he never denied the existence of a god, some evidence suggests that Hitler wasn't any kind of mainstream Christian in his last years either. He seemed to have become a believer in what he calls "the Lawgiver" or "Providence," a supernatural force that he thought guided the struggle between races of humanity and would ensure the victory of the Aryan people in the end. Just as I do with God in Chapter 3, I picture "the Lawgiver" smacking his imaginary forehead in utter disbelief at such human nonsense.

Most historians now agree that the Calles government had overreached, and the response was predictable. A peasant revolt known as the Cristero Rebellion raged against the government for more than two years. In 1934, a new president rolled back the penalties Calles put in place, and an uneasy truce was restored between God and country in Mexico.

Examining the horrors of a Cultural Revolution in China

Chinese history just boggles my mind. I'm sure the Westernness of my brain doesn't help, but China seems like a complicated collision of kingdoms and dynasties and philosophies rising and falling and merging and splitting over the course of more than 4,000 years. It's completely fascinating, but I just can't wrap my head around it. Even when it comes down to a single era, like the Cultural Revolution of the 20th century, the complexity stuns me, but that period is important to this discussion.

The Qing Dynasty, the last of the ruling dynasties of China, collapsed in 1911 and was replaced by the Republic of China, a chaotic era in which feuding warlords fought for control of the central government, finally erupting into 23 years of civil war. The Communist Party of China won in 1949. Like the Community Party in the Soviet Union, this government was officially atheistic.

In 1966, the Communist Party of Mao Zedong (also spelled _Mao Tse-tung_) announced the beginning of a Cultural Revolution to finish the political revolution and thrust China forward into a supposedly shiny future. It didn't quite work out that way, partly because it was crammed with contradictions. "Four Great Rights" were granted to the people, including freedom of speech and association. But in the same breath, certain ideas were forbidden, including anything that sounded like the pre-revolutionary days, including what was called the "Four Olds" — Old Customs, Old Culture, Old Habits, and Old Ideas. These "Olds" did include some real obstacles to human progress, though few people today would argue that the benefits gained for Chinese society were worth the horrific costs that followed.

The Party saw religion as one of the ways the "Four Olds" were carried forward — the main enemies of progress. Mao created a terrifying paramilitary movement called the _Red Guards_ — young people full of revolutionary certainties who became Mao's proxies in every school and village, spying on parents, teachers, and friends to catch and report any pre-revolutionary ideas or actions, including religious ones. Mao issued an order forbidding the police to interfere with the actions of the Red Guard. Temples and churches were closed or destroyed, and religion was portrayed as a "bourgeois" tool of foreign elements who were opposed to China's best interests. Clergy and monks of all faiths were rounded up and detained in "re-education camps." Thousands of people were tortured or killed.

Like Stalin's Soviet Union, Mao's Cultural Revolution underlined the point that no worldview can be trusted with absolute power, and that enforced atheism is every bit as bad, both in principle and in practice, as enforced religion.

Birthing Modern Humanism

Getting a handle on the birth of an idea can be difficult, but a few tools can help. Google's Ngram Viewer is one of them. Type in any word or phrase and Ngram scans millions of books, and then creates a graph that shows how common the word is over time. It's like a glimpse into the maternity ward of ideas. And the idea of modern humanism is no exception.

The word *humanism* started in the 15th century, although at that point it described the study of the ancient classics, not a secular worldview. For four centuries Ngram shows a mostly flat line for humanism, meaning the word didn't appear in many books. Then suddenly a wobble shows up in the 1850s, then a bump. After gestating for 400 years, the idea of modern humanism was born.

Zoom in to the year 1853 and the details come into focus. An organization called the British Humanistic Religious Association formed to promote knowledge of science, philosophy, and the arts. It was a step in the direction of modern humanism.

The line starts a steady climb through the end of the 19th century. And just as it had been with "atheism" centuries earlier, the phrase *secular humanism* was used as a put-down in the early going, an accusation mocking the efforts of people like Felix Adler to create religions that are both ethical and God-optional. As the 20th century starts, the Ngram continues skyward as more people, movements, and organizations adopted humanism as a preferred label for an ethical life philosophy without supernatural beliefs.

The following sections introduce some of those key people, movements, and organizations.

Redefining God: John Dewey

Few people can claim a greater influence on American culture than the philosopher John Dewey (1859–1952). In the course of a long career, Dewey practically reinvented the American system of education from the bottom up. He was also a key figure in the rebirth of modern humanism. But his approach was controversial, even among humanists — partly because he wanted to keep using the word God, even though he didn't believe such a being existed.

A lot of atheists and humanists today are pretty much allergic to religious language and ritual. For some, such reminders of religion bring up too many bad memories or resentments. Others don't want to be assumed to be religious, an assumption that makes them disappear into the mainstream and reinforces the idea that atheists are rare.

But Dewey, writing in the 1930s, was coming from a very different place. Though an atheist himself, he wasn't allergic to religion. In fact, he worried aloud that there was a growing "crisis in religion" as increasing knowledge of the world made it harder for people to be religious.

Are you wondering why an atheist wanted people to keep believing in God? Well he didn't, really. Like Felix Adler in the 19th century (see Chapter 7), Dewey said he wanted to rescue the religious impulse, to keep religious language and ritual, *even if people no longer believed in God.* This may seem strange at first, but it's very similar to Unitarian Universalism today, which I describe in the "Doing Religion With an Optional God" section later in this chapter. Religion, he said, is a way to gather in community, to focus on ideals, and to take positive action together. Wouldn't want to lose that just because God is off the clock.

But Dewey went even further than most UUs when he said *Let's keep using the word God, but mean something else* — not a supernatural being, but community, ideals, whatever it was that made people want to strive to be their best. That, he said, is "God."

This designation is a big problem for a lot of people, religious and secular alike, even today. If someone thinks the supernatural God is an important idea to preserve, they want to know that when someone says "God," she means *God.* And if someone thinks belief in a supernatural God is a harmful thing, it doesn't help when the very word is redefined to mean pretty much anything. Suppose I'm a researcher dedicated to the fight against cancer, and the word "cancer" is suddenly redefined to include backyard gardening. My efforts will begin to look a bit bizarre: *You're fighting against cancer? But that's one of my favorite hobbies!*

Not long after Dewey proposed this redefinition, the United States entered the Cold War, religion became entwined with patriotism, and God was added to the currency and the Pledge of Allegiance. If "God" has been redefined to mean anything a person wants it to mean, arguing that church-state lines have been crossed becomes very difficult.

With or without religious language, Dewey's ideas profoundly influenced modern humanism and liberal religion, including Ethical Culture and Unitarian Universalism.

Making manifestos and declarations

Even though religious doubt has been around for thousands of years, it was a new idea to many in the early 20th century. And it was certainly new to have it traipsing around the world stage. Prominent humanists of this era felt it was time to define humanism and the humanist movement more clearly.

Creating A Humanist Manifesto

If an idea or movement is new, it helps to have a framing document — something that outlines what it's all about, why there's a need for it, and what its supporters consider important and true. Humanism got its first such document in 1933 with *A Humanist Manifesto.*

The word "manifesto" can be a little jarring to modern ears, sounding like a thrown gauntlet, a defiant challenge. It can be that, but a manifesto is just an attempt to *manifest* an idea, to take something abstract and make it solid and clear — something humanism really needed in the early 20th century.

Even as humanism tried to find its legs around this time, religion was going through an identity crisis of its own. As science advanced into areas once explained by religion, a Social Gospel movement turned the attention of many churches away from abstractions like salvation and grace and toward the alleviation of suffering — feeding the hungry, housing the homeless, caring for the sick. Good stuff. But the chaos of the First World War gave rise to a new revival of fundamentalism that quickly swamped the Social Gospel movement in a new tide of superstition.

A Humanist Manifesto was an attempt to capture the ideas of humanism in the midst of that swirling mess, with 15 statements of naturalistic belief. It was also a challenge to the supernaturalists of the time. Beliefs should be based not on revelation, it said, but on reason and science.

You may think the 34 signers of this Humanist Manifesto of 1933 were ardent rejecters of religion. But like John Dewey, who was one of the signers, they weren't looking to throw out religion. In fact, nearly half of them were ministers or theologians. They were advocating a new *kind* of religion — one with all of the supernatural elements whittled out — calling it "religious humanism."

It was common for humanism at this point to brim with optimism about human potential. Supernaturalism was on the way out. Science was marching forward, bringing progress and plenty in its wake. The new religion (as they called it) of humanism, informed by science and driven by reason and compassion, would lead humanity forward into a bright future by pushing aside harmful and reactionary beliefs.

Or so they thought.

Declaring a global movement

Something astonishing happened in many developed countries after World War II — a rapid, dramatic, and often unexpected shift to the secular. I've heard dozens of possible reasons for this, from the use of religious hatred by the Third Reich to the introduction of universal health care. Whatever the reason, it quickly became clear that some kind of international umbrella organization was needed to connect and represent the many atheist, humanist, and other freethought organizations suddenly popping up around the world. In 1952, the International Humanist and Ethical Union (IHEU) was created at a World Humanist Congress in Amsterdam.

Now think about it for a moment: What would a world congress of nonbelievers have sounded like to people like Protagoras (see Chapter 4), al-Raw⊠nd⊠ (refer to Chapter 5), Jean Meslier (see Chapter 6), and Percy Shelley (check out Chapter 10), all of whom hid their unbelief or suffered severely for not doing so? I can imagine them flying in to Amsterdam as representatives.

The first order of business for the World Humanist Congress was drawing up the Amsterdam Declaration, an accessible, cross-cultural statement of principles to unify a growing global movement.

Embracing the secular: Paul Kurtz and Humanist Manifesto II

By the 1970s, many humanists felt it was time to manifest humanism clearly yet again — and this time, that meant a clear step away from religion. The answer was *Humanist Manifesto II,* and the leader of the effort was the American philosopher Paul Kurtz (1925-2012).

Forty years had passed at this point since the first Humanist Manifesto, and a lot had happened to blunt the optimism of that first attempt: Fascism, the Holocaust, the Cold War, and the very real possibility that the world would meet its end in a global thermonuclear fireball. It had been a sobering and difficult 40 years.

So when Kurtz sat down with Edwin Wilson to craft a new manifesto, they began by acknowledging that a little more realism was needed. In addition to broad statements against weapons of mass destruction and racism and in support of universal human rights, *Humanist Manifesto II* got quite specific, saying for example that divorce, birth control, and abortion should be universally available, and that an international court should be established to try those accused of war crimes and other crimes against humanity.

But one of the main differences in Manifesto II was a much more secular attitude. The Manifesto was to be "a design for a secular society on a planetary scale," and the signers were identified as nontheists who "find insufficient evidence for belief in the supernatural." Hard to get much clearer than that.

Manifesto II also made a not-too-subtle slap at earlier attempts to reclaim religious language, rituals, and ideas: "Some humanists believe we should reinterpret traditional religions and reinvest them with meanings appropriate to the current situation." *(We're looking at you, Dewey!)* "Such redefinitions, however, often perpetuate old dependencies and escapisms; they easily become obscurantist, impeding the free use of the intellect. We need, instead, radically new human purposes and goals . . . Humans are responsible for what we are or will become. No deity will save us; we must save ourselves."

Throughout his career, Kurtz revived and promoted the term "secular humanism," making the separation from religious humanism clear and complete. In the 1980s, Jerry Falwell, leader of a fundamentalist Christian political revival called the Moral Majority, seized on the term "secular humanism," painting a picture of a dark, powerful cultural force threatening morality and faith in the United States. In doing so, he exaggerated what was actually a small philosophical movement at the time. "Do we want secular humanism to take over the hearts, minds, souls, and spirits of our children and grandchildren?" he asked. "Or, are we willing to fight the good fight for their sakes?"

The American Humanist Association at the time — the main US national organization of secular humanists at the time — had only about 4,000 members.

Kurtz later established several important national humanist organizations, including the Center for Inquiry, the Council for Secular Humanism, Prometheus Books, and the Institute for Science and Human Values.

Building a philosophy of humanism: Corliss Lamont

The horrors of the Second World War knocked the heady confidence in humanity's future out of many humanists. A clear exception was American philosopher Corliss Lamont, a thinker who took the shining football of *A Humanist Manifesto* and ran with it for the rest of his long and productive life.

Lamont's brilliant career as a professor at Harvard, Columbia, and Cornell would have been enough accomplishment for most people. But his biggest contributions were as a defender of individual rights, challenging the US government in several legal battles over civil liberties and the right to privacy. (If you're a US citizen, Lamont is one of the reasons the US government can't intercept your mail, even if they think it includes "communist propaganda.") But he also found time to become one of the most eloquent and thoughtful advocates of humanism in the late 20th century.

His direct influence on humanism came mostly in the form of a single book —
The Philosophy of Humanism. Based on a course he taught at Columbia, the
book captured humanism for the first time not just as a way of thinking about
enormous questions about religion or death or meaning, but as a complete
philosophy of life without supernatural beliefs. (For more on this terrific little
book, flip to Chapter 11.)

Disagreeing with Gandhi

Gandhi was one of those saintly few whose character and judgment tran-
scended culture and point of view. How can somebody disagree with a guy
who taught a nation how to overthrow 300 years of colonial rule without
firing a shot?

These sections introduce two people who liked and respected Gandhi enormously but disagreed strongly with him on some key issues, including the
place of religion in Indian life. Both knew him personally, and both were atheists. One fought for social equality in India, whereas the other rose to lead
the new nation, handling national power intelligently and ethically.

Leading a religious nation: The atheist Jawaharlal Nehru

Jawaharlal Nehru (1889–1964) spent a lot of his time in prison while fighting
for the freedom of his people. He eventually rose to lead his nation, establishing a new order in place of British colonial rule.

Nehru was a great admirer of Gandhi, especially his focus on nonviolent
action. At the same time, Nehru, who was an atheist, criticized Gandhi's use
of religion to define India as it moved toward independence, worrying that
it made people passive, and worst of all, that it stopped them from thinking.
"Religion, in India and elsewhere has filled me with horror," he wrote in his
autobiography, "and I have frequently condemned it and wished to make a
clean sweep of it."

He wrote his autobiography in 1936, including those clear renunciations of
religion, and *still* became Prime Minister of India in 1947, which is pretty
much unthinkable in most countries. But India is unique in ways that make
this possible. A long history of multiple religions living cheek-and-jowl with
each other, including atheistic religions like Jainism, made tolerance fairly
high. And even though Nehru had strong criticisms for religion, he recognized the need to live peacefully together. "The only alternative to coexistence," he said, "is codestruction."

Nehru helped draft India's first independent constitution, and his influence was clear. Many of the values he laid out during the independence movement are stamped into the document, including guarantees of freedom of religion and association, equality for all regardless of caste or color, and the establishment of India as a "secular democratic republic." It's right in the first sentence of the Preamble.

It often comes as a shock when people who know India as a very religious country find out that it's officially secular. But that makes it very much the same as the United States. Our founders also knew that the only way to protect religious freedom for all is to take government itself out of the religion game entirely.

In a way, Nehru's atheism was the perfect qualification for the first prime minister of a country with deep and varied religious roots. Starting with a Hindu leader would most likely have infuriated Muslims and other religious minorities, and a Muslim president would have frosted the Hindus no end. An atheist with a strong commitment to religious freedom was much less likely to play favorites.

Nehru guided the new country through its challenging early years before dying in office in 1964 and leaving behind a single clear request: "I wish to declare with all earnestness that I do not want any religious ceremonies performed for me after my death. I do not believe in such ceremonies, and to submit to them, even as a matter of form, would be hypocrisy and an attempt to delude ourselves and others."

So of course Nehru was cremated in accordance with Hindu rites on the banks of the Yamuna River.

Pressing Gandhi on social issues: Gora

Goparaju Ramachandra Rao, better known as Gora, was an atheist activist and social reformer active in India in the middle of the 20th century, just as Gandhi was making headlines with his first nonviolent campaigns.

Gora wanted nothing more than to have a conversation with Gandhi — about religion, about atheism, and about the social change they both wanted so desperately. But penetrating Gandhi's inner circle wasn't easy. Gora decided on a time-tested technique — making a complete nuisance of himself.

He peppered Gandhi with short letters requesting an interview. When that didn't work, he joined Gandhi's *ashram* (spiritual retreat), working and meditating and just generally trotting around on the margins of Gandhi's view like a puppy. Finally Gandhi relented, granting Gora a series of interviews.

Gandhi told Gora he had heard of his work in the villages and asked him to tell him about it.

Gora described an innovative program of monthly "cosmopolitan dinners" in which people of all castes came together in an attempt to break down the barriers throughout Indian society. Some members of the program refused to attend public functions or wedding celebrations unless they included cosmopolitan dinners. He also described adult literacy classes held for the general public, especially the Harijan. (Gora had done his homework, so he knew Gandhi preferred "Harijan," or "Child of God," to the term "untouchables.")

Gandhi noted that Gora could do those things just as easily without atheism.

"True," said Gora, explaining that his method was atheism, just as Gandhi's was Hinduism. Both were systems that could be used as the means to an end — the improvement of life for the downtrodden. Gora described the advantages of atheism for breaking down barriers between people, because barriers of caste and religion have no significance to an atheist. All are human beings, he said, adding that atheism also put man on his own legs, because no divine will or fate controls his actions. Breaking down these barriers released free will in the Harijan, he said, releasing them from the inferiority into which they had been pressed for all the centuries they were made to believe that they were "fated" to be untouchables. Religion silences questioning about how and why, he said. Atheism restores the ability to question one's place.

This didn't sit well with Gandhi, who said he would consider fasting because atheism was spreading.

Gora responded immediately: He would fast against Gandhi's fast.

"You will fast?" Gandhi asked, incredulously.

Yes, Gora replied, and then asked Gandhi *why* he would fast. Tell me how atheism is wrong, he said, and I will change.

Gandhi paused for a while, and then told Gora that he could see how deep was his conviction in atheism. But then Gandhi suddenly stiffened. It's the present behavior of the people that's allowing atheism to spread, he said.

See what happened there? It's something just about every atheist has seen. I can tell someone directly that I have devoted my life to feeding the hungry and working for human rights, earning the Nobel Peace Prize in the process, but if I say that atheism has motivated me to do so, all the good seems to fall away, and it's a spreading cancer to be stopped.

But Gora persisted through a series of interviews, chipping away at Gandhi's resistance. And with each one, Gandhi seemed to open up to the idea that two people can work toward the same ends from entirely different starting points.

Gandhi ended the last talk by showing an encouraging change of heart. He said he saw that high ideals were just as present in atheism as in theism, and that he recognized they were both seekers of truth, both hard workers, and both willing to change when they were wrong. He said he would support Gora in his work with the Harijan, even though their beliefs differed.

Now there was a breakthrough, and it was all Gora had been seeking. He spent the rest of his life working to improve the conditions of the Harijan and for the advancement of the atheist perspective in India. That's a life very well spent.

Meeting the "Most Hated"

Journalists and cultural commentators have often conferred the title of "Most Hated Woman (or Man) in America" on controversial figures. Some of the recipients of this moniker have been criminals, but just as often the designation has gone to someone who held strong opinions outside of accepted norms.

The following sections introduce four people who bore the "Most Hated" label for their atheist beliefs.

The "Most Hated Man in Kentucky": Charles Chilton Moore

After a short career as a minister in Kentucky, Charles Chilton Moore (1837–1906) gradually grew disgusted with Christian endorsements of slavery in the Bible and in pulpits around the US South. He stepped down from his post and eventually came to doubt the Bible even more. He started calling himself a Deist (see Chapter 2), then an agnostic, and finally an atheist.

In 1884, Moore started a newspaper called the *Blue Grass Blade* with the explicit purpose of promoting freethought and atheism — the first such periodical ever. His editorials against religion drew shock and outrage, and he began to receive regular death threats. In 1894 he said, "If there is a devil, Bourbon County [Kentucky] is nearer and dearer to his heart than any place of its size on earth" — and earned himself a stint in jail for it.

In 1903, Moore solicited letters from his readers on the topic "Why I Am an Atheist." Letters flooded in from people in all walks of life — men and women, rich and poor, educated and not, farmers, teachers, housewives, doctors, the works. Reading the stories not of philosophers and famous authors but of regular folks grappling with the same big questions is incredibly moving. As a result of his trials and his newspaper, Moore earned the epithet of "Most Hated Man in Kentucky."

As usual, rumors of a deathbed conversion to Christianity made the rounds after Moore's death in 1906, and his wife and his publisher were left to deny them.

The "Most Hated Woman in America," Part 1: Emma Goldman

Around the turn of the 20th century, "Red Emma" Goldman (1869–1940) was the convenient embodiment of everything bad and scary to the sensibilities of the time: anarchy, communism, free speech, gay rights, pacifism, reproductive freedom, prison reform, free love — oh, and atheism.

Any challenger of the powers that be who writes and speaks for more than a year or so will eventually be challenging the powers in wartime. For Goldman it was the First World War, and sure enough, she was accused of treasonous activity for criticizing the US government, the war itself, and the draft. It couldn't have helped that she published a powerful essay called "The Philosophy of Atheism" in 1916 — one of the most powerful and eloquent defenses of the worldview written to that point.

Goldman managed to step on just about every exposed nerve in the United States of her time. People in the United States particularly hated and feared *anarchism* (the desire to live without government) because an anarchist had assassinated President William McKinley a few years earlier — not long after hearing an Emma Goldman speech. People hated and feared pacifism because the United States was at war. People hated and feared atheism and communism because fears that the Bolshevik Revolution would spread to the workers of the United States had spawned the Red Scare of 1919. So it was an especially bad time to be Emma Goldman — or an especially good one, depending on how you look at it.

In 1917, as the United States prepared to enter the war and the Bolsheviks took power in Russia, the American fears of the time converged to earn Goldman the undisputed title of "Most Hated Woman in America." FBI Director J. Edgar Hoover seized on the national mood, arrested Goldman for speaking against the draft, and deported her to Russia, her birthplace, in 1919.

The "Most Hated Woman in Britain": Margaret Knight

The mild-mannered Margaret Knight (1903–1983) seemed like a Girl Scout compared to other atheists on the "Most Hated" list. But a mere ten minutes talking about moral education on BBC Radio in 1955 was enough to earn Knight a whole slew of nasty nicknames, including "The Unholy Mrs. Knight" and "The Most Hated Woman in Britain."

Knight had been a student at Cambridge when a little bit of Bertrand Russell reading helped her find what she called the "moral courage" to give up her religious beliefs. "It was as if a fresh, cleansing wind swept through the stuffy room that contained the relics of my religious beliefs," she said years later. "I let them go with a profound sense of relief, and ever since I have lived happily without them."

In the years after the Second World War, immigration from Eastern Europe and India quickly changed the ethnic and religious face of Britain. The BBC made a good effort to keep up, inviting a wider variety of belief perspectives on its radio programs. In 1955, Knight, then a professor of psychology, delivered two short radio addresses on the BBC Home Service under the title "Morals without Religion."

Her tone was civil and her thesis simple: moral education should be separated from religious education so that all people, regardless of their perspective, can have a shared understanding of it.

Knight was stepping on a raw nerve here. In addition to ethnic and racial diversity, the United Kingdom after WWII was rapidly going secular. Both church attendance and reported belief were way down and sinking fast. To many listeners, Knight's broadcasts seemed to confirm the suspicion that religion was "under attack" in Britain.

Though she reported a good deal of positive feedback, most of the public response was outraged. "Don't let this woman fool you," said one editorial. "She looks — doesn't she — just like the typical housewife; cool, comfortable, harmless. But Mrs. Margaret Knight is a menace. A dangerous woman. Make no mistake about that."

But in a later book on the subject, Knight shared one letter from a listener in Germany that she found especially moving:

Please accept the gratitude from an unknown man who has seen in your talk the sunrising of a new epoch based on the simple reflection; to do the good because it is good and not because you have to expect to be recompensed after your death. Being myself a victim of Nazi oppression I think that we all have to teach our children the supreme ethics based on facts and not on legends in the deepest interest for the future generations.

The "Most Hated Woman in America," Part II: Madalyn Murray O'Hair

In the 1960s and 1970s, Madalyn Murray O'Hair was the face of atheism in the United States. O'Hair was founder and president of American Atheists and a plaintiff in a landmark decision by the US Supreme Court that banned compulsory Bible readings in public schools (see the next section for more discussion).

O'Hair was the embodiment of the nightmares of a Middle America still immersed in the psychological terror of the Cold War and who saw religion as the defining difference between the United States and the Soviet Union. It made little difference to the brash O'Hair, who pursued church-state separation with an unapologetic fervor, going after everything from "under God" in the Pledge of Allegiance to "In God We Trust" on the currency, quickly earning her turn as the "Most Hated Woman in America." When she wasn't at the Supreme Court, she was on the talk shows where she delighted in provoking religious opponents into spitting fits of rage.

Though even atheists are divided over Madalyn's approach, there's no denying her impact. The legal precedents she helped establish were a huge step forward in securing religious freedom for all Americans, regardless of their perspective.

Courting the Separation of Church and State

Church-state separation — the principle that government should be separate from organized religion, shouldn't endorse any particular religion, and shouldn't restrict the religious freedom of its citizens — took a number of leaps forward in the 20th century. Almost every new national constitution in the century included religious freedom as a guarantee, and many specifically included church-state separation as a way of achieving that.

In the United States, the Supreme Court reached several key decisions that helped rebuild the wall of separation that had been seriously eroded over the years in American public schools. When a Pennsylvania student named

Ellory Schempp protested his high school's daily Bible reading requirement by bringing a Qur'an to read instead, he was sent to the principal's office. His father sued, and the case began wending its way up through the system.

In 1960, atheist activist Madalyn Murray O'Hair sued to protest the same requirement in her son's Baltimore school (refer to the previous section for more on O'Hair). The two cases were merged, and in 1963, the US Supreme Court ruled 8–1 that mandatory Bible readings in public schools were a violation of church-state separation. And in 1962, the Court ruled that organized, mandatory prayer in schools was also unconstitutional.

Notice the word "mandatory." Individual prayer wasn't banned, and even organized group prayer is still allowed as long as the school doesn't lead it and it isn't mandatory for all students, which is a very reasonable compromise — but one very widely misrepresented and misunderstood.

Canada, which not only allowed but mandated Bible reading and the Lord's Prayer at the start of each school day for most of its history, banned the practice in 1996 as a restraint on religious freedom.

A few attempts at separating church and state have failed. A 1970 suit to remove "In God We Trust" from US currency failed on the weird argument that it wasn't a theological statement. And in 2010, the Ninth Circuit court in California ruled that the words "under God" shouldn't be in the Pledge of Allegiance, but the Supreme Court overturned that one on procedural grounds.

Suing to protect religious freedom for all

Here is a timeline of some key 20th century decisions of the US Supreme Court related to the separation of church and state:

- **1947:** States must provide the same guarantees of religious freedom as the federal government.

- **1948:** Religious instruction disallowed in public schools.

- **1952:** Religious instruction allowed off school property during school hours.

- **1962:** Teacher-led prayer disallowed in public schools.

- **1963:** Bible-reading and recitations of the Lord's Prayer disallowed in public schools.

- **1973:** States will fund textbooks and teachers' salaries in religious schools.

- **1987:** Court strikes down the Creation Act, which had mandated that creationism be taught alongside evolution in public school science classrooms.

- **1989:** Religious displays depicting only one religion banned.

- **1992:** Prayers given by clergy as a part of an official public school graduation ceremony disallowed.

Keeping fear alive with urban legends

Countless urban legends exist about atheists, from the arrogant atheist professor humiliated by a humble Christian student (or by Albert Einstein, or a US Marine, or God) to the new US penny design that won't include the motto "In God We Trust" because of an atheist lawsuit (not true). The same fear that brought the wrath of Britain down on poor Margaret Knight is at work in these cases as well — that the presence of nonbelievers in the culture means religion is under attack.

The granddaddy of all atheist urban legends is "Petition 2493" — a supposed petition filed by atheist Madalyn Murray O'Hair asking the US Federal Communications Commission (FCC) to ban all religious programming (or televangelists in one variant, or the use of the word "God" in another) from broadcast television. For more

than 30 years the legend has stayed alive, most recently in forwarded e-mails. The names of the threatened shows and televangelists change, but the basic story remains the same. The petition as described was never real — just a perfect rumor trapped in the amber of a common fear.

This kind of thing isn't entirely harmless. In addition to adding to the general fearfulness and mistrust between people — never a good thing — it has cost quite a bit of taxpayer money. At one point in the late 1980s, the FCC was receiving an estimated 150,000 pieces of mail per month protesting the nonexistent petition. And despite the FCC's best efforts, including a dedicated web page and multiple press releases, the deluge continues to this day.

Separation issues are about religious freedom for everyone, not just atheists. When government endorses a religious view, it's usually guaranteed to be the majority one, which in the United States means mainline Protestantism. That's why minority religions are interested in securing that separation just as much as atheists are. In 1999, a lawsuit in Texas sought to end the reading of prayers at public school football games. The plaintiffs weren't atheists, but a Mormon family and a Catholic family. The prayers didn't reflect their beliefs either.

People have countless opportunities to express beliefs, to come together with others who share those beliefs, and to put their beliefs into practice in their lives and even in the shared culture. But when people of different beliefs are each other's captive audiences, it makes sense to follow that lovely ethical idea found in all of traditions — treat others as you would like to be treated. Making sure one person isn't forcing her rituals or beliefs on another is an important part of that principle.

Doing Religion with an Optional God: Unitarian Universalism

Unitarian Universalism is a fascinating religious denomination. It was formed in 1961 as the merger of two older concepts:

- ✔ Unitarianism, the belief that God is one person, not three (leaving Jesus entirely human)
- ✔ Universalism, the belief that everyone is saved, regardless of action or creed (leaving hell out of business)

Both of these ideas popped up early in Christian history — the fourth century — and the early church fathers slapped both of them down as heresies, executing or otherwise punishing many who professed those beliefs.

But you can't keep a good idea down, and both reemerged in the late 18th and early 19th century as their own Christian denominations. They ran on parallel tracks for more than a century, agitating for the abolition of slavery, getting arrested on the same picket lines for women's voting rights, protesting wars, and feeding the hungry — the kinds of things nondogmatic churches did really well. Both continued to get harsh treatment from mainstream Christianity. Finally, in 1961, they consummated the union and merged to become Unitarian Universalism (or UUism).

Since that time, UUs have developed an interesting and courageous experiment — a religious denomination built around something other than beliefs. Like Ethical Culture, UU is creedless. That doesn't mean individuals sitting in the UU pews don't have beliefs, just that their community is built around something else — shared values and principles like the worth and dignity of every person, justice and compassion, and a free search for truth and meaning.

So what does UUism have to do with atheism? The majority of Unitarian Universalists are humanists (both religious and secular), atheists, or agnostics. Most have left belief in God behind, but they still want to do many of those things religious communities do — creating communities of mutual support, coming together to do good, reflecting on values and ethics, marking life landmarks, and more.

Some atheists say UU feels too much like church, and some believers say it doesn't feel enough like church. They both have other options. For everyone in the middle, UU is worth looking into.

Burying God, Keeping Jesus: The Death of God Theologians

For most of its history, the rainbow of disbelief left out the color black. Welcome to "Death of God" theology, a movement of radical theologians in the mid-1960s who declared that God is no longer relevant in the modern world, and therefore no longer exists. (Refer to Chapter 2 for more about the rainbow of disbelief.) The small, esoteric movement even had its moment in the spotlight, capturing the cover of *TIME* magazine in April 1966 — a black cover with read letters asking "Is God Dead?"

When I first heard of this movement, several questions popped to mind: So you mean God was alive, but now is dead? Or he never existed, and now that's been figured out? Or he existed, but only as a mental construct that no longer works?

Which is it? Depends on which Death-of-Godder you ask. Some felt that Christianity had simply outlived its usefulness as an explanation of the world, and that God, once believable, no longer was. One suggested that God was kept alive by faith, like Tinkerbell, and that a renewed sense of festivity and fantasy can bring him back to life. One of the most prominent, Thomas J.J. Altizer, made the startling suggestion that God was alive, then *fully* inhabited Christ, then literally died on the cross, at which point his spirit went out into the world.

Personally, I've never known quite what to make of the Death of God theologians, which so far hasn't lost me any sleep. Though I share the opinion that God isn't real, I can't shake the idea that they were simply making up the rest of it as they went. Being theologians, I guess you'd say.

Although their theories on what God once was and what exactly happened to him were all over the map, they seemed to agree on one thing — it's all about Jesus now. He's no longer divine, they said, just a great teacher, but he can still serve as a helpful focal point for morality.

Skipping Yahweh: Humanistic Judaism

Imagine a clergy member informing the congregation that he or she no longer believes in God. That declaration has to be one of the most dramatic human moments imaginable. This person, the one who led many of them to faith or reinforced it when it was flagging, who quoted chapter and verse in times of need or loss, who may have even preached against unbelief — this person of all people is an *atheist*.

Given the shock, anger, and betrayal many would naturally feel in this situation, you can easily see why the 18th century priest Jean Meslier waited until he was dead (see Chapter 10) and 20th century minister Dan Barker sent a letter. But in 1963, Rabbi Sherwin Wine actually walked to the front of his synagogue in Windsor, Ontario, faced a congregation expecting a typical Saturday service, and told them that he no longer believed in God — but that he still considered himself a Jew.

All of the major religions are about more than supernatural beliefs. Certain traditions, rituals, ethics, language, symbols, and ways of living are just as much a part of that religious identity. Judaism was always about more than God, and Wine wanted to keep all the rest.

As he stood in front of the murmuring crowd, he obviously knew people would be shocked. But I'm sure he also knew that he couldn't possibly be the only one in the room who felt as he did. So after he announced that he'd be stepping down, he invited anyone else who happened to feel the same to come with him to create . . . well, whatever would be next. He didn't really know.

Eight families came forward to help figure out "what's next." They ended up forming a whole new kind of Jewish congregation, a nontheistic one, right across the river in Detroit — the Birmingham Temple. Wine created a new humanistic liturgy that reflected Jewish culture, identity, and history and taught humanist ethics without reference to God.

Like Motown music and the Model-T Ford, this brilliant idea didn't stay in Detroit for long. The idea spread first around the United States and then around the world as Humanistic Judaism. Today the movement has more than 40,000 members and is recognized as one of the five branches of Judaism itself.

Imagining the same thing happening in Christianity may be difficult at first — but why should it be? It would work just the same and satisfy the same need. In fact, I'll bet you a dollar that within the next ten years, some priest somewhere is going to walk out of his collar, leaving God behind but bringing the rest of his Catholic identity and values with him to create Humanistic Catholicism. Now hold the book at arm's length and move it up and down to shake on it. Okay, that's a bet.

Reconciling Science and Religion (Or Not) Again: Gould's NOMA

Looking back at the century as it drew to a close, paleontologist Stephen Jay Gould noticed that the Catholic Church had been gradually and tentatively extending an olive branch to science. In 1950, Pope Pius XII called evolution "a legitimate matter of inquiry" on which "Catholics are free to form their own opinions." When John Paul II went even further in 1996, calling evolution "more than a hypothesis," and citing "significant argument[s] in favor of the theory," Gould thought it was high time to reach for that branch. And he did so in 1997, proposing a new way of looking at the relationship of science and religion.

Science and religion are concerned with different things, he said, and as long as they stay out of each other's areas of concern, there's no need for conflict. This general idea wasn't actually new. Pope Leo XIII made a similar proposal in 1893. But new or old, Gould's proposal reopened the important discussion about whether or how science and religion can live together.

Each of the two has "a legitimate magisterium, or domain of teaching authority," Gould said. Science deals with observable fact, and religion deals with morality and meaning. The two domains don't overlap, he said, so there shouldn't be a problem. Many people have agreed with him, including many fellow atheists and agnostics who are eager to move beyond the culture war.

But others, including prominent scientists and philosophers, have pointed to serious problems with the idea. It's hard to find a religion anywhere that doesn't make claims of fact, from miracles to the effectiveness of prayer to whether a giant flood ever covered the Earth. And several sciences, including neuroscience and psychology, have recently made enormous contributions to understanding what morality is and how it operates. There's even been scientific progress in defining morality by improving people's understanding of what increases or decreases suffering. So the domains do overlap, they say, enormously and inevitably.

Even though many of these critics are just as eager to form a better relationship between science and religion, this idea just doesn't work for them. Either way, there was no better time to begin asking these questions than the cusp of the 21st century.

Chapter 9

Voicing a New Atheism, and a New Humanism, for the 21st Century

*T*he beginning of the 21st century saw the birth of a more confrontational brand of atheism, one that challenges the ill effects of religion without apology. At the vanguard of this movement-within-a-movement are four prominent writers who've boosted atheism into the center of the cultural conversation.

The new century has also seen a broadening of the freethought movement, including a gentler, more cooperative and humanistic strain of atheism. It may get less media attention, but even the blogger PZ Myers — as confrontational an atheist as you're going to find — calls humanistic atheism "the heart of an atheist movement that will endure and grow. Ignore it," he adds, "and we can expect atheism to fade away."

This chapter explores atheism in a new era of fast growth and rising public awareness.

Tracing the Birth of the 21st-Century Atheist Movement

Social movements are often born in a single, defining moment. You can trace the birth of the 21st century atheist movement to a single moment — the terrorist attacks of September 11, 2001. Though atheists and humanists had been around for centuries, challenging religious ideas and working for their own place at the cultural table, the horror and clarity of that moment — especially the clear part played by religion — was the last straw and a call to action for countless nonreligious people.

Adopting President Bush's frequent praising of "faith-based initiatives" in American communities, many atheists pointed out that the terrorist attacks of 9/11 were also a "faith-based initiative" — and that religion could no longer get a free pass from criticism and challenge.

Other movements have been jumpstarted in similar ways. Black Americans had been working for equal rights for almost a century after emancipation when Rosa Parks was arrested for sitting in the white section of a public bus in Montgomery, Alabama. That clear injustice struck a chord. It was the last straw, and a full-blown social movement for civil rights was born.

Gays and lesbians had been working for social acceptance and equal rights long before the raid at the Stonewall Bar in Greenwich Village, but that single event proved to be the last straw, a tipping point that created a powerful social movement for gay rights.

Feeling "Deep Grief and Fierce Anger": The Four Horsemen

Ask an atheist what he or she was feeling on September 11, and you'll typically get two answers:

✔ That terrible mix of fear, anguish, uncertainty, and grief that everyone else was feeling

✔ Anger and determination to speak out and challenge religion more than ever before

Add a feeling of slack-jawed exasperation when it seemed like everyone else, from the president to my Aunt Diane, was responding to an act of religious insanity by *dropping to their knees in prayer*. Politicians started lacing their speeches with calls for God's protection, and some prominent evangelists even blamed atheists in part for the attack, calling it God's revenge for "secularizing America." The president spoke of the need for a "crusade" against those who had committed the crime, alluding to Matthew 12:30 ("He who is not with me is against me") as he called for allies in a war against a country that had nothing to do with the attack.

It was surreal. And among its many other effects, this painful time gave birth to the modern freethought movement.

Being a direct, unapologetic public atheist in a hyper-religious time and place is difficult, but several prominent voices rose to the challenge. Among them were four authors whose bestselling books criticizing religion came out on each other's heels, all within a few years of the attacks and each other. Their books became rallying points for "The New Atheism," and those authors — biologist Richard Dawkins, philosopher Daniel Dennett, journalist Christopher Hitchens, and neuroscientist Sam Harris — became known, with ironic tongue in cheek, as "The Four Horsemen of the New Atheism."

The first of these books, Harris's *The End of Faith,* wasn't published until three years after September 11, 2001. But plenty else had been written and said in those three years, including an astonishing, clear-headed essay written by Dawkins in the raw and frantic days immediately following the attack.

The following sections describe some key aspects of the atheist response to this horrifying moment.

Sounding the alarm: Richard Dawkins on "the elephant in the room"

On September 15, 2001, less than 96 hours after the attacks of September 11, a compelling essay by Richard Dawkins appeared in the *Guardian* newspaper in the United Kingdom. Commentators and politicians at the time were doing what they've done for centuries — saying that a religiously inspired tragedy, in this case the 9/11 attacks, wasn't really about religion at all. It was about politics, or culture clash, or something else . . . *anything* but religion.

"They hate us for our freedom," President Bush said, not worrying whether that actually made any sense. Countless religious progressives claimed the attacks had been inspired by religious extremism, attempting to place a firewall between that extremism and religion in general.

The purpose of Dawkins's remarkable essay was to make the case that religion was an "elephant in the room" that everybody was too polite to talk about, and that religion wasn't just incidentally involved but had played an essential, indispensable part in the tragedy — that the tragedy literally *couldn't have happened without it.*

He starts by imagining someone coming up with the idea of crashing airplanes into buildings to strike terror into a hated nation. The reason itself may not have been religious in origin — it could just as easily have been political. Ah, but how to do it? You would need some sort of guidance system to keep the planes on course until they hit the buildings.

He considers a few options, including a pigeon trained to peck at a target in exchange for food pellets — something that was actually tested in World War II. But getting the pigeon and the necessary targeting equipment on the plane would be too difficult. To pull off such an attack, you really need . . . a human being. But involving a human presents a problem. He couldn't be trusted to stay on target because he'd know that to do so would mean his own end as well.

Then Dawkins's imaginary terrorist event planner hits on an idea: What if some young men could be convinced that death isn't the end after all? Better still, what if they can be made to believe that a heroic death (like the murder of several thousand infidels) would be followed by a trip straight to a paradise with 72 virgins to call his own?

Suddenly you have your guidance system. Whatever the origin of the desire to wreak havoc, religion provided the means to focus it, to amplify it, and to make it a reality.

Dawkins assured his readers that he wasn't making light of the tragedy. On the contrary, he said he was motivated by a "deep grief and fierce anger" — and this grief and anger heralded a whole new day for his approach to religion. "My last vestige of 'hands off religion' respect disappeared in the smoke and choking dust of September 11· 2001," he said, "followed by the 'National Day of Prayer,' when prelates and pastors did their tremulous Martin Luther King impersonations and urged people of mutually incompatible faiths to hold hands, *united in homage to the very force that caused the problem in the first place.*"

September 11 was by no means the first straw on the atheist's back. But for many, it was definitely the last.

Joining (or rejoining) the battle: Harris, Dennett, Hitchens . . . and Dawkins again

A book, especially one that is groundbreaking and unique, always takes some time to put together. But in the weeks and months that followed September 11, 2001, four writers and thinkers began working independently on books that would transform the discussion of religion and raise the profile of atheism higher than ever before.

The close timing of their books and the similarity of their messages — that religion shouldn't just be automatically tolerated but should be held to the same critical standard of reason as everything else in human life — caused them to be clumped together in the public mind. They came to be called "The Four Horsemen" and their approach "The New Atheism."

Between the summer of 2004 and the summer of 2006, atheism went from buzzing gadfly on the fringe of the culture to a high profile hot topic. The movement gained a face and a voice. Even though many atheists and humanists protested that this more aggressive, confrontational voice didn't speak for them, it did something every movement needs — staked a claim at the outer edge, allowing the other atheists and humanists to set up their tents in the huge new space they helped define.

These sections introduce these four writers. For a more in-depth look at the books they wrote that changed atheism, head over to Chapter 13.

Sam Harris

The first of the four voices to appear in book form was probably the least likely — a previously unpublished and little known student of philosophy and the human mind by the name of Sam Harris. When he started knocking on publishers' doors in 2003 with a broadside against religion called *The End of Faith,* he was stepping completely out of the shadows. The book did find a publisher, which officially started the four-act opera of smart, articulate, non-word-mincing atheist bestsellers.

So without much of a résumé, how did Sam Harris get the attention of publishers and eventually the world? He did it the old-fashioned way — by writing and thinking original thoughts with extraordinary clarity and intelligence. He later earned his PhD in neuroscience and wrote several other bestsellers, including *Letter to a Christian Nation, The Moral Landscape,* and *Lying.*

Richard Dawkins

Richard Dawkins was next with *The God Delusion,* a more general but no less powerful critique of religion. By the time Dawkins stepped up to the atheist plate, he had 30 years in the big leagues as a well-known public explainer of science. Because of his high profile and his 9/11-inspired commitment to take the gloves off and say what needs saying, Dawkins became the poster child and lightning rod for the New Atheist movement. (Harris preferred his privacy and quiet meditation over public smack downs.)

When you read *The God Delusion* — and I really recommend that you do — you're likely to be surprised by the tone. Religious critics have spared little effort painting Dawkins as a shrill and strident lunatic. Doing so is easier than answering his arguments, I suppose. And although he can be very direct at times, Dawkins's approach is so much less maniacal than the public caricature that you'll keep checking the cover to be sure you're reading the right book.

For added effect, listen to the audiobook, read by Dawkins. His accent — a cross between a BBC newsreader and Professor McGonagall — is about as far from shrill as you can get.

Daniel Dennett

Act Three of the Four Horsemen is Daniel Dennett, a philosopher at Tufts University who looks like Santa Claus and thinks like Socrates. He comes across in person and even in writing like an uncle who came up with a really neat idea while fishing and can't wait to tell you — and the idea ends up changing the way you see the world. His book *Breaking the Spell* is the work of a scholar who finds religion rather fascinating but not true, and by the way not a very good idea. But fascinating!

Dennett brings a calm, scholarly voice to the conversation. He sees religion as a direct consequence of who we are and what we've been through as a species. Of the Four Horsemen, Dennett is the one who seems most interested in figuring religion out and finding practical ways to break the spell it holds over people.

Christopher Hitchens

The last Horseman is Christopher Hitchens, who wasn't a bit nice — and what a waste of good venom if he had been. Hitchens was a *polemicist,* someone who used words to perform drive-by surgery without the patient's permission. He wrote from a place of deep conviction, and though he could be bitterly funny, he didn't play games or mince words. This passion, combined with incredible gifts as a writer, resulted in some of the most brilliant, witty, and devastating English prose of the past half century.

Hitchens's interests and targets went way beyond atheism. He tore apart Bill Clinton, Henry Kissinger, capitalism, the Left, the Right, and even Mother Teresa before turning his attention to religion itself. The 2007 book that earned his Horsemanship has the typically uncompromising title *God Is Not Great: How Religion Poisons Everything.* (More on that in Chapter 13.)

Hearing the Chorus of New Atheists: We Are Here, We Are Here, We Are Here!

Whether the New Atheist books made a lot more atheists, or just empowered a lot of people who were already atheists to stand up a little taller and speak up a little louder, is hard to say. Probably both. Either way, a huge chorus of new atheist voices and awareness campaigns rose up to join them in the decade after 9/11. Some are dedicated to "the end of faith," whereas others focus on reaching out to the closeted nonreligious — estimated to number more than 50 million in the United States alone.

In both cases, it's a bit like the Whos on the speck in *Horton Hears a Who!* shouting, "We are *here*, we are *here*, we are *here!*" to get the outside world to see and hear them. Buoyed by their greater numbers and higher profile, atheists are ready to be recognized as a valid and viable part of the culture.

Some signs indicate that this recognition is beginning to take root. After the 2012 re-election of US President Barack Obama, several pollsters noted that the nonreligious had been among Obama's most crucial voting blocs. One researcher with the Pew Forum on Religion and Public Life called it "a striking development in American politics," adding that "the religiously unaffiliated are a very important, politically consequential group."

The following sections describe a few ways that atheists and other nonreligious people have attempted to make their presence better known.

Calling out from billboards and buses

Billboard and bus advertising campaigns by atheist groups have received a lot of attention in recent years. The first in recent years went up in January 2008 with a simple message — "Don't Believe in God? You Are Not Alone" — against a blue sky. Others take direct aim at religion. Examples include the following:

- ✔ **Are You Good Without God? Millions Are:** Also against a blue sky background. FreeThoughtAction, American Humanist Association, and the United Coalition of Reason sponsored this billboard.

- ✔ **Imagine No Religion / Beware of Dogma:** Letters appeared in stained glass design on this billboard by the Freedom From Religion Foundation.

- ✔ **We Are All Atheists About Most Gods. Some of Us Just Go One God Further:** The British Humanist Association sponsored this billboard.

- ✔ **There's Probably No God. Now Stop Worrying and Enjoy Your Life:** The British Humanist Association also sponsored this one.

- ✔ **You Know It's a Myth. This Season, Celebrate REASON!** This billboard included the three wise men following the Star of Bethlehem in the background, brought to you by American Atheists.

- ✔ **You Know It's a Myth . . .And You Have a Choice:** These billboards appeared in both Hebrew and Arabic. American Atheists sponsored them.

- ✔ **"I read the Bible. Now I'm a Proud Atheist." Julia Sweeney, Comedian, Playwright . . . Atheist:** This billboard was one of a series spotlighting celebrity atheists, sponsored by the Freedom From Religion Foundation.

- ✔ **Please Don't Label Me. Let Me Grow Up and Choose for Myself:** This billboard showed happy, bouncing kids, along with phrases like "Christian Child," "Atheist Child," and "Marxist Child" in the background, courtesy of the British Humanist Association.

- **You Don't Need God — to hope, to care, to love, to live:** The Center for Inquiry backed this billboard.

- **You KNOW they're all SCAMS:** This ad included houses of worship from several religions — another billboard from American Atheists.

- **Mormonism: God Is a Space Alien, Baptizes Dead People, Big Money, Big Bigotry — Join American Atheists!:** Subheading read "Atheism: Simply Reasonable." The background included a man in Mormon sacred garments, also known as "magic underwear." You guessed it: American Atheists.

- **Doubts About Religion? You're One of Many:** It included photos of one famous African American atheist (such as Langston Hughes) and one present-day African American atheist, sponsored by African Americans for Humanism.

- **One Nation Indivisible:** The original phrase from the US Pledge of Allegiance (before "Under God" was inserted in 1954) appears over an American flag backdrop. The North Carolina Secular Association backed this billboard.

One of my favorites is a brilliant Facebook campaign by the American Humanist Association. Each ad captures a public statement that reflects a humanistic approach to life, then notes that it "Sounds Like Humanism." One features a photo of the Dalai Lama saying, "The time has come to find a way of thinking about spirituality and ethics beyond religion altogether," followed by the phrase, "Sounds Like Humanism." The campaign to date has also featured quotes by Albert Einstein, Hillary Clinton, Bertrand Russell, Ronald Reagan, and NFL linebacker Brendon Ayanbadejo.

The point is a good one —humanist values look an awful lot like human values, because they are.

The tone of these various campaigns runs the gamut from confrontation to mild invitation to funny to thoughtful. Which tone is adopted has a lot to do with the sponsoring organization and its goals. For instance, American Atheists sees itself as "the Marines of the movement," so their messages tend to be confrontational. Others like the American Humanist Association take a more humanistic tone, as you may expect. Not that it always changes the public reception. Even the most inoffensive messages, like those that just say some people don't believe, are often refused by advertising or bus companies, and many are vandalized.

You probably won't be surprised to discover that opinion among atheists is split about these campaigns. Some love the aggressive ones and think the simple blue-sky messages are too mamby-pamby. Others like the simple messages letting nonbelievers know they're not alone and think the messages attacking religious beliefs are tin-eared and counterproductive.

Coming out with the Out Campaign

The Out Campaign, a project of the Richard Dawkins Foundation for Reason and Science, encourages atheists to be open about their beliefs to their families, friends, and communities. It was inspired by the LGBT movement, which urged gays and lesbians to be out as well. As soon as people realized that gays and lesbians weren't some shadowy figures "somewhere out there" but were also among their friends and loved ones, their attitudes toward gays and lesbians began to shift.

The same reasoning works with atheism: As soon as friends and loved ones know that good and normal folks like Cousin Sue or that nice Mr. Williams down the street are atheists, the perception of atheism as something sinister and far away begins to melt.

The Out Campaign introduced the red capital A as a symbol of atheism — a clever reference to the scarlet "A" worn by Hester Prynne as a mark of religious disapproval in *The Scarlet Letter.* (See more about this symbol and others in Chapter 14.)

The campaign encourages atheists to

- Come out of the closet to encourage others to do so
- Reach out to help spread a positive view of atheism
- Speak out about their beliefs and values, helping people realize that atheists don't always fit stereotypes and are a very diverse group
- Keep out religion from public schools and government
- Stand out and become visible in their communities by being involved in public life and community service

Rallying around reason

Big public rallies are another favorite way for atheists to make themselves visible and heard. Rallying is a peculiarly American thing, probably because the need for visibility is so great here.

The first big attempt was the Godless Americans March on Washington in November 2002 when more than 2,000 atheists, agnostics, and humanists came together for a mile-long parade and rally on the National Mall. Leaders in the movement spoke about the importance of keeping religion and government separate and the need for atheists to assert a greater presence in the culture. Musicians played and a religious counter-demonstration briefly blocked the parade — it was a classic, all-American event on the national front lawn, but with a godless twist.

March 2012 saw the following two major rallies for the nonreligious.

Celebrating reason with the Reason Rally

The Reason Rally — "Woodstock for atheists and skeptics" — brought more than 20,000 nonbelievers back to the National Mall in Washington. And the growth in the movement since the Godless March ten years earlier was immediately clear. Big headliners including Richard Dawkins, Adam Savage (co-host of the television program *Mythbusters,* a favorite of skeptics), blogger PZ Myers, and comedian Tim Minchin highlighted this event, and two sitting politicians — Congressman Pete Stark, who's an atheist, and Senator Tom Harkin, who's not — addressed the rally by videotape.

After so many years on the fringes of the culture, atheists began to feel like they were sitting at the grown-ups' table.

People who'd also been at the Godless March ten years earlier noticed another change. The 2002 event had mostly consisted of white men older than 40. But the 2012 Reason Rally included about as many women as men, a much greater ethnic diversity, and skewed really young — mostly younger than 30. The rally was another indication that the freethought movement was growing and changing in very good ways.

Rolling with Rock Beyond Belief

The second major rally of the year was Rock Beyond Belief, which was held in response to an evangelical festival held in 2010 at Fort Bragg, North Carolina.

The 2010 event held on the base was called Rock the Fort. Created by evangelist Billy Graham's organization, it quickly became clear that the event was meant to bring soldiers to Jesus. "Find friends and relatives who need Christ," said the website, "pray for them, and invite them to the Rock the Fort event where they will hear the message of salvation." The festival had already appeared at several other bases and was co-sponsored by the Army's Religious Support Office.

Many soldiers at Fort Bragg began to express their discomfort with a specifically Christian evangelical event being held on a US military base. Some were members of minority faiths and some were atheists, but most of those complaining were actually Christians themselves who had simply read the Constitution.

When the Military Religious Freedom Foundation asked that the event be cancelled, the base commander said there was no violation, and that Fort Bragg "would provide the same level of support to any other group."

Well okay then. Sgt. Justin Griffith, an atheist stationed at Fort Bragg, took the base commander at his word, applying for a permit to hold an event called Rock Beyond Belief. Unlike Rock the Fort, this one wouldn't be about converting people. It would simply celebrate secular values and salute the presence of the nonreligious in the military — a presence often vigorously denied (see Chapter 19). Griffin even had prominent scientist and atheist Richard Dawkins agree to speak and received a $50,000 donation from the Stiefel Freethought Foundation.

Shortly after the request was filed, stonewalling began. Despite the Fort Bragg legal staff strongly recommending that the base's support be identical to Rock the Fort, base commanders said Rock Beyond Belief would be limited to a small indoor venue, and they refused to give the estimated $40,000 in financial support that the religious event had received. The evangelical event had included a parachuting demonstration by evangelical soldiers, so Griffith planned to include a parachuting demonstration by atheist soldiers. (Such demonstrations haven't traditionally gone well indoors.)

Given the unequal treatment, Griffith reluctantly cancelled the event and appealed the decision.

Eventually, after a civil but strongly expressed outcry from the freethought community, Fort Bragg reversed its course. The base leadership allowed the event to proceed on the main parade field, the same place Rock the Fort had been, and matched all financial support. It took place on March 31, included several speakers and live bands — and yes, atheist paratroopers. It was a great success.

Griffith said afterward that the hope wasn't to have an atheist event for every Christian event. Instead, he said the base shouldn't have any sectarian events of any kind. But as long as there was one, the Constitution says there must be room for others.

Welcoming the young and the godless

The youngest generation of the nonreligious — the young Millennials, 18 to 29 years old — are coming into their own faster than any previous generation of atheists and humanists. They have the lowest level of religious identity and belief of any generation, even when those generations were the same age. Only 54 percent believe in a personal God — the kind that receives prayers, intervenes in human affairs, and cares if you've been naughty or nice.

They're more comfortable being out — in part because so many of their friends are also nonreligious — and they're more likely than older atheists to find common ground and cooperate with religious people.

That doesn't mean they're pushovers. The young Millennials are also making a name for themselves in secular activism, especially in protecting the separation of church and state.

Let me introduce a couple of these courageous young people.

Jessica Ahlquist

In 2010, an anonymous parent at a Rhode Island high school contacted the American Civil Liberties Union (ACLU) about a prayer on a permanent banner affixed to the wall of a local high school auditorium since 1963 — the year after the US Supreme Court banned teacher-led prayers in public schools.

"Our Heavenly Father," the prayer begins, "grant us each day the desire to do our best, to grow mentally and morally as well as physically, to be kind and helpful," and so on. It's a nice enough prayer — but "Our Heavenly Father" makes it a specifically Christian one, excluding even other religions, not to mention the nonreligious. That's not constitutional; the government is required to remain neutral in matters of religion.

A student at the school named Jessica Ahlquist, who was raised Catholic but is now an atheist, became an informal spokesperson in favor of the prayer's removal, speaking at several raucous and angry school board meetings. "[The prayer] seemed like it was saying, every time I saw it, 'You don't belong here,'" she said.

She also researched Roger Williams, who founded the colony of Rhode Island after he was banished from Massachusetts Bay Colony for religious opinions that weren't in the majority, and shared her findings with the board.

New England, one of the two most secular regions of the country, may seem a strange place for this to play out, but Rhode Island is an exception — the most religious state in a secular region.

After the board voted 4–3 to keep the prayer banner, the ACLU filed suit and asked Jessica to serve as plaintiff. She agreed —and then began receiving violent threats from fellow students and the public. Her own state representative called Jessica "an evil little thing" on local radio. Two florists refused to deliver flowers ordered for her by supporters during the trial.

But the atheist community nationwide offered tremendous support, including $62,000 raised for her college education.

When asked about the local community's reaction, Jessica said, "They might see it as a very negative thing right now, but I'm defending their Constitution, too." I couldn't have put it better myself.

In January 2012, the US District Court for Rhode Island ruled in favor of the banner's removal, and it was taken down in March of that year.

Such protests aren't about attacking Christianity. They're attempts to create a culture in which individuals and families can truly make their own choices in matters of belief, and no one religion is allowed to dominate these shared spaces. (For more on why this issue is important for everyone, including religious people, see Chapter 8.)

Duncan Henderson

In 1984, the US Congress enacted the Equal Access Act, which says that any club at a federally funded school must have the same access to meeting spaces and other resources as all other clubs. Religious groups and individuals who wanted prayer clubs and the like originally urged Congress to pass the law. As long as attendance is voluntary, the group is student-initiated, and it's not disruptive, you're good to go.

The act has permitted the formation of religious clubs in high schools across the United States, and rightly so. If they're student-led, they should absolutely be allowed. But the act also protects and allows gay and lesbian clubs, atheists clubs — the works. So when Duncan Henderson, a student in Auburn, Alabama, wanted to form a freethought club at his junior high school to counter the feeling of isolation he and other atheist students felt in the ultra-religious state, it should have been a no-brainer.

"I had just 'come out' in seventh grade," he told a local reporter. "And I had a few friends that I knew were nonreligious. And as we got older, we started hanging out more, and I was like, 'You know what? I really want a group for us to not be badmouthed constantly by the majority of the school.'"

But he faced stiff opposition from school administrators, as well as bullying and even death threats from fellow students — one of whom told Duncan he would shoot him "and every other atheist with a shotgun."

When he went on to Auburn High School, Duncan tried again. This time he found an ally in Dr. Todd Freeman, the school principal, who quickly stepped in to become the club's sponsor — even though he himself is a Christian.

"Our kids have a right to meet," he told the local TV station. "And they have a right to establish a club, and it's not my prerogative to necessarily agree or disagree with positions of clubs, but it is my prerogative and responsibility to make sure they have the right to have the club. I could see where there would be resistance, but it's not really a question because it's law."

Despite differences in perspective, it's amazing what's possible when well-informed people of good will work together.

Secular Student Alliance

Do you want tangible proof that the young nonreligious are growing by leaps and bounds, driving the growth of the whole movement? Look no further than the Secular Student Alliance (SSA), one of the most positive and dynamic organizations in freethought today.

Launched in November 2001 in Columbus, Ohio, SSA supports nontheistic students in the United States with leadership training, guest speakers, resources, and organizational support. In 2003 the SSA had 42 campus groups in their network. In 2009 it had 143 groups. At this writing (2012), it's up to 413 groups, and every indication is that the growth will continue.

Founding new organizations

Several new nontheistic organizations have sprung up since the beginning of the century, including but not limited to:

- ✔ **The Richard Dawkins Foundation for Reason and Science** (www.richarddawkins.net): This nonprofit was created "to support scientific education, critical thinking and evidence-based understanding of the natural world . . . to overcome religious fundamentalism, superstition, intolerance and suffering."

- ✔ **The Secular Coalition for America** (www.secular.org): This political advocacy group represents atheists in Washington, DC, with a mission "to increase the visibility, amplify the diversity of, and respect for, the growing voice of the nontheistic community in the United States, and to protect and strengthen the secular character of government as the best guarantee of freedom for all."

- ✔ **Project Reason** (www.project-reason.org): Author Sam Harris created this 501(c)(3) organization to "promote scientific knowledge and secular values within society."

- ✔ **Recovering from Religion** (www.recoveringfromreligion.org): A nonprofit organization providing support for individuals leaving religious affiliations, especially those who experience severe ostracizing or retribution. Also sponsors the Secular Therapist Project (SecularTherapy.org) to help nontheistic individuals find therapists who are also nontheistic.

Spreading Humanism Worldwide

As the religious landscape shifts worldwide — including more religion in the global South and less in the global North — humanism has stepped forward as a compelling life philosophy that goes beyond disbelief in gods, giving a framework for meaning, ethics, community, and compassionate action. In the process, a movement-within-a-movement called New Humanism offers an alternative to the more confrontational approach of the New Atheists.

New Humanists can be just as critical of religion as New Atheists, but they generally choose to de-emphasize differences, spending more time building bridges and emphasizing common ground between the religious and nonreligious. Some just turn their focus away from religion entirely, working instead on building vibrant and effective humanist communities to meet many of the same human needs.

These sections explore the softer, more humanistic side of religious disbelief in the early 21st century and how it's making its way around the world.

Creating humanist chaplaincies at Harvard and beyond

If a phrase like "humanist chaplaincy" makes your head hurt, you're not alone. But like other terms that used to be contradictions — "female congressman," for example, or "Microsoft Works" — it's just an example of language lagging behind reality.

A *chaplain* has traditionally been a minister who serves as a counselor or conducts religious services for members of an otherwise secular institution, like a military unit, a college, or a hospital. Because nonreligious people have no less need for personal counseling or emotional support, and because many of them like to participate in rites of passage and other rituals, humanist chaplains have begun taking a place beside the religious ones.

Current humanist chaplaincies are found at

- American University (Washington, DC)
- Columbia University (New York)
- Glasgow Caledonian University (United Kingdom)
- Harvard University (Massachusetts)

> ✔ Rutgers University (New Jersey)
>
> ✔ University Hospitals Leicester (United Kingdom)
>
> ✔ University of Leeds (United Kingdom)
>
> ✔ The British, Dutch, and Belgian Armed Forces

The Military Association of Atheist and Freethinkers in the United States is working hard to get humanist chaplains on this side of the pond. Some organizations are offering training and support to humanist chaplains both in Europe and the United States.

One of the keystones of humanism in recent years has been the Humanist Chaplaincy at Harvard University. It was established in 1977, but it's only since a secular humanist rabbi named Greg Epstein became Harvard's Humanist Chaplain in the autumn of 2005 that the Harvard Humanists have become a leading voice in global humanism. In addition to hosting high profile events, giving awards to prominent humanists, launching a Humanist Community Project (see "Moving beyond words" at the end of this chapter), and establishing a strong humanist presence in community service and interfaith work.

In 2007, the Harvard Humanist Chaplaincy celebrated its 30th anniversary by hosting an event called The New Humanism. It was designed to counter the growing public perception that the more aggressive New Atheism was the only nonreligious game in town. It gave its name to the growing new humanist movement and spawned a thoughtful new online magazine called The New Humanism (www.thenewhumanism.org) that's become a mouthpiece for that movement. And Epstein's book *Good Without God* has become one of a small handful of must-reads for those hoping to understand how nonreligious people see and interact with the world, and how they sort out ethical questions without a religious framework.

Epstein has also become a lightning rod for many atheists because of his criticism of the in-your-face tactics and tone of the New Atheists, including Dawkins, Hitchens, and blogger PZ Myers.

Setting a place at the table — national and international humanism

National and international humanist associations have played a huge part in promoting humanism as a meaningful and rewarding life stance, including the American, Canadian, and British Humanist Associations, as well as the International Humanist and Ethical Union.

The Brits have a bit of a leg up on the Americans, mostly because Britain went secular so quickly in the late 20th century, giving secular Britons the critical mass that allows a much greater presence in the culture. For comparison, the US Congress currently has just one representative who is religiously unaffiliated, but the British Parliament has more than 100 openly nonreligious members in the All-Party Parliamentary Humanist Group. Although the nonreligious are at 20 percent in the United States, British surveys put the UK nonreligious as high as 76 percent. That kind of thing makes a big difference when you're trying to get yourself heard.

That's not to say it's all drumstick lollies and peppermint humbugs for the British humanists, of course. The humanist voice still encounters some resistance to real equality in UK culture. One 21st century example is Thought for the Day, a brief daily reading on BBC Radio 4 that offers "reflections from a faith perspective on issues and people in the news." In 2002, the BHA and the National Secular Society asked the news service to include the humanist perspective as well.

When the request was denied, the Humanist Society of Scotland created Thought for the World, a daily secular podcast on which prominent British humanists offered reflections on daily life and events from a humanist perspective — and much more interesting (frankly) than the pablum served up by Thought for the Day. See if you agree — search online for it and have a listen.

The American Humanist Association does a terrific job making the humanist voice heard in the United States, with public awareness programs, charity work, and local chapter support for those individuals who identify as humanists.

Then of course there's the International Humanist and Ethical Union, which I discuss in Chapter 8. The IHEU continues to form that international umbrella few nonreligious folks could have dreamed of just a few generations ago — a kind of United Nations for world humanism.

Promoting humanism in Africa

Africa has had a troubled history in modern times — hundreds of years of colonialism and slave trading, followed by a century of combat, genocides, epidemics of malaria and AIDS, and excruciating poverty. The religious history has also been strange and unique. A century ago, only one percent of the world's Christians lived in sub-Saharan Africa. Then evangelical Christianity swept into the vacuum left when the European powers went home. Today, more than 25 percent of the world's Christians live in this region. Africa is quickly becoming the new face of Christianity.

Some of the results of this process have been neutral or good. But there's also been an increase in antigay intolerance, including a proposed national law in Uganda to make homosexuality a crime punishable by death. Uganda has also suffered from the longest running civil war in history as the Lord's Resistance Army fought for three decades to instill a Ten Commandments-based government in Uganda.

In the midst, a small but steady humanist movement has formed in several countries including Uganda and Nigeria. Being an African humanist right now isn't easy. Leo Igwe, the most prominent Nigerian humanist and a former IHEU representative, is leading a difficult struggle against witchcraft accusations in West Africa. Women accused of being witches are rounded up from their villages and relocated to witch camps in Northern Ghana. While trying to draw world attention to this practice and the abduction of witch children, Leo has been arrested and beaten more than once, and his family has been threatened. But he persists in fighting this abuse of human rights — a powerful way to apply humanist values to a real-world problem.

Uganda humanists have started a small but successful network of humanist schools, providing science- and critical-thinking–based schools as an alternative to religious schools in the country. And one of the most prominent political columnists at the *Uganda Daily Monitor* is an articulate humanist and atheist named Alan Tacca.

"Part of the reason why Africans are deeply religious, spiritual and supernatural in outlook is because the people have given up hope of achieving justice and happiness in this life and in this world," he wrote in his column. "Humanists must be involved in changing and challenging unjust institutions, customs, and traditions . . . For humanism to flourish in Africa, humanists must take the quest for justice and human emancipation seriously."

Tacca makes a call to move beyond the exchange of ideas into social and political action to improve the human condition. That's why African humanists are among the most active and passionate in global humanism, lobbying or petitioning their governments to take action against injustice — and not just injustice against humanists, but (like Igwe's work in witch camps and Tacca's calls for basic human rights) injustice against humans.

Atheists and theists alike in Africa often point to *Ubuntu,* a southern African humanistic philosophy of life, as a positive ethic that binds people together. Ubuntu is about recognizing the ways in which people depend on each other, and treating others with kindness, compassion, and a sense of kinship regardless of their relation to you or their perspective. One of the best things about Ubuntu is the fact that religious believers (such as Archbishop Desmond Tutu) and secular humanists alike embrace it. And it's become a powerful way for African nontheists to frame their humanism in a culturally relevant way.

Exploding into a Thriving Online Community

There's not much problem going public if you're a new religious believer. But if a person begins to explore religious doubts, or even starts to consider him or herself an atheist, he or she can have a lot of anxiety about the reaction of the outside world. Atheists also don't have many gathering places — no atheist churches on every corner. Add the fact that the recent growth in atheism has happened in the dawn of the Digital Age, and it makes sense that the atheists mostly "get together" and communicate online.

These sections take a closer look at how the Internet has facilitated breaking down barriers so that atheists can meet and a few of the different sites that connect nonreligious people.

Considering how the Internet has helped

Before the Internet, doing a proper investigation of religion was much more difficult. The Internet was made of paper. Websites were called "books" and kept in big brick servers called "libraries" which had to be visited physically, with your body.

The Internet offers several advantages for atheists and other nonbelievers:

- ✔ **The Internet has made connecting with other likeminded folks easier.** Before the World Wide Web, it often took half a lifetime for someone like me to really become a part of the humanist movement that is now such a big part of who I am. The Internet makes it easy to do in a few weeks what I didn't achieve in 25 years.

- ✔ **The Internet's anonymity helps.** A person usually needs some time to feel secure enough in his or her identity as an atheist before openly wearing the identity in the real world. Until then, it's often SaganFan514 talking to OneLessGod about secular ethics in an online atheist discussion forum.

- ✔ **The Internet provides a relatively safe haven for discussion.** Many commenters talk about feeling safe in online atheist forums; they can kick off their shoes and be with people who see the world in the same way. This is especially true of atheists in areas where religion overwhelms everyday life. "It's refreshing to come home after a long day in the Bible Belt and have people who I know are on my side making jokes I wanted to during the day but instead had to hold my tongue and keep quiet for fear of losing friends and influence at my school," said one recent online forum comment. "Without these little jokes and articles I feel my life would be just a little harder to manage."

Surfing to some popular atheist websites

In addition to blogs (see Chapter 13), several websites have been created specifically for atheists to meet, chat, vent, laugh, and just generally make plans to take over the world. The Secular Web (www.infidels.org) was one of the first. Founded in 1995 to provide resources about atheism and skepticism, the site includes a huge library of essays, debate transcripts, atheist arguments, and book reviews, as well as a discussion forum and several other resources. For about the first decade of its existence, the Secular Web was the only game in town, and it played an important role as the new-born modern atheist movement toddled into the 21st century.

In early 2008, a new social networking site called Atheist Nexus (www.atheist nexus.org) was launched — a kind of Facebook for atheists. Because a couple of recent deconverts from Christianity launched the site — one of whom was a fundamentalist minister, no less — some atheists greeted it with skepticism at first. Was it a trick, a trap, a scam of some sort?

It was nothing of the kind. And after the site's credibility was established, the atheist community giddily ran in and began filling out their profiles, writing blogs, posting videos, and forming groups around common interests, such as

- Jewish Atheists
- Gay Atheists
- Parenting Little Heathens
- Atheists Who Were Muslim
- Eco-Logical (environmentalists)
- Humane Atheists (animal lovers)
- Amateur Radio Atheists
- Godless Bowlers
- Ex-Amish Atheists
- Black Atheists
- Undercover Atheists (for those still in the closet)

Atheist Nexus currently has more than 28,000 members.

But the 800-pound gorilla of online atheism at the moment is reddit — specifically the atheism subreddit of reddit. A *reddit* is a social news website that calls itself "The front page of the Internet." Users post short text content or links, which other users vote up or down. The more a submission is upvoted, the more people will see it, because it rises to the top of the news feed. Reddit is divided into communities ("subreddits") by topic, including atheism (reddit.com/r/atheism).

As of late 2012, more than 1.3 million people were subscribed as atheist redditors, making it one of the 20 largest subreddits on the site. Interestingly, not a single religious subreddit has yet made it into the top 50.

Maturing as a Movement

In recent years, many atheists and humanists have come to feel that the freethought movement has passed a watershed, one that separates our toddlerhood from . . . say our adolescence. Thanks to the higher profile and easier accessibility of atheism, especially online, the process of going from doubter to atheist and connecting with others is much, much faster. As a result, atheists can move on to the next questions much earlier in their lives, including:

- ✔ What does it mean to be an ethical atheist in the world?
- ✔ What are my responsibilities to other people and to myself?
- ✔ How should I act toward people who don't share my worldview?
- ✔ How can I find a sense of community and act on my values?

Consensus on these questions isn't always possible, which is fine. The fact that people in the movement are even asking them, and asking them much earlier, is a sign that the movement is maturing. The following sections explore some of the symptoms of this change.

Making accommodations — is "interfaith" a bad word?

Some of the biggest questions in atheism right now revolve around "interfaith" issues. Should atheist organizations have anything to do with religious organizations? Should they find common ground to cooperate and work together when values and goals overlap, or is that a way of indirectly "promoting religion" and therefore bad?

A terminology problem complicates these questions from the start. If groups from two different faiths work together, it's called "interfaith" work. But what do you call it when atheism works together with religion? Is it still *interfaith?*

The very word "interfaith" makes some atheists see red. Atheism isn't a faith by any traditional definition, of course. And a lot of atheist organizations want nothing to do with any such efforts anyway, no matter what they are called. They sometimes call atheists who do cooperate with religious people or organizations "accommodationists," which is meant to sound like "appeasers" before the Second World War. They're often seen as sellouts, milquetoasts, and traitors to the revolution.

But a large and growing number of atheist and humanist organizations and people don't think accommodating others is such a bad idea. They think reaching across belief lines and finding common ground despite differences is one of the healthiest and most productive things we can be doing right now. *(Full disclosure: I'm one of those people.)* They tend to shrug at the word "interfaith," saying the language just hasn't caught up with the reality yet, and the important thing is the cooperation, not the label.

Many local and national freethought groups have begun building alliances and working cooperatively with religious groups in their communities. The Secular Student Alliance does a lot of this, which makes sense, because young atheists and humanists tend to be much more open to reaching across the aisle than nonbelievers in their parents' and grandparents' generations.

Moving beyond words

Books, blogs, speeches, debates, discussions — for most of its history, atheism and humanism have been about exchanging ideas. Words, words, words. This suits a lot of us just fine (see Chapter 14 for more information).

But a large and growing number are looking for something more, including a greater sense of belonging, of fellowship, of common purpose. They've had groups for years. But what they're looking for are *communities.*

The early 21st century has seen a rapid rise in humanist communities of many kinds, as well as related efforts to put humanist values to work in the world. These sections explore the ongoing experiments in building humanist communities and putting them to work beyond words.

Building a new kind of community

Church communities at their best can satisfy a lot of human needs, including

- ✔ Social connection to others
- ✔ Building a framework for meaning and purpose
- ✔ Providing mutual support
- ✔ Coming together to be inspired and to do good

In recent years, a growing number of communities have started popping up that try to satisfy those human needs without the overlay of supernatural beliefs. Unitarian Universalism, a fascinating denomination that's built around values and principles, not shared beliefs is one such group. Ethical Culture is another. They have rituals and symbols, they inspire, and they come together to make the world a better place. All good things, and none that require a God.

Countless others are also coming from different directions but working toward the same goal of building meaningful communities, including several I mention in Chapter 18. But they're often disconnected from each other, doing their own thing, which keeps them from learning from each other what works and what doesn't. The Harvard Humanists have launched a Humanist Community Project for the specific purpose of helping these diverse humanistic communities connect with each other, sharing ideas and hard-won experiences.

As church attendance in the United States continues to drop by as many as three million people per year, I'm glad these folks are doing the hard work of figuring out what comes next. The human needs don't go away just because you walk out of those church doors.

Seeing humanism at work

As these new communities form, they're finding that active humanism — including compassionate action to help others — is an effective and satisfying glue for nontheistic communities.

Groups that struggled to attract and keep members when their programming consisted of monthly meetings with a speaker and discussion are growing by leaps and bounds as soon as they start to address their members' social and emotional needs. They're as likely to have a barbecue as a lecture now, and when a member is ill or having a hard time, the group becomes a community of support. Community volunteering is becoming a more regular part of what atheist and humanist groups do. And simple things like childcare at meetings or humanist "Sunday schools" to learn about ethics have helped make the movement more family-friendly and multigenerational.

In other words, atheist and humanist groups in the 21st century are finding that they can come together as a result of their shared atheism, but that doesn't have to define what they do together. All that's needed is to be humans together.

Part III

Reading the Great Works of Atheism

The 5th Wave   By Rich Tennant

"A cookbook for atheists?! Who cooks without praying?"

In this part . . .

This part goes back to Square One and retraces the steps of atheism through the ages, this time using important written works in every era as stepping stones. Here you can discover some of the forbidden or lost works that laid the foundations of atheism, as well as the powerful arguments against belief in God that emerged in more recent times. If you're looking for additions to your reading list, this is the place to find them.

Chapter 10

Uncovering Lost, Secret, Censored, and Forbidden Works

*B*efore the authors known as the New Atheists topped the bestseller lists, before abolitionists and feminists decried the unhelpful role of religion in their struggles, even before the broadsides of the Enlightenment, history was sprinkled with tiny, tantalizing fragments of atheist and agnostic thought.

In the struggle to be heard, religious doubt was saddled with plenty of disadvantages. Fear kept most of the doubters quiet in the first place, and whatever they did write had only the tiniest chance of surviving beyond its own era. If people don't like what a book says, they're much less likely to pass it along to the next generation. It's that simple. And if an idea was only spoken rather than written down, it's even less likely to be passed on.

Such a selective process can end up painting a pretty inaccurate and frankly boring picture of what life was like in a given place and time. Imagine if only a few of the most popular movies in a given decade were passed on to future generations. We'd end up with a really narrow and distorted view of that era. *Harry Potter* movies are great, but do they capture the breadth and depth of filmmaking in the first decade of this century? Hardly. But if people pass only those films down to future generations from that decade, those future folks will think we were a pretty one-note culture.

That's exactly what happens when an era packs only a few favorite ideas in the care package it sends to posterity. It gives the false impression that everybody in that time and place thought and believed the same. It's misleading *and* boring.

The nonmainstream books that do survive are often scrubbed of their unorthodox religious opinions — by editors, by family members, and sometimes even by the authors themselves. And nothing is scrubbed out quite as thoroughly as atheism.

In this chapter I give a quick and selective tour of some books that don't survive the process, at least not in one piece — books that are lost, secret, censored, or forbidden.

Speaking Volumes in Two Sentences: Protagoras's On the Gods

Protagoras of Abdera, a fifth century BCE Greek philosopher often called the first agnostic, challenged religion, fled Athens under a death sentence, and died in a shipwreck. (Refer to Chapter 4 for more on his life.)

Before he endured these ordeals, Protagoras wrote a book. I'd really like to read this book, but it's not going to happen — the fickle roller coaster of history rolled into modern times with an empty seat where Protagoras's most important book used to be.

The title of the lost book doesn't say much about its importance. Like countless others written at the time, it's simply called *On the Gods*. But the first two sentences — the only ones that have survived — are anything but common:

Concerning the gods, I have no means of knowing whether they exist or not or of what sort they may be. Many things prevent knowledge, including the obscurity of the subject and the brevity of human life.

That passage may not look too shocking from your comfy seat in the 21st century, but it was shocking enough in ancient times to keep philosophers buzzing about Protagoras throughout the Classical period and down through the centuries.

The Athenians may have been successful in erasing the book from history, but Protagoras's agnosticism, trapped in the amber of those two memorable, sensible sentences, survives to this day, quoted in the works of others.

Hearing Echoes of the Lost Sutras of Cārvāka

Cārvāka was the name of one of the strongest schools of atheist materialism in ancient India. It burst into the conversation of that fascinating culture as early as the sixth century BCE. Cārvāka was one of the earliest philosophies to spend time working out the implications of materialism, a simple but powerful idea.

Materialism is the idea that everything in the universe is made of matter or energy, or derives from them. Materialists don't believe that souls, spirits, ghosts, deities, and any other nonmaterial entities you can think of are real.

Disbelieving in ghosts and souls and such doesn't mean that something like human consciousness isn't real. It obviously is. Materialism just says it doesn't have an existence independent of the matter that creates it — a human brain. My consciousness — my "me" — results not from an immortal soul that can outlive my body, but from the natural activity of my material brain. Just as the music is over when the band stops playing, materialism says I will cease to be when my brain stops "playing" me into existence.

I'm not thrilled about that idea, and I doubt the followers of Cārvāka were either. But as far as I can tell, none of us gets a vote, and I am as convinced as they were that it's true.

Like many Indian schools of thought, Cārvāka created little books called sūtras to sum up their point of view. A *sūtra* is a text that captures complex ideas in a collection of short, pithy sayings. Sutra-like texts from various cultures outside of India include

- ✔ Benjamin Franklin's *Poor Richard's Almanac*
- ✔ Mao's *Little Red Book*
- ✔ The *Analects* of Confucius
- ✔ Even *Chicken Soup for the Soul* by Jack Canfield and Mark Victor Hansen

The *Bārhaspatya-sūtras* captured the most important Cārvāka ideas. Written around the third century BCE, these sūtras have been lost except for a few fragments quoted in other (mostly unfriendly) sources. Many of those surviving bits criticize or contradict religious doctrines directly, saying

- ✔ Religion is a human invention.
- ✔ Nothing is wrong with sensual pleasure.
- ✔ Death is the end of existence.
- ✔ Direct experience is the only valid kind of evidence.
- ✔ Hindu religious rituals are ignorant and unmanly.
- ✔ The authors of the Vedas, the sacred books of Hinduism, are "buffoons, knaves, and demons."

Given how forceful their criticisms of religion were, it's not too surprising that the powers that be persecuted the followers of Cārvāka, or that most of their texts — including the *Bārhaspatya-sūtras* — conveniently went missing.

Listening to Al-Razi on "Fraudulent" Muhammad

Sometimes the dividing line between a culture's prized and hated books runs right down the middle of a single author. The tenth century Persian physician and philosopher Abu Bakr al-Razi was just such an author, and *On the Refutation of Revealed Religions* is a book on the naughty side of the line.

I can only imagine the confusion among friends and admirers of al-Razi. They couldn't help loving his incredible contributions to science and medicine — alleviating suffering, defining new disease treatments, isolating new compounds, showing endless compassion for the less fortunate, and saving countless lives. But I have to think there were some awkward silences when he called Muhammad a fraud and all religion a hoax.

The same cloud of confusion befuddled the admirers of other famous religious doubters, from Thomas Jefferson to Thomas Edison to Susan B. Anthony to Albert Einstein. Their cultures bent over backwards to celebrate their achievements without drawing any attention to their doubt. Al-Razi presented the very same challenge to his tenth century Islamic fans.

On the Refutation of Revealed Religions dismantled the whole idea of prophecy, brick by rational brick, arguing among other things that it makes zero sense for Allah to give prophetic knowledge to a few rather than to everyone at once.

Al-Razi encouraged a really fertile line of questioning: If you were God/Allah, would it make a lick of sense to do things the way they have been done? Most people take for granted the idea that the deity revealed truth through a few chosen prophets. Moses talked to a bush, Joseph Smith found golden plates, Muhammad talked to Gabriel, and Jesus talked . . . to himself, I guess. But when you put yourself in the Holy Loafers for just a minute, it starts to look like an odd way of doing things. It does make sense, though, as a way for a few ambitious folks with a healthy prophet motive to get things started.

Not too many people have had the chance to follow al-Razi's reasoning. Many of the more than 200 books he wrote have survived to be enshrined in the annals of Islamic history. But these stinging critiques of religion, for some reason, were misplaced along the way.

Discovering the First Explicitly Atheist Book — Theophrastus Redivivus

Sometime in the 1650s, just as the Scientific Revolution was breaking into a run, several copies of an anonymous book began circulating around Europe — a book filled to the brim with forceful arguments against belief in God.

Theophrastus redivivus started by declaring that every great philosopher in every age has been an atheist (whether he could openly admit it or not), that all religions are fictions, and that anyone claiming to have proof of the existence of a god is lying or mentally ill. That was just on the first *page*.

The rest was a collection of arguments against belief by writers and thinkers through the ages — a kind of freethought anthology — and the first book-length work of atheist thought produced in Europe.

Passed secretly from hand to hand and house to house, *Theophrastus* touched off a century of whispered discussions and arguments about the existence of God and spawned more than 200 anonymous pamphlets, essays, and handwritten books arguing against religious belief, known collectively as the *clandestina*.

It's hard to really get inside the mind of a person from the 17th century, to fully grasp how different the world looked before all those later centuries happened. Atheism wasn't just a weird minority opinion at the time. For most people, it was completely *unthinkable* that God didn't exist. A 17th-century understanding of science — no matter what century a person actually lives in — makes it bone-crushingly obvious that an intelligent designer created the world. As a result, atheism fascinated and repelled the 17th-century mind. Some people in the period even considered atheism to be evidence of serious mental illness. And you know what? If I were alive in the 17th century, before science began to really fill in the gaps, I'd probably have to agree.

Around 1700, a different breed of atheist tract appeared, one that didn't just collect atheist opinion from the past but made new and compelling arguments for atheism and against religious belief, including some informed by the new Scientific Revolution. The ball set rolling by *Theophrastus* was headed straight for the Age of Reason, knocking over the pins of superstition as it went.

The impact of the clandestina was huge. Many of the main arguments and ideas of the Enlightenment started in these secret, anonymous documents. After centuries of religion arguing with itself through the Reformation and several religious wars, the very idea of religious belief was finally getting a sustained challenge.

But unlike those religious wars, the atheist's main weapons, then as now, were words, arguments, and ideas.

Making a Whispered Myth Real: The Treatise of the Three Impostors

The rumor of a book that called Jesus a liar and fake, spoken in hushed voices, started as far back as the 13th century. Sure, it said the same about Moses and Muhammad — but impugning the character of Jesus was the real attention-getter in medieval Europe.

All the whisperers seemed to agree on the title of this rumored book — *The Treatise of the Three Impostors* — as well as the basic thrust, that the three biggest prophets of all time were liars. But no one could agree on who wrote the mysterious thing. Some pointed to Averroes, a 12th-century Islamic overachiever in the al-Razi mold. Others even suggested Holy Roman Emperor Frederick II, who went to war with two Popes and famously refused to believe anything that reason couldn't explain. *(Red flag!)* As the centuries rolled by, everyone with a reputation for religious skepticism joined the lineup of possible authors — even if they were born centuries after the birth of the rumor.

Funny thing, though: Even as the rumor passed from one generation to the next, nobody ever seemed to have seen the actual book.

Then all at once, in the late 17th century, copies of *The Treatise of the Three Impostors* were everywhere. Europe, already reeling from scores of secret manifestos challenging and ridiculing religious belief, suddenly had another shocker to deal with.

And what a shocker it was! Religion, said the anonymous author, was born of ignorance and is full of "vain and ridiculous opinions." Ideas of God are "silly," and the clergy use those ideas to keep the common people in "deplorable blindness." Jesus, Moses, and Muhammad were "impostors" who intentionally duped their followers with the equivalent of magic tricks. Even the existence of God was seriously doubtful.

The smoldering embers of debate created by the earlier clandestina burst into a bonfire when this mythical manuscript suddenly came to life.

But who wrote it?

My money (and the money of most of the historians who've weighed in) is on John Toland, an Irish philosopher and satirist. Toland was in his 20s and expressing suspiciously rational opinions at the time the "ancient manuscript" suddenly appeared. He was among the first to claim that he'd found a copy — I'm betting he was the very first — which he quickly disseminated to philosopher friends. And within a decade, Toland was writing one treatise after another attacking Christianity and questioning every religious assumption he could get his hands on.

If John Toland didn't write *Three Impostors,* I'm the Pope.

Within a few years of its sudden appearance, *The Treatise of the Three Impostors* was the most widely read of the anonymous atheist documents coursing around Europe, setting the stage for the Enlightenment and the French Revolution.

Expelling the Atheist: Shelley's Necessity of Atheism

Even as late as the 19th century, blasphemy was still an actual, arrestable crime in England. Simply standing up in public and expressing the opinion that God didn't exist could, and often did, get a person locked up.

The poet Percy Bysshe Shelley was never one to hold back an opinion — and despite the laws against blasphemy, this included his opinion that God was pretend. While an Oxford student in 1811, Shelley wrote a strongly worded and well-reasoned pamphlet titled "The Necessity of Atheism," printed up a few hundred copies, and quietly scattered them around the Oxford grounds.

Just expressing an atheist opinion out loud was enough to set the wheels of British justice in motion at this time. But Shelley went beyond that, arguing (pretty convincingly, if you ask me) that atheism was a *necessary* position — the only one that could be reasonably held.

Shelley examined three types of evidence — human senses, human reason, and the testimony of others — dismantling each in turn as a valid foundation for belief. Having done so in under a thousand words, he concluded that atheism wasn't just sound and reasonable, but the only real choice left standing.

In his one act of caution (possibly ever), Shelley left his name off the pamphlet, signing only "An Atheist." No one who knew Shelley was fooled by this act; between the mastery of language and the sheer cheeky nerve of it all, every finger pointed right at the 19-year-old poet. Within the week, he was hauled in front of the wall of frowns that was the Oxford Council of Deans.

When one of the deans asked him point blank if he wrote the pamphlet, Shelley didn't admit to it, but he didn't deny it either. As a result, he was suspended from Oxford and sent home, furious.

Percy and his father (a Member of Parliament without the slightest sense of humor) couldn't stand each other, and this latest development made things much worse. Without Percy's permission, the elder Shelley worked out a deal with Oxford to let his son back in. Just one condition — Percy had to publicly renounce his atheism. *Oh, fat chance,* said Shelley, or probably something more poetic — at which point he was permanently expelled from Oxford.

This expulsion had such a devastating effect on his career that he was forced to settle for becoming one of the finest poets in the history of the English language.

Disguising Darwin's Autobiography

In 1876, just a few years before his death, Charles Darwin jotted down a few recollections of his life. He mostly skipped over his biggest achievements, which were already well enough known. Instead, he focused on the development of his opinions and character, which made it much more fun to read. He barely touched on the writing of entire books but spent almost two pages describing his ingenious method for stealing fruit from trees as a child. (It *was* pretty clever.) So in these jottings, which eventually became his autobiography, you get a good look inside the private head of a man whose public work fundamentally changed what it means to be human.

Darwin finished the book, stuck it in a drawer, watched his grandkids play for another six years, and then died — at which point his son Francis began to think about what to do with the document.

The choice may seem obvious at first: He's Darwin after all, and this was his autobiography, so you publish it, right? But Francis had to deal with two knotty questions, and the answers to these questions weren't obvious:

- ✔ **Did Dad want it published?** In the first pages of the manuscript, Darwin said he was writing because he thought it may interest his children and their children to read it. He'd have loved to have such a thing from his own grandfather, he wrote, even if it was "short and dull." So he decided to give his children and grandchildren a record of his own thoughts. But would he have wanted the rest of the world to see it?

- ✔ **If so, would he have wanted it *all* published?** Darwin included not just his scientific opinions, but also his religious ones — or should I say his *irreligious* ones — which were guaranteed to raise hackles if those opinions got out and started wandering the streets of Victorian England.

Most people familiar with the current cultural debate over evolution may think Darwin would have relished raising a hackle or three. But they don't know Darwin. The man whose theory overturned the most cherished assumptions of the human race was actually a conflict-avoider of the first rank. After publishing *On the Origin of Species,* he retreated to his home to study orchids, leaving the pitched debate to friends like Thomas Huxley. Was this a man who'd want his religious opinions trotted out after his death?

If I were Francis, I'm not sure what I'd have thought.

When it came to religion, the path Darwin took was a really interesting one. He was so religious as a young man that he planned to be a minister. But a five-year voyage around the world as a naturalist on the *Beagle* brought a very different Darwin back to England. He put aside his plans for the ministry and gradually did the same with his supernatural beliefs.

The *Autobiography* gives a full, personal account of his changing opinions. He decided in the end that the Old Testament was "manifestly false" and to be trusted no more than "the beliefs of any barbarian." He said that "fixed laws" and not divine will governed the world, and that all morality can be derived without reference to God. Disbelief crept over him slowly but was at last complete, he said, and he "never since doubted for a single second that my conclusion was correct."

Reading the manuscript after Charles's death, his wife Emma — a deeply religious Christian — was worried about what would happen to his reputation if his views were known. Though there was no end to her penciled concerns, one passage especially troubled her. Charles wrote

I can indeed hardly see how anyone ought to wish Christianity to be true, for if so the plain language of the text seems to show that the men who do not believe, and this would include my Father, Brother and almost all of my friends, will be everlastingly punished. And this is a damnable doctrine.

Emma bracketed that passage and wrote in the margin

I should dislike the passage in brackets to be published. It seems to me raw. Nothing can be said too severe upon the doctrine of everlasting punishment for disbelief — but very few now wd. call that 'Christianity,' (tho' the words are there).

In all, Emma marked up nearly 20 pages of the document for deletion, telling Francis that his father's true religious views must not be made public. In some cases, her edits precisely reversed what Charles meant to say. If you read this

I liked the thought of being a country clergyman . . . I did not then in the least doubt the strict and literal truth of every word in the Bible, I soon persuaded myself that our creed must be fully accepted.

. . . you're likely to think Darwin remained a Christian. But the original passage told a different story:

I liked the thought of being a country clergyman . . . I did not then in the least doubt the strict and literal truth of every word in the Bible, I soon persuaded myself that our creed must be fully accepted. *It never struck me how illogical it was to say that I believed in what I could not understand and what is in fact unintelligible.*

At first Francis disagreed strongly with his mother's wishes, and for five years after Charles's death, the Darwin family nearly came to blows over it. They were on the verge of actually suing each other when Francis finally relented. He published his father's *Autobiography* with his mother's requested edits, leaving very little hint of Charles's agnosticism.

So if it didn't end up in the published *Autobiography*, how do modern readers know his real views? For that, another member of the Darwin family deserves the thanks — Nora Barlow, niece of Francis and granddaughter of Charles, who got her hands on the original in 1958, restored all the omitted passages and published Charles's unabridged *Autobiography* for the first time with religious critiques and agnosticism intact.

Lying about the dying: Tales of deathbed conversion

Years after the death of Charles Darwin, a story emerged that the agnostic scientist converted to Christianity on his deathbed.

That was to be expected — the story I mean, not the conversion, which never happened. After a famous atheist or agnostic dies, or even a heretic or a member of a minority faith, you can hardly count to ten before someone somewhere claims that the person converted in the final moments. The supposed conversions always seem to occur, rather conveniently, with no one present but the dying person and the storyteller. Because it bolsters the faith of the faithful, and because the best material witness is no longer taking questions, many religious believers are quick to believe and spread such stories. Thomas Paine, Martin Luther, Voltaire, Thomas Edison, Jean-Paul Sartre, John Lennon, and countless others have been subjects of false deathbed conversion tales.

For sheer nerve, though, it's hard to beat the tale invented by Lady Elizabeth Hope. The British evangelist claimed in 1915 to have heard Charles Darwin renounce evolution and accept Jesus on his deathbed. Fortunately, several of those who were *actually* present during Darwin's last days, including his daughter Henrietta and son Francis, were still alive in 1915 to denounce the fiction.

"Lady Hope's account of my father's views on religion is quite untrue," said Francis. "I have publicly accused her of falsehood, but have not seen any reply."

Henrietta added, "I was present at his deathbed, Lady Hope was not present during his last illness, or any illness. I believe he never even saw her, but in any case she had no influence over him in any department of thought or belief. He never recanted any of his scientific views, either then or earlier."

When the temptation arises to misrepresent a person's religious views on his or her deathbed, the Ninth Commandment — the one that prohibits bearing false witness — is often the hardest to keep.

Censoring Himself . . . for Awhile: Mark Twain

After an autobiography is finished, it's pretty odd for the author to wait very long to release it. After a lifetime at the mercy of the press and biographers, most public figures are eager for the chance to tell their stories in their own words. But sometimes, concerns about the reaction to their opinions outweigh that eagerness. Such was the case with Mark Twain.

Twain's concern about revealing his own anti-religious opinions led him to hold back much of his later writing from publication, including some stinging anti-religious commentary.

"I expose to the world only my trimmed and perfumed and carefully barbered public opinions," he wrote in his final years, "and conceal carefully, cautiously, wisely, my private ones." As he evolved through his life from practicing Presbyterian to mild Deist to an increasingly sharp religious critic, Twain's writings begin to show a deepening disgust with religion.

His complete *Autobiography* is thought to include some of his most direct anti-religious views. I say it's "thought to" include them because I haven't read his complete *Autobiography* yet. That's not because I don't have a library card, but because Twain specified that only an abridged version — "trimmed and perfumed," you may say — be released upon his death. He then gave instructions (in a Preface titled "As from the Grave") for new editions to be released every 25 years, each with a little more material:

From the first, second, third, and fourth editions all sound and sane expressions of opinion must be left out. There may be a market for that kind of wares a century from now. There is no hurry. Wait and see . . . The editions should be issued twenty-five years apart. Many things that must be left out of the first will be proper for the second; many things that must be left out of both will be proper for the third; into the fourth or at least the fifth the whole Autobiography can go, unexpurgated.

At this writing, the century mark has finally passed, though only one of three volumes has so far seen the light of day. But even that is enough to get a good taste of the uncensored Twain to come.

Here's a passage:

There is one notable thing about our Christianity: bad, bloody, merciless, money-grabbing and predatory as it is — in our country particularly, and in all other Christian countries in a somewhat modified degree — it is still a hundred times better than the Christianity of the Bible, with its prodigious crime — the invention of Hell. Measured by our Christianity of to-day, bad as it is, hypocritical as it is, empty and hollow as it is, neither the Deity nor His Son is a Christian, nor qualified for that moderately high place. Ours is a terrible religion. The fleets of the world could swim in spacious comfort in the innocent blood it has spilt.

It doesn't get much clearer than that.

Chapter 11

Sampling Important Works: Deep Thoughts, Big Thinkers

In This Chapter

▶ Encountering serious thinkers in every age

▶ Being grateful for the help of unorthodox believers

▶ Clearing the cobwebs of superstition

▶ Creating a new way of thinking

*O*ne of the best ways to see the development of atheist thinking through the years is by reading key books that challenge religious assumptions and lay out a vision of a world without gods. That's a tough nut to crack in the early going, because (as I show in Chapter 10) most atheist and agnostic opinion before the Renaissance disappeared not long after it was written.

When the late 18th century clocked in, you started to get the opposite problem: The climate for freethought in Europe improved dramatically, and the result was an avalanche of new thinking and a huge increase in new works. Now the trick was figuring out *what* to read.

This chapter attempts to do the impossible — choose a small number of works that illustrate the development of atheist, agnostic, and humanist thought from ancient times through the end of the 20th century. This list is nowhere near complete, and I even manage to leave out a lot of my personal favorites. I try to make up for that by listing a few additional titles in the sidebars, and I devote Chapter 12 to the 21st century.

Spotting the Survivors

The books that have survived from ancient and medieval times aren't necessarily better or more important than those that didn't. In some cases, they're just incredibly lucky. I start with two books that are both lucky and important, leaving their mark on the development of ideas in their own time and throughout history — one from ancient Rome, the other from 11th century China.

Musing on the Nature of Things with Lucretius

It's hard to think of a single book with a greater impact on the world than *De rerum natura* (*On the Nature of Things*). Written by the Roman poet and philosopher Lucretius in the first century BCE, *De rerum* is an attempt to explain the whole system of thought of Epicurus, who felt the greatest impediment to human happiness was fear, and that the greatest source of fear was the idea of gods.

I introduce materialism in Chapter 10, which is the idea that everything in the universe is made of (or derived from) matter or energy. Like many powerful ideas, the materialist point of view appears independently in several different cultures, and Epicurus was one of several Greeks running with it right around the same time as the Indian philosophers — in the third century BCE.

Two centuries later, Lucretius wrote *De rerum natura* to convince a friend that Epicurus was right about the nature of things. The gods, if they exist at all, are too blissful and serene in their perfection to care about what humans do. Gods didn't create the universe; a natural product of a few physical laws did, acting on a few basic types of particles — mixing and combining them to create everything there is.

The purpose of *De rerum* was to explain how this could be, and it does so with incredible grace and conviction — in 7,400 lines of poetry, no less. Sitting down and writing a book that explained everything in a time when pretty much everything still lacked explanation may have been daunting. But that's exactly what Lucretius set out to do.

He started by going after superstition with all his rhetorical guns blazing. Humans everywhere lay crushed beneath religion, which he depicts as a hideous, glowering beast. Then, he said, Epicurus "raised his mortal eyes" to confront and tame the terror so that humankind could live without fear.

Lucretius often empathized with the reader, acknowledging for example that talking or thinking about such things is hard. A person tends to shiver a bit at the idea of stepping on holy ground with a hammer in hand. But was it really holy ground? Isn't it true, he asked, that religion has been the author of at least as many profane horrors as holy goods? He had a particular disgust with the stories in many religions of parents sacrificing their children to please the gods. He cited a story from Greek mythology — the slaying of Iphigenia by her father Agamemnon as a sacrifice to the gods so his ships could have favorable winds toward Troy — but would also have been familiar with the story of Abraham and Isaac. Though Abraham's knife (unlike

Agamemnon's) didn't quite find his child's throat, Abraham's willingness to murder an innocent child without questioning the order is rightly held up by religious critics as an act of insane immorality, one directly endorsed by God. (Had Lucretius lived a century later, after Christ, he would have known yet another religious story in which a father sacrifices his son to high praise.)

Lucretius found such acts to be such a perfect illustration of the evil religion contains that he put them front and center in *De rerum.* "Such are the crimes to which religion leads," he warned.

Lucretius continued assailing religion and superstition, stanza after stanza, citing Epicurus at every turn. "Religion now is under foot," he said. Thanks to the efforts of Epicurus and others, humanity can find its way out from under the weight of religion and turn to understanding the world as it really is.

One of the most common questions atheists are asked, even today, is why they have to criticize religion — why they can't simply believe what they believe and leave religion alone. Lucretius attempted to answer this question. Seeing and exploring the universe as a natural, material place is impossible without first addressing and removing the supernatural assumptions that overlay so much of human culture and the human mind. (Scan the sections near the end of this chapter and you can see the same thing at work in this book: First I present "Clearing the Way," then "Building a New Vision.")

After getting religion out of the way, Lucretius described the world as seen by Democritus and Epicurus, a natural world that operates without the intervention of gods. Matter can't be created or destroyed, he said, anticipating the law of conservation of mass by 2,000 years. The universe is full of atoms — "the seeds of things," he called them — which combine and split apart in endless combinations to make everything.

He tackled the fear of death by arguing as a materialist that the soul (or consciousness) is a product of the body. After the body dies, consciousness goes with it. That leaves no sensation of any kind after death, which means no possibility of suffering or torment at the hands of the gods.

De rerum natura goes on, page after remarkable page, spelling out theories of the senses, sex, love, sleep, dreams, the changing seasons, social order, politics, planetary motion, weather, earthquakes, disease, and emotions — an incredible and comprehensive catalog of everything a curious person might conceivably wonder about the universe. In doing so, Lucretius got an astonishing number of things right.

It's an arresting thought that the Scientific Revolution ends up simply confirming a lot of things that occurred off the top of a few observant and curious Greco-Roman heads.

The masterpiece that nearly slipped through the fingers of humanity

De rerum natura is easily one of the most important books of all time. Its way of looking at the world had been lost in the crush of religious orthodoxy during the Middle Ages, but after the manuscript was rediscovered in 1417, it had an immediate, profound, and lasting effect on the intellectual course of the Western world.

But that rediscovery came incredibly close to not happening at all.

Lost manuscripts from ancient Greece and Rome had begun to re-emerge in the 15th century, some from the Arab world, others from monasteries around the continent, where a few Catholic monastic orders had preserved and recopied ancient books (see Chapter 6 for more about this). Renaissance humanists eagerly fanned out across Europe in search of these lost treasures.

Poggio Bracciolini was one such book hunter. Between his duties as a papal secretary, Poggio traveled throughout Europe, finding several key classical texts in the process. When he pulled *De rerum natura* off the shelf of the Fulda monastery in the middle of what is now Germany, he recognized the author's name right away. Lucretius was mentioned with great admiration in the works of Cicero and other early historians, but all of his works were thought to be lost at this point. They very nearly were — 15 centuries after the death of Lucretius, Poggio Bracciolini was holding the last crumbling copy of the philosopher's only known book.

Poggio had copies made and distributed to many influential thinkers, and the world would never be the same. Many scholars argued that *De rerum natura* jolted the European mind and imagination so powerfully that it served as the starting bell for the Renaissance, the Scientific Revolution, and the Enlightenment — even the modern world itself.

It's just about unbearable to realize how close it came to being lost forever.

Correcting the Unenlightened with Chang

By the Middle Ages, the practical, secular philosophy of Confucianism was groaning under the weight of superstitious beliefs that had accrued since Confucius's time. That's the fate of any system of thought that isn't constantly discussed, re-examined, and renewed. Nonsense and sloppy thinking gradually crept over it like vines over a wall, until you couldn't even see the bricks underneath. By the ninth century, supernatural ideas and rituals from Chinese folk religion had strangled the secular usefulness out of Confucianism.

Through the careful reading of ancient Confucian texts, some philosophers in this period were able to get a clear enough view of the original to see that it was worth restoring, and Neo-Confucianism was born.

The purpose of Neo-Confucianism was to restore the clear thinking and practical ethics of Confucianism for the betterment of Chinese society by cleansing it of supernatural and mystical ideas. One of the most important Neo-Confucians is Chang Tsai (1020–1077), and his most influential book was *Correcting the Unenlightened,* which presented his vision for restoring rational Confucianism.

Just as it had been a thousand years earlier (see Chapter 4), *t'ien* was an important focus for Chang's generation. The word translates loosely as "heaven," but it literally means, "that which causes the world to be as it is." If a philosopher believed in gods, *t'ien* was the gods. For secular philosophers like Chang and Xun Zi, it meant natural, physical laws and principles.

Not surprisingly, Chang's book reads a lot like *De rerum natura.* They were both talking about the nature of things, and both doing it without gods. After the gods have been set aside, the natural world begins to reveal itself much more clearly and sensibly.

The two books have another similarity. Just like Lucretius started by slaying the "hideous, glowering" beast of religion, so Chang knew he had to be decisive in getting the gods out of his readers' minds before he could describe the Confucian system. When I say "t'ien," he wrote, remember that

- ✔ T'ien makes things happen on Earth without sharing the concerns of people.
- ✔ T'ien is without consciousness or sympathy.
- ✔ T'ien doesn't act with purpose, and it never has.

It was a big step in the direction of understanding the world naturalistically.

I'm sure that Chang, like most people, would have preferred to live in a universe that cares about people and is responsive to their needs. But he thought it best to see the world as it really is and respond accordingly, instead of seeing it as he wished it to be and wondering why *t'ien* never seemed to pick up the darn phone.

Chang felt that human nature is essentially good, but that people are at their very best when they're in harmony with *t'ien* — the principles of the natural world.

Most important for a secular philosophy, Chang emphasized that rational explanations are at the heart of even the most mysterious or bizarre things. If something seems mysterious, he said, keep asking questions until you get to the source of it — and there you will find a rational explanation.

Chang Tsai and the other Neo-Confucians succeeded brilliantly in bringing secular Confucianism back to life. By the 13th century, it was back on top as the ethical and social compass of Chinese culture.

Appreciating Unorthodox Believers

The first challenges to religious ideas often come not from outright unbelievers but from *heretics* — believers who see the shortcomings of traditional beliefs and practices and are willing to bang the drum to get things fixed.

A special kind of courage is required to bang that drum from inside the temple. As I say in Chapter 5 and elsewhere, heretics were usually considered a much bigger threat to the Establishment than complete nonbelievers because heretics were much more likely to end up splitting the church into separate movements in competition for the souls (and pennies) of the faithful.

The period from the early Renaissance to the French Revolution was brimming with courageous heretics, including

- ✔ Michael Servetus, a Spanish theologian burned in 1553 for opposing infant baptism and believing God to be a single being, not three

- ✔ Giordano Bruno, a Dominican friar burned in 1600 for his (accurate) belief that stars were actually other suns circled by "innumerable worlds"

- ✔ Baruch Spinoza, a Dutch philosopher kicked out of the Jewish community in Amsterdam in the 1650s for supposedly "abominable deeds" and "monstrous heresies"

Spinoza's expulsion order by the Jewish authorities was especially intense, including a magnificent series of curses that sounded (ironically) like Pharaoh cursing Moses in *The Ten Commandments:* "Cursed be he by day and cursed be he by night," said the order. "Cursed be he when he lies down, and cursed be he when he rises up; cursed be he when he goes out, and cursed be he when he comes in. The Lord will not spare him; the anger and wrath of the Lord will rage against this man, and bring upon him all the curses which are written in this book, and the Lord will blot out his name from under heaven" . . . and on it goes. No one was to speak to him, or approach within ten feet, give him a place to stay, or (most important of all) read anything he wrote.

So what did he do to earn this expulsion? He wasn't an atheist, but his views departed so far from Jewish orthodoxy that he may as well have been. He didn't believe the soul was immortal, for example, didn't believe God intervened in the world, and didn't think the Old Testament came from God or applied any longer to the Jews.

Identifying the Index of Forbidden Books

The *Index Librorum Prohibitorum,* or Index of Prohibited Books, was a list of books deemed injurious to morality or faith by the Catholic Church. The List was published and updated each year starting in 1559.

As might be expected, the Index looks like a recommended reading list for freethinkers, from the scientific works of Johannes Kepler, Nicolaus Copernicus, and Galileo Galilei to the

philosophy of Michel de Montaigne, Baruch Spinoza, David Hume, and Jean-Paul Sartre to the eye-opening satires of Jonathan Swift and Desiderius Erasmus.

By 1966, the whole idea of forbidding books had become impractical and the Catholic Church's cultural monopoly a dim memory. The Index began to look like a quaint antique, and the Church abolished it.

All three of these heretics, along with countless others, had their works placed on the Catholic Church's Index of Forbidden Books — a feather in the cap of any heretic worthy of the term.

Praising Folly with Erasmus

In 1509, while on holiday in England, a Dutch monk named Desiderius Erasmus wrote an incredibly courageous little book. It was no scowling, accusatory broadside against the Church, like Martin Luther would write eight years later. No, this was a howling, *laughing* broadside against the Church, and all humanity — one that quickly became a continental bestseller.

The first time I read this amazing book, I had two immediate thoughts, complete with mental exclamation marks:

- ✔ "It sounds like it was written last week!"
- ✔ "I can't believe he wasn't killed for this!"

But it wasn't, and he wasn't.

Erasmus felt that the Catholic Church of his time — a church of which he was a part — had become broken, unethical, and deeply corrupted. But the world itself wasn't much better. So he enlisted the goddess Folly to give a speech praising humanity for all it did to promote and celebrate her work by spreading and promoting foolishness. *The Praise of Folly* was the result.

Starting outside the church doors was a masterstroke. Folly first praises the foolishness of philosophers, then of her fellow gods — a nice touch. She takes extended jabs at parents, at women and men, at warriors and artists, at poets and politicians, at doctors and princes and commoners. She thanks several national characters, from the Germans to the Turks, for doing her work for her. She even spends a bit of time mocking science in its cradle.

Then gradually, ever so gradually, she begins praising the priests and scholars of the Holy Catholic Church, first for their back-bending theologies (written as if they knew the Mother of God personally and visited Hell every weekend, he says), then for their laziness — and finally for their greed, their ignorance, and their rank immorality and galling hypocrisy.

Ah, ha ha *ha!*

It's simply brilliant. For the first 80 pages or so, Erasmus softened his readers, got them laughing at everyone around them, even at themselves. So when the men of the Church stepped into the crosshairs, why, it only seemed fair, especially because Erasmus was one of them! But the point was clear enough to get tongues wagging and brains working all over Europe. Not a good combination for the Church.

Erasmus was a friend and mutual admirer of Martin Luther, and a lot of historians think *The Praise of Folly* prepared the ground for the Protestant Reformation that began a few years later. But Erasmus was also a close friend of Pope Julian II, and the book was after all just a lark. *Ha ha ha!*

If he hadn't made it funny, hadn't included other targets, and didn't have friends in high places, Erasmus really may have met his end at the stake. Other heretics did, and for an awful lot less.

As it was, Pope Paul IV put all of Erasmus's books, including *The Praise of Folly,* on the Index of Forbidden Books in 1559. But by that time, Erasmus was safely dead, and at any rate it was way too late to get the genie back in the bottle. The ideas were out there. The Reformation, the Enlightenment, and the course of freethought — up to and including atheism — flew right out of that hilarious, ingenious bottle.

Reasoning with Paine

Thomas Paine (1737–1809) is a perfect example of a religious believer whose out-of-the-box thinking about religion made him an inspiration not just to other out-of-the-box believers, but also to atheists and agnostics who had entirely thrown away the box.

Born in England, Paine became a corset maker, and then became involved in local activism, irritating many people as change makers tend to do. He met Benjamin Franklin, moved to the Colonies, and became quickly embroiled in revolutionary activities.

In 1776 Paine wrote *Common Sense,* a pamphlet credited with bolstering support for the idea of independence among the colonists. (One British Loyalist warned him that without the monarchy, the Colonies would quickly "degenerate into democracy." Now there's a telling phrase.) Paine took a job working for Congress, got fired, and then moved to France, where he quickly became embroiled in revolutionary activities. When power changed hands in 1793, he was arrested and imprisoned.

There, in a French prison, Paine earned his place in freethought history by writing *The Age of Reason,* one of the most powerfully reasoned, clear, and compelling assaults on traditional religion ever written.

Not that Paine was an atheist. In fact, it was his concern that revolutionary France was throwing the baby out with the bathwater by abolishing all religion that led him to write *The Age of Reason* in the first place, "lest in the general wreck of superstition, of false systems of government and false theology, we lose sight of morality, of humanity and of the theology that is true."

Paine was a Deist, and "the true Deist has but one Deity," he said. "His religion consists in contemplating the power, wisdom, and benignity of the Deity in his works, and in endeavoring to imitate him in everything moral, scientifical, and mechanical." (For more on Deism, check out Chapter 2.)

Like Erasmus before him, Paine knew how to prepare an audience to hear what he had to say. He started with a clear statement of his own position. He believed

- In one God, and hoped for an afterlife
- In the equality of man
- That religious duties included doing justice, loving mercy, and making others happy
- That all established churches were human inventions created to terrify and enslave people and make money
- That all people nonetheless have the right to believe in the doctrines of those churches, or in any religious idea to which their conscience leads

Paine then moved to a theme familiar to the Islamic heretics I write about in Chapters 5 and 10 — that the testimony of self-proclaimed prophets is a pretty weak and suspicious reason for believing. Paine's position on prophecy can be summed up as follows: If God speaks to you, fine, but don't expect me to put any stock in your testimony. Instead, I look to the natural world, which is the bible of the Deist.

More help from unorthodox friends

Other key books by unconventional religious believers rattling the orthodox cage include the following:

- ✔ **The Jefferson Bible:** In 1803, during his off hours while serving as President of the United States, Thomas Jefferson took a pair of scissors to the New Testament, cutting out everything miraculous or supernatural, leaving behind only the moral philosophy and basic human story of Jesus. It's hard to miss the resemblance to the Neo-Confucians' attempt to trim the supernatural away from Confucian teachings (see Chapter 5 for more information on that).

- ✔ **Dialogues Concerning Natural Religion:** David Hume wrote this dialogue among three fictional friends about the nature of God and how much (or how little) humanity can ever know about God. Most scholars agree that Philo, the most skeptical of the three, is a stand-in for Hume's own vaguely Deistic opinions.

- ✔ **The Gospel of Christian Atheism:** Thomas J.J. Altizer was one of several religious thinkers in the mid 1960s to articulate a "death of God" theology. Though some others in the movement believed that God never really existed, Altizer suggested that he did exist, but then literally died as Christ on the cross. It was an odd idea, but one that offered another way of conceiving of a world without God, urging people to focus on the moral message of Jesus instead.

- ✔ **A New Christianity for a New World:** One of several books by Bishop John Shelby Spong, who has to be the most radical prominent clergyman of all time. Spong urges Christianity to "change or die," and the changes he suggests include recognizing that no supernatural God exists, that all miracle stories are false, that the sacrifice narrative of Christ is wrongheaded and barbaric, and that scripture bears no ethical relevance in modern life.

In other words: Just do away with God, the Bible, miracles, and Christ on the cross, and Christianity will be fine.

In Part II of *The Age of Reason*, Paine turns a hot light on that *other* Bible — the Judeo-Christian one — which he calls pure mythology. Book by book, he decimates the Bible for factual errors and internal contradictions. Although biblical critics today point out those (massive) contradictions all the time, Paine was among the first to apply this secular technique to the sacred book — and that book didn't come out smelling like a rose, but like something entirely else.

Even more important to Paine was the grotesque immorality he saw in nearly every book of the Bible — especially (though by no means entirely) the Old Testament. For many readers in his time, seeing his list of rape, murder, enslavement, and genocide, all directly sanctioned by God in the Bible, was a genuinely shock, the first they'd heard of these terrible things being in the Good Book. Then as now, the pulpit filtered most Biblical knowledge before it reached the congregants. And though plenty of hellfire found its way into the sermons of the late 18th century, the devil was in the details, and the truly nasty details were news to most of Paine's readers.

The Age of Reason sparked new interest in Deism as a way of doing religion. And though not an atheist himself, Paine's forceful arguments against dogmas and superstitions make *The Age of Reason* a natural and important part of the written legacy of freethought.

Despite his clear statements of belief, his relentless dismantling of the Christian religion led to the false charge that he *was* an atheist. He spent the last years of his life back in the United States, shunned and isolated for his views. Only six people attended the funeral of one of the founders of his country.

"He had lived long, did some good and much harm," said one obituary.

Clearing the Way

Europe needed a few hundred years to wake from its medieval nap. The rediscovery of the classics spurred the Scientific Revolution and a new, secular way of seeing the world and being in it.

By the 18th century, a cultural and intellectual movement called the Age of Enlightenment caught fire. The thinkers at the heart of the movement wanted to spur progress and improve society by embracing and increasing knowledge. Just as I've argued for earlier periods, the first task was to get unhelpful ways of thinking out of the way. And just like earlier thinkers, those in the Enlightenment saw superstitious and supernatural ideas as the most unhelpful of all, and therefore the ideas most in need of a swift kick out the door.

Before a new, secular worldview could be built, they say, it was necessary to "break the spell" of the old ways of thinking. That process continued far beyond the Enlightenment, through the 19th and 20th centuries and well into the 21st. These sections present three important works of exactly this kind, ideas intended to clear people's minds and cultures of supernatural beliefs.

Hiding disbelief with an atheist priest

Few double lives are more compelling to imagine than that of an atheist priest, but that was exactly the situation for Jean Meslier.

The year was 1689 and France had recently finished nearly a century of bitter religious warfare when Jean Meslier became a parish priest — "to please my parents," he said. For 40 years he performed his job, doing his best to ease and improve the lives of his parishioners. But upon his death in 1729, those same parishioners made an astonishing find — four handwritten copies of a memoir in which Meslier revealed that he was an atheist and pretty much always had been.

The subtitle — "Clear and Evident Demonstrations of the Vanity and Falsity of All the Religions of the World" — says all you need to know about his point of view. Imagining the whole scene is quite dramatic. Every day for the last ten years of his life, Meslier finished his priestly duties, and then returned home, picked up a quill, and bent to attack the very religion and God he had spent the day serving. The result wasn't the first book-length work written from an atheist perspective — just the first one with a name on it.

That's right — the first openly atheist author was also a Catholic priest.

He really can't be blamed for keeping it secret while he was alive. Blasphemy was still a capital crime in France at the time. Meslier addressed the book to his parishioners and framed as a heartfelt apology for his part in deceiving them. Telling his parishioners would have been too dangerous while he was alive, he said, so he decided to do so after his death.

Meslier thought everything through to the last detail. To ensure that his parishioners saw the book he wrote for them, he registered it with the town clerks, telling them to deliver the four copies to his congregation when he died.

In the course of 93 chapters, Meslier said that

- Priests are "pious morons" eager to deceive others with "illusions, errors, lies, and fictions" so they can control them.
- He felt "pain and extreme loathing" for speaking against his true beliefs and for keeping people in the "stupid errors, the vain superstitions, and the idolatries that I hated, condemned, and detested to the core."
- Christianity is no less false, vain, or idolatrous than any other religion.
- All religions are human creations and God doesn't exist.
- He had come very close to "bursting out with indignation" hundreds of times, but was afraid of the consequences.
- The Gospels are filled with contradictions, which he pointed out in detail.
- Religion is the cause of war and division among people.
- In addition to the good, the Bible is filled with deeply immoral teachings.
- People don't need the priests — it's the other way around.

Historians know that the Catholic authorities found the memoir and immediately read it because Meslier was buried in an unknown location with no marker and no mention in the parish register. He just disappeared without a trace — except for his book.

Even worse than the treatment of Meslier's body was the treatment his book received at the hands of Voltaire 30 years later. Eager to promote his own Deism (refer to Chapter 2), Voltaire published an abridged version of the memoir, omitting all references to Meslier's atheism so he too would appear to have been a Deist who revolted against Catholicism. Voltaire even created a completely fictional statement by Meslier, saying he "begged God" to restore the "natural religion" that Christianity had drifted away from. (We know it's fictional because it doesn't appear in the original manuscripts — only in Voltaire's mash-up.)

Despite that dishonesty, Voltaire is the one to thank for bringing Meslier's memoir to the attention of the thinkers and doers of the Enlightenment — even if he played dress-up with it first.

Promoting Good Sense with d'Holbach

Paris was Mecca for the Enlightenment philosophers in the late 1700s — though I don't think they'd be too thrilled by *that* analogy. It was the place to be if you were a thinker looking to change European culture, a place where ideas were currency and progress was in the air. And no one stood nearer the vortex of these powerful new ideas than Paul-Henri Thiry, Baron d'Holbach (1723–1789). D'Holbach created a *salon* in Paris, a place for great thinkers to discuss and debate the ideas that ended up driving the engine of the Enlightenment.

Like many in his circle, d'Holbach saw religion not only as false but also as an obstacle to morality. In 1761 he published *Christianity Unveiled,* the first of his many broadsides against religion.

Helping modern-day Mesliers: The Clergy Project

There's no good way to know how many clergymen in the 18th century were actually non-believers like Jean Meslier. But in recent years that scenario has become so common that an online community called The Clergy Project (www.clergyproject.org) was created to provide support for ministers, priests, and other members of the clergy who are in this difficult situation.

It's not unusual for a member of the clergy to have his or her entire identity tied to that role, which ultimately rests on a set of assumed beliefs. Even today, a minister or priest who announces a loss of those beliefs risks losing his or her entire community and support system, not to mention income and sometimes even family. Many who have done so have become the targets of strong feelings of anger and betrayal from their former flocks.

For these and other reasons, a clergyperson who has a change of heart commonly keeps it to him or herself. The Clergy Project, which currently includes more than 400 members, allows clergy in this situation to provide each other with support and advice.

But he was just getting started. Seven years later, he published *The System of Nature,* a book that picked up where Lucretius left off nearly 2,000 years earlier, describing the nature of things in a materialistic universe without gods.

But just as Lucretius and others discovered before him, you can't describe the natural world until you get the supernatural one out of the way, so the book included powerful and compelling arguments against religious belief, which d'Holbach called the chief sources of ignorance, servitude, and hatred.

After that case was made, d'Holbach presented a very convincing case for morality without God. There are many reasons to act morally, he said. You just need to have good sense and reflect on what is good for you and for those around you. It's to my advantage to be good, and to my disadvantage to be bad. The world will make my path smooth if I behave well, and it will make my life miserable if I behave badly. Reflection, backed up with real-world consequences, forms the basis for real morality — not the fear of God.

The book touched off excitement from some and an explosion of outrage from others. Among the furious were the Deist Voltaire and the Calvinist Frederick the Great, both of whom wrote scathing replies. This reaction didn't worry d'Holbach too much because he had taken the wise precaution of publishing both books under a false name. So although many suspected him as the author, they couldn't convincingly tie the noose around d'Holbach's neck.

Not many people would have been eager to string d'Holbach up anyway. He had a reputation for incredible kindness and generosity, and everyone with any power in Paris seemed to have experienced it at one time or another. The Calvinist writer/philosopher Rousseau even based a fictional character, a highly moral atheist, on d'Holbach. That was some good press for d'Holbach, and helpful if you're going to make a career attacking sacred cows.

It was a long book, and pretty dense in spots. As a result, it didn't really penetrate to the common people, and they were the ones d'Holbach really wanted to reach. So a few years later, he released a shorter, more accessible version — a kind of *System of Nature For Dummies* — and called it *Good Sense, or Natural Ideas Opposed to Supernatural.* It was an instant bestseller, which didn't help the blood pressure of the higher-ups one bit. The Catholic Church even threatened to cut off financial support to the French crown if the two books weren't suppressed.

Too late! Once again, a useful genie had been uncorked. Baron d'Holbach's works ended up having a tremendous impact on the Enlightenment, especially the developing concept of human rights. Enlightenment ideas challenged traditional power structures around the world, and crucial documents including the US Bill of Rights, the French Declaration of the Rights of Man and of the Citizen, and the UN's Universal Declaration of Human Rights are all rooted directly in Enlightenment principles — which in turn were born in works like d'Holbach's *Good Sense.*

"Changing the way people think" — the *Encyclopédie*

One of the most incredible things to come out of the French Enlightenment was the *Encyclopédie* — a 35-volume masterpiece with more than 75,000 articles by dozens of contributors, intended by its editor-in-chief, the atheist philosopher Denis Diderot, "to change the way people think."

Endorsed in the early going by the French government, the radical and antireligious nature of many of the articles drew condemnation from the Catholic Church. The French government officially banned the project to mollify the Church but allowed work to continue in secret — partly because the project employed several hundred people. The resulting work captured the essence of Enlightenment thought in amazing depth and detail.

Rejecting Christianity with Russell

The English philosopher Bertrand Russell (1872–1970) offered some of the clearest, easy-to-understand arguments against religious belief. His essay "Why I Am Not a Christian" has been called one of the most influential works of the 20th century and is on the very short list of great works of atheist thought.

On the surface, the soft-spoken Russell didn't seem like the kind of person to get in trouble. Yet he spent most of a long life in trouble of various kinds, mostly for standing up for unpopular positions in which he strongly believed. His loud moral opposition to Britain's involvement in the First World War got him thrown in prison, and there's no end to the grief he got for his antireligious writings and speeches.

His view of religion is made crystal clear: religion is "a disease born of fear and as a source of untold misery to the human race," he said in another essay. Not that it hasn't made *some* contributions, he admitted — religion had a hand in creating the calendar, and it caused Egyptian priests to keep track of eclipses so carefully that they could eventually predict them. "These two services I am prepared to acknowledge," he said, "but I do not know of any others."

Russell began "Why I Am Not a Christian" by defining a Christian as a person who believes in God and immortality and who thinks Christ was the best and wisest of men.

Then, using the clarity of thought and expression that was his trademark, Russell explained why each of these three beliefs was unsustainable, refuting each of the traditional arguments for God's existence in turn, then those for immortality.

At last he turned to the moral character of Jesus Christ. After granting a few worthwhile moral teachings, Russell turned to what he called "one very serious defect" in Christ's moral character — his belief in the existence and acceptability of an everlasting hell.

As Russell often did when his criticisms got close to the bone, he lightened the moment. "You will find that in the Gospels Christ said, 'Ye serpents, ye generation of vipers, how can ye escape the damnation of Hell.' That was said to people who did not like His preaching. It is not really to my mind quite the best tone." It's true that Christ threatened damnation over and over throughout the Gospels, usually not for moral shortcomings but for disbelief or insufficient respect. For this and other reasons — his odd cursing of figs and pigs, for example — Russell found himself unable to consider Christ "the best and wisest of men."

In the end he returned to religion itself, which he thought was primarily based in fear of the unknown and the desire for protection in times of trouble, adding that science had done a great deal to reduce the unknown and to provide protection from the chaos of the natural world.

"A good world needs knowledge, kindliness, and courage," he said. "It does not need a regretful hankering after the past or a fettering of the free intelligence by the words uttered long ago by ignorant men. It needs a fearless outlook and free intelligence."

Building a New Vision

Religious criticism is all well and good — but at some point it's time to start building a new vision, describing what the world looks like after gods are out of the way. These sections look at three works that do exactly that.

Drawing crowds with Robert Ingersoll

The last half of the 19th century was something of a golden age for freethought in the United States and United Kingdom, and a lot of the credit has to go to the public speeches of Robert Green Ingersoll (1833–1899).

Traveling orators were a popular form of educational entertainment in the 19th century. Robert Ingersoll, a former Illinois state politician whose radically progressive religious and political views eventually made him unelectable, was among the most famous of these speechmakers.

The Illinois Republican Party had urged him to run for governor but wanted him to hide his agnosticism. He thought it would be unethical to conceal information from the public and refused. But leaving politics didn't mean people wouldn't come out to listen to him speak — and that's just what they did, by the thousands, hearing Ingersoll on subjects from education to politics to women's rights to religion. His outspoken and eloquent views on religion earned him his fame and a nickname — "The Great Agnostic."

A lot of important works in the history of freethought are . . . well, a little dry. That's what makes Ingersoll's speeches so huge. They were eloquent. They were moving. They *inspired.* He often spoke without notes for up to two hours at a go, every sentence a beautifully crafted, quotable pearl. His ability to build an argument from the ground up, bringing the audience with him step by step, helped to make religious unbelief a viable position for many who had frankly never thought it could be.

Though his talks had plenty of religious criticism in them, he went beyond that, sharing a vision of what the world looked like to a person without religious beliefs. In a speech titled "Why I Am an Agnostic," his description of the feeling that came over him when at last he walked away from religious belief ran counter to the common assumption of the faithful but echoed the actual experience of many, many others:

> When I became convinced that the Universe is natural, that all the ghosts and gods are myths, there entered into my brain, into my soul, into every drop of my blood, the sense, the feeling, the joy of freedom. The walls of my prison crumbled and fell, the dungeon was flooded with light, and all the bolts, and bars, and manacles became dust. I was no longer a servant, a serf or a slave. There was for me no master in all the wide world — not even in infinite space. I was free — free to think, to express my thoughts — free to live to my own ideal — free to live for myself and those I loved — free to use all my faculties, all my senses — free to spread imagination's wings — free to investigate, to guess and dream and hope . . . I stood erect and fearlessly, joyously, faced all worlds . . . We can fill our lives with generous deeds, with loving words, with art and song, and all the ecstasies of love. We can flood our years with sunshine — with the divine climate of kindness, and we can drain to the last drop the golden cup of joy.

See what I mean? It was a kind of epic poetry, and it captivated his audiences like nothing else could. No one did more to ignite and fan the flames of this "golden age" of freethought than The Great Agnostic. His influence was brought forward beyond his immediate audience when shortly after his death in 1899, his brother-in-law collected Ingersoll's best-known speeches for publication as *The Works of Robert G. Ingersoll.*

Imagining a humanist world with Lamont

The American philosopher Corliss Lamont (1902–1995) was best known for suing the US government a few times over civil liberties — cases that set the stage for important gains in personal liberty and rights of association. But he was also an influential philosopher and teacher who wrote *The Philosophy of Humanism,* a book that's been called "the definitive study of humanism."

I have a warm place in my heart for this book. Back when I was first exploring organized freethought, I joined the American Humanist Association, and *The Philosophy of Humanism* was sent along with my welcome packet. Now I'd already figured out what I thought of religion, so I didn't need another book debunking arguments I'd already rejected. I needed something that described the *implications* of the decision I'd already made, one that answered the main question on my mind: "Okay, so I'm a humanist. Now what?"

That, in a nutshell, is what Lamont's book does.

Lamont started by defining and describing humanism, as I do for atheism in Part I of this book, then he traced the long tradition of humanist thought (as I do in Parts II and III), and finally finished by describing the values and perspectives of the humanist . . . as I do for atheism in Part IV. Great minds, and all that.

While I'm borrowing ideas from Corliss, I hope I've managed to borrow one of the things he was most famous for — a sense of fun and wonder and optimism. Search online for "Corliss Lamont" and the first image you'll see is Corliss grinning like a jack-o-lantern. When I first picked up his book, I still had the image of atheists as a sour bunch of grumps back then, and I really had my doubts about joining them in any official way. Lamont showed me that I could be a nonbeliever who was full of joy, interested in knocking things down when necessary, as Lamont himself did, but also in building them up.

The last section of his book, "The Affirmation of Life," is like the end of an Ingersoll speech — an inspiring tribute to what's possible when people bring their best selves to the task of being human.

I'll admit that the final chapter, "A Humanist Civilization," tips into Pollyanna just a bit. Lamont drew a picture of a relentlessly shiny world that has moved beyond religion and healed of its injuries, a culture in which education gets more money than war, freedom of expression is absolute, and the collective good trumps the greed of individuals. Because humans would still be at the wheel in such a world, I'm not quite *that* optimistic. I also don't spend a lot of time envisioning a world without religion. Neither the religious nor the secular are going away, in my humble opinion. We're all in this together for the long haul.

But as I note in Chapter 2, humanist ideals don't have to be limited to a secular worldview. It's just about putting this world and this life first, no matter what else you believe. This attempt to describe a civilization built on those humanist ideals was the first one I'd seen, and it still inspires me and many others.

It's also hard to disagree with the book's final sentence: "Humanism assigns to us nothing less than the task of being our own savior and redeemer." It's all up to human beings.

Waxing miraculous with Dawkins

For people more familiar with his work challenging religion, British biologist Richard Dawkins (b. 1941) may seem a strange choice for a section about building a positive vision. But his contribution to building that vision has been as big a part of his work as clearing superstitions out of the way. His popular science writing has emphasized understanding and a sense of wonder in equal parts, and one essay in particular has become one of the most treasured examples of the wonder of a naturalistic view.

"To Live at All Is Miracle Enough" tackled a question atheists hear all too often: *How can you find meaning and purpose in life without God and the promise of eternal life? Or, as it's often put, Without God, how can you get out of bed in the morning?*

Dawkins began by putting human existence in perspective. That each person is born at all is a stroke of incalculable luck. Uncounted trillions of people could have been here instead of you if any one of a trillion tiny things had happened differently — if your mom and dad married other people, or married each other but conceived in a different month, or a different sperm won the race to the egg . . . And you'd have to do the same for your grandparents, all of them, and a hundred thousand generations before them. But things happened just as they did, says Dawkins, so the countless other possible combinations of DNA never came to pass. Instead, "in the teeth of these stupefying odds, it is you and I, in our ordinariness, that are here."

Dawkins spun out this thread of improbability with great skill, making the reader feel the incredible good fortune of being alive, even for a short time. As I continue to read and reread this essay over the years, I begin to feel a bit piggy for ever complaining that my life won't last forever, and plenty grateful that it happened at all.

Dawkins brought it home in a memorable passage that has made "To Live at All" one of the favorite readings for humanist funerals, like a 23rd Psalm for the nonbeliever:

After sleeping through a hundred million centuries we have finally opened our eyes on a sumptuous planet, sparkling with colour, bountiful with life. Within decades we must close our eyes again. Isn't it a noble, an enlightened way of spending our brief time in the sun, to work at understanding the universe and how we have come to wake up in it? This is how I answer when I am asked — as I am surprisingly often — why I bother to get up in the mornings.

Squeezing in a few more recommended texts

Including all of the worthwhile works that relate to or support an atheistic worldview is impossible. I address several others in Chapters 12 and 13, including the recent flurry of high-profile best sellers. Here are a few more that simply must get a nod:

✔ **"The Philosophy of Atheism":** Written by Emma Goldman, this essay, which appeared in *Mother Earth* magazine in 1916, does for the atheist perspective what Corliss Lamont does for humanism. It's a very strong, compelling vision.

✔ **Atheism: The Case Against God (Prometheus):** More than a generation before the "New Atheists," George Smith penned this powerful set of arguments for rejecting belief in God.

✔ **The Blind Watchmaker (Norton):** In 1802, a theologian named William Paley made an analogy. If you find a watch on the ground while out hiking, you wouldn't think it was natural. Its complexity would instantly suggest the existence of a watchmaker. Same with the complex universe, he says, which likewise suggests an intelligent creator. In *The Blind Watchmaker*, author Richard Dawkins shows that the compelling illusion of design is actually created by the process of natural selection.

✔ **The Demon-Haunted World (Ballantine):** Not specifically a work of atheism, but a brilliant, wide-ranging assault by the agnostic Carl Sagan on bad thinking of all kinds, and a case for science as a "candle in the dark" of ignorance and superstition.

Chapter 12

Laughing in Disbelief: Challenging the Divine with Humor

....

In This Chapter

▶ Satirizing sacred cows

▶ Worshipping false gods . . . to make a point

▶ Blaspheming in multimedia

....

Devoting a chapter to humor may seem strange in this book, but in addition to just being one of the best things in life, humor plays a huge part in softening up the big, serious topic of religion. Humor cuts religion down to human size so you can think about it, play with it — and yes, laugh about it.

If you want to ask challenging questions about religion, having a sense of humor helps. Knowing that some people won't find it funny — especially when it's their own sacred cows being milked — is also helpful. Like Toto pulling back the curtain to reveal the sad little man behind the Wizard, laughter can pull back the cloak of sacredness around religion so people can see its humble human origin.

Sacred has at least two definitions:

✔ It can mark something as special, awe-inspiring, and deserving of respect. This definition is no problem. Even the nonreligious can hold things sacred by that definition.

✔ It can also mean *hands off — this idea can't be questioned.* This definition is a big problem. So how can you question the unquestionable? By rejecting the very idea of unquestionable ideas.

One of the sacred principles of freethought — that's "sacred" by the first definition — is that no question is unaskable, no authority unquestionable. One of the greatest, time-tested ways of busting through the wall of immunity that surrounds religion is laughter.

The agnostic Mark Twain knew this better than anyone. "Power, money, persuasion, supplication, persecution — these can lift at a colossal humbug," says the character of Little Satan in *The Mysterious Stranger*, "push it a little, weaken it a little, century by century — but only laughter can blow it to rags and atoms at a blast."

It's true. A timeless connection exists between comedy and truth. Comedy theorists note that a joke is often funniest when it reveals something that's true but hidden by a fig leaf. The laugh comes as the fig leaf is yanked away, and the strength of the laugh is what comedian Lenny Bruce called a Geiger counter for the truthfulness of the joke. If no truth is revealed, then it isn't as funny. The laugh's strength often depends on how obvious the revealed truth is after that fig leaf is gone.

Institutions, ideas, nations, and people who stand on firm foundations can endure a joke or two at their expense. But if the foundation is built on sand — well, to quote Twain again, "No God and no religion can survive ridicule."

This chapter offers a small, selective taste of the long and glorious history of humor used to challenge religious ideas.

Getting Satirical

Religion is a favorite target of humorists, and satire is one of their sharpest tools. Almost every example in this chapter falls under the category of satire. Nearly all were also greeted in its time with cries that they was really just a cheap shot — that it was "mere ridicule."

So what does ridicule really mean? *Ridicule* is the claim that something is worthy of contempt — that it's literally "ridiculous." Some things are, of course. It can be a potent weapon against tyrants and frauds of all kinds. The brutal dictator Slobodan Milošević started losing his grip on power when he became the subject of ridicule and was no longer taken seriously. Ridicule is a powerful tool for breaking down walls of immunity.

But satire is a different animal. *Satire* uses wit to shine a bright light on human vices and follies. Ridicule is sometimes just an attack for its own sake, but satire always has a point to make, a critique to offer. Ridicule can be rude, even crude. Satire intends more and better. Ridicule points and laughs at the naked emperor. Satire wants to change the world.

The following are three brilliant examples of satire lampooning religion in order to draw attention to its shortcomings.

Mark Twain

For most of his life, Mark Twain (1835–1910) stayed away from religious targets, which is why most people don't even know he was an agnostic.

But toward the end of his life, the gloves were off. "The Bible . . . has noble poetry in it; and some clever fables; and some blood-drenched history; and some good morals; and a wealth of obscenity; and upwards of a thousand lies," he said in *Following the Equator.* "Faith is believing something you know ain't true . . . If Christ were here now, there is one thing he would not be — a Christian . . . If there is a God, he is a malign thug."

Huckleberry Finn it ain't. You probably notice some bitterness there and not much humor. Twain was writing through a lot of personal pain at this point. But in some of his last contributions, he managed to make a heartfelt case that religion is both false and ridiculous. And he did it by using the beautiful, devastating weapon of satire.

Several of Twain's best humorous assaults on religion weren't published until after his death — in fact, in 1972, a few years after the first moon landing. The delay was his idea. "I expose to the world only my trimmed and perfumed and carefully barbered public opinions," he wrote near the end of his life, "and conceal carefully, cautiously, wisely, my private ones" — including his true thoughts about religion. He instructed his editors to only gradually release some of his less "perfumed" thoughts over the course of a century after his death. Here I discuss two examples.

"Thoughts of God"

In the essay "Thoughts of God," Twain skewered what is now called "intelligent design theory" by wondering what kind of being would ever create the fly on purpose.

> Not one of us could have planned the fly, not one of us could have constructed him," he said, "and no one would have considered it wise to try, except under an assumed name." He imagines the moment the fly is created and sent into the world — to persecute sick children, settle on the open wounds of soldiers, spreading disease and death. "Go forth," says the fly's Creator, "to please Me and increase My glory, Who made the fly."

It's a wicked, dark humor, but it's still humor. It strips away the protection of sacredness and calls the perfection of the world into question in a few sentences. It makes me think. If Twain succeeded, I'm not just entertained but more convinced that he has a point. That's good satire.

"Little Bessie Would Assist Providence"

In his essay "Little Bessie Would Assist Providence," Twain put innocent and unanswerable questions in the mouth of a four-year-old girl:

> **Bessie:** Mama, why did the neighbor boy die of typhus?
>
> **Mama:** It was God's judgment for his sins.
>
> **Bessie:** Why did the roof fall on that kind man who was trying to save the old woman from the fire?
>
> **Mama:** Don't ask me why, because I don't know. I only know it was to discipline some one, or be a judgment upon somebody, or to show His power.
>
> **Bessie:** You know the lightning came last week, mama, and struck the new church, and burnt it down. Was it to discipline the church?

The questions keep coming in rapid fire. Mom does the best she can to give the party line, and Bessie comes to the only conclusions she can: that God sends all the troubles and pains and diseases and horrors in mercy and kindness to discipline us. So it's the duty of every parent to help God by killing and starving their children and giving them diseases, she says — "and brother Eddie needs disciplining, right away! I know where you can get the smallpox for him, and the itch, and the diphtheria, and bone-rot, and heart disease, and consumption, and . . ."

When her frazzled mama faints dead away, Bessie figures it's the heat.

George Carlin

The comedian George Carlin (1937–2008) made a career of bursting sacred balloons. And he wasn't above ridicule when he felt something was ridiculous.

In one routine he noted that God has a list of ten things that you should not do. Then Carlin's voice rose as he described a place God created, "full of fire and smoke and burning and torture and anguish," to lock you away forever if you break any of the rules.

"But He loves you," Carlin added quietly.

See that, right there? *That's* the fig-leaf moment. Under this particular leaf was the contradiction between eternal damnation and a loving God, captured in four perfectly placed words, delivered by Carlin with a sudden softening of tone — *but He loves you.* The contradiction is funny and true — and it's funny *because* it's true.

Carlin's work reframed religion to drive home a point. Instead of praying to God, he said he'd started praying to the tough guy actor Joe Pesci, because "he looks like a guy who can get things done." Carlin noticed that "all the prayers I now offer to Joe Pesci are being answered at about the same 50 percent rate. Half the time I get what I want, half the time I don't. Same as God, 50-50."

In another routine, he boiled the Ten Commandments down to two, including "Thou shalt try real hard not to kill anyone, unless of course they pray to a different invisible man than you."

Like a lot of comedians, Carlin's work is sometimes dismissed as lowbrow entertainment. That's about as far off the mark as you can get. George Carlin is a thinking person's comedian if ever there was — and an articulate atheist.

The Onion

The Onion (www.theonion.com) is a parody news organization found both online and in print. Its fake news stories deliver some of the smartest satire available, and one of its favorite targets is religion.

A favorite example of mine is an article with the headline, "Pope Calls for Greater Understanding between Catholics, Hellbound" in which Pope John Paul II is said to have called upon the world's Catholics to build a bridge of friendship between themselves and "the eternally damned."

It continues for several paragraphs, contrasting the idea of earnestly reaching out to others in friendship and love while still maintaining that they're going to hell.

Two weeks after the attacks of September 11, 2001, while other comedy outlets were frozen in place, *The Onion* ran an article titled, "God Angrily Clarifies 'No Kill' Rule."

Some other Onion favorites include the following:

- Sumerians Look On In Confusion As God Creates World
- Evangelical Scientists Refute Gravity with New 'Intelligent Falling' Theory
- Gay Teen Worried He Might Be Christian
- God Answers Prayers of Paralyzed Little Boy: 'No', Says God
- Christian Right Lobbies To Overturn Second Law of Thermodynamics
- Pope Vows to Get Church Pedophilia Down to Acceptable Levels
- God Cites 'Moving In Mysterious Ways' as Motive in Killing of 3,000 Papua New Guineans

Poking orthodoxy in the eye: Voltaire

In the 18th century, Voltaire (who wasn't an atheist but a Deist) railed against intolerance, tyranny, and superstition by using satire. His best-known bust is the only one I know carved with a smirk.

In his short story "Micromégas," Voltaire goes after one of the most essential elements of most religions — human specialness. A traveler from another world visits Earth. He is 20,000 feet tall and more than 400 Earth years old and hails from a planet 21 million times larger than Earth. Banished from his planet for 800 years for writing a heretical book about insects, he takes the opportunity to travel, makes a tiny friend on Saturn (who is just 6,000 feet tall), and then heads to Earth.

At first the two are convinced the planet is uninhabited, then (like a scene from *Horton Hears*

a Who!) realize that very tiny beings live down below. They both agree that the beings are far too small to have any intelligence — then to their shock, they realize the little things are *speaking.*

Short story shorter, they eventually learn that humans are convinced the entire universe was made for them, and the two giants nearly shake the planet to pieces with their laughter. It's a pretty direct comment on one of the centerpieces of the Christian worldview — that the human species is the center of God's concern (more on that in Chapter 3).

I haven't done it justice here. Search online for it and enjoy.

None is just a cheap laugh for its own sake. Each is a critique of some aspect of religious belief or practice, including young earth creationism, intelligent design, homophobia, prayer, the Catholic sex abuse scandal, and the problem of evil.

As Erasmus and Voltaire both demonstrated (see the nearby sidebar), the ability to laugh at religious ideas that are harmful is a powerful way to get a serious conversation started.

The Power of Parody: The Church of the Flying Spaghetti Monster

One of the most effective ways to make a satirical point is to pretend you're on the same team as the target — then hoist it with its own petard. A great example on the political side is Stephen Colbert, a comedian who pretends to be an enthusiastic conservative so he can ridicule conservatism in its own language. What Colbert does for politics, the Church of the Flying Spaghetti Monster (FSM) does for religion.

FSM was born in 2005, shortly after the Kansas State Board of Education voted to introduce "intelligent design" (ID) into the state science curriculum. Board member Kathy Martin said at the time that evolution had been proven false, whereas intelligent design was "science-based and strong in facts," and so deserved equal time in the classroom.

The response was swift and strong. Many supporters of ID wrote in to praise the decision as a victory for all that's good. The board also received letters from scientists, educators, parents, and members of the general public decrying the policy, including one signed by 38 Nobel laureates urging the board to reverse the decision.

FAMOUS FREETHINKER

One of the more creative responses was an open letter to the board by Bobby Henderson, a recent graduate of the Oregon State University physics program. The letter pretended to agree with the board's decision to allow multiple points of view, then claimed that another religious perspective, one based on the worship of a Flying Spaghetti Monster, also deserved to be included.

It was a classic, straight-faced satire in the Stephen Colbert mold, and it was brilliant.

"I think we can all agree that it is important for students to hear multiple viewpoints so they can choose for themselves the theory that makes the most sense to them," he said in the letter. But he added that he was concerned students would only hear one Intelligent Design theory. He and many others around the world, he said, believed that the world was created by a Flying Spaghetti Monster. Henderson asked that the science curriculum be split not two but three ways, teaching Intelligent Design, Flying Spaghetti Monsterism, and what Henderson calls "logical conjecture based on overwhelming observable evidence."

Henderson's satirical letter spread like wildfire online. The Associated Press praised it as "a clever and effective argument" and the *Daily Telegraph* said it was "a masterstroke, which underlined the absurdity of Intelligent Design."

The following year, four of the six religious conservatives on the Kansas board who had approved the nonsensical policy lost their seats in an election, and the new board quickly voted to reject the change.

Many credit Henderson's letter for showing how untenable the board's position was. In the end, by yanking the board's fig leaf away, satire may have been even more powerful than the serious objections of 38 Nobel laureates.

Missing the joke: Poe's Law

The Internet has developed its own set of rules, laws, and adages — attempts to explain or describe aspects of the online experience. "Poe's Law," named for its originator, Nathan Poe, notes that it's pretty much impossible to create a parody of religious fundamentalism that won't be mistaken for the real thing.

The website for Landover Baptist Church (www.landoverbaptist.org) is a perfect example of Poe's Law in action. The site is filled with over-the-top characters like Pastor Deacon Fred and Betty Bowers (America's Best Christian), as well as pronouncements, suppressed sexuality, and moral calls to action that are so close to religious fundamentalism in the real world that it's hard to be sure they're kidding.

To complicate matters, another site called Objective:Ministries (www.objective ministries.org) has an ongoing project to shut down Landover Baptist, calling it an "anti-Christian fraud." But it turns out Objective:Ministries is *itself* a parody site.

And how can I be sure it isn't serious? Well . . . I guess I can't.

But that wasn't the end, not by a long shot. The Church of the Flying Spaghetti Monster has since exploded into a worldwide phenomenon, especially on college campuses. Along the way, it has developed its own rituals, scripture, and words and phrases including the following:

- ✔ Pastafarian: A worshipper of the Flying Spaghetti Monster
- ✔ "I Have Been Touched by His Noodly Appendage": I am blessed
- ✔ The Olive Garden of Eden: Where it all began
- ✔ Antipasti: People opposed to Pastafarianism
- ✔ The Eight "I'd Really Rather You Didn'ts": Instructions for moral living
- ✔ RAmen: Said at the conclusion of a Pastafarian prayer

Now lest you think FSMism is just an extended joke — amusing but not all that powerful — try explaining to a Pastafarian exactly why her religion is fake and another (take your pick) isn't. Arguing that the hearsay and revelations of one prophet are inherently more valid than those of another isn't easy.

Or you may want to talk to Nico Alm, an Austrian Pastafarian who learned that his government forbade hats in driver's license photos *unless* they are of religious significance — then showed up to the driver's bureau wearing a pasta strainer on his head, claiming it was a religious mandate for worshippers of the FSM. When the government failed to come up with a decisive way to distinguish Pastafarianism from any other belief claim, Alm got his wish.

Skewering the Sacred Musically: Tim Minchin

British-Australian musician/comedian Tim Minchin (b. 1975) has quickly become the musical voice of atheism and skepticism — and an insanely funny one at that. Like so many of the comedians in this chapter, Minchin's material is tremendously smart and thought-provoking — a perfect example of the power of comedy to reveal the truth about sensitive subjects.

Examples include

✓ "Storm," a nine-minute beat poem about the collision of his skepticism with the starry-eyed gullibility of another guest at a dinner party.

✓ "Thank You, God," a relentlessly upbeat tongue-in-cheek prayer thanking God for fixing a woman's cataracts while continuing to give countless babies malaria.

✓ "Pope Song," which crams 84 obscenities into two minutes while outlining the child sex abuse scandal in the Catholic Church and the Vatican's inadequate response. The obscenities are central to the point, as Minchin points out in the last few bars: *If the language in this song offends you more than the idea that the Pope protected priests who were abusing children, then you need to check your values.* (I may have paraphrased that a bit.)

✓ "The Good Book," a toe-tapping square dance tune about the consequences of using the nastier parts of the Bible (such as the story of Abraham's willingness to kill Isaac) as a moral guide.

✓ "White Wine in the Sun" isn't a comedy, but a heartfelt rendition of the meaning of family at the holidays for a religious nonbeliever. It's an anthem for the humanist heart.

Minchin never offends just for the sake of it. In every case, he's using edgy comedy and crossing lines to get the listener's attention — and yes, as always, to yank that fig leaf away, revealing the truth.

Blaspheming at the Movies: Life of Brian

In the late 1970s, fresh off the success of their film *Monty Python and the Holy Grail*, the members of the British comedy group Monty Python were asked what the title of their next film would be. Without missing a beat, Eric Idle answered, *"Jesus Christ: Lust for Glory."*

It was meant to be a joke, but the more they thought about it, the more there seemed to be something there. No one had ever written a comedy set in Biblical times. Why not?

Because it's bloody hard, that's why not. The cloak of sacredness, which I mention earlier in this chapter, is like a wet blanket. The more they tried to work up a direct satire of Christ, the more it fizzled. But they didn't give up on the idea, and after months of research began to identify the problem — and the solution. As Python member John Cleese said, the founders of great religions tend to be extremely intelligent people with good ideas that are instantly mangled and misinterpreted by their followers — who also tended to turn them into gods (or sons thereof).

That's where the comedy is — not in the words of the Sermon on the Mount, but in the way Bob and Martha mishear it from the back of the crowd ("Blessed are the cheesemakers?!")

Messiah fever was very much in the air in first century Judea. There was no shortage of people claiming to be The One — or having others claim it for them. *Life of Brian* (1979) is built not around the life of Jesus, but on the life of Brian, an average putz born the same night in the manger next door. Brian eventually becomes the unwilling focus of a cult of worship, and there begins some of the best religious satire ever written.

One scene captures the history of Western religion in 60 seconds. When Brian, pursued by an adoring crowd, loses his shoe, one follower stops and picks it up, then declares loudly that it's a sign — they must *all* take off one shoe! Another follower loudly insists that no, it's clearly a sign that all shoes must be gathered up. Yet another insists it's a *sandal,* not a shoe, while another urges the crowd to forget the shoes and gather around a gourd Brian had touched. The crowd splits into bickering factions.

When they all catch up to Brian the next morning, he scolds them. "Look, you've got it all wrong! You don't need to follow me! You don't need to follow anybody! You've got to think for yourselves! You're all individuals!"

"Yes!" the crowd replies in perfect unison. *"We're all individuals!"*

Christ appears only briefly in the film and is never joked about directly. This wasn't skittishness on the part of the Pythons — as their BBC overlords could attest, they never hesitated to go wherever the comedy was. But in this case, the best material was in imagining the guaranteed nonsense all around him.

Of course this nuance had little effect on the controversy that followed — as controversy always does whenever the sacred veil is breached. The film was banned in several countries, protests were held across the United States, and commentators decried the supposed attack on Christianity. Most hadn't seen the film, of course, and the protests only created a larger demand, as such things always do.

Some of the Pythons were atheists or agnostics, while others held religious views. But all saw terrific value in bringing smart satire to bear on human religion, *especially* on the things that are declared off limits.

Bringing the Blasphemy Home on TV

The three most successful animated television series today all include a huge amount of humor aimed at religion, and atheists and agnostics created all three.

The following three shows have drawn the predictable wrath of religious groups and social conservatives for their irreverent treatment of religion. But irreverence is very much the point of comedy — that's how to bust through that veil of sacredness and ask otherwise unaskable questions. Whether any given plotline or joke goes too far is up to the individual viewer. For many people, believers and nonbelievers alike, shows like these play a valuable role in knocking the big questions down to manageable size.

The Simpsons

Religious belief and practice get more airtime in *The Simpsons* than just about any other aspect of culture. The Simpsons go to church and say grace before dinner, they have a conservative Christian next-door neighbor, and they shop at a convenience store run by a Hindu. Bart Simpson's favorite entertainer is a Jewish clown, and little sister Lisa becomes a Buddhist. Homer meets God, Bart sells his soul, and the family briefly joins a cult called the Movementarians.

You can't swing a three-eyed Jesus fish in Springfield without hitting a religious reference, and the result is some savvy insight into the role of religion in today's culture. Series creator Matt Groening identifies as an agnostic — the ideal position for an equal opportunity satirist of religion.

South Park

The edgy and risky animated series *South Park* sprang from nontheistic heads — in this case, atheists Trey Parker and Matt Stone. *South Park* goes after its targets relentlessly, sparing no one, including Parker and Stone's fellow unbelievers:

- In one episode, a boy is fostered into a "strict agnostic" home in which a tyrannical father demands absolute uncertainty. The correct answer to any question is "I don't know," and Dr. Pepper is declared the only proper drink for an agnostic because "nobody's sure what flavor it is."

- The boys seek the origin of Easter traditions, only to learn (in mysterious Da Vinci Code fashion) that St. Peter was actually a rabbit.

- In the midst of the Catholic child sexual abuse scandals, the local priest goes to the Vatican to demand a better response, only to learn that the doctrine of celibacy for priests can't be changed because the document it was written on has been lost.

- A family of Mormons moves to town, and one of the boys is drawn in by their kindness, then repulsed when he learns the Mormon origin story, then convinced that the family's kindness is more important than the odd beliefs of their church.

- After an episode in which Scientology is lampooned — largely through a straightforward description of its beliefs — Isaac Hayes, one of the voice actors for the series who is himself a Scientologist, quit the show.

- One character travels to the future to find that everyone is an atheist. There's no more religious war — instead, the United Atheist Alliance now battles the Unified Atheist League, shouting "Oh my Science!" as they die.

- An episode in which a character in a bear suit is said to be the prophet Muhammad drew death threats from a New York-based Islamic group and was censored by the Comedy Central network — even though the suit opens at the end to reveal not Muhammad inside, but Santa Claus.

Family Guy

Family Guy is the brainchild of Seth MacFarland, another atheist who mines the rich material of religion. In the course of the series, his characters have founded a religion that worships the TV character Fonzi; converted to Hinduism, Mormonism, and Jehovah's Witnesses; and time-traveled to meet Jesus in person. God burns down the local bar while trying to impress a woman by lighting her cigarette with a lightning bolt, and Brian (the dog) identifies as an atheist. In one unusually serious episode, the Christian Scientist parents of a boy with leukemia rely on prayer in lieu of medical treatment, leading two of the main characters to kidnap the boy so he can be treated.

Downloading Disbelief

Some of the best expressions of atheist humor live (like many atheists) online. These sections take a closer look at three examples.

Mr. Deity

After hearing religious leaders try to explain how a loving God could allow the deaths of 230,000 people in the 2004 Indian Ocean tsunami, film director Brian Keith Dalton sketched out a brief satire in which God — played by Dalton as a kind of self-absorbed Hollywood film producer — works with his assistant Larry to figure out what evil would be allowed to exist.

Far from making light of the tragedy, Dalton was asking one of the oldest questions in religious thought, first proposed by Epicurus: God is said to be all-good and all-powerful. Yet evil exists. Either

- ✔ God wants to abolish evil but can't, in which case he's not all-powerful; or

- ✔ He can but doesn't want to, in which case he's not all-good; or

- ✔ He can abolish evil *and* wants to — but then, why is there evil?

The sketch became the script for a short web video, which in turn became the pilot episode of "Mr. Deity," a web series exploring (and lampooning) religion.

Other topics from the first five seasons include the following:

- ✔ Mr. Deity asks Jesus to do him a "really big favor" — go to Earth, live a sinless life, and die in agony.

- ✔ Mr. Deity explains how he handles prayers (by voice mail).

- ✔ Mr. Deity is outraged to learn that humans are attributing the Bible to him, when in fact they entirely left him out of the editorial process, and it makes him look "schizoid."

- ✔ Lucifer (also known as Lucy), the Deity's wife, hires the philosopher Nietzsche to kill Mr. Deity (see Chapter 7).

Dalton was Mormon until his late 20s, and several episodes take particular aim at Mormon theology, including the idea that dark skin is a curse from God. Dalton now identifies as an atheist.

Jesus and Mo

It sounds like the setup for a bad movie — or a really good comic strip. Jesus and Muhammad share an apartment. Once in a while they head downstairs to the Cock and Bull Pub, order a couple of beers from the atheist barmaid, and talk about (and criticize) each other's religions. Moses sometimes tags along.

That's the simply premise of *Jesus and Mo* (www.jesusandmo.net), a webcomic that's been turning out thoughtful and funny religious satire twice a week since 2005. Each of the two main characters sees the flaws in the other's religion, meaning one or the other serves as the voice of reason in a given strip.

When religion itself is satirized, the atheist barmaid is the voice of reason and a kind of Greek chorus for both. And Moses, being a prophet shared by both religions, creates a useful triangle for certain topics.

So how does the cartoonist get away with drawing Muhammad, something that Islam prohibits? It's not Muhammad, he says, but a body double.

Adding a layer to the joke, the atheist barmaid never appears in the frame because, as the website explains, "it is forbidden."

Eternal Earthbound Pets

When the Rapture comes, and Christians are taken up to glory, what will happen to the loving pets they leave behind? That's the question posed by one of the most original religious satires I've ever seen, a website called "Eternal Earthbound Pets" (www.eternal-earthbound-pets.com).

The website claims to be a group of dedicated animal lovers who are also confirmed atheists, meaning they'll still be on Earth after the Rapture leaves Christian pets ownerless. For a nominal fee of $135, Eternal Earthbound Pets guarantees that if the Rapture occurs within ten years of payment, one pet per residence would be cared for after the Christian owner is raptured away.

The "company" confirms that each of their representatives had properly blasphemed in accordance with Mark 3:29, which promises that whoever blasphemes against the Holy Spirit will never be forgiven. That guarantees they will be left behind when Christ returns, leaving them free to provide the needed petsitting.

In case anyone can't decide whether it's serious or satire, the website answers the most important question of all: Is this a joke?

The answer: "Yes."

Chapter 13

Reawakening Passionate Disbelief: Key Works of the 21st Century

In This Chapter

▶ Igniting a rebirth of compelling atheist authors

▶ Blogging disbelief

▶ Living a complete life without gods

Within five years of the destruction of the World Trade Center by Islamic terrorists, four prominent atheist authors published bestselling broadsides against religious belief, ushering in an uncompromising, confrontational movement known as "New Atheism."

This side of atheism in the 21st century — the angry and outspoken side — gets the most attention. But another side exists as well, one less interested in confrontation than in finding common ground with religious people while focusing on secular ways to fulfill the human needs that have usually been addressed through religion. And just as the New Atheists have their books and prominent voices, so do the more humanistic co-existers.

This chapter looks at the prominent works that sparked both New Atheism and the New Humanism that rose in its wake.

Sparking an Atheist Renaissance

Like most eras in the history of atheist thought, books were the catalysts that kicked the 21st century into gear. Several atheist authors poured their passion and intellect into key works that touched off a powerful new movement in the first decade of the new century, bringing religion and atheism back to the center of the cultural conversation.

This section introduces six of those works — two histories that set the stage and four books that articulate a more forceful, uncompromising form of atheism than the West had ever seen before.

Setting the stage: Hecht and Jacoby

When most people think of the authors who launched the atheist renaissance in the 21st century, they think of the "The Four Horsemen" — Richard Dawkins, Sam Harris, Daniel Dennett, and Christopher Hitchens — and their earthshaking bestsellers. They were first called the "Four Horsemen" (an ironic nod to the Four Horsemen of the Apocalypse) after appearing in a filmed discussion of the same name, and each of their books earns a section in this chapter.

But the Four Horsemen weren't the first writers to open the topic of atheism in the 21st century. The following two important histories played a big part in establishing the long, impressive legacy of doubters and freethinkers. They're the giants on whose shoulders modern atheism stands.

Doubt: A History

Written by Jennifer Michael Hecht, *Doubt: A History* (HarperOne) is terrifically readable and smart excursion through the long history of people doubting the religious claims and beliefs of their times.

Hecht wanted to call it *A History of Atheism,* but her publisher balked. It was 2003, before Dawkins and the rest sold millions of books by opening up an unabashed can of New Atheism. The publisher retitled the book, although Hecht said the content was still pretty much the same as it would have been under the title she wanted.

The book starts back in the Indian atheistic philosophy of Cārvāka and comes forward to the 21st century, tracing the development of religious doubt from roots to branches.

Freethinkers: A History of American Secularism

In 2004, another great work of history. *Freethinkers: A History of American Secularism* (Holt) by Susan Jacoby was released, giving a kind of gravitas to the American freethought movement by showing in great historical detail what secularists had long suspected — that atheists, agnostics, and other unorthodox thinkers were present and active in every era and every progressive social movement in the United States, from feminism to abolition to women's voting rights to civil rights.

Jacoby also argues that this important presence has been intentionally erased from history by those individuals who prefer a religious narrative for the national story. That's one of the most striking things about her book — that so many key figures have been forgotten, or their accomplishments downplayed, because of their (ir)religious views.

Jacoby writes with the clear and engaging prose of the best modern historians. Freethinkers weren't merely present in these crucial moments in national history, she says. Far from being incidental, their freethought values played a huge part in coloring those moments and movements.

Urging The End of Faith – Sam Harris

There seems to be one emblematic atheist at a time in the world — one name that springs to mind when someone mentions the word "atheist." In the 1960s and 1970s, it was Madalyn Murray O'Hair (see Chapter 8). In the early 21st century, Richard Dawkins wears the crown. But it wasn't Dawkins's book *The God Delusion* that launched The New Atheism. It was Sam Harris's *The End of Faith* (WW Norton).

In many ways, Harris was an unlikely icebreaker for the new movement. He's an atheist, but he doesn't like the label, because it defines him in terms of religion. He's also a devoted practitioner of Zen meditation and speaks of the value of mystical experiences, things that make some atheists go cross-eyed. But he's equally clear that these pursuits don't have to have anything to do with religion or anything supernatural. In fact, he thinks it's high time we got rid of religion entirely. That's what *The End of Faith* is about.

It's a frankly intolerant book, which immediately makes it a hard sell. Tolerance is one of those things most people have learned to embrace as an unquestioned value. But Harris argues forcefully (and really well) that people don't tolerate everything, and they shouldn't. Violence against innocents, for example, isn't tolerated. So if religion leads to violence against innocents, it shouldn't be tolerated either.

By drawing a straight line between religion and the attacks of September 11 (among many other things, large and small), Harris argues that religion isn't just false but something people can no longer *afford* to tolerate. It belongs to the infancy of humanity, he says, and it needs to be set aside before it does irreparable harm to the planet and the people who live on it.

Harris says he started writing the book during the difficult period following the September 11 attacks, so religious extremism was his first target — but not his last. He's also critical of religious moderates, who he says provide cover for extremists by opposing all criticism of faith.

The book makes a scientific examination of belief itself, arguing that beliefs have inevitable consequences, and that mutually exclusive belief systems lead inevitably to conflict and even violence. The only solution for everyone's sake is to set aside irrational beliefs and speak to each other and make decisions on the basis of rational discourse.

So it starts with Islam, which Harris calls a "cult of death," but it certainly doesn't stop there. Harris argues that Islam's uniquely positioned at this point in history to do the most damage, but he says other religions that refuse to submit to reason and challenge hold the same seeds of destruction.

The book ends with an interesting chapter on spirituality, which Harris argues is independent of religion (see more on this in Chapter 16). In fact, what passes for spirituality in the West is, he says, a sad shadow of the real thing. He believes that real spirituality, achieved through practices including meditation, causes a person's perspective to be "radically transformed," but that people should approach it in rational terms, not in ways distorted by supernatural ideas.

The End of Faith was published in August 2004 and received the PEN/Martha Albrand Award for First Nonfiction in 2005, at which point it hit No. 4 on the New York Times Best Seller List.

Like most truly worthwhile books, readers have found plenty to agree and disagree with in *The End of Faith*. But whatever your perspective, it's hard to deny that it's the product of an astonishing, original mind, and one that has greatly enriched the conversation.

Diagnosing The God Delusion with Richard Dawkins

Biologist Richard Dawkins's *The God Delusion* (Houghton Mifflin Harcourt) brought all the prestige of its author with it when it hit in 2006. Dawkins had been best known as a popularizer of science for the first 25 years of his career, so he was merely famous at this point, not yet infamous. He'd proposed a book critical of religion to his publisher years earlier, but the publisher had discouraged it, fearing Dawkins would distract from his reputation as a science writer. But since September 11, 2001, he'd become ever more vocal in his criticism of, and contempt for, all religion.

When he returned to his publishers with the idea, he found them more receptive — something Dawkins credited to "four years of [President] Bush." A bestseller was born — and with it, some real public infamy.

The level of that infamy is a little surprising to many of his readers, because despite what you may have heard, *The God Delusion* isn't all that contemptuous in tone. It can be direct in its criticism at times, but given its reputation, you'd think it was a frothing rant. Most people who actually have read it agree that it's nothing of the kind. In fact, if I were to rank the books of the Four Horsemen on a Contempt-o-Meter, Dawkins would be third, well behind Hitchens and Harris.

As he correctly points out in the Preface to the paperback edition, the language and tone in the book is much less contemptuous and ranting than, say, your average restaurant review. But because religion has a traditional free pass from direct critique, challenges to religion that are milder than those aimed at somebody's recipe for lobster thermidor are met with howls of protest and fainting spells. That's unfortunate, Dawkins says, because the cooks in those restaurants are real people with real feelings, while blasphemy is a victimless crime.

When he does build up a head of steam, Dawkins's irritation tends to be aimed at televangelists and ayatollahs or at bad ideas themselves more than at the everyday believer. And it isn't just off-the-cuff opinion he offers. At every point, Dawkins supports his claims with arguments and illustrations.

Disagreeing with Dawkins is certainly possible, and many people do. But dismissing his work as an unhinged rant is hard to do after you've read the book. So if you're an intelligent religious person with enough confidence to hear some challenging ideas, you'll probably do just fine reading *The God Delusion.*

The book defines a delusion as a belief held despite clear and compelling evidence against it, and Dawkins puts God in that category. He spells out the reasons it's important to challenge religion:

✔ Because in addition to whatever good it does, religion has also done some serious harm.

✔ Because among the harm has been the active obstruction of the good, including stem cell research, women's rights, sound reproductive policy, civil rights, and science education.

✔ Because religion causes many people to pass their moral decision making to religious authorities and scriptures, which are steeped in Bronze Age ideas.

✔ Because it leads people to be satisfied with not understanding the world.

✔ Because everyone benefits when everyone's decision making is grounded in the same rules of evidence and reason.

He then goes through his own reasons for believing God doesn't exist (many of which are similar to those I include in Chapter 3), the roots of religion, the natural basis for morality, and suggestions for the way forward.

Dawkins writes that he hopes to the book will "raise consciousness" by illustrating four main ideas:

✔ That atheists can be "happy, balanced, moral, and intellectually fulfilled."

✔ That science provides better explanations of the world than religion.

✔ That children shouldn't be labeled by their parents' beliefs, meaning terms like "Catholic child" or "Muslim child" or "atheist child" should sound as strange and inappropriate to our ears as "Marxist child" or "Republican child."

✔ That far from being ashamed, atheists should be proud of their willingness to question religious belief, which is evidence of a healthy, independent mind.

The response to the book has been predictable and focuses mostly on tone. The best thing readers of any perspective can do is read it themselves and decide.

Breaking the Spell with Daniel Dennett

In 2006, a professor of philosophy at Tufts University named Daniel Dennett came out with the most scholarly and measured of the "Horsemen" books. *Breaking the Spell: Religion as a Natural Phenomenon* (Viking) argues that religion is a natural consequence of being human, and that people can and should study religion and the scientific claims it makes.

The middle of the book does just that, using biology and social science to figure out where religion came from and how it evolved into what is today. By the time he gets to the meat — the actual effects of religion in the world — Dennett's done an excellent job preparing the reader for his conclusions that religious people can certainly be moral and have meaningful lives, but that religion itself shouldn't get the credit for that, and can actually get in the way.

Maybe the best way to sum up Dennett's description of religion as a natural human thing is this: Religion is a way of looking at the world that worked really well a hundred thousand years ago when people lived in small, separate tribes and had no better way to understand the world or control their own behavior. But now that those tribes are all knitted together into a big interdependent world of seven billion people — with a lot of things that go seriously bang — people need to take a hard look at the way they think and the things they believe.

And that in the end is Dennett's reasonable proposition — not that any one way of thinking is thrown out, but that everyone agree to the simple notion that all ideas should be open to discussion, and that everyone must work together to find out what's true and what's good.

If you're a religious person who wants to hear from the other side, but having your beliefs forcefully challenged makes you queasy, Dennett is a good start. He has the careful approach of an academic, following up nearly every claim with something like, "Of course I could be wrong," or "More research is needed." In the end, his conclusions are almost identical to Dawkins and Harris, but you may feel less tension in your neck and shoulders.

Arguing that God Is Not Great with Christopher Hitchens

Christopher Hitchens, a British journalist and public intellectual who died in 2011, seemed to have spent every day of his remarkable life absorbing knowledge and handing out opinions. He seemed to have read everything, known everyone, and retained more about the world than three standard lifetimes would allow. Combine that with the fact that he clearly didn't care what anyone thought of him and you get one of the most intelligent, forceful, and unapologetic voices of the past century, not to mention a hugely satisfying read — unless he's slitting the throat of one of your own sacred cows.

Just about every Hitchens reader has had the experience of seeing his own cows gutted, by the way — and not just the religious. I was a staunch opponent of the Iraq War, and Hitchens was a strong supporter of that war. Waving away someone as sharp as Hitchens wasn't easy when he ripped into my own conclusions, so I have some sympathy for religious readers when he goes after their beliefs.

He did have the courage of his convictions. When he claimed that waterboarding (an "enhanced interrogation tactic" by which a subject experiences the sensation of slowly being drowned) wasn't torture, he accepted a challenge to be waterboarded himself. When he ended the experiment in terror after five seconds, he made it clear that he'd been wrong: "If waterboarding does not constitute torture," he said, "then there is no such thing as torture."

Hitchens weighed in on most of the major issues of his times, and his 2007 book *God Is Not Great: How Religion Poisons Everything* (Twelve Books) was his biggest contribution on the topic of religion. His title and subtitle perfectly capture what he meant to say: that God as described in the Bible is a contemptible figure, and that religion poisons everything it touches. It's violent, irrational, and intolerant, he says, supports and defends racism, tribalism, and bigotry, promotes ignorance and is hostile to open questioning, contemptuous of women and coercive toward children. He then provides arguments and anecdotes gathered from his wide-ranging knowledge and experience to support his conclusions.

A typical example from early in the book: When asked by a conservative radio host if Hitchens were alone in an unfamiliar city at night and a group of strangers began to approach him, would he feel safer or less safe knowing that they had just come from a prayer meeting? He replied with personal stories from Belfast, Beirut, Bombay, Belgrade, Bethlehem and Baghdad —"just to stay within the letter B," he said — showing why in each case he would indeed feel threatened if he knew the group of men approaching him were coming from a religious observance.

His course through the topic is unpredictable, which is part of the fun of reading him. He discusses the *fatwa* against Salman Rushdie, weird religious fears of ham, why he thinks the New Testament is even worse than the Old, and whether religion tends to make people behave better. Yet by the end, even though the path has been winding, there's a feeling that he left no stone unturned.

In the end, he answers one of the questions that every critic of religion must answer: Why do you care? Why can't you just allow people to believe as they wish? His answer is that he would happily do so if religion didn't intrude into every aspect of life, from public policy to private morality. If they would only leave me alone, he said, I would gladly return the favor. Because they are incapable of doing this, he said, the battle was joined.

If you're a religious person, and the experience of having your heartfelt beliefs mercilessly challenged by a first-rate intelligence with no manners isn't appealing — you may want to avoid this book. If on the other hand you're looking for the very best from every side of the discussion, and you're willing to absorb some very sharp arrows, then strap in, hold on, and open that cover.

Continuing the Conversation: Great Blogs

The 21st century has seen the rise of several entirely new media. And because so much atheist community takes place online, a discussion of "great works" of atheism in this century can't just stop at books. It has to include a powerful and influential new way of getting thoughts into other heads: the blog.

Hundreds of high-profile blogs explore and express atheism today. This section introduces five blogs that represent the breadth and depth of these voices.

Reflecting intelligently: Greta Christina's Blog

Greta Christina is a San Francisco-based writer whose blog — called simply "Greta Christina's Blog" (freethoughtsblogs.com/greta) — is one of the best, most thoughtful expressions of atheist thought around. Instead of responding to the day's news, Greta tends to write longer reflections on themes and issues in and around atheism. When I want to know what a smart and thoughtful atheist thinks about an issue that I care about, I turn first to Greta Christina.

Her blog is well-informed but not academic, drawing more on her own experiences and insights than anything else. I feel like I'm reading the thoughts of someone who *pays attention,* then reacts intelligently.

That doesn't mean she's always sober and calm. She can also be hilarious, emotional, and profane. One of the common themes in Greta's work is why atheists are often angry about what goes on in culture, and why that anger is justified. She's written a book about it (*Why Are You Atheists So Angry?,* Pitchstone Publishing) and was the main reason I thought of writing the section in Chapter 14 of this book about atheist anger.

If I could read only one atheist blog, it would be Greta Christina's Blog. And for one of the best imaginable introductions to atheism, visit her home page and browse the sidebar titled "Favorite Posts: Atheism." Every post is gold.

Commenting on the current: Friendly Atheist

Hemant Mehta isn't a philosopher or a scientist. He's a 30-ish high school math teacher in Chicago who started writing a popular blog called "Friendly Atheist" (patheos.com/blogs/friendlyatheist) in 2006 — right around the time he sold his soul.

In January 2006, Mehta, who's been an atheist since he was 14, made an offer on the public auction site eBay to attend church one day for every $10 bid by the top bidder and write about the experience in an atheist newsletter he edited.

The winning bid of $504 came from Jim Henderson, a minister in Seattle, who asked Hemant to attend several different churches. Hemant's experience of doing so resulted in national media coverage, the book *I Sold My Soul on eBay* (WaterBrook), and "Friendly Atheist," one of the most popular atheist blogs by every measure.

Friendly Atheist is like the pulse of the freethought community. If something is happening anywhere in the world that has some connection to atheism or humanism, it's a good bet that Hemant will post about it the day it happens — often as many as four to six times a day. The posts tend to be short, smart, and clever, and the comment threads offer a place for atheists to gather and discuss news that impacts their community. A terrific resource and a great read.

Leading the Marines: Pharyngula

Paul Zachary "PZ" Myers is the undisputed heavyweight of the atheist blogosphere. He's a pretty unlikely candidate for the job — in his own words, a "third-rate liberal intellectual at a third-rate university" — but since Myers began holding forth on science and atheism in a big way in 2005, his Pharyngula blog (`freethoughts.com/pharyngula`) has built a massive and devoted following.

Named for a stage of embryonic development, Pharyngula started out with a focus on biology, with special attention to cephalopods — octopuses, squids, and such, Myers's research interest — and became the journal *Nature*'s top-ranked blog by a scientist in 2006. Myers gradually began to address religion more often, especially "intelligent design" theory, and to advocate for atheism and naturalism. Within a couple of years, those topics had become the main focus of the blog.

Pharyngula isn't friendly atheism. If there's one voice in atheism less filtered and less concerned with niceties than Christopher Hitchens, it's Myers. He's known for a brutal willingness to eviscerate those he sees as fools, cutting them off at the knees with stinging contempt and sarcastic wit that takes no prisoners — and that includes fellow atheists, especially those he sees as too soft toward religion.

One famous episode in the blog's history, nicknamed "Crackergate," occurred after a student at the University of Central Florida removed a consecrated communion wafer from a Catholic Mass. The local Catholic community erupted in outrage, including claims that (because Catholics believe the wafer turns into the actual body of Christ when consecrated) he had essentially kidnapped God.

After the student received media attention and multiple death threats, Myers commented on his blog that the wafer the student had removed was after all "just a cracker" and that the reactions were "petty and stupid." Myers then asked his readers to send consecrated wafers to him, promising to "show you sacrilege, gladly" by treating the items with "profound disrespect and heinous cracker abuse, all photographed and presented here on the web."

The Catholic League demanded that the university fire him. The university acted like a university and did nothing of the kind. Myers and his family received countless death threats and hate mail, and the atheist community erupted into its own internal debates about whether Myers had gone too far.

Later than month, Myers posted a photo of his kitchen garbage can. In it was a banana peel, coffee grounds, pages from both the Qur'an and *The God Delusion* — and a consecrated wafer, pierced with a rusty nail. He wrote that nothing must be held sacred, that it's essential to question everything. Though the outrage continued unabated, many others felt that an important point had been made, and that the inclusion of *The God Delusion* — which Myers pointed out was "only paper" — was an inspired decision.

Pharyngula has also been a forceful supporter of women's rights within the freethought movement, speaking in defense of several prominent women who came under attack for their views in 2011 and 2012.

So if you're looking for the most unfiltered possible version of the New Atheism, a voice that makes Christopher Hitchens sound like Shirley Temple watching kittens at play, Pharyngula is it.

Building bridges: Non-Prophet Status

If you want to have all of your preconceptions about atheists and atheism shattered, look no farther than Non-Prophet Status (nonprophetstatus. com), a blog founded by interfaith activist and atheist Chris Stedman and featuring eight outstanding contributors. The blog is described as "a forum for stories promoting atheist-interfaith cooperation that hopes to catalyze a movement in which religious and secular folks not only coexist peacefully but collaborate around shared values."

For a soft-spoken 20-something from the upper Midwest, Stedman has done a lot of world-shaking. He's the Interfaith and Community Service Fellow for the Humanist Chaplaincy at Harvard University, Emeritus Managing Director of State of Formation at the Journal of Inter-Religious Dialogue, and holds an MA in religion from Meadville Lombard Theological School at the University of Chicago.

Chris grew up Christian, and then began to question the church when he came out as gay and felt the sting of judgment from those around him. He eventually decided he didn't believe in God, but he continued to see the benefits religious people got from their involvement in religious communities. His work now is focused on achieving those same benefits for the nonreligious and encouraging bridge-building between worldviews along the way.

The middle isn't an easy place to stand. Stedman takes a lot of grief and abuse from both sides — from the religious for being an atheist, and from atheists for consorting with the religious and for criticizing the New Atheist approach. But Chris also has a lot of supporters on both sides who see tremendous courage, integrity, and restraint in the work he does to build those bridges.

Other blogs and podcasts worth a good look

The Internet is overflowing with other blogs that present an interesting and insightful look into atheism. Here are a few others that I suggest you check out:

✔ **Daylight Atheism:** Adam Lee's smart and thoughtful blog (`bigthink.com/blogs/daylight-atheism`) includes essays rather than reactions to news of the day. It's one of the best voices in atheist opinion.

✔ **Blackfemlens:** Sikivu Hutchinson writes this powerfully provocative blog (`blackfemlens.org`), which is a passionately intelligent voice on the intersection of feminism, atheism, religion, and the black experience in America.

✔ **Dispatches from the Culture Wars:** Journalist Ed Brayton writes this blog (`freethoughtblogs.com/dispatches`). It's intelligent snark from the trenches, delivered three to four times a day.

✔ **American Freethought:** This podcast (`americanfreethought.com`)

features some of the best interviews and commentary in atheism today.

✔ **Freethought Radio and Podcast:** Hosted by former minister and current atheist icon Dan Barker and Annie Laurie Gaylor of the Freedom From Religion Foundation, this program (`ffrf.org/news/radio`) offers up-to-the-minute news and commentary from an atheist perspective.

✔ **Epiphenom:** A personal favorite, this blog (`ephiphenom.fieldofscience.com/`) by British medical writer Tomas Rees looks at the science of religion and nonbelief.

✔ **Butterflies and Wheels:** Another brilliant and thoughtful look at atheism and religion as it happens, written by author and columnist Ophelia Benson (`freethoughtblogs.com/butterfliesandwheels`).

For even more atheist blogsurfing, search online for "Atheist Blogroll."

If you're interested in seeing this kind of conversation and connection between different worldviews, Non-Prophet Status is the place to watch it happen. Check out the later section, "Building bridges with the religious" for more on what Stedman has written.

Providing perspective: Skepchick

Founded in 2005, Skepchick (`skepchick.org`) is the place to go for lively and intelligent blogging from the perspective of skeptical and/or atheist women. Described as "an organization dedicated to promoting skepticism and critical thinking among women around the world," Skepchick is a collaboration of 18 writers, including a PhD in astronomy, a cultural anthropologist, a computational quantum chemist, an attorney, a former Muslim, the director of African Americans for Humanism, an artist, a couple of biologists, a pharmacologist, and an entomologist.

Writing with "intelligence, curiosity, and occasional snark," the contributors tackle topics including science, skepticism, feminism, atheism, secularism, and pseudoscience with writing that is crisp and engaging. Skepchick is one of the great destination blogs in freethought.

Going beyond the Intellectual: The Complete Life without Gods

Letting go of supernatural beliefs is just the beginning of building a secular life. As ever-larger numbers of people walk away from those beliefs, a growing need for resources exploring ways to live a satisfying and complete life without religion exists.

These sections present a number of recent books that go beyond intellectual questions, addressing meaning, spirituality, inspiration, and ethics for the nonreligious.

Getting godlessly spiritual

The title of *The Little Book of Atheist Spirituality* (Viking) by André Comte-Sponville often draws a chuckle. Some see a contradiction in "atheist spirituality," whereas others assume the book is a lightweight, touchy-feely book that substitutes religion with the Age of Aquarius. Fortunately it's much better than that — a thought-provoking, accessible little book that tackles all of those important intangibles that a human being runs into after she's given up the gods.

Comte-Sponville writes with the relaxed confidence of the European atheist he happens to be. For anyone deafened by the culture war, this kind of book is like hearing new music that's refreshing and surprising. The author has advantages, of course — atheism doesn't cause as many fits of the vapors among French philosophers as it does in Alabama. That leaves him freer to think and build instead of reacting and defending quite so much, so he can raise intriguing new questions instead of answering the same tired batch. He thinks about community and loyalty, the ways people stay attached to ideals and committed to each other after faith is gone, and how people think about and react to the death of loved ones without the traditional supports.

He has no interest in attacking religion and the religious. "Humanity is far too weak and life far too difficult for people to go around spitting on each other's faiths," he says. "I loathe fanaticisms of all kinds, including atheistic fanaticism." So he's not looking to de-convert anyone — just to understand and live his own life, and to help others do so. His book is a tolerant atheist perspective much less often heard, and a welcome addition to the 21st century atheist chorus.

"Truth, not faith, is what sets us free," he says at the end of this marvelous little book. "We are already in the kingdom. Eternity is now."

Flipping the idea of holiness

Chet Raymo is a physicist who occupies the challenging middle ground between religion and irreligion. Calling himself a "religious naturalist," Raymo says he "attend[s] to this infinitely mysterious world with reverence, awe, thanksgiving, praise," which he notes are "all religious qualities," but doesn't think there's a supernatural God at the root of it all.

In *When God is Gone, Everything is Holy* (Sorin Books), Raymo suggests that supernatural beliefs put limits on people's experience of what he calls "holiness" — the wonder and mystery of the world — and that letting go of those beliefs can release that quality into the wider world. What was once mundane is now a full part of the mystery — and that includes all of humanity.

As Chris Stedman and others have found, being in that middle ground draws fire from both sides. Raymo's use of words like "holy" and "mystery," as well as his desire to hold on to some of the Catholic perspective of his youth, doesn't sit well with some atheists. But others — especially those who are also in that middle ground, like Unitarian Universalists — find a lot of value and wisdom in Raymo's approach.

Creating a humanist Bible

A few years back, British atheist philosopher A.C. Grayling had an arresting thought: How would world history have been different if the writers of the Bible used Greek and Roman philosophy instead of local religions as their sources? But they didn't so Grayling did. The result is *The Good Book: A Humanist Bible* (Walker & Co.).

Despite the title, Grayling didn't mean for his humanist bible to shove the Bible bible aside. He wanted to create a secular contribution to the age-old conversation humanity has with itself about the good. So he did what the creators of the Bible did — selected texts from a number of different sources, then edited them, wove them together, and added a bit of his own thoughts to make it flow.

But here's the twist: It's not just a collection of excerpts, an approach that's been done a thousand times before. Instead, Grayling put everything into a kind of biblical structure, with chapters and verses, allowing the reader to really imagine that the original may have turned out very differently with different sources. If you know Plato and Aristotle, you'll see their ideas pop up in this or that verse, but without citation. It's a completely different way of experiencing their work, and you get the same kind of narrative flow you get from scriptures. Well worth a look.

Seeking the good without God

In Chapter 9, I introduce the Humanist Community at Harvard University and Greg Epstein, the humanist chaplain who runs it. Both Greg and his organization play a crucial part in global humanism today, and Greg's 2009 book *Good Without God: What A Billion Nonreligious People Do Believe* (William Morrow) is a great contribution to the discussion of human ethics and life without belief in God.

Epstein is a relentlessly energetic and positive guy who's devoted his adult life to studying humanism and putting it into action. If anyone can make the case for that transition from words to actions in a secular context, he's the one. *Good Without God* argues that there's nothing theoretical about the ability of humanists to lead meaningful and compassionate lives — they're already doing it.

Some aspects of Epstein's work and "New Humanism" in general have drawn sharp criticism from within the atheist community, from the idea of a humanist chaplain to participation in interfaith dialogue and cooperation to his criticism of the tactics of New Atheists, both stated and implied.

Good Without God followed several New Atheist books onto the New York Times Best Seller list and has become a useful catch phrase for billboards, organizations, and events promoting this less confrontational form of unbelief.

Building bridges with the religious

Chris Stedman became an evangelical Christian in his teens. But when he came out as gay, and that community turned its back on him, he began to question his beliefs. Eventually he decided he was an atheist.

Change a detail here and there and you have the story of many an atheist. But Stedman's story took a different turn after he left the fold. Instead of diving into his new secular life without a backward glance, or glancing back only to berate, Stedman recognized that not everything he'd lost had been bad. He also became aware that for all of the obvious differences, the religious and nonreligious shared a lot of common ground, more than either side usually saw.

Stedman had become a "faitheist" — a derogatory name some atheists use to describe other atheists who they see as too accommodating toward religion. Eventually he wrote a memoir of his experiences and co-opted the word for his title: *Faitheist: How an Atheist Found Common Ground with the Religious* (Beacon Press).

Unlike many of the other books in this chapter, *Faitheist* isn't a collection of arguments or a work of history. It's a story, specifically a memoir of Stedman's own complicated path through religion and into atheism. He went through the phases so many former believers describe — thinking he could fix Christianity, looking East for another religion, deciding religion was garbage but God was real, and then finally, in an instant, getting rid of God as well.

But as he engaged in the atheist community, he began to feel that something was missing. They had the intellectual side of life managed really well. But he felt that the more emotional, humane side of life, the side that religion had fulfilled for him, received too little attention.

The last chapters of the book describe Stedman's re-engagement with religion — not for its beliefs, which he still rejected, but for what it seemed to know about satisfying human need — as well as his breakthrough work as an atheist in the interfaith movement.

Other recent books that are worth a look

Even a short and painfully incomplete list of recommended books by 21st century atheist authors should include the following:

- *The Portable Atheist* **(Debate Editorial):** Written by Christopher Hitchens, it's an excellent collection of short readings from religious doubters in every era.

- *Infidel* **(Free Press):** Ayaan Hirsi Ali wrote the gripping story of a young woman in an Islamic family who escaped an arranged marriage to become an articulate advocate of atheism and women's rights in the West.

- *Nonbeliever Nation: The Rise of Secular Americans* **(Palgrave Macmillan):** This book, written by David Niose, is a snapshot of the nonreligious in America today, with a smart and potent analysis of what it all means for American culture.

- *Letter to a Christian Nation* **(Knopf):** It's a breathtaking response from Sam Harris to critics of *The End of Faith*, written in the form of a long letter (or a short book).

- *Confessions of a Buddhist Atheist* **(Spiegel & Grau):** A former Tibetan Buddhist monk, Stephen Batchelor, keeps the Buddhism while losing the supernatural beliefs that have grown up around it in the centuries since its founding.

- *Godless: How an Evangelical Preacher Became One of America's Leading Atheists* **(Ulysses):** A 21st century version Jean Meslier, Dan Barker vividly recounts the story of his deep engagement with Christianity as a minister, followed by his loss of belief and subsequent work to fight against the negative effects of religion.

- *The God Virus: How Religion Infects Our Lives and Culture* **(IPC Press):** Darrel Ray takes a scientifically-informed look at how religion acts as a cultural virus, replicating itself from one person or generation to the next.

Part IV
Living a Full Life without Belief in God

The 5th Wave   By Rich Tennant

"We had three exorcisms performed on him, but it turned out he just needed a really good nasal decongestant."

In this part . . .

What's it actually like to be an atheist? How do they think about meaning, ethics, and death? How many nonbelievers are there in the world today, and how is their influence growing? How do the nonreligious get some of the benefits of church without the detriments . . . and without the actual church?

These are all good questions. This part answers these and dozens more. Here you can get a snapshot of atheism today — how disbelief differs by generation, gender, and ethnicity, where atheists live and how they express their beliefs, and just what it's like to be an atheist, meeting the many challenges of being human without a supernatural safety net.

Chapter 14

Getting Personal with Atheism Today

. . . .

In This Chapter

▶ Counting atheists worldwide

▶ Discovering who and where they are

▶ Asking why they are (sometimes) angry

▶ Seeking and celebrating diversity in the movement

. . . .

*I*n addition to grand questions and deep history, there are some simpler questions to answer about atheists — like who they are, what they're like, where and how they live, and just how many we're talking about.

This chapter attempts to get past common misconceptions and ask a few basic questions about atheists to provide a truer picture of people who just happen to think no gods are knocking about. Some of the answers may surprise you. I hope so, because they still surprise me.

Counting Heads: The Growing Nontheistic Presence around the World

Getting a handle on religious nonbelief worldwide is a tricky thing for several reasons:

✔ In most cultures, atheism has a real stigma associated to it. As a result, many nonbelievers don't admit their atheism when asked by a pollster. Many people even make false claims about their own churchgoing behavior. One poll in an Ohio county in the early 1990s counted heads in every church in the county on a given Sunday morning and found 20 percent of the population there. But when they conducted a countywide poll that week to ask whether people had been in church that Sunday, 36 percent said yes!

Asking the question worldwide: Are you religious?

In 2005 and again in 2012, Gallup asked 50,000 people worldwide the following question: "Do you consider yourself a religious person, not a religious person, or a convinced atheist?"

The wording isn't great, because atheists can reasonably choose the second or third choices, and many people would see "convinced" as "certain," which few atheists are (see Chapter 2). Even so, the results are interesting:

✔ In Ireland, those who chose "religious" dropped from 69 percent to 47 percent in seven years — the largest drop in the world.

✔ China had the highest percentage of "convinced atheists" in 2012 at 47 percent. Japan had 31 percent and France 29 percent.

✔ The most religious countries are in Africa, South America, and Eastern Europe.

✔ Though "nonreligious" polls at 20 percent in other surveys, only 1 percent of US respondents in the Gallup poll chose "convinced atheist" in 2005; it rose to 5 percent in 2012 . . . the same as Saudi Arabia.

✔ Atheism has its false negatives. If someone identifies as "Unitarian," he will usually be counted as Christian, even though most Unitarian Universalists are nontheists of one stripe or another. The same goes with Buddhists, most of whom are also nontheistic.

✔ How the questions are asked varies from country to country, year to year, and poll to poll, which makes them difficult to compare. Until recently, many polls of religious belief didn't even include "None" as an option.

So you can get a pretty good idea how many Mormons and Muslims and Methodists exist in the world, but counting nonbelievers is like counting beads of mercury — while wearing plastic mittens — in the rain.

As of 2012, the best estimates put people who don't believe in a supernatural God at around 16 percent of the world's population, or 1.1 billion.

Figuring Out the Who, What, and Where of Atheism

Despite the many uncertainties, a lot is known about atheists, thanks in part to recent efforts to get a clearer picture worldwide. The American Religious Identification Survey (ARIS), the Pew Center surveys, the European Values Survey, and several others have brought that picture into much better focus. The snapshot of atheism around the world, which I discuss in this chapter, is possible in large part because of their work.

The next sections describe how hard it is to find, count, and otherwise learn about atheists — and what some determined people have found when they tried anyway.

Mapping religion and doubt: Atheists hiding in plain sight

Maps showing the different world religions are misleading and don't accurately depict nonbelievers, let alone religions themselves. One color-coded map, titled "World Religions," which is currently available for use in classrooms, charts the religious beliefs held in countries around the world — and each country earns exactly one color.

As a result, it looks like India has nothing but Hindus, which must come as a shock to the 200 million others there. The light blue of Christianity covers 80 percent of the globe, even though just 33 percent of the world's population is actually Christian, and all of those blue countries are home to millions of people with dozens of other worldviews. Islam covers Northern Africa and the Middle East in solid green. China and Southeast Asia are all pink Buddhists. And tiny red Israel marks the only apparent Jews in the world while ignoring the one in four Israelis who aren't Jewish. The indigenous religions of Africa, Asia, and the Americas are all invisible.

It's all much too neat and clean.

The false perception this map creates really matters. To see why, do the same with gender. Use green for countries that are majority male and red for those that are majority female. The resulting solid red Earth gives the impression that no men live on the planet, which I'm almost sure isn't true.

This kind of majority shorthand is a real problem for nonbelievers all over the globe. On this map they don't seem to exist at all. In fact, one in six people on Earth today is a nonbeliever. But the numbers are just the beginning of the story. It's also interesting to see how different all of those nonbelievers are from each other. A lot of that difference comes from their unique histories. In the next section, I mess up the neat colors of the map of world religions by introducing some fascinating national and regional characters in global disbelief.

Disbelieving differently around the world

From a country of atheist Lutherans to a province of atheist Catholics, here are some of the most interesting spots on the globe for religious disbelief.

Scandinavia

Norway, Denmark, and Sweden are three of the four least religious countries on Earth, but you wouldn't know that on the surface. In fact, nearly 80 percent of Norwegians belong to the Lutheran Church of Norway, for example, but 72 percent say they don't believe in God. Only 3 percent attend church more than monthly, and most don't attend at all. Membership has more to do with cultural identity than belief.

Scandinavians tend not so much toward outright atheism as *apatheism,* meaning religion is just off the radar. Sociologist Phil Zuckerman says that when he asks a Swede, Norwegian, or Dane about their religious beliefs, they tend to look perplexed, like someone had asked for the karmic profile of their crown chakra. More than 80 percent said religion is unimportant in their daily lives. And by almost every measure, they're the most ethical, orderly, nonviolent societies in the world. (Refer to Chapter 15 for more on the ethical and orderly Scandinavians.)

Québec

Québec was historically the most religious of the Canadian provinces by a mile (sorry, I mean by 1.609 kilometers). The French permitted only Catholics to settle what was then called New France, so it isn't surprising that as late as the 1960s, 83 percent of the population was still Catholic.

In the early 21st century, Québec is still about 83 percent Catholic — but it's now the *least* religious province by a wide margin. It has the lowest regular church attendance of all provinces (10 percent) and the lowest percent of people who consider themselves religious at all (22 percent, compared to 36 percent for all Canada).

So how do you go from the most religious province to the least religious without losing any Catholics? It's simple. Well no, it's not — these things never are. But it's *interesting.*

Surrounded by English-speaking Protestants, French Canadians are eager to keep their unique identity — and "French" goes with "Catholic" in Canada even more than it does with "fries" in the United States. Yet educated Catholics are among the most likely of all religious identities to quit believing. But in Québec, you can't throw off Catholicism without also throwing off your Frenchness.

So even as they've stopped believing, most Catholic Québécois have remained "cultural Catholics." There's no better proof of the change than a 2002 referendum to switch the provincial school system from Catholic to secular. The referendum passed easily and with very little fuss.

Growing in disbelief: The American picture

The American Religious Identification Survey (ARIS) and the Pew Forum have this to say about the nonreligious ("the Nones") in the United States:

✔ In the 1990s, the nonreligious grew by 1.3 million adults every year.

✔ Nones are now one-fifth of US adults, but a third of those aged 18 to 29.

✔ Though one in five Americans identifies as having no religion, in terms of actual beliefs and behaviors, it's about one in four.

✔ Regarding belief in the supernatural, most Nones are best classified as agnostics or deists (59 percent).

✔ Twenty-four percent of current Nones and 35 percent of first generation Nones are former Catholics.

✔ Disbelief isn't a class thing. Nones are very similar to the general population in terms of education and income.

✔ Most Nones are first generation. Only 32 percent of current Nones report they were nonbelievers at age 12.

✔ Politically, 21 percent of independents are Nones, 16 percent of Democrats, and 8 percent of Republicans.

United States: The Unchurched Belt(s)

Most people know about the Bible Belt. Journalist H.L. Mencken first came up with that description in 1924 for the Southeastern quarter of the United States, a place with about 2.5 Baptist churches per person.

Less well known — and much less catchy — is the Unchurched Belt, a region along the Pacific coast so named in 1985 for having the lowest church attendance and lowest professed belief in the country.

The Unchurched Belt originally included Washington, Oregon, and California, all with 22 to 25 percent nonreligious populations. But by 2000, California had become more religious (mostly because of an increase in the Catholic Hispanic population) while New England became even less religious than it was before. The top US states for nonreligious identity in 2012 are

✔ Vermont (34 percent)

✔ New Hampshire (29 percent)

✔ Wyoming (28 percent)

✔ Alaska (27 percent)

✔ Maine (25 percent)

✔ Washington (25 percent)

✔ Nevada (24 percent)

✔ Oregon (24 percent)

So the "Bible Belt" isn't really any kind of a Belt at the moment. Stuck on opposite ends of the continent, the two relatively secular zones look more like the Unchurched Earring-and-1980s-Mobile-Phone.

Comparing the United States and United Kingdom

On the face of it, the United States and United Kingdom are like siblings. But when it comes to religious culture, they're about as different as they can be:

- ✔ The United States has no state religion, no prayer or Bible study in public schools, and belief in God is really high, around 82 percent.

- ✔ The United Kingdom has a state religion, religious education and prayer services in the schools, and belief in God is really low, around 38 percent.

- ✔ US politicians must wear religion on their sleeves. Presidents often end speeches with "God bless America." When the Democrats didn't include a 2008 platform reference to "God-given potential" in the 2012 platform, a firestorm erupted among conservatives, and Democrats put it in.

- ✔ British politicians almost never make religious references while in office. When Prime Minister Tony Blair suggested ending a speech with "God bless Britain," a firestorm erupted among his advisors, so he took it out.

- ✔ For many years, exactly one member of the US Congress publicly identified as nontheistic (Pete Stark, D-California).

- ✔ At this writing, more than 100 nontheistic members of the British Parliament are members of the All-Party Parliamentary Humanist Group.

In some ways, the differences may not be quite as great as they appear. Though Pete Stark lost his Congressional re-election bid in 2012, a silent poll released by the Secular Coalition for America in the same year found that 28 of the 535 members of Congress didn't believe in a higher power.

Talkin' about My (Kids') Generation

Some things tend to increase as a person gets older — political conservatism, for example, and the willingness to wear socks with sandals. Belief in God and religious identity also tend to increase slightly with age. So when ARIS 2008 showed the "nonreligious" percentage in the United States shrinking as people get older, it wasn't a big surprise. Among respondents who are

- ✔ Age 18 to 29, 22 percent are nonreligious.

- ✔ Age 30 to 49, 17 percent are nonreligious.

- ✔ Age 50 to 69, 13 percent are nonreligious.

- ✔ Age 70 and older, just 7 percent are nonreligious.

An interesting twist: The Millennials — including that 18 to 29 group — have the lowest level of religious identity and belief *even when compared to the other generations when they were that age.* So they're likely to keep a pretty high percent of nonbelievers as they get older.

The more you break down the question, the less traditionally religious these young people are. A 2012 Georgetown study found that only 54 percent believe in a "personal God" — the kind that loves, smites, hears prayers, and forgives (or declines to do so).

A Pew study also shows that the glue of family faith is losing its stick in the younger generation. While just 7 percent of people 65 and older have ever left the faith in which they were raised to become nonreligious, that number rises to 13 percent for people in their 30s and 40s and 18 percent of those currently under 30. That's 18 percent who have already left religion at a pretty young age. These kids are much more willing to choose a worldview for themselves rather than stick with the one they were born into.

The Millennials' disenchantment with religion is less about beliefs than social attitudes. When asked to choose descriptions that reflect what they think of Christianity today,

- ✔ Fifty-eight percent said "hypocritical."
- ✔ Sixty-two percent said "judgmental."
- ✔ Sixty-four percent said "anti-gay."

Those answers include the responses of Millennials who are Christians. The nonreligious were even higher in these negative responses.

These results don't mean the young Nones are all flocking to organized freethought. Some are, but many in the Millennial Generation are either turned off by the atmosphere of culture war or haven't been motivated by their own experiences to connect with a worldview in any formal way. A lot of them see their nontheism as a more incidental part of who they are than older atheists do.

This more passive atheism drives a lot of older atheists crazy. But the passivity isn't all bad, because it partly results from progress the older generation has made in normalizing the worldview.

Those atheists working for even further progress sometimes forget how much better things are now for nontheists than just a generation ago. In addition to greater numbers and higher visibility, bestselling books and high-profile blogs are now available articulating the atheist worldview, as well as a thriving, connected, international community. Yes, nontheists still have plenty of reason for concern (see the next section), but the situation is improving.

Symbolizing atheism and humanism

Having a symbol is useful for a worldview. Muslims have the star and crescent, Jews have the Star of David, and Christians have the cross. So what symbol do atheists and humanists have?

For a long time nothing represented atheism or humanism as global movements. That's partly because consensus on *anything,* especially something like a shared symbol, is hard to come by among freethinkers, for reasons contained in that very word. Before nontheists even get close to arguing over various designs, we'll generally spend a year or two arguing whether we should even *have* a symbol — which is why no one has to worry too much about atheists taking over the world.

In 1965, with the international Humanist movement taking off in a big way, the British Humanist Association hosted a competition to create a symbol. (They like the capital H on Humanism, so I'll do that here.) The winning entry (see the following figure), submitted by London artist Dennis Barrington, was a letter "H" with a large black dot above the crossbar, like the head of a person with arms raised. Clever and concise, it's been the go-to symbol of humanism, and Humanism, ever since.

Atheism also gained a couple of symbols in recent years. A contest in 2008 resulted in a protracted debate over whether there should even *be* a symbol; then some good jokes (my favorite suggested we just adopt the @ sign,

so every e-mail would identify the sender as an atheist); and finally some nice, thoughtful entries.

The winner, designed by Michigan graphic artist and retired schoolteacher Diane Reed, has a bit of a Star Trek vibe — not a negative with this crowd — with a sharp letter "A" wrapped in a circle representing the natural universe. Attractive, positive, and jewelry-friendly.

Perhaps my favorite for sheer cleverness is the symbol for the "Out Campaign," an effort by the Richard Dawkins Foundation to encourage atheists to help improve the public image of atheism by coming out of the closet. Displaying the symbol itself on clothing or jewelry or in social media and explaining what it means when asked has become one low-key way to come out. The symbol is an italic capital "A" in scarlet red (offered here in black to save you a few bucks — you're welcome). It's a clever reference to the letter "A" worn by Hester Prynne in Nathaniel Hawthorne's *The Scarlet Letter* to mark her as an adulteress, but now worn by atheists as an unashamed symbol of an unfairly maligned worldview.

It may seem ironic that creating a better culture and community for younger nontheists makes it easier for them to decline to join it, but that's the way cultural movements work. Ask a feminist who fought for better treatment of women through the 1960s and '70s, only to have her own daughter grow up so far removed from the struggle that she takes the progress for granted and asks her mom, "Why is it *always* about gender with you?" Same with racial progress, sexual orientation, and countless others. Maddening as it is to the veterans of each movement, it's actually a sign of progress when our kids can roll their eyes at us.

Answering the Question: "Why Are Atheists So Angry?"

Things are much better for atheists than they were a while ago. If that's the case, why are atheists so angry? I hear this question quite a bit. But despite high-profile court cases and protests when religion pokes its nose where it shouldn't be, not all atheists are angry.

Even those atheists who are (rightfully) angry about discrimination and ignorance aren't angry most of the time. Greta Christina, one of the great atheist bloggers and the main source for this section, notes that she's usually quite cheerful, that her life is full of joy and pleasure, and that she's conscious of how fortunate she is. Same with me and with most atheists I know.

Greta continues by saying that some things are indeed worth being angry about, and that anger over injustice and mistreatment of anyone is valid, moral, useful, and necessary. Right again. You and I may or may not agree about what counts as injustice, but I'm sure you'll agree that injustice is worth getting angry about.

To illustrate this, allow me to describe some issues around the attacks of September 11, 2001, a day that galvanized the freethought movement in several ways. The attacks were every bit as heartbreaking and terrifying for atheists as for religious people. But a few elements added a unique pinch to the pain and rage felt by those who don't believe in God.

Try to put yourself in the shoes of a nonbeliever — someone who is dedicated to being a good, honest, productive person, who was equally devastated by that terrible day, but who doesn't believe in God. From that perspective, consider the following:

✔ Religious extremism played an essential role in the motivation and the execution of the attack.

✔ The media hastily downplayed the role of religion.

- ✔ The response to a religiously motivated attack was a national call for prayer.

- ✔ The president claimed that he was doing God's will by launching two wars in response, including one on a country with no connection to the attack.

- ✔ Prominent televangelist Jerry Falwell said the attack was God's wrath for those who tried to "secularize America," including feminists, gays and lesbians, and organizations working to secure the constitutional rights of all Americans.

- ✔ The speeches and ceremonies commemorating the tragedy included religious language and symbols — including a Christian "cross" from the wreckage — without ever acknowledging that hundreds of those who died were nonreligious.

- ✔ Some subsequently used the tragedy to stir up hatred toward Muslims generally, including the controversy over a proposed, entirely peaceful Islamic community center several blocks away from the site.

- ✔ For some time, patriotism and Christian religious belief became intertwined like never before.

Even as I write that list, I'm tugged between emotions that are very common for atheists. First, the pain and outrage I felt all those years ago well back into my heart, including the parts that colored it differently for me as a nonbeliever. But the second major emotion is a feeling that I ought to *pull back,* that I shouldn't let my anger show. Then I remember that there are things to be angry about, and indifference in the face of injustice can be frankly immoral.

Here's a greatly abbreviated list of other things that bring out the hurt and anger of many atheists:

- ✔ Several polls show that atheists, despite an extremely low incidence of violence and incarceration (see the nearby sidebar), are the most mistrusted minority in the United States. Most people say they would rather have just about anyone else dating their daughter or serving as President.

- ✔ Atheists routinely and without justification are accused of being immoral *because* they aren't believers in any gods (See Chapter 15 for more on atheism and morality)

- ✔ Atheists in the military and children in public schools are sometimes required to engage in religious rituals or prayers, are proselytized, or are punished or ostracized for not belonging to the religious majority.

- ✔ Seven US states still prohibit atheists from running for public office — something unthinkable for any other worldview. If any state prohibited Jews from running for office, it would and should be a national outrage quickly corrected.

✔ Entire organizations, buckets of scarce resources, and continuous lawsuits are required to keep creationism and other religious ideas out of public school science classrooms and in the hands of families and churches where they belong.

✔ Religious concepts such as "life begins at conception" have derailed important and humane public policy, including stem cell research and sensible reproductive rights.

✔ The Catholic Church, by its opposition to sensible birth control, has unleashed a humanitarian catastrophe on developing countries.

✔ Many children are abused with the idea that God would punish them eternally for honest doubts or very normal human thoughts.

✔ Countless thousands of children have been sexually exploited by generations of priests abusing their trust and authority.

✔ Sexuality, one of the most beautiful and enjoyable parts of being human, is often depicted by religion as shameful. Estimating the emotional damage done to generations of believing teens by some religious attitudes toward the natural and harmless practice of masturbation, for example, is hard.

✔ Though many religious people and institutions have worked hard on the right side of social issues, traditional religious ideas have often formed the greatest obstacles to moral and social progress, including the abolition of slavery, women's voting rights, sensible reproductive rights, gay equality, and countless others.

✔ Many individual atheists have been shunned and disowned by their religious families.

✔ Many people believe religious ideas should be granted special protection from challenge simply because they're religious.

Again, this list is seriously abbreviated. Hopefully it's enough to show that atheists aren't angry just for the sake of it, or for imagined slights, or for merely feeling "offended." There are real injustices at work here.

Opening Up the Freethought Movement

For most of the history of the organized freethought movement, atheists have tended toward a particular type. If police were profiling atheists 20 years ago, for example, they may have been told to watch for

✔ A white male in his 60s or 70s

✔ Scientifically oriented, well-read, well-educated

✔ Grey-to-white hair and beard

✔ Driving a mid-sized vehicle with multiple incendiary bumper stickers

Officers would have been cautioned to expect an argument — suspect may be armed with syllogisms. Aside from the car, they'd have essentially been looking for Socrates.

I doubt too many bulletins like that were ever issued, because these guys also tended not to rob gas stations. If you walked into any freethought meeting in the late 20th century, you'd have mostly seen this guy standing around in small groups talking to others very much like him about biblical contradictions, something silly the Pope said, or the latest discovery in particle physics. And though both women and men are atheists of this kind, most of these folks have been men.

I call this classic, lecture-and-debate-minded atheist Harry.

I love Harry. Harry has been the backbone of organized freethought for most of its history. But another kind of nonbeliever also exists. It's not that they aren't intellectual, but they're not interested in talking quite so exclusively about science and philosophy. They're looking to create community, connect with others, and work for social justice and the common good. And though both women and men are atheists of both kinds, this more socially and community-oriented atheist tends more often to be a woman.

I call this more community-oriented nonbeliever Sally.

The following sections explore the role of gender in the atheist and humanist community and digs a little further into this Harry-and-Sally distinction.

Speaking of gender

The gender divide in the freethought movement isn't imaginary. ARIS shows women are much more likely than men to be religious and to stay religious. Even if they were raised without religion, they're less likely to *stay* nonreligious than men who were raised that way. So it isn't too surprising that (with important exception) men have dominated the organized secular movement.

Making generalizations about gender is always a risky business. Remember that plenty of men and women are on both sides of this Harry/Sally fence. Madalyn Murray O'Hair (see Chapter 8) was a classic Harry, for example, and there have been several other prominent women in leadership positions who fit the same description. On the other side, Greg Epstein (refer to Chapter 13) and Sherwin Wine (see Chapter 8) are both Sallys, and I have a lot of Sally in myself as well. But both gender and the Harry/Sally difference have become important factors in organized atheism today. And because this chapter is about atheism today, in I wade.

The gender balance in organized atheism is getting better, but slowly. Susan Jacoby, a great historian of the secular movement, estimates that her audiences have gone from about 90 percent male a decade ago to about 75 percent male in 2012. It should improve more quickly now, because the split is more even for atheists under 30.

Honoring Harry — the "classic" atheists, and what they built

People who fit the profile of Harry — science-minded, often (not always) white, and often (not always) male — created today's organized freethought movement. They were able to do so because they didn't have the same social and emotional needs as many others — needs the church often satisfies. That's why they were able to walk out of those church doors and build this brand new thing around science, reason, and ideas instead of community and emotion.

It makes sense that the Harrys built a movement nothing like the churches they'd just walked away from. Many of them had been wounded by religion, so they wanted nothing that looked or felt anything like it. Harrys also tend to be proudly individualistic and even solitary. A word like "community" can make them nauseous, and getting together in a room to sing about love and brotherhood is somewhere around a tax audit on their list of dreaded tortures. In fact, they often go to great lengths to separate themselves from anything that feels too much like religion, preferring to exchange rational ideas while working to keep religion out of politics and public life.

When polls in the early 2000s began suggesting that 40 million Americans were nonreligious, some of the Harrys began looking around the room at their meetings and wondering where the other 39.8 million people were. Some shrugged and said "Nonbelievers just aren't joiners." Harrys are nonjoiners, but not all nonbelievers are.

Seeing Sally — the "community" atheists, and what they need

In recent years, many atheists and humanists have begun to feel that the freethought movement was built too narrowly, serving only those who were already in it, and they started looking for ways to open the doors more widely for atheists different from themselves — the "Sallys."

Whether male or female, Sallys don't believe in God any more than the Harrys do. The Sallys of the 20th-century freethought movement felt as if their needs weren't being met. Sallys are every bit as intelligent and committed, but the Sallys didn't find the freethought movement that Harrys built appealing, so they often stayed in communities, usually progressive churches, built to serve those needs. They weren't there for the theology, just for the community, which makes them a lot like most of the believers sitting in the pews around them. (Check out Chapter 18 for more discussion.)

Sallys are more interested in working for social justice than talking about contradictions in the Bible. They see tremendous value in having a supportive community around them and in joining with others to work for a better world. At some point, many Sallys become deeply conflicted about staying in a church community, especially if they feel the doctrines of that church are opposed to the very values of openness and tolerance they want to promote. But when they look at organized atheist and humanist groups, they often see too little community and too little compassionate action.

Many in the freethought movement have seen the problem and feel that it's high time to start meeting the needs of nonbelievers beyond the traditional lecture-and-debate Harry types, including this community-seeking doer of good deeds. And though both genders are involved, it's no surprise that many of the leaders of this new effort to refocus atheist attention are women. One recent example is "Atheism+," a label that says, "I'm an atheist, *plus* I care about social justice and equality and inclusiveness." Atheists have always cared about these compassionate issues, but this new effort seeks to place them closer to the front and center of attention and action. (For more on A+, see Chapter 2.)

Considering race and ethnicity

The gender balance isn't the only thing that's shifting in the atheist landscape; in recent years, the movement has also gained a much greater presence of nonwhite nonbelievers.

Religion has never just been about beliefs. It's also about community and identity and a whole lot more. This is especially true in racial or cultural minority communities. The French-speaking Québecois I mention earlier in this chapter are a prime example, their Catholicism wrapped up so tightly with their Frenchness that it ends up having literally nothing to do with beliefs. Many of those Québec Catholics who no longer believe in God keep calling themselves Catholic so they don't disappear into the Protestant English speakers around them.

The same is true in communities of color surrounded by white majorities. African American atheists like Sikivu Hutchinson and Norm Allen have written powerfully about the especially strong, angry reaction they get from others in the black community when they identify as atheists, as if they're renouncing not just God but their race and community as well. Ditto for Latinos, for whom Catholicism is often a big part of cultural identity.

Despite those challenges, the landscape is shifting. In 1990, just 6 percent of African Americans identified as nonreligious. By 2008, that number had nearly doubled to 11 percent. You can also see the shifting landscape among the nonreligious overall:

- ✔ In 1990, nonreligious Americans were 80 percent white, 10 percent black, and 4 percent Hispanic
- ✔ By 2008, nonreligious Americans were 72 percent white, 8 percent black, and 12 percent Hispanic

In other words, the general population is looking more nonreligious, and the nonreligious are looking more like the general population.

Like the presence of more women, the greater presence in recent years of African Americans, Hispanics, and other nonbelievers of color in organized atheism and humanism is another force increasing the focus on social justice and humanitarian work among atheists and humanists.

Creating a Satisfying Community for Nonbelievers of Every Stripe

As the human landscape of freethought changes, the focus of the freethought community changes as well. The greater presence of women, young people, families, and people of color is expanding the agenda of the nonreligious community and changing the very picture of who atheists are and what they do.

In addition to the traditional program of monthly meetings and discussions, the freethought movement is placing a greater emphasis on volunteering, social activities, social justice and human rights activism, family programming (including childcare and babysitting coops), and mutual support in times of need.

At the higher levels, atheists and humanists are asserting a stronger voice in social and political issues. National organizations like the Secular Coalition for America provide a unified voice with lobbyists and information campaigns on issues of importance to the nontheistic community. Experiments like the Humanist Community Project at Harvard University are helping nontheists build, grow, and improve mutually supportive freethinking communities that attend to the very human needs that churches have addressed for centuries — but without the need to claim belief in a God.

No social movement goes through changes this profound without internal struggles, and the freethought movement is no exception. Some atheists prefer the traditional movement focus of challenging religion and encouraging a secular society and worry that they'll be shoved to the side. New movements like the social justice–oriented Atheism+ has brought some of these worries to the surface.

More than one person has observed that "we're behaving like a bunch of Protestants," splitting and arguing and pretty much excommunicating each other. (I joke about the excommunicating. I think.)

Similar struggles happened as the civil rights, women's rights, and gay rights movements gradually came into their own. Call it growing pains. Getting everyone pulling together is easiest when you're all storming the castle together. But after the goal begins to take shape around you, people within a movement are bound to fight amongst themselves about what to do after they get inside. When passionate people with different visions collide, it isn't always pretty. Think of Martin Luther King, Jr. and Malcolm X — two people devoted to civil rights for African Americans, but with very different visions of how to get there. Though the challenges of nonbelievers don't nearly rise to the struggles of African Americans in the 1960s, there's no reason this movement should be immune to some of the difficulties that theirs endured.

Other efforts have focused on creating a more comfortable landing place for closeted atheists and others who share the worldview but haven't embraced the identity. The Brights Network is an effort to offer a positive label for a naturalistic worldview using the noun "Bright" (as in "I am a Bright"). Billboard campaigns with simple text such as "Don't believe in God? You are not alone" and the "Out Campaign" of the Richard Dawkins Foundation have invited atheists to help improve the public perception of atheism by letting those people who love them know that they're atheists.

Like earlier movements, the freethought movement is likely to come through this growing process best if it's responsive not only to the traditional atheist, but to the needs of nonbelievers of every kind. And every indication suggests that it's headed that way — just not along a straight line.

Taking a Quick Look at Issues around the World

As atheists in the United States grapple with gender, race, and privilege, church-state separation, and a greater focus on social justice, atheists in other countries have their own concerns — sometimes similar, and sometimes quite different. As I write this:

- Atheists in Egypt and Indonesia are in prison on charges of blasphemy.

- The International Humanist and Ethical Union is urging the repeal of Pakistan's blasphemy laws after mob violence against Christians and the assassination of two politicians who supported the repeal.

- After rescuing three kidnapped children accused of witchcraft in Ghana and being beaten and arrested in the process, Nigerian humanist Leo Igwe is now conducting a field investigation of "witch camps" holding thousands of women against their will in Northern Ghana.

- Atheists in Ireland continue to challenge a blasphemy law there by posting online quotations critical of religion.

- British humanists are working to keep creationism out of science classrooms and to oppose special protection for religion in politics.

- Humanist organizations in Ghana and Uganda are fighting antigay legislation that's backed by religious and political organizations.

- The Atheist Centre in India continues its decades-long struggle against the caste system.

In some cases, atheists and humanists are alone in these efforts, or even fighting religious resistance to change. But in a growing number of cases, they're finding common cause with progressive religious groups, working together on these key issues. The future is likely to have even more of these alliances between religious and nonreligious people of goodwill who share the same goals and human values.

Chapter 15

Being Good with or without God

*M*illions of people around the world are walking away from religion every year. In Chapter 14, I describe how fast church attendance is dropping and religious belief is plummeting in dozens of countries. A billion people now walk the Earth without a single god in their heads.

If it were true that people need religious belief in order to behave themselves, all this secularizing would add up to a moral emergency. But be not afraid, for this chapter brings good news! Religion can be the source of moral principles, but religion is no more necessary to being a moral person than a high-fiber diet. As moral development researcher Larry Nucci puts it, people's understanding of morality around the world is very much the same whether they're of "one religion, another religion, or no religion at all."

That's good news all right — but it does make the work of understanding morality a little more challenging. You can't just ask one question and figure out whether someone is likely to behave well. But whatever is true has always been true, and it's better for people to really understand this crucial bit of human life than to only think they understand.

More reasons to be optimistic about human morality exist than we usually recognize, and there are just as many reasons not to worry about the growing presence of atheists, agnostics, and humanists in today's culture. When it comes to being and doing good, atheists are more like their religious friends and neighbors — for better and worse — than either group often thinks.

By showing that people can be good with or without God, this chapter can make people less afraid of each other, and even of themselves. So a defense of morality without religion ends up really being a defense of human nature itself. That's what most of this chapter is about: not atheist morality, but plain old natural human morality. Take a look at the research and focus the lens a bit better, and it turns out, surprisingly, that humans aren't so bad after all.

Defining Morality

What is morality? What does it mean to be a moral person? The first question seems easy enough: *Morality* is about distinguishing between good and bad, or right and wrong. But that's where it starts to get complicated, because people don't always agree on what's right and wrong.

Some people decide whether something is right based on a holy book or by a person in authority. Atheists (and many believers as well) see a problem with this approach. Because the various holy books and authorities say different things, having discussions about right and wrong is more difficult than it should be. And if a scripture instructs followers to harm others, people outside of that book's influence should be permitted to say it's a bad source of moral guidance.

(Not that any holy book would do that, of course. Ahem.)

The same is true for authority. I shouldn't consider something good just because someone else, even a greatly admired person, suggested it, without also thinking independently about whether it makes sense. (See the nearby sidebar for one psychologist's work in the way individuals define morality.)

For a chapter on morality without God, using a definition from an atheist makes sense. Neuroscientist Sam Harris says that morality is concerned with "the well-being of conscious creatures." If something contributes to that well-being, it's moral. If it detracts from it, it's immoral.

Not all atheists agree with that definition — but that's par for the course. For my purposes here, think of morality as an effort to strive as much as possible for the well-being of conscious creatures.

Figuring out how individuals define morality

Psychologist Jonathan Haidt has done fascinating work on personal definitions of morality. He identified five moral "foundations":

- ✔ Fairness
- ✔ Avoiding harm
- ✔ Loyalty
- ✔ Purity
- ✔ Authority

He then ran a survey to see where people place the most importance. Some think an act is immoral if it's somehow impure. Some think an act of disloyalty is a very big deal morally. Others are concerned with fairness or whether something harms people, whereas some think challenging authority is immoral. Most people are some combination of these, with more or less weight in each category.

One really interesting result: Haidt found that political liberals care most about fairness and avoiding harm, and a lot less about loyalty, purity, and authority. In other words, liberals (and most atheists) don't usually think a sex act is immoral because it isn't the standard, "pure" version, and they don't think there's anything wrong with challenging an authority figure.

But they're very concerned when someone is harmed or treated unfairly.

Political conservatives are more concerned about loyalty, purity, and authority than liberals and less concerned about fairness and avoiding harm. Still concerned, of course, but less so.

Being Good without a Belief in God

The idea that concepts of right and wrong have to come from a supernatural source is as old as sin. In the Genesis story, Adam and Eve were expelled from the garden for eating fruit they were told not to eat. Don't forget that the fruit was from the tree of the knowledge of good and evil. And the problem wasn't the fruit itself so much as the act of disobedience.

At the heart of this fascinating story is the idea that only God *can* know the difference between right and wrong. Morality is said to be a complete mystery to humanity, so all humans can do is follow his instructions. And when Adam and Eve failed to do that, they put the whole moral universe at risk.

So when I claim that people can know right from wrong without God's help, I know I'm yanking at some very deep roots. And when I say people can even *be* good without God, it's time to explain just how that works. Read on.

Why bother being good at all?

After I gave a talk several years ago, an audience member introduced himself as a Christian with a Bible-based morality. Without the guidance of God and the Bible, he said, he wouldn't have any way of knowing right from wrong, much less any reason to be good.

I could have gone many ways with this. I could have asked why he hadn't cut his hair the way the Bible says to, for example (Leviticus 19:27). But that's a parlor game, and I could tell he was serious.

I could also tell that he was a decent guy, and I didn't believe for a minute that his decency would evaporate if he suddenly learned there was no God. I believed he would still know right from wrong and would still have plenty of reasons to be good. The same ones I have, in fact. But rather than lecture him, I figured I'd get him to tell me what those reasons are himself. So I shrugged and asked, "Why should I even *care* about being good?"

His eyes widened. "Why should you even *care?* Because society would fall apart without morality! Relationships would be impossible without trust. If everyone were free to do as he pleased, it would be hell on Earth! You'd have to be looking over your shoulder all the time."

Then he smiled. "And even if you don't believe in God's judgment, you'd probably spend your life in jail for your crimes."

I nodded. "A great list. You just described all the reasons I'm good, and you did it without needing the Bible or God."

He looked mad for a second, then sheepish, like he'd fallen for a trick. But it wasn't a trick at all — just a simple demonstration that everyone, even those who find the Bible a useful source of moral guidance, can also find *reasons* to be good. For example:

- ✔ I know what it feels like to be harmed or cheated or lied to, so I empathize with others and try not to harm, cheat, or lie to them.
- ✔ When my empathy is overwhelmed by my own selfishness or greed, I get real human consequences from those around me.
- ✔ Like most people, I want to be liked and respected by those around me, not held in contempt.
- ✔ I don't want to be looking over my shoulder to see if those I've hurt are coming after me. If I treat people well, I can relax.
- ✔ The cooperation and goodwill of those people around me makes my life easier.
- ✔ I have self-respect, which is based in part on how I treat others.
- ✔ I don't want to be punished for breaking the rules of the society in which I live.
- ✔ I can't really ask others to behave morally if I don't behave morally myself.

This list can go on for pages. Some reasons are lofty and some are down to earth. Some may also be in the Bible, but they don't rely on scripture or God — they simply make sense. I can figure them out. In fact, moral development experts say most people figure out the ethical principles that make for a moral life not from books or teachers but through their own interactions with others — on the playground, on sports teams, in their families, and in other social groups — before they're out of elementary school.

These principles don't guarantee my good behavior, but neither does any religious doctrine. In both cases, whenever a person loses his or her moral sense, plenty of other people and social institutions are willing to straighten that person out. Everyone makes moral decisions large and small a hundred times a day. And when those decisions are made well, everyone benefits.

Chucking Stalin and the Inquisition — and getting serious about morality

Neither religious belief nor religious disbelief is a guarantee of good behavior. Incentives like greed, power, anger, resentment, fear, or desperation can overwhelm the moral incentives listed earlier in the previous section, which can make an atheist *or* a believer behave badly.

Still, plenty of people in both camps spend an enormous amount of energy trying to paint the other side as immoral by using the bad behavior of famous monsters — dictators or criminals drunk on greed, power, anger, and all the rest — as an indictment of everyone who shares the monster's religious (or nonreligious) label.

But using the horrendous acts of Grand Inquisitor Torquemada, or Adolf Hitler, or Fred Phelps to draw conclusions about the average Ned Flanders Christian is a stretch. Likewise, thinking that Idi Amin or Osama bin Laden are any reflection on the moral character of my Muslim neighbors ignores all the other variables that made the famous monsters what they were.

The same applies to Joseph Stalin, Mao Zedong, and other atheists with immoral behavior to answer for. Like the religious villains, their actions say more about unchecked power than about their opinions of gods. And drawing conclusions about what it means to be an everyday atheist from Stalin is as silly as doubting the ethics of a passing Quaker because Torquemada lost his moral compass.

This brings me to a moral point worth noting. People of all worldviews should be judged on the moral standards they actually live by and endorse. Most Christians today think burning people at the stake is a bad idea, and most are outraged when Pastor Fred Phelps and members of his Westboro Baptist Church picket soldiers' funerals with signs claiming to know that God hates gays. Few Muslims embrace the ethics of Idi Amin or Osama bin Laden. And most atheists think Stalin was an immoral criminal. Those opinions matter more than the labels they happen to share.

If someone does endorse the violence and hatred that made these monsters infamous — now *that's* something worth objecting to. But as I argue in "Framing the question right" later in this chapter, the rest of the people in a given worldview should get credit for showing a lot more human decency.

Being good without God — a quick history

Most atheists will readily admit that a lot of religious believers are good people. From Martin Luther King, Jr. to the Dalai Lama to Mr. Rogers to my dear, sweet mother-in-law, I have no trouble coming up with countless examples of people who do their religion proud.

But many religious people to think that nonbelievers simply can't be moral people. This idea found its way into a good number of the sermons I heard in 25 years as a churchgoing nonbeliever. Not all religious people think it, of course, but many have, and many do, and that misconception has caused a good deal of personal pain among atheists and other nonbelievers.

When the philosopher Pierre Bayle said in 1681 that an atheist could be just as virtuous as a Christian, and that there's no reason atheists couldn't form a moral society of their own, Christian Europe fell off its chair. He eventually lost his teaching job in the Netherlands for saying such things.

Funny thing, though: Three centuries later, the Netherlands is majority nontheistic. And Bayle was right — it's one of the most peaceful, orderly, nonviolent societies on Earth. (More on that shortly in "The Scandinavians" section.)

But the misconception that atheists can't be good is a persistent one. So before I turn to how morality works without supernatural religion, I want to offer a few cameos from the history of goodness without God. (See Chapter 4 for a deeper discussion of these three.)

The Confucians

Confucianism is a philosophy that's all about ethics, self-improvement, virtue, altruism, and compassionate action — and all without appealing to gods for help or clarification. Confucius articulated the earliest known version of the Golden Rule: "What you do not wish for yourself, do not do to others." Check out Chapter 4 for more on Confucianism.

Epicureans

The philosopher Epicurus and his followers in ancient Greece, most of whom were atheist, agnostic, or deistic, were among the first to talk about justice as a social contract between people — an agreement not to do harm to each other.

The Jains

Jainism is a nontheistic religion centered on peace and nonviolence. Jains have been at the forefront of social and moral issues in India for centuries, all without reference to gods. Refer to Chapter 4 for additional insight into the Jains.

The Reformers

Atheists and agnostics have done courageous work on major moral issues of their times, such as

- ✔ Pioneers of women's rights including Susan B. Anthony, Matilda Joslyn Gage, Elizabeth Cady Stanton, Simone de Beauvoir, and Gloria Steinem

- ✔ Slavery abolitionists including Frances Wright, Ernestine Rose, Frederick Douglass, and Lydia Maria Child

- ✔ Advocates of social equality, prison reform, and fair labor practices including Jeremy Bentham, Robert Owen, J.S. Mill, Felix Adler, Emma Goldman, Gora, and Jane Addams

- ✔ Advocates of reproductive rights including Margaret Sanger and Katha Pollitt

- ✔ Protestors against war and militarism including Bertrand Russell, Kate Hudson, Jane Addams, Noam Chomsky, and Aldous Huxley

(See Chapters 7 and 8 for more on these reformers.)

Moral society without God — the Scandinavians

One of the clearest arguments that people can be deeply good without believing in God is happening right now in the Scandinavian countries — Denmark, Norway, and Sweden. By nearly every measure, these societies are some of the least religious in human history. Between 65 and 78 percent of the population expresses no belief in God, and regular church attendance hovers around 3 to 5 percent.

But instead of teeming with depravity and violence, sociologist Phil Zuckerman notes that these countries are "moral, stable, humane, and deeply good." They top the world in nearly every marker of a civilized society, including low crime rates, high literacy, low unemployment, and some of the highest GDPs per capita on Earth.

And when it comes to generosity, the Scandinavians make up three of the top four countries in aid per capita given to poor countries. The (highly religious) United States does all right, giving $97 per person to developing countries in 2010. But secular Sweden gave $483 per person, doubting Denmark gave $517, and nonreligious Norway gave an incredible $936 for every man, woman, and child in their country to struggling nations — nearly ten times the level of the United States. A pretty moving and impressive commitment to moral values, I'd say, all from countries with very little religious belief.

The compassionate humanists

Nontheists have always been generous people. But in recent years an effort has evolved to specifically organize giving and volunteering around the values of that worldview, including mutual care and responsibility. If humanity wants a better world with less suffering and more justice, and there's no supernatural power to make it happen — well, then it's up to humans.

Several major nontheistic groups launched disaster relief efforts after the 2004 Indian Ocean tsunami, including SHARE (by the Council for Secular Humanism) Non-Believers Giving Aid (by the Richard Dawkins Foundation), and Humanist Charities (by the American Humanist Association).

In 2010, a humanist membership organization called Foundation Beyond Belief was created to focus and encourage generosity in the nontheistic community. (Full disclosure: I'm the executive director.) As of late 2012, the atheist and humanist members of the Foundation have raised more than $750,000 for charities around the world and created a network of humanist volunteer teams in 23 cities across the United States.

Digging Up the Natural Roots of Morality

For as long as people have been thinking about the difference between good and bad, two ideas have competed for attention:

- ✔ The human understanding of the good comes from outside of humanity — God being the usual suspect.
- ✔ The human understanding of the good is woven into the human mind, a natural part of being human.

For a long time this was considered a toss-up, and a tie generally goes to the Big Guy. But the last century or so has seen a huge amount of new understanding of how humans are put together. Fields like neuroscience, genetics, and biochemistry have shed much more light on how people know right from wrong — and why they tend more often than not to choose the right.

As with so many other discoveries, the resulting picture leaves little for God to do. Behaving well turns out to be highly adaptive. It aids survival. So evolution has naturally selected a tendency to be good, which puts moral understanding and behavior deep in the fabric of who and what human beings are.

That's a shocking claim to many people, even those who accept evolution. Sure, evolution can explain sex and aggression and hunger and fear — but isn't evolution about "survival of the fittest," and "nature, red in tooth and claw"? How can that ever lead to morality?

As it turns out, evolution not only *can* select for moral behavior, it really *must*. Even so, morality isn't foolproof. Some evolved tendencies that were helpful a million years back aren't the least bit helpful in the modern world. In those cases, humans have developed social norms, rules, and laws to protect each other from each other. The biologist David Lehti gives an arresting example: If you think of the way other social species on Earth behave, it's frankly amazing that dozens of unrelated adult males can be confined together on a plane for hours with dozens of fertile females, yet everybody arrives at the gate in Cleveland alive and unharmed. Left to its own devices, evolution would tend to work against that happy outcome. Yet it happens ten thousand times a day because people have developed a social morality that thankfully trumps evolved human tendencies when it needs to.

That doesn't mean people are saints, not by a long shot. No one is (including saints). But we have a stronger inclination to be moral than immoral, and science points to several reasons why. These sections look at the natural roots of morality, as well as the ways society patches the gaps when human nature fails to keep people behaving.

Clarifying "survival of the fittest"

The phrase "survival of the fittest" brings to mind a world in which the strongest survive by pummeling the weak. That's about as far from Harris's definition of morality as you can get — and if that were the contribution of evolution to morality, it wouldn't be much of a contribution at all. More like something to overcome!

But that's not what the phrase means. "Survival of the fittest" doesn't refer to physical fitness, but whether your traits are the best *fit* for your environment. An animal's survival may depend on being puny so it can disappear under a rock when predators come by, while his bulky, muscular friend can't hide and gets eaten. So "fitness" isn't just about strength or the ability to squash others. In many cases, it's about the ability to cooperate with them.

Cooperation and empathy have been a much better fit for the conditions of human life than "pummel thy neighbor" ever could be. To see why, just imagine two Stone Age populations, one with a genetic tendency to kill each other, the other with a tendency to help each other. Which population is likely to still be around ten generations down the line, passing on those genes and tendencies to their kids? Not the one with murder as a national pastime, I'll tell you that. "Every man for himself" is a terrible group survival strategy.

This natural cooperation and empathy is strongest in a person's "in-group" — those closest and most similar to him or her. As I describe in the next section, when it comes to living peacefully with "out-groups" — those who look and act differently from a given person — evolution offers some real challenges. Racism, nationalism, militarism, and the overblown fear of immigrants are among the less helpful things humans have inherited by natural selection, and getting over those fear-driven things is one of the biggest moral challenges facing the modern world.

Being afraid — and getting over it

Things have never been worse in the world than they are today. I know this because my e-mail inbox says so:

- ✔ Rapists are using sinister new tactics, like recordings of crying babies, to lure and capture their victims.
- ✔ Child abduction rates have risen 444 percent since 1982.
- ✔ Violent crime is spiraling out of control.

Slight problem, though — *all of these claims are untrue.* No police department has ever reported a rape or attempted rape using this tactic — or any of a dozen others that frantic e-mails warn about. Child abduction rates, always extremely low, have remained level or declined in recent decades. And violent crime in the United States and United Kingdom has actually been declining steadily since the early 1990s. US figures for 2010, the most recent year on record, show the lowest level of violent crime in recorded history in *every category*.

But who would know, given the constant moral panic, the insistence that no one is safe in "this day and age"?

Fear is one of the greatest drivers of religious belief. This makes sense — if the world has gone violently mad, there's real comfort in the idea that someone with infinite power and goodness is in control. But religion isn't responsible for the perpetual paranoia, though it often contributes to keeping fear alive. The original culprit, the biological parent of human fears, is evolution.

Imagine a sunny Wednesday afternoon a million years ago. Two pre-human ancestors are walking through the high grass on the African savannah. Suddenly there's a blur of movement off to the left! One of them assumes it's something fun and goes in for a hug. The other jumps 15 feet straight up and grabs a tree limb. Even if it's just a fluffy bunny nine times out of ten, which of these guys is more likely to pass on his genes to the next generation? *(Hint: Look up.)*

Counting the incarcerated

New inmates in the US federal prison system are asked their religious identity so officials can make accommodations in diet or schedule and know which clergy (if any) to call in times of need. I contacted the Federal Bureau of Prisons for information about the religious identification of prisoners. The results were interesting:

✔ Most religions have about the same percentage in prison as in the general population. Mainline Protestants, for example, make up 31 percent of the US population and 32 percent of the federal prison population.

✔ A few religions are slightly overrepresented in prison, and some are underrepresented. Mormons are an example of the latter, making up 1.3 percent of the US population but just 0.3 percent of the federal prison population.

You can't draw direct moral conclusions from these data alone, of course. For one thing, a strong correlation exists between the average income in a given religion and the ability of its members to stay out of prison. Other sociological factors enter in as well.

One major exception to the pattern does exist — one worldview that's right on the national average in income but is *hugely* underrepresented in prisons: atheists.

About five percent of Americans identify not just as nonreligious but specifically as atheists. But only 0.09 percent of the federal prison population identifies as atheists — 50 times fewer than would be expected.

Remember that the data are taken at the time of entry, so conversions in the pen won't show up, just their worldviews around the time their crimes were committed. The result contradicts popular assumptions about atheists. Although an atheist is regarded by much of society as inherently immoral, he or she is among the least likely people to end up in a federal prison. I don't think this is because the legal system has a crush on atheists. Neither do I think it means atheists are necessarily more virtuous. But at the very least, it should give pause to those who think they're *less* virtuous.

In a long-ago world that was bent on killing us, no trait would have been more useful for survival than perpetual, sweaty paranoia. That's why humans have inherited a strong tendency to assume that every shadow and sound is a threat, which in turn kept them alive and reproducing. Whenever I come upstairs from a dark basement, I feel a tingling on the back of my neck, my step quickens, and my heart races just a bit — even though my basement, unlike basements on the ancient savannah, rarely contains a cheetah.

That creepy feeling is less relevant now, but half a million years ago it was plenty useful for keeping predators of all kinds at bay — including the strange, unfamiliar humans from over the hill. By the time high blood pressure killed off one of my ancient ancestors at 22, he'd already have several jittery, paranoid offspring pounding espressos and cradling stone shotguns through the long, terrifying night.

Even as evolution has given people a tendency to cooperate with their immediate community, it also makes them fear and distrust those who are different. That worked at one time. But in a close-packed world of seven billion people of countless different colors, creeds, and kinds, such overblown fear and distrust isn't as helpful for survival. People are in greater control of their environment than ever before, but the human brain hasn't had a chance to catch up.

So people stay afraid, keep believing that things have never been worse — and keep clinging to the comfort of religious ideas.

When religious ideas help people recognize their shared humanity, conquer their fears, and enlarge the circle of those they love and trust (as they often do), such ideas are part of the moral solution in the modern world. But when religious ideas reinforce ancient fears and hatreds, drawing lines and narrowing the circle of love and trust (as they often do), those ideas are part of the moral problem.

Framing the question right — why do people (mostly) behave so well?

Why are people so darn moral?

That's not a question you hear every day. Try asking that out loud at your next family gathering and you'll probably get incredulous laughter. Everyone "knows" how depraved people are and how much worse things are getting by the day. To say otherwise seems completely daft.

But a moment's thought and a few statistics say otherwise.

Putting good and bad behavior in perspective

Most people behave pretty well most of the time. Immoral behavior is the exception, not the rule. Acts of cruelty and unfairness are noticed much more than kind or neutral acts. I tend to remember the three jerks who cut me off on the freeway on my way to work , but who ever notices the 10,000 people who could have done so, but didn't?

Likewise, the news media reliably gather up and report on every murder, rape, and robbery in a given day, which gives the false impression that murder, rape, and robbery are happening constantly pretty much everywhere. In fact, the opposite is true — these things are newsworthy precisely *because they are rare.* The vast majority of the acts most people perform in a given day aren't immoral in the least.

In addition to less bad stuff going on, there's more good. The World Giving Index shows that the world is becoming a more charitable place, with steady annual increases in volunteering time and the willingness to help a stranger.

One recent study focused on the wide gap between how ethical people are and how unethical people *think* they are. One group took a math test in which they could easily cheat. Another group watched on tape, then were asked to predict whether they themselves would cheat in the same circumstances. Actual cheating was much less common than predicted. Researchers think that's because emotions are stronger when you're experiencing an ethical dilemma than when you're just thinking about it, and past research shows that emotions actually *help* people make the right moral decisions — the opposite of what is commonly thought.

No, the world isn't a perfect place, and it never will be. But a lot can be gained in the quality of human life by recognizing that it's much better, and people are much better, than you or I often think.

Playing nice

A lot of studies confirm our stronger tendency toward moral behavior. But isolating the variables out in the real world can be difficult. As a result, many researchers have been turning to a world where variables are under greater control — the world of video and online gaming.

For those who think human culture is losing its moral grip, these games are a convenient target. When they aren't accused of sucking the brains out of children, video and online games are accused of greasing the slippery slope that's plunging humanity into an abyss of immorality. After the Columbine High School killers were found to have played the violent video game Doom, many felt the case was closed. Violence in fantasy became violence in real life, they said — even though many experts consider such game play to be an expression of violent tendencies, or even a helpful release, not the cause.

And even though some games and situations do make me wonder about the human species, research in moral decision making using gaming scenarios is reinforcing the conclusion that people are actually surprisingly moral — even in situations you'd think would surely go the other way.

One such study looked at an online role-playing game called Pardus — a virtual life game in which hundreds of thousands of people assume other identities and interact in a completely artificial environment. Spaceships move through a universe perpetually at war, while players forge alliances, trade, battle, and build with other players. Almost no rules are in place to guide behavior in the game. Seems like a perfect place for human nature to go berserk — survival of the fittest in its usual, misunderstood meaning.

But when the researchers tracked the behavior of 400,000 players in the game, assessing millions of individual human interactions by those players, they found that only 2 percent of all actions were aggressive in any way. Most players (who didn't know they were being watched) most of the time behaved in a way the researchers described as social and compassionate — even without specified rules. One researcher noted that far from anarchy, the result is participants organizing themselves as a social group with good intentions.

Even in a virtual world without consequences or rules in which individuals with masked identities *travel around in armed spaceships,* people tend more often than not to behave pretty well. So maybe I shouldn't be too surprised that the real world — complete with social approval and disapproval, rules and consequences, and with far fewer starfighters — functions even better. And sure enough, similar studies in the workplace, in family settings, and in communities of various sizes and types have shown the same result — though people tend to mostly notice the bad exceptions, most people most of the time behave well.

Suddenly the whole moral question is a lot less frantic. Instead of seeking a way to somehow become moral, you're left with the interesting but less urgent question of why most people most of the time already *are* moral, with and without religion — and the collective desire to work on the times they aren't.

Discovering "moral molecules" and mirrors in your head

Science has only recently begun to really plumb the depths of the incredible three-pound blob of jelly that is the human brain. And one of the things research is uncovering is the complex, evolved mechanism humans have that reinforces their morality.

The role that the oxytocin molecule plays in sexual attraction and arousal has been known for a while, as well as its role in maternal feelings and bonding between people. But recent studies have also shown an important connection between oxytocin and moral behavior. When oxytocin is released, trust goes up and fear recedes. Individuals are more likely to feel empathy for others and therefore more likely to behave morally towards them. Subjects were 80 percent more likely to make generous decisions in simulated scenarios after getting a nasal injection of oxytocin. And on the flipside, it turns out psychopaths are bad at producing oxytocin. So it makes sense that Paul Zak, one of the top researchers in this area, calls oxytocin "the moral molecule."

A moral molecule would be a big hit with natural selection, of course, because fear and mistrust prevent societies from flourishing, whereas cooperation, empathy, and trust help them survive and thrive.

Okay, I've saved my favorite for last: the mirror neuron.

In your head are some neurons that fire whenever you do something. Pick up a marble, yawn, or slam your shin into a trailer hitch, and these neurons get busy. Scientists have known this for a long time.

But in the past decade or so, they've discovered that these same neurons also fire when you see someone *else* picking up a marble, yawning, or slamming a shin. They are the reason you wince when you see a car door slam on somebody else's fingers, and yawn when someone else yawns. They're called *mirror neurons,* and they have the powerful capacity to make you feel, quite directly, what somebody else is feeling.

You probably see where I'm going with this. The implications are huge. Mirror neurons make people vulnerable to the experiences and feelings of others. They go beyond sympathy (the concern for someone else's well-being) to empathy — the ability to feel what someone else is feeling.

If Bill Clinton could really "feel your pain" like he said he did, his mirror neurons were helping him do that.

So why did mirror neurons evolve? Like any evolutionary "why" question, it helps to think about what the absence of the feature would have meant. Mirror neurons make teaching and learning much easier, for one. All primates have them, so it turns out monkey see, monkey do is a matter of hardware, not just software. When Cave-Kid saw Mom or Dad starting a fire, or picking berries, or spearing dinner on the hoof, mirror neurons would have made it easier to duplicate the task. Populations without this cool adaptive anomaly would have had a selective disadvantage, resulting in fewer survivors over time, and *voilà!* Mirror neurons became the norm.

Then there's the selective advantage of being good. Without the hard-wired ability to feel what someone else feels, individuals really could be islands unto themselves, indifferent to each other's pain and suffering. Picture one population of mutually indifferent, self-centered creatures, and another in which empathy is the norm. Which population is going to survive to pass on its genes?

The most powerful human moral concept is the Reciprocity Principle: Treat others as you would like to be treated. Christians may recognize their Golden Rule in that, but its origin is much older and its presence much more universal than a single religion or philosophy (see the nearby sidebar). It's the heart of human morality, something people generally figure out on their own by age six. And mirror neurons are a continuous, helpful nudge.

Little effort is needed to see the root of empathy, sympathy, compassion, conscience, cooperation, guilt, and a whole lot of other useful tendencies in this remarkable neural system. It's just one more reason humanity is still here after all these years.

Recognizing the changing nature of morality

I often hear that religion and God are necessary because they offer an unchanging moral code. It sounds very reassuring. But a moment's reflection shows that an unchanging moral code is the last thing we want or need.

Most people wouldn't want to live in a world governed by the moral norms of Bronze Age Mediterranean cultures — say about 3,500 years ago. Women were considered the property of their husbands. Slavery was accepted as the rightful dominance of the strong over the weak. It was considered a holy duty to stone gays, fortune tellers, and disobedient children to death. This is the period in which the Old Testament was written, in which each of these actions was endorsed as morally correct. But finding a living Christian or Jew who thinks these things are morally correct now is nearly impossible. Our moral understanding, thankfully, has changed.

The Pharisees in the New Testament apparently tried to evolve their morality a bit, but Jesus seemed to be irritated by that, scolding them for no longer observing the instruction to kill disobedient children (Mark 7:9–13). And women still had a miserable time of it, ordered to "obey their husbands as gods." Again, most modern believers have now moved past that Bronze Age morality.

In Europe in the Middle Ages, guilt was decided not by evidence but by trials of fire, water, and combat. Fortunately the ethics of fairness have changed since then. It was also considered a pressing moral duty to identify and burn witches. Not so much today (except in some parts of Africa — see Chapter 14 for a description of atheists working to protect women accused of witchcraft in Ghana).

Humanity finds its way forward, changing moral norms over time. Slavery ended in the United States and United Kingdom in the 19th century, a change in moral norms driven by courageous atheists, as well as theists who in many cases had to find the moral courage to ignore their own scriptures. Women, whose inequality was considered morally neutral or even good for most of history, were finally granted the vote and other rights in several countries by the early 20th century.

But there was more progress to be made. Despite many moral improvements in the United States, interracial marriage was still illegal in many states until 1967, and a woman couldn't get contraception without her husband's permission — both "moral" positions that have since changed for the better.

This list could go on, but you get the idea.

Don't be seduced by the idea that unchanging moral norms would be good. Such norms do change over time, and despite dire warnings of moral chaos, most people of all beliefs eventually agree that the changes in moral understanding I've listed here have been big improvements. When someone feels a change isn't for the best, it's time to have a discussion. But wishing away the ability to change the human mind about morality isn't good for anyone.

Exercising the moral muscle

Whenever someone is a particular saint or sinner, people commonly look to that person's upbringing for clues. Surely something her parents did (or didn't do) set the stage for her selfless acts (or terrible crimes). Religious conservatives often cry out after heinous acts like mass shootings that morality is declining because children are no longer raised to honor and obey parents, authorities, and God; to follow instructions without question; and to know the Ten Commandments. They say the acts are a result of parenting gone wrong.

One conservative religious parenting book after another cites "permissive parenting" as the cause of a supposed moral decline, and obedience and discipline as the solution. "Obedience is the foundation for all character," In his book on Christian parenting, Baptist pastor Jack Hyles called obedience the foundation of character, of the home, and of society. A list of the 100 most frequent words in John MacArthur's *What the Bible Says About Parenting* includes duty, authority, obedience, fear, command, law, and submit.

Not all Christian parenting advice runs that way. *Parenting With Love and Laughter: Finding God in Family Life* doesn't include a single one of those nasty obsessions in its top 100. And that book shares fully half of its top 50 words — and a lot of its other values — with *Parenting Beyond Belief,* my own book for nonreligious parents. Both of these books emphasize involving kids in ethical decision making and inviting them to ask the reasons behind the rules — and neither book counts "Because I said so" as a valid reason. As is often the case, religious moderates have more in common with the nonreligious than they do with fundamentalists.

Parenting styles do strongly affect children's ethical development. But is unquestioning obedience really the way to go, or do the less authoritarian books have it right?

Moral development research consistently recommends the less authoritarian approach. Dr. Joan Grusec, a leader in this field, says parents who demand unquestioning obedience are actually *less* likely to raise ethical kids than those who emphasize reasoning and questioning. That's the exact opposite of popular opinion.

Comparing rescuers and non-rescuers in Nazi Europe

In one especially powerful study, 700 survivors of Nazi Europe were interviewed, including *rescuers* (people who actively helped others hide or escape, often at great risk to themselves) and *non-rescuers* (people who were either passive in the face of the atrocities or actively involved). The researchers asked both groups about their upbringing — specifically how their parents taught them values and ethics.

Almost everyone described growing up in a home where morality was taken seriously. But when the questions turned to how that was done, an astonishing pattern emerged. The non-rescuers were 21 times more likely to have been raised in families that emphasized *obedience to authority*. Rules were meant to be followed without question — in other words, the rules were taught by indoctrination. If a child

asked why a given rule was in place, the parent was likely to say, "Because I said so."

Rescuers, on the other hand, were three times more likely than non-rescuers to identify reasoning as an element of their moral education. *Explained,* the authors said, was one of the most common words used by rescuers in describing their parents' ways of talking about rules and ethical ideas. The parents *explained* why something was right or wrong and allowed the children to ask further questions. This in turn gave the kids experience not just at rule-following but at thinking morally.

When the Nazis rose to power, most of those raised to obey authority kept obeying authority, while those taught to think morally kept thinking morally — and were able to see that this particular authority should be resisted.

Indoctrinating kids to rules (teaching by rote without encouraging independent thought or challenge) is one of the worst things parents can do to develop the ethical judgment of their children. Researcher Larry Nucci has said indoctrination is worse than doing nothing, because it actually interferes with a child's moral development. Yet conservative commentators urge parents to indoctrinate because it feels so decisive. People with nondogmatic worldviews, including atheists, have an easier time walking away from the rule-following approach to ethics. That's a good thing, because the questioning path leads more reliably to ethical adults who will question both commands and commandments rather than boldly do whatever they're told.

Grasping ethical incentives — carrots and sticks

I've always found it interesting that Christianity offers release from the greatest human fear — death — but then backs up this awesome gift with the threat of hell if you don't accept it.

That's not all that unusual, really — in fact, it's downright human. Most morality works in the same carrot-and-stick fashion. People are offered a chance to be good for goodness' sake, or for the approval of others, or for a piece of candy — and if they still choose to break the rules, it's The Stick.

I remember seeing a perfect example of the carrot-and-stick a few years ago as I stood in line at an amusement park. A teenage boy wearing a Christian day camp T-shirt ducked under several of the rails and cut in front of us in line.

Two minutes later, his bright pink tie-dyed Jesus-fish shirt was spotted by one of the camp counselors. The counselor walked over and reasoned with the lad using the reciprocity principle:

"Michael, what are you doing? How would you like it if these nice people all cut in front of you?"

(And then, wait for it...)

"If I see that again, you're out of the park."

That's the carrot and stick. Drive the speed limit and everyone is safer, including you. Not enough for ya? Here's a $120 ticket. Have a nice day.

When I am told, as I often am, that my atheism is a license for mass murder, I try to point out that

- ✔ Despite being an atheist for my entire adult life, I've never taken advantage of that supposed license, nor have any of the atheists I know.
- ✔ I have countless reasons *not* to do such a thing, including a lack of motivation, an abundance of empathy, my desire to be thought well of, a brain full of oxytocin, and all the rest of the incentives from this chapter.
- ✔ And if those fail . . . I'm pretty sure murder still carries legal penalties.

In other words, even if all positive appeals to principle failed to reach me, an earthly stick is ready and waiting right behind that carrot.

As I point out at the beginning of this chapter, no matter what their worldview, the overwhelming majority of people don't need to feel that stick across their bottoms. You and I are both surrounded every day by people happily nibbling on the various carrots they get for behaving well. Only rarely are the moral sticks needed. But society has evolved those penalties for use whenever they are needed.

Recognizing different levels of morality

In thinking about morality without religion or scriptures or God, it helps to recognize that some kinds of morality are much more impressive than others. If not getting arrested is my moral high water mark — well, I should want to aim a little higher than that. On the other end of the spectrum (as Gandhi, Bertrand Russell, and Martin Luther King, Jr. can attest), getting arrested can be a sign that you've aimed *really* high.

Psychologist Lawrence Kohlberg saw six stages on the moral ladder, each higher and better developed than the last:

- **Fear of punishment:** The first and lowest kind of morality is fear of punishment. Threats of spanking are in this category, as is hell. If someone tells me I should believe in God so I don't go to hell, I always think, "Ooh, that's some low Kohlberg you've got there." (I don't say that out loud, of course, because "low Kohlberg" is considered offensive in some cultures.)

- **Hope of reward:** Only slightly higher is stage two, the hope of reward. Being good only on condition of a gumball isn't the most impressive moral code. Lollipops and heaven are also stage two.

- **Social approval and disapproval:** Stage three is a killer, at least for me. I take it very hard when people disapprove of my actions, especially when it's people I respect. When those same people are happy with me, I feel like Thor. This isn't the highest form of morality, but it's not bad, and it's a potent one for many people.

- **Rule following:** The fourth level of morality is following laws and rules. Most civil codes are based on Level 4, and those folks who want the Ten Commandments posted in every school are appealing to this middling level of morality.

- **Social contract:** If you have a Stage 5 understanding of morality, you recognize that laws and rules are made by humans and can be changed by humans. (This is the point where some religious folks scream "Moral relativism!" and swallow their tongues.) The earlier section, "Recognizing the changing nature of morality," is all about Level 5.

- **Universal ethical principles:** The sixth and highest level of moral development is reached when a person is willing to violate rules and laws if they contradict higher principles, even at the risk of punishment, social disapproval, or sometimes death.

  Name a true moral hero, religious (Thomas More, Martin Luther King, Jr., Jesus Christ) or nonreligious (Thomas Paine, Bertrand Russell, Ernestine Rose), and they'll probably be working at Level Six at least some of the time.

Sharing a golden, human idea

The ethic of reciprocity (or the Golden Rule) is universal, belonging not to any one religion or philosophy but to all humanity. Some variations throughout history include the following:

- **Zoroastrianism (seventh century BCE):** "That nature alone is good which refrains from doing unto another whatsoever is not good for itself." — Dadistan-i Dinik 94-5

- **Jainism (fifth century BCE):** "A man should treat all creatures in the world as he himself would like to be treated." — Sutrakritinga; Wisdom of the Living Religions #69, I:II:33

- **Buddhism (fourth century BCE):** "Hurt not others in ways that you yourself would find hurtful." — Udanavarga 5,18

- **Classical Greece (fourth century BCE):** "May I do to others as I would that they should do unto me." — Plato

- **Hinduism (fourth century BCE):** "This is the sum of duty: Do not do to others what would cause you pain if done to you." — Mahabharata 5,1517

- **Confucianism (fourth century BCE):** "Surely it is the maxim of loving-kindness: Do not unto others that you would not have them do unto you." — Analects 15,23

- **Christianity (first century CE):** "Do unto others as you would have them do unto you." — Matthew 7:12

- **Judaism (third century):** "What is hateful to you, do not do to your fellowman. This is the entire Law; all the rest is commentary." — Talmud, Shabbat 3id

- **Islam (seventh century):** "No man is a true believer unless he desireth for his brother that which he desireth for himself." — Azizullah, Hadith 150

- **Taoism (12th century):** "Regard your neighbor's gain as your own gain and your neighbor's loss as your own loss." — T'ai Shang Kan Ying P'ien

- **Baha'i (19th century):** "Lay not on any soul a load that you would not wish to be laid upon you, and desire not for anyone the things you would not desire for yourself." — Baha'u'llah, Gleanings, LXVI:8

- **Wicca (20th century):** "Ain' it harm none, do what thou wilt." — The Wiccan Rede

Some say treating someone as *they* wish to be treated is better, not as *you* wish to be treated. You could, after all, be a masochist. So there's the Platinum Rule: "Treat others the way they want to be treated."

So what's the humanist Golden Rule? Any one of them. That's one of the benefits of a philosophy that doesn't have a dogma of its own. An atheist or humanist can range through all of human thought to find the best, and leave the rest behind.

"Some of the time" is a key point. Everyone responds to moral incentives at many levels. As a secular humanist, my goal is to aim for the highest levels of moral expression as much of the time as possible. But even if I act on universal moral principles every other Tuesday, I'll spend a lot of the time in between just hoping for the approval of others, following rules, or trying not to get hurt. We all do that, no matter what our beliefs. It's just good to aim higher when we can.

Keeping two moral ideas in view

Being able to put human morality into words is helpful. And as it happens, two simple ethical concepts underline just about all of human morality. They are as follows:

- ✔ **Reciprocity:** *Reciprocity* is the idea that I should treat others as I wish to be treated. No matter where or when people live or what their religion is, if any, the ethic of reciprocity is part of their culture and moral system. By simply interacting with others, people learn that treating others as they would like to be treated is a good idea. Children internalize this early on, usually by age 7 or 8 at the latest. Harvard Humanist chaplain Greg Epstein notes that no religion or ethical philosophy ever completely misses this concept — and that it makes perfect sense without reference to a God. (See the nearby sidebar for different ways various religions and philosophies have phrased the ethic of reciprocity.)

- ✔ **Universalizability:** *Universalizability* — also known (without saving a single syllable) as the *categorical imperative* — is another idea so simple that kids understand it. When I threw my ice cream stick on the ground and my mom said, "What if everyone did that?", she was appealing to my ability to see that I'd done a thing that wasn't universalizable. I pictured myself swimming in a ten-foot drift of ice cream sticks. Fun, but sticky, and even at five years old, I didn't do sticky. Given a minute, I could probably have thought of ten other reasons it was not good for everyone to throw their ice cream sticks on the ground. *Reasons,* not doctrines.

Naming a moral idea isn't the same as following it, of course. But for the many reasons already discussed in this chapter, religious believers and atheists alike tend to follow these moral principles more often than not. In fact, it's harder to derail a person from basically moral tendencies than people often think.

Character development specialist Marvin Berkowitz puts it this way: if a kid grows up in a basically pro-social family and culture, the child tends to develop into a good person. Religion is just one way to frame a moral life. There are countless other ways to do so without any reference to God.

Chapter 16

Seeing the World Naturally

God isn't the only one who's gone missing in the atheist worldview. When someone decides that humans actually created the Creator, not the other way around, the rest of the supernatural world tends to follow God out the door. Just as Santa Claus generally takes the Easter Bunny, the Tooth Fairy, and the rest with him when he goes, most people who set aside the idea of gods quickly see faeries, goblins, demons, ghosts, and all other magical beings as products of the same fevered human imagination.

What's left when the supernatural explanations disappear are *natural* explanations — those that don't rely on a realm outside of the universe we know. Instead of making room for beings that play by a different set of rules, it's safe to assume until proven otherwise that everything is part of the same natural universe, playing the same natural game — and humans can set themselves to the fascinating task of understanding that game without a religious filter in the way.

The absence of magic and miracles doesn't remotely mean the absence of wonder and awe. All of those things that are awe-inspiring about existence remain so — they simply have different, natural explanations. In fact, many atheists who were once religious describe a much *deeper* sense of wonder after all this spectacular stuff turns out to be not a divine design, but the result of unguided physical processes. Seriously, how much more wonderful is that?

This chapter explores the way the world looks to a mind firmly anchored in the natural world.

Feeling Freedom and Relief

Some atheists never really had religious beliefs in the first place. Their view was naturalistic from the beginning. For those atheists who did have supernatural beliefs, the stories of losing those beliefs are amazing in their variety. Some people describe slipping out of belief quite easily and without drama. Others describe personal pain, especially if religious friends and family react badly. But after they finally set aside religious beliefs, an amazing similarity exists in the feelings they describe. The most common by far are *freedom* and *relief.*

I should add *surprise* as another common feeling. Many religious people have been told for years that a loss of faith is followed by a loss of all hope and joy. When that turns out not to be the case, and the world is every bit as beautiful and life as precious and worthwhile as it was the day before — for a lot of new atheists, it's a very pleasant surprise.

The freedom and relief often come from the realization — sometimes for the first time ever — that their thoughts are their own, that their fate is in their own hands, that they aren't pawns in someone else's chess game but autonomous human beings. Atheists who grew up in conservative religious homes often experience this feeling most strongly, but others often speak of this sudden change of perspective as well.

And contrary to another common assumption, no one has an urge to suddenly go on a violent rampage. Good people of faith become good people without faith. Instead of seeking to do harm, the feeling of freedom and relief is often followed by an overwhelming sense of personal responsibility.

Accepting Responsibility and Accountability

When the last remnant of religious faith is gone, people tend to realize that with nobody minding the store, it's up to human beings to care for each other, to work for justice, to comfort those who suffer or grieve, and to make this life as good as it can be for as many people as possible. It's up to humanity to accept the responsibility we had formerly given over to God.

In a religious context, people can just leave these concerns in God's hands, or feel as if something's been accomplished when a prayer is uttered. Many religious believers don't take that easy way out, of course. They follow up their prayers with real human effort. (Good thing they do, because that's how things actually get done.)

But for people without religious belief, handing off the responsibility isn't even an option. The easy illusion of doing good by dropping a line to the divine is no longer available. Instead, nonbelievers know they have to pick up the shovels, send in the donations, give the blood, hold the hands, and feed the hungry mouths themselves.

The same is true of accountability. If you believe in God, you may feel a greater accountability because somebody's watching you all the time. But Christian belief (among several other traditions) comes with a very useful Get Out of Sin Free card — divine forgiveness. No matter what you've done you'll be forgiven (with one exception — see Mark 3:29). You only have to ask, and some traditions even dispense with that part.

When televangelist Jimmy Swaggart was caught committing adultery with a prostitute in 1988, he tearfully begged God for forgiveness as the cameras rolled. "I have sinned against you, my Lord," he said, "and I would ask that your precious blood would wash and cleanse every stain until it is in the seas of God's forgiveness."

Atheists don't have that mighty handy option. They have to be accountable to other human beings with no guarantee of forgiveness. That tends to make atheists more careful than we might be if we believed in a reset button.

(Swaggart's bid for forgiveness worked, by the way — until he was caught doing the same thing again three years later. When his congregation proved less forgiving the second time, Swaggart said, "The Lord told me it's flat none of your business." Darn that human accountability!)

Atheists do have to be careful not to substitute secular prayers for religious ones. We can spend all day "Liking" charities on Facebook without feeding a single hungry child. So in place of accountability to the divine, we have to hold each other accountable for our actions and our inactions. The more someone relied on accountability to God in their religious life, the more they may need human accountability in his shiny new secular life.

But it's not as if atheists are taking over from God. If he isn't there, he never was. All the effort, love, and support people have ever had has come from other people. A new nonbeliever is simply recognizing this for the first time.

Setting Aside Bronze-Age Ideas

Traditional religions are literally conservative by nature. A big part of their purpose is to *conserve* a set of beliefs, rituals, values, and traditions from the past. Scriptures and priesthoods and catechisms set these ideas in stone, making change difficult, and sometimes even impossible.

As a result, religions rooted in the cultures of the Bronze Age or Iron Age (3600 BCE–200 CE) tended to carry the beliefs, rituals, values, and traditions of those eras into the modern era with little change, even as the cultures around them adapted and changed over time. It's like trapping those values in amber so they don't spoil during the voyage to the 21st century and beyond. Some of these values are worth preserving — love your neighbor, that's very nice — but others really needed to spoil and be gone.

A worldview that isn't tied to the past by scriptures and catechisms, one with values grounded in the natural world and in human society, is better able to change and adapt over time. By constantly examining their values and beliefs, people holding a naturalistic worldview are well equipped to keep and renew good values and ideas while leaving the bad ones in the past.

The following sections explore ways in which a nonreligious worldview can more easily dispense with outdated and undesirable ideas.

Thinking about virtues and vices

Virtues are qualities admired and rewarded by a given culture. Or to borrow from author Sam Harris (see Chapter 9), you may say a virtue is something that promotes the wellbeing of conscious creatures. Moral systems often define virtues and then encourage people in different ways to strive for them.

A *vice* is the flipside of virtue, something a given culture frowns upon and discourages. You may also define a vice as something that's either unfair or harmful to another person or animal, or to the environment.

The naturalistic view tends to focus on fairness and harm in defining vices. If something isn't unfair and no one is harmed, an atheist would say it probably shouldn't be considered a vice. Traditional religious views include things like purity, loyalty, and respect for authority in their moral codes. (See Chapter 15 for more on moral codes.) That's how things like sex and patriotism get treated as moral questions more often than secular people think they should.

A lot of the behaviors defined as virtues in the Bronze Age could get you arrested today. The Bible presents Abraham's unquestioning faith as a virtue, for example, when he dutifully follows God's instruction to kill his innocent son Isaac. The knife was in motion by the time an angel's hand stayed it. He passed the test. By the religious standards of the Bronze Age, he was a virtuous man because he was willing to do whatever he was commanded to do by his superior — in this case, God.

Suggesting a few humanistic virtues

Virtues don't always come easy — in fact, a virtue that comes easy isn't much of a virtue. Virtues should be qualities to strive for, a list built by the consensus of people in a given family, community, nation, or planet.

Here's one list of naturalistic virtues — amendable, arguable, and always incomplete:

✔ **Humility:** Surprised? Don't be. I'm descended not just from apes but from bacteria, and I share 98 percent of my DNA with chimpanzees. I live on a tiny speck in a universe so vast I can't even really grasp it, and my life is a fleeting blip in cosmic time. Though atheists don't always exhibit it, deep humility is a natural fit with a natural worldview.

✔ **Empathy:** Empathy is natural (see Chapter 15), but that doesn't mean it's always easy. I have to overcome my equally natural selfishness to feel what others feel, to be compassionate.

✔ **Courage:** Paul Kurtz (check out Chapter 8) called courage "the first humanistic virtue." I'm a fragile mortal living in an indifferent universe. It takes real courage to honestly face this fact. I get that courage from within myself and from those around me who were born into the same daunting reality.

✔ **Honesty:** Honesty is what made me naturalistic in the first place. I need to extend that honesty into every aspect of my life.

✔ **Openness:** I'm as prone as anyone to cling stubbornly to my opinions. Openness means staying open to the possibility that I may still be wrong. It also means accepting and being open to differences among people. Openness is a much better word than "tolerance," in my opinion.

✔ **Clear thinking:** There's often a bright line drawn between thinking and ethics, and that line doesn't belong there. As I describe in Chapter 15, people can and should think about the reasons to behave morally. And clear thinking — including the ability to get our own biases out of the way — has huge benefits in every aspect of human life.

✔ **Generosity:** In the absence of a God, we humans are all we've got. Generosity — of resources, of time, of spirit — is the best way to get the best possible world.

✔ **Gratitude:** In the naturalistic view, gratitude is directed to people, not to a god. Sometimes I don't even need someone to thank. I can be grateful for my health and family, for all the advantages I enjoy, and for the opportunity to extend those advantages to others. I often think about the incredible odds against ever being born, and I'm speechless with gratitude for being one of the lucky few who made it into the world.

Three thousand years later, the Nazi defendants at Nuremberg (ironically) offered Abraham's defense — that they were only following orders. The secular international tribunal at Nuremberg, working from a moral code that had come a long way since the Bronze Age, now had a different term for following orders to murder innocents. It wasn't a virtue any more — it was a vice, a crime against humanity.

Few religious people today would follow Abraham's example, which is good, although the story of Abraham and Isaac is still told and retold as an inspiring example of ultimate faith. I can't imagine what it's like to carry a bronze millstone like that when you've moved on morally yourself.

Atheists have it easier. We can look at an idea and say, "That's immoral, and here's why." No need to struggle, wrestle, or bend over backwards to explain the difference between our current understanding of right and wrong and the one trapped in amber by scriptures we've inherited. If something from any influential book or thinker is reconsidered in the light of new evidence or a better moral consensus, we're free to change it or throw it away.

Not that we jump at the chance. Despite our self-image as 100 percent sober and rational, we atheists can kick and scream and cry as much as anyone when our most treasured preconceptions are challenged. We're human that way. But in the end, we don't have sacredness to hide behind, so the more level and less biased heads in the room will keep things moving forward.

Enlightened nonbelievers have joined with enlightened believers to end slavery, improve race relations, promote the rights of women, gays, and lesbians, and create an international system of law — more often despite scriptures than because of them. I admire those believers who challenge their own sacred books when necessary, and I'm glad I don't have to figure out how to do that myself.

Embracing doubt

Certainty is comforting. But a big part of embracing the naturalistic worldview is letting go of the addiction to being certain — or at least thinking I am.

Phrases like "I don't know," "I'm not sure," and "nobody knows for sure" are a good sign that someone has embraced honest doubt. A naturalistic worldview includes the ability to say, for example, "What was there before the Big Bang? Nobody knows" — and mean it. It means avoiding the temptation to add " . . . no one knows but God." As comforting as it is to think that someone somewhere has all the answers, even if we don't know them ourselves, atheists agree with the philosopher David Hume, who said that God is just the answer you get if you don't ask enough questions.

The problem with "certainty" is that it closes doors. *Skepticism* (withholding judgment until sufficient evidence is available) is the right alternative to certainty — and skepticism is not, despite some claims, a negative thing, not the same as cynicism. It's a core value for humanists and scientists alike. If I declare that I know the answer to a given question beyond any doubt, there's no more investigation. Sometimes my assumption is right. But just as often, the answer I've latched onto will turn out to be wrong. Skepticism, which keeps the door open, is a better option. It allows me to keep asking questions, which means getting really comfortable with doubt.

Rethinking sex and sexuality

When it comes to sex and gender, the Bronze Age wasn't the most enlightened time. Religions born in this period have conserved and transmitted these ideas up to the present day. As a result, sex itself is often wrapped up in a confusion of mixed messages — to paraphrase country singer Butch Hancock, religions with Bronze Age roots often call sex a dirty, nasty thing . . . that I should save for someone I love.

Though many religious people have moved beyond these fearful notions, many others keep following their scriptures regarding sex and gender — even though the rest of society has long since outgrown them.

Being free of ancient scriptures and unchangeable ideas means the nonreligious can easily adapt and change their attitudes as cultures and ethics mature. (For more on changing moral standards, and why it's a very good thing, see Chapter 15.) No area of human life is in greater need of an update since the Bronze Age than sexuality and gender.

Atheists and humanists don't have a separate set of ethics related to sex. The same questions of responsibility and consequences apply as with everything else. Does a particular sexual practice harm anyone? Has everybody involved given informed consent? If so, then have a blast. Sex is a natural part of being human, and evolution, not Satan, has made it enjoyable. That's why every one of your ancestors had sex. And a good thing, or this book would have one less reader.

The following sections highlight a couple of harmless sexual practices that tend to give some religions a stroke.

Masturbation

The roots of society's odd attitudes toward masturbation are intertwined with the age-old distrust of bodily pleasures. That distrust probably didn't originate in religion. Religion is simply a place to put humanity's most beloved ideas for safekeeping — both good and bad. So when it comes to perpetuating and reinforcing fearful attitudes toward the safest sex of all, it's hard to beat scriptural religion.

Ancient attitudes toward masturbation have been carefully preserved in several traditional religions — often in amazingly over-the-top language. The Catholic catechism calls masturbation "an intrinsically and gravely disordered action," and a popular 19th century Jewish theologian called it "a graver sin than any other in the Torah." The Torah includes the first five books of the Bible, by the way, so masturbation is apparently worse than anything forbidden in the Ten Commandments, including murder. Mormonism teaches that "masturbation is a sinful habit that robs one of the Spirit," while Shi'a Islam forbids it completely, quoting sect founder Imam Ali as saying "one who masturbates commits a sin equal to killing me eighty times."

Twenty I could see . . . but *eighty?*

In the naturalistic view, masturbation is a non-issue. The question of consent is irrelevant, because it's a solo activity. And every one of the urban legends — you'll go blind, you'll grow hair on your palms, you'll make yourself sterile — is nonsense grounded in the ancient distrust of physical pleasure. Because people with a naturalistic worldview are free of the scriptures and traditions that preserve fears about the practice, they can see masturbation for what it is — a healthy, harmless release and expression of our naturally-evolved sexuality. No harm, no foul, no sin. Have fun.

Homosexuality

Nontheists tend to come down solidly on the side of equal rights across the board for gays and lesbians. Why? Because once again, no one is harmed by any sexual relationship between consenting adults, regardless of the genders, races, or anything else that's involved. What consenting adults do in their own lives is simply none of my business, up to and including sex and marriage.

Although the opposition to gay equality is almost entirely grounded in conservative religion, just as opposition to interracial marriage was half a century ago, supporters of gay equality include religious moderates and non-believers. It's yet another clue that religious moderates have a lot more in common with the nonreligious than they do with fundamentalists.

Thinking about gender

Though gender equality in the developed world has come a long way since the Bronze Age, most of that progress has happened in the last 200 years. Women were considered the property of their husbands in several early cultures, and gender roles and behaviors have been tightly defined for most of Western history. Women weren't allowed to participate in cultural leadership, were mostly confined to hearth and home, and had few of the human rights that are now taken for granted. Men enjoyed more individual rights but were also confined to their own set of gender roles and behaviors.

The ball that began rolling in the Enlightenment gathered speed in the 19th and 20th centuries. But as with other social advances, progress was opposed at every step by orthodox religion.

Like the liberal religious, those individuals with a naturalistic viewpoint have been better able to adapt to changing gender roles, and in many cases to lead the change. Not coincidentally, most of the major figures in feminism from the beginning have been atheists, agnostics, and others who were free of dogmatic scriptures and traditions. Neither is it surprising that those women pointed straight at those scriptures and traditions as the heart of the problem. "The Bible and the Church have been the greatest stumbling blocks in the way of women's emancipation," said Elizabeth Cady Stanton. "The whole tone of Church teaching in regard to women is, to the last degree, contemptuous and degrading." (See more about feminism and freethought in Chapter 7.)

Recognizing that religion has been part of the problem doesn't mean a naturalistic view is an instant ticket to enlightenment. The organized freethought movement has had to take a hard look in the mirror recently concerning equal treatment for women to be sure the playing field is genuinely level for women in the movement. (Check out Chapter 14 for more information.) But the fact that freethinkers do so without unhelpful memos from the Bronze Age gives me much more confidence in that process than I'd have otherwise.

Accepting Mortality

My attitude toward death is straightforward: I'm opposed to it. Most people agree with me on that, no matter what they think happens afterward. The greatest challenge of being alive is knowing that someday I won't be any more. Even worse is the realization that those people I love aren't immortal either. Two thumbs way down for that.

One way to respond to the difficult fact of mortality is to imagine that we don't really die after all — we just go somewhere else where we'll meet up again some day with those we love. I like that idea. But people with a natural worldview don't think that wishing makes it so. We'd rather meet our situation honestly.

The Greek philosopher Epicurus (refer to Chapters 4 and 11) said people are mostly afraid of death because they don't really grasp nonexistence. Humanity has to really grasp that death is the end of experience. "As long as I exist," he said, "Death does not. Once Death exists, I will not. Why should I fear something I will never experience?"

Not bad.

He also offered the *symmetry argument:* You're living between two bookends of nonexistence. You didn't exist for millions of years before you were born, and (to paraphrase Twain) it didn't inconvenience you a bit. If your nonexistence before birth wasn't such a terrible thing, your future nonexistence shouldn't be either. It's literally the same thing — except for your ability to anticipate the next one. And you'll continue to live in the memory of those who loved you, and in your accomplishments in this world — especially the ways you made that world better than you found it. That also helps.

These consolations help people to accept mortality without religious consolations. One bonus: When you do away with the idea of heaven, hell goes with it. No devils, no demons, no flames to worry about. Nonexistence means the end of all worry and pain. That, to me and many other atheists, is the real promise of absolute peace.

Saying goodbye . . . for real

Atheists who were never religious have always understood death as final. When we lose a loved one, we mourn a permanent loss. But those who once believed in an afterlife often describe a "second grieving." After she gave up her Catholic belief, Julia Sweeney said she realized she had to go and basically kill off everyone she ever knew who died, because she hadn't *really* thought of them as dead before.

As any grief expert will tell you, facing and experiencing grief is much healthier than denial. As long as the possibility of an afterlife has a toehold on someone's mind and heart, there can be a bit of avoidance at work, an asterisk that keeps that person from really recognizing and mourning the loss. I've heard Julia's refrain over and over from people who are no longer religious — that they had to go back and mourn those they'd lost all over again because they hadn't really thought of them as gone.

If instead you accept your death and others' deaths as final — just as naturally as most people accept the death of a beloved pet as final — you can do the hard but important work of really saying goodbye.

Embracing life's limits

Recognizing that death is real can lend an urgency and preciousness to life itself. That's the upside of death: it makes life much more meaningful, which is even more important than the honest goodbye.

The book and film *Tuck Everlasting,* a story of a family that drinks from a spring that gives eternal life, perfectly captured this idea. They are 87 years into their immortality at the time of the story — and they hate it. Removed from the cycle of life and death, they don't change or grow older, and they feel as if life is passing them by. As one character puts it, death is not to be feared as much as the unlived life. You don't have to live forever — you just have to live." Perfect.

Life is made much more precious by the fact that it doesn't last forever. Understanding this life as a lucky shot at consciousness has the power to make every moment incredibly precious. You should wake up every morning laughing with delight that you're here at all, not crying because it won't last forever.

Gaping in New Wonder at Reality

I am a piece of the universe that woke up.

Every atom in my body has been around since the beginning of time, and because matter can't be destroyed, every bit will continue to be here until the end of the universe. And, to paraphrase the phenomenal (agnostic) writer Bill Bryson in *A Short History of Nearly Everything,* every atom in your body has almost certainly gone through stars and millions of other creatures on its way to becoming part of you. You're kind of wonderful that way.

The astonishing history of your atoms is just one example of the wonder that the naturalistic view holds in store, a brand of wonder that traditional religious wonder can't touch — at least not so far. The astronomer Carl Sagan once said a religion that focused not on ancient scriptures but on the magnificent universe revealed by science would inspire awe far beyond current religious wonder. Until then, the nonreligious will keep all of that natural wonder warm.

Considering whether an atheist can be spiritual

Poor spirituality. The word's been so stretched and abused that it's hard to know what somebody means when they use it. When a Christian friend asked me how my family and I achieve spirituality in our home without religion, I asked what she meant by spirituality.

"Well . . . spirituality," she said. "You know — having a personal relationship with Jesus Christ and accepting him into your life as Lord and Savior."

Yes, doing that without religion would be a neat trick. If spirituality is to have any real human value, I prefer using a definition that doesn't exclude 90 percent of the people who have ever lived.

Those who say they are "spiritual but not religious" get a lot of grief from all sides. That's what happens when you try to find a place in the middle. But they're really making a claim that I'm about to make — that traditional, organized religion can be a source of spirituality, but it certainly doesn't have a monopoly on it. To understand why, let me define spirituality in a way that doesn't depend on religion.

Spirituality at its best is about *being awake*. It's the attempt to transcend the mundane, sleepwalking experience of life everyone falls into, to tap into the wonder of being a conscious and grateful thing in the midst of an astonishing world. It can happen in a religious context, but it doesn't require it. Religion can sometimes enhance that awareness and awakeness, but just as often it can get in the way of being really aware and awake.

Some atheists have no interest in such things, but many do. For those who do, the following naturalistic practices can pull a person out of the everyday and put the brain in a different gear:

- **Meditation:** If meditation seems like the opposite of being awake, you're missing the point. Meditation is about being awake to your own existence, being present in the moment, not being highly caffeinated. And meditation is a great way to get yourself focused in the present.

- **Flow state:** When you're completely in the moment, so intensely focused on the activity at hand that you lose track of time, then suddenly look up at the clock and realize it is midnight — that's the flow state. It's one of the most deeply satisfying and meaningful states a person can enter. It's secular spirituality.

Some people get engrossed in a hobby like painting or woodworking for their sense of flow. Some play music or sing or compose. Others can lose themselves in deep conversation or intense reading. Flow state can happen when playing sports, or even getting deep into a video game. (Yes, I just connected video gaming to spirituality, and I'm not the first. Search online for "video games spirituality" to see what I mean.) After you recognize that spirituality doesn't have to be religious, and that flow is what you're after, all sorts of possibilities open up for reaching that wonderful, optimal state of mind. Then you can say, "I'm flowy, not religious" — or even, "I'm not religious, just awake."

Welcoming natural wonder

Many people feel that a worldview without God must be cold and devoid of wonder. But people who've left religion often say exactly the opposite. Not that religion keeps a person from marveling at a sunset or a newborn baby, of course. But these new naturalists often find that discovering about the natural processes behind such wonders gives a deeper and more profound appreciation of just how very wonderful they are — one much more astonishing than "God did it."

For a small sample of natural wonder, consider the following:

- You are star material that knows it exists.

- The Earth is hurtling through space at 68,400 miles per hour.

✔ The continents are moving under your feet at the rate fingernails grow.

✔ Your DNA is about half your mom's and half your dad's.

✔ Your memories, your ideas, even your identity take the form of a constantly recomposed electrochemical symphony playing in your head.

✔ You're related by shared descent to every living thing on Earth — not just apes, but whales, bacteria, redwoods, and your front lawn . . . even bananas.

✔ A bolt of lightning instantly heats trillions of air molecules hotter than the sun. The superheated molecules explode out of the way with a *crack*, leaving a miles-long vacuum behind. The deep rumble that follows is trillions of molecules crashing back in to fill the void.

✔ About a trillion such stars are in the galaxy, which is one of a hundred billion galaxies spread across 12 billion light years in a universe made of a curved fabric woven of space and time in which hydrogen, given the proper conditions, eventually evolves into Justin Bieber.

✔ . . . Make that Stephen Hawking.

Natural processes explain each of these points, and each fundamentally changes the way I look at the world.

A lot remains unknown, but what humanity has learned hasn't dispelled a sense of wonder one bit. Understanding doesn't kill wonder, it *feeds* it. Atheists find that the incredible wonder of a natural universe completely eclipses the wonder of a universe that's controlled by an unseen hand.

Grasping the implications of evolution

Creationists sometimes warn of the dire consequences of accepting evolution. "If you teach children they are descended from animals, they'll act like animals" is one common warning, and "Survival of the fittest justifies endless cruelty" is another. (I address both of these in Chapter 15.) But devote enough time to finding out more about evolution in depth, and you can find that the real implications are beautiful, ennobling, and eye-opening.

If religion teaches that humans are essentially fallen angels, science teaches that humans are risen apes. The first can produce a feeling of shame and unworthiness, like you've let yourself down. But the second makes me feel astonished and grateful that humanity has come as far as it has. It's the natural point of view, informed by science, that makes me optimistic and proud. Yes, people sometimes behave like baboons. But people have also cured polio, measured the universe, formed the United Nations, and written *Charlotte's Web*. Humanity can always do better, but considering that the ancestors of humans were bacteria, I'd say humanity is doing all right.

Realizing that I'm an animal doesn't make me want to "act like an animal" — it makes me feel a deep kinship with other living things. That's one of the greatest implications of a worldview informed by evolution. A walk in the woods becomes a family reunion. And when I grasp that I'm not the end product of evolution, just a tiny twig on the immense and complex tree of life, the pride I felt in the previous paragraph is tempered with a nice dose of humility — and again, wonder.

Discovering and Defining Life's Meaning

If you don't believe there's a God whose divine plan gives your life meaning, you get to figure out your life's meaning for yourself.

You'd think that the freedom to decide for yourself what your life is all about would appeal to people — especially in the United States, a country with a serious fetish for individual freedom. But the idea of figuring out meaning on their own seems to scare a lot of people. They worry that a life without God would also be a life without meaning.

As with so many other topics in this book, God can be a useful frame for the search for meaning and purpose. A religious person may say:

I didn't know what God's purpose was for me. I prayed about it day and night, and finally, after many unfulfilling years, God led me to [insert meaningful thing here]. I've never been happier or more fulfilled. I know in my heart that I've discovered God's purpose for my life.

A nonreligious person may have the same experience and put it this way:

I didn't know what the right purpose was for me. I thought about it day and night, and finally, after many unfulfilling years, all that serious reflection led me to [insert meaningful thing here]. I've never been happier or more fulfilled. I know in my heart that I've discovered the right purpose for my life.

Once again, a religious and a nonreligious person are less different than they tend to think. One person directs her thinking to an idea of God; the other directs her thinking to her own mind. One feels led by God; the other feels led by her own reflection and self-knowledge. Both knew when they weren't fulfilled and when they finally were.

Given a choice, I prefer making my own choices, and I think most atheists would say the same. Life is so much more meaningful that way. I chose the person I married, and we chose the house we live in. We chose to have children and how to raise them. She chose to be a teacher; I chose to be a writer.

And in every case, the fact that we made our own choices made those experiences so much more meaningful than they would have been if someone else selected us for each other, assigned us to have kids, and chosen our house and careers. Even if they were the same choices we'd have made, the satisfaction clearly would have been so much less.

Meaning and purpose in a natural worldview aren't really that different from a religious one. Being uncertain about your purpose or feeling like your life doesn't have the meaning you wish it had can be unsettling. For some, the idea of God helps. But those who don't believe in a God get to drive the whole scary, exhilarating road themselves.

As I said before, I wouldn't have it any other way.

Raising Children to Think Independently

One of the most heartfelt values for most atheists is the freedom to think for themselves. So it makes sense that most atheist parents also want to protect their kids' rights to think for themselves.

My parents gave me a strong curiosity about the world and the freedom to think for myself about it, which I'm incredibly grateful for. They never made me feel that I was expected to believe as they did, and they never said I couldn't or shouldn't ask certain questions. I worked out my beliefs for myself, building the foundation of my understanding of the world brick by brick.

The result of that process is the deep satisfaction of really knowing what I believe is true and why I believe it, because I placed every brick in that foundation myself. No one handed me settled answers to the big questions, and I was never told to believe something just because so-and-so said it was true. I know the reasoning and experience behind every opinion I hold.

I can't begin to tell you how much that means to me.

As a parent, I've always urged my kids to get outside of my oversized influence as a dad and think independently. Whenever they ask for my opinion, especially about the big unknowables, I tell them what I think, but I always follow it up with a reminder that they should find other people who believe differently and talk to them — and that in the end, they get to work it out for themselves.

So when my daughter was about eight and asked, "Did Jesus really come alive after he was dead?" I said, "I don't think so, no. I think that's just a story so we feel better about death. But talk to Grandma Barbara. I know she thinks it really happened. Then you can make up your own mind and even change your mind back and forth a thousand times if you want."

I didn't know at first if other atheist parents took this approach, but I eventually learned it's by far the most common. One 2006 survey of parents in the United States and Canada indicated that nearly 90 percent who identified as "very religious" said they raised they children specifically to believe as they do, while more than 90 percent of the parents who identified as atheists said they wanted their kids to make their own choices in religious identity. A larger 2012 parent survey by the author Wendy Thomas Russell had an almost identical result.

And why is that? Why do atheists leave such an important thing to chance? Consider these reasons:

- ✔ **They don't actually leave it to "chance."** They leave it to their kids.

- ✔ **Some want to steer clear of what they experienced as kids.** Many atheists were told what to believe when they were kids, and sometimes even frightened into religious belief with ideas of hell or the wrath of God. That's given them a serious allergy to indoctrination of any kind, so they work hard to avoid doing it in reverse. And those like me who had an independent process want their kids to have the same advantage they enjoyed.

As a result, very few atheists raise their children specifically as atheists. They try to keep all labels off them for as long as possible until they can choose their own.

If my kids end up choosing a religious identity, I'm confident it will be one of the many positive expressions, one that matches the values of honesty, curiosity, and compassion with which they were raised. If they choose something I think is less positive, I'm sure we'll talk about it, just like we do about anything else. But I won't disown them, and I certainly won't love them any less — another approach that atheist parents and liberal religious parents tend to share.

Chapter 17

Being an Atheist in a Religious World

In This Chapter

▶ Seeing our religious culture through nonreligious eyes

▶ Getting to know about religion, even if you aren't religious

▶ Choosing battles, making peace

▶ Being an atheist in a religious family

*R*eligion has a huge influence and presence in the world. Five out of six people identify as theistic believers of one kind or another, and the world's history and cultures are steeped in religious ideas.

I sometimes refer to atheists as people who have "set religion aside," but that's a little misleading. An atheist can't set religion aside any more than someone who rides a bike to work can set traffic aside. Even in relatively secular countries like the United Kingdom or Norway, religion continues to show up in public ceremonies and rites of passage, cultural identity, and even the architecture of the buildings. In the United States, a country with a much higher level of professed faith, religion is in everything from political speeches to public policy, from the daily Pledge of Allegiance to US currency, from public remembrances to the family dinner table.

This chapter explores some of the issues around being an atheist in a religious world.

Living in a Mostly Religious Culture

Like any minority, part of the challenge of being an atheist is figuring out how to live among the majority. An atheist has to ask him or herself many questions: Should I be open about my beliefs, or be quiet and let others assume I'm one of them? Do I skip religious rituals and traditions, or modify them, or just smile and go along? How can I assert my right to freedom of belief in a way that doesn't trample on the rights of others — and how should I respond when others trample on me? Can I challenge beliefs that I think are harmful or dishonest? If I have kids, do I raise them as atheists, or raise them to make their own decisions? If I want them to decide for themselves, how can I make sure I'm not forcing my own views on them?

In the following sections, I look at some of the more public questions and some of the ways atheists choose to answer them.

Choosing battles, knowing rules

Most Western countries have some level of freedom of religion for individuals. Official religious tolerance is often a practical solution to stop people from killing each other over differences of belief. Today, such freedoms are commonly accepted as a natural thread in the fabric of a civilized society. Everybody fully understands what "freedom of religion" means, and all conflicts are happily in the past.

Yeah . . . okay, maybe not so much. Conflict between worldviews is still common despite religious freedoms for these reasons:

- ✔ Religious belief is deeply personal, and the visible existence of contradictory points of view can feel threatening.

- ✔ Some religions have a stated plan to convert the world (such as "The Great Commission") or believe that their nation is theirs by divine right or history (orthodox Jews in Israel, for instance, or Christian Dominionists in the United States).

- ✔ Some atheists see eliminating religion as an ultimate goal and "accommodation" of religion as an obstacle to that goal.

- ✔ The line between exercising my own beliefs and stepping on the rights of others can be unclear.

- ✔ Not everyone recognizes the right to openly criticize other worldviews, or where that line should be.

- ✔ Many are not aware that freedom of religion includes the right to not believe at all — that "freedom of religion includes freedom *from* religion."

When living with religious diversity, people still have a lot of misunderstanding, a lot of sharp elbows, and a lot of outrage. In addition to conflicts between religions (such as the "Ground Zero Mosque" controversy in Manhattan), you may have heard about atheists protesting when religion ends up somewhere they think it shouldn't be. It may be a politician making religious arguments against stem cell research, the Ten Commandments carved in stone outside a courthouse, a prayer over the loudspeaker before a high school football game, or references to God on money and in the Pledge of Allegiance. It can feel like the religious majority is forcing itself on everyone else, trampling my rights to self-determination in the process.

A lot of religious believers get angry about these challenges, feeling like their own freedom of expression is under attack. The rights of Christians and other religious believers to worship and believe freely in their own hearts, homes, and church communities must never be infringed. At the same time, no one else should be required to bend the knee or participate in religious rituals that aren't their own in our shared spaces.

When the Southern Baptist denomination was founded in 1845, they really understood this concept. They were a tiny minority, and they didn't want some majority vision of God forced on them or on their kids. So the Southern Baptist Convention wrote strong support for the separation of church and state and freedom of religion into their founding documents. "The state has no right to impose penalties for religious opinions of any kind," they said. They fought tooth and nail to be sure public officials and public schools were never endorsing any form of religion. That's for the home and church, they said.

But after they became the largest Protestant denomination in the United States, Baptist churches became the greatest violators of church-state separation, endorsing candidates from the pulpit, pushing for Christian prayer in public schools, directly lobbying for public policies that match their values . . . and they forgot what all that separation nonsense was ever about — even though their official documents still clearly favor separation.

That's okay — atheists, Jews, Hindus, and all the rest of the minority worldviews down here in the cheap seats will remember for them. Protecting the rights of those outside of the majority is a battle worth choosing, for the sake of *everyone's* religious freedom.

Grappling with church-state issues in public school and in the public square

Pursuing your own beliefs in your heart and home is easy. The challenge comes when lives overlap with the lives of other people who have their own visions, their own way of doing things. Public policy, public schools, public parks and roads and buildings — this is where it gets tricky. But the goal of a free society is worth the work. And a big part of meeting the challenge is understanding what the separation of church and state is really about.

Most atheists feel the same way as I do — that not everyone needs to believe the same. Good thing too, because universal agreement on religious questions is never going to happen. I also don't need to be protected from offense, which should also be a relief — it's too much to ask others to keep from offending me. There's no way to know what's going to offend each and every person.

On the other hand, it's reasonable for you and me both to live without having to take part in someone else's religion, or to see our shared government playing favorites with one worldview over another. And asking that our kids be able to go to a school that doesn't promote another religion is also reasonable. That means government and schools need to stay out of the practice of religion entirely. Those are decisions best made at home.

When you hear a parent raising a concern about religion in the schools — sometimes an atheist parent, but just as often not — notice that it's rarely about "offense." The school should not promote or favor one worldview over another because doing so interferes with the rights and responsibilities of the parents to raise their children as they see fit.

There's a good way to drive this point home. Suppose I'm the principal of your child's middle school. I rise at the PTA meeting and announce that I'm in favor of putting God back in schools. Starting Monday, we'll open each day with a prayer, and we'll be teaching creation instead of evolution. A loud cheer goes up. Finally, our prayers have been answered! As I'm carried out on jubilant shoulders, I announce that we'll be praying to Chac-Xib-Chac, the Mayan god of blood sacrifice, and it's the Mayan creation story that'll be taught as true. I'd get a quick plunge to the floor — and I'd deserve it. I shouldn't force any religion on your child. Those decisions are best made at home.

If on the other hand I said our prayers would be specifically Catholic — that we would pray to Mother Mary and invoke the name of the Holy Father each morning, for example —Baptists and Methodists would be lined up outside my office, and rightly so. The same goes for my own worldview. If I heard that a teacher at my child's school was advocating atheism — saying specifically that God doesn't exist, and telling the kids they should believe the same — I'd be the very first parent demanding the teacher's head on a plate.

Some people try to solve the problem by suggesting schools can use "interdenominational prayers." But no prayer accommodates all concepts of God. Not all religions have gods that are prayed to, for one thing. Others aren't called "God," and some faiths consider it blasphemous to say or even write the name "God." One religion I know of even includes a specific instruction not to pray in public, ever, but to only pray alone in your room. (You may have heard of this religion — it's Christianity, and the instruction is Matthew 6:5–6.) And I haven't yet heard an actual prayer that fits with my point of view as an atheist. So no, "interdenominational prayers" aren't the answer. Secular schools are the answer.

Remember that "secular" doesn't mean the same as "atheistic." Secular schools are *neutral* on religious questions, leaving those questions where they belong — in the hands of individual families.

The same applies to all other aspects of a shared government. It's just as intrusive to have "In God We Trust" or the Ten Commandments in a federal courthouse as it would be to have "Praise Allah the Merciful," or "No Worries, God is Pretend."

Allow the statements and symbols of a single religious viewpoint into government buildings, and the next thing you know, it'll be on money! Okay, so it *is* on US money. Given these examples, I hope you agree that it really shouldn't be. (In fact it wasn't always there. The US Founders preferred a secular motto — *E pluribus unum* — but "In God We Trust" was added to currency during the Second Red Scare of the 1950s to distinguish the United States from the godless Communists.)

Despite every effort by the founders of this country to clearly define and protect religious liberty, it continues to be a real challenge, something each generation has to grapple with and rediscover. That's okay — as hard as that is to do, it's the best way to keep everyone's shared values alive and maturing. (See more about the US Founding Fathers in Chapter 6.)

Living in the closet

A few years ago I had a terrific conversation with one of my wife's cousins, a Southern Baptist whom I deeply admire and respect. He'd just found out I was an atheist, and he chatted me up about it for two good hours. No conversion attempts, just a good chat. At the end he said, "I hope you don't mind me bending your ear for so long. I just don't know any other atheists."

"Actually," I said, "I'm pretty sure you do." The odds are very good that he knows several people who are somewhere on the "rainbow of disbelief" I describe in Chapter 2. But the stigma attached to atheism is so large — especially where he lives, in the US South — that most of those individuals who don't believe in God stay closeted, sharing their opinion with few people or no one at all. In many cases, they continue going to church, continue bowing their heads at the table, and even continue their professions of faith. (As I note in my description of the Clergy Project in Chapter 11, some atheists are even in the pulpit.) Any other nonbelievers around them are probably under the same camouflage, so all of them continue assuming they're alone. And the many believers around them, family and friends, continue in their belief that all the atheists are somewhere out there in Hollywood, New York, or Beijing.

You can easily assume that every parent on your block, everyone cheering in the stands at the soccer game, or everyone walking the aisles of the supermarket is a churchgoing believer. But it's never true. No matter where you live, even in the Bible Belt of the southern United States, atheists, agnostics, and humanists are in your community. Surveys put the nonreligious population around 20 percent in the United States, or more than 50 million people, and a much higher percentage in Canada and the United Kingdom. (Check out Chapter 14 for specific numbers for different countries.)

Being public about that worldview in some places is easier. In others, the vast majority of nonbelievers remain quiet and closeted, even as they go through the motions of belief.

Coming out of the closet

An atheist or other nonbeliever may choose to keep his or her opinions quiet for many reasons. The first and most common is the fear of how those around him or her would receive such an announcement of unbelief.

The comedian Julia Sweeney describes the reaction of her Catholic mother when she found out Julia was an atheist. "Not believing in God is one thing," her mother said. "But an *atheist*?!" Comedy aside, Julia describes the real difficulties her parents had accepting her decision. Her dad said she had betrayed her family, her school, and her city — Spokane, Washington, in which Catholicism is the largest religious presence. Both parents said they would no longer speak to her, and her father told her not to come to his funeral.

Just try and stop me, she thought.

Eventually, gradually, her parents came around. Her father even ended up telling Julia he was proud of her for saying what she really thought — though he still figured Satan was involved somehow.

That's a quick summary of one coming-out story — a long, complex process crammed into a few sentences. A thousand variations exist, some smoother, and some much rougher. Some atheists describe being harassed, abused, or completely cut off by their families. Some atheist teens have been disowned and kicked out of their homes. But many others who expected a bad reaction say it went surprisingly well, even resulting in a stronger, more honest relationship with friends and family. The response depends on dozens of things: the religion of the family, how orthodox they are, where they live, how strong the family relationships already are, and much more.

Coming out atheist parallels many of the concerns of lesbian, gay, bisexual, and transgender (LGBT) people as they struggle with the same decision. Both atheists and gays know that many of those around them, including people they love and care about, consider both religious disbelief and homosexuality to be immoral or even evil. The thought of losing valued relationships or even being shunned completely by family and friends is painful and frightening. Many decide that coming out isn't worth the risk.

There's also the question of models — examples of others in the culture who have the same identity. Many LGBT people remained closeted, especially in the early years of the gay rights movement, because it often seemed there was only one way to be publicly gay — stereotypically flamboyant and sexually extroverted. As more people from all walks of life came out as LGBT, including many who didn't fit the stereotype, others felt more comfortable leaving the closet as well. They had models, ways to be LGBT that matched their own personalities and values.

The same dynamic is true of atheists. Some remain closeted in part because the only atheist they've seen is the angry atheist, the culture warrior girded for battle against religion. They've stopped believing, they're looking for options, but they see only two choices — continue pretending belief to keep friends and family intact, or immediately declare war on them and all they stand for. And many atheists just aren't interested in signing up for that confrontation.

As I say in Chapter 14, the "culture warrior" approach is often very well justified. But knowing that it isn't the only one available is important. When I was a doubting teen, the only atheist I'd ever heard of was Madalyn Murray O'Hair (see Chapter 8). She did courageous and important work — and she terrified me! She was so confident, so aggressive, and so unrelenting in her attacks on religion. Years later I'd agree with much of her outrage. But at 15, I couldn't identify with it. So without other role models, I remained closeted for years.

Eventually I stumbled on the amazing history of freethinkers that I present in Parts II and III of this book, and I went from isolation to the company of giants. Just as important, I became part of a tradition with a thousand different ways to be. But that history is largely unknown. Between that and relatively few visible role models, it's no surprise that only a tiny fraction of the more than 50 million nonreligious Americans are open about what they believe.

Fortunately, both are changing. Many books published in the past decade tell the bigger story of religious doubt, including that long and impressive history. And just as there are countless public examples now of "how to be" gay or lesbian, there's a growing public spectrum of religious disbelief as well, including atheists, agnostics, and humanists who

✔ Make a point of working together with religious people

✔ Stand up for the religious freedom of believers

✔ Call themselves religious, even without believing in God (see Chapter 8)

✔ Create communities with rituals, traditions, and mutual support

✔ Focus on doing compassionate work rather than debating theology

✔ Are just plain normal people

They aren't always in the media spotlight, but if someone cares enough to look, they can certainly be found.

How and whether to come out depends on many things, including whether an atheist is a dependent minor or a self-sufficient adult. The full topic is beyond the space available here and beyond the purpose of this book. (Greta Christina, one of the great atheist bloggers I talk about in Chapter 13, is writing a whole book on the subject as I speak.) But check out the nearby sidebar for a few observations and tips.

Coming out atheist: Issues and tips

Whether you're coming out as a nonbeliever or think you may have a family member who is, here are a few thoughts to remember:

✔ Coming out is a personal decision. No one should force an individual into or out of it.

✔ If you're coming out as an atheist and anticipate a bad reaction, be sure to establish a supportive community first —friends, selected family members, online, and so on.

✔ If you're coming out as an atheist to loved ones, let them know that most of who you are hasn't changed. You still feel, value, hope, care, dream, act, think, and love as you did before. And if you want to have your choice respected, let them know clearly that you respect their own choice to believe, even if you question the beliefs themselves.

✔ Take one step at a time. The moment you come out isn't the best time to get into a point-by-point refutation of the family religion. Focus on the relationship first.

✔ If you're religious, and a loved one comes out to you as an atheist, know that she may assume the worst. Let the person know that you still respect and love her as an individual, even if you disagree. You may be surprised over time how little has changed between you. And if you agree, tell her! It's always a nice surprise.

✔ Sometimes coming out is traumatic and results in broken relationships. But more often, it goes much better than people think it will.

✔ Know that coming out normalizes disbelief, which makes it easier for others to do so. It also helps reduce the general fear of difference when a religious person learns that someone they know is an atheist.

Deciding how to interact with religion and the religious

After I decided I wasn't a religious believer, another set of questions confronted me:

- ✔ I've rejected religious belief, but how should I behave toward religion itself?

- ✔ Am I supposed to be opposing it, challenging it, defeating it — or learning to live with it — or pretending that it isn't there?

- ✔ Even more important, how should I interact with religious *people?*

These answers aren't always obvious. Most atheists feel that at least some religious ideas aren't just untrue but also harmful to a shared culture and to the rights of people in that culture. Granting blanket immunity to religious ideas seems wrong. But many of the people atheists know and love are religious, and the atheists don't want to attack them while they're attacking the more problematic parts of religion . . . or do they? By continuing to support a belief system that has some toxic ideas, aren't the believers themselves part of the problem?

For many atheists, answering these questions means doing the following:

1. **Separating beliefs from the people that hold them as much as possible.**

   I can love and respect many people I know while thoroughly disliking and opposing some of their views. After those two levels of respect are separated, the answers become clearer.

2. **Recognizing that not all religious belief is the same.**

   Saying "I hate all religion" is a bit silly when the word *religion* runs the gamut from "kill your neighbor" to "love your neighbor." Many religious people hold views that are entirely benign and inspire them to good, compassionate work. Although a world with a lot more believers like Rev. Fred "God Hates Fags" Phelps would be a nightmare; a world with a lot more Liberal Quakers would be pretty nice.

   Not all atheists see much difference between types of religion. I didn't when I was 25, but I do now. Atheists can change and grow in their worldview, just as religious believers can. Though not everyone goes the same direction, it helps to remember that atheists also go through stages and changes in their perspective, and how they act toward and think about religion and religious people often . . . *evolves.*

Many atheists think they should engage religious people and institutions in just the way they wish to be engaged themselves, as co-participants in the world. Atheists can and should loudly protest the intolerance, ignorance and fear that is born of religion while at the same time loudly applauding religious people and institutions whenever they show charity, tolerance, empathy, honesty, and any of our other shared values.

I call this *engaged coexistence*. Believers and nonbelievers are going to be sharing this little planet for the long haul, so the best everyone can do is work together to pay the rent and remind each other to keep our feet off the furniture.

Notice that coexistence doesn't mean people can't talk about their differences, even challenge each others' assumptions when it really matters. Doing so is *essential*. Beliefs that stay in my head and affect no one else are one thing. But when my beliefs are out in the world affecting other people, I no longer have the right to expect immunity from challenge. So if you think a belief of mine is leading me to treat others unfairly, or causing harm, or spreading ignorance, you have every right to call me on it, to convince me that I'm wrong — to try to change my mind.

And because I'm human, I'll probably dodge and weave and bluster and fudge. It's what people do. But I'd appreciate it if you persist anyway. It's the only way forward.

Of course it's a two-way street — or in the case of a pluralistic society like this one, a hundred-way street. Everyone's free to think and believe independently. But if I think your belief is harmful, it's time for a family meeting. Sometimes that means questioning the Jehovah's Witness at the door — though if it's just some minor point of theology, I'd rather not. Sometimes I'm in the mood to lock horns in an online forum — though sometimes, especially as I get older, I'd rather not. But when the stakes are huge, and a particular religious view is blocking promising medical therapies, or marginalizing a segment of the society, or encouraging my nation into war — those are the times I try to find my voice and engage.

Other people have different thresholds, and more power to them. The key to engaged coexistence is remembering that people deserve respect, but ideas must earn it.

Getting Religiously Literate

In 2010, a Pew Forum survey offered a quiz of basic religious knowledge to US respondents of various worldviews. Mainline Protestants and Catholics both averaged around 16 correct out of 32 — about half right. Mormons averaged 20.3, while Jewish respondents averaged 20.5. That's pretty good, but it's still just second place.

A few more stats about religious knowledge

Of US respondents to a 2010 Pew Forum survey of religious knowledge:

✔ Only 55 percent knew that the Golden Rule isn't one of the Ten Commandments.

✔ Just 54 percent knew that the Qur'an is the holy book of Islam.

✔ Fewer than half could name all four Gospels (Matthew, Mark, Luke, John).

✔ Fewer than a quarter knew that public school teachers can read from the Bible as an example of literature.

✔ Only 18 percent knew that traditionally Protestants, not Catholics, teach that salvation comes through faith alone.

So who was the top group, the most religiously literate of all? Why, it's atheists and agnostics at 20.9, about two-thirds correct.

On questions about Christianity — including several about the Bible — Mormons and white evangelical Protestants do best, with 7.9 and 7.3 out of 12 (respectively). Jews and atheists/agnostics know the most about other world religions like Islam, Buddhism, and Hinduism. (Christians tend to do badly on that one.) Fewer than half of Americans know that the Dalai Lama is Buddhist, and less than 40 percent know that Vishnu and Shiva are associated with Hinduism.

Forty-five percent of US Catholics don't know that their church teaches that the Communion bread and wine actually become the body and blood of Christ, whereas more than half of US Protestants don't know that Martin Luther founded their branch of Christianity.

When it comes to religion, Europe and the United States are mirror images. Americans tend to be deeply religious but know very little *about* religion; Europeans are overwhelmingly secular but tend to know a huge amount *about* religion.

This actually makes sense:

✔ Atheists most often become atheists after examining and challenging the religion into which they were born and then continuing with others.

✔ Atheists are often challenged to defend their position, so they tend to know the arguments for and against belief, and they learn a lot about religion in the process (see Chapter 3).

✔ Atheists often find religion fascinating, which is why we cared enough to look into it.

The following sections further explore how and why atheists know so much about religion.

Understanding why religious literacy matters (for everyone)

Why is religious knowledge important, including the religions of other cultures, even if you aren't religious? There are three very good reasons:

- ✔ **To understand the world:** It starts with understanding. If most of the people on Earth identify as religious, see the world through religious eyes, and express themselves to some degree in religious terms, you will spend a really unhelpful amount of time being baffled by the world if you don't have some basic understanding of religion. And the more understanding, the better. Knowing about not just the majority religion, but also other religions around the world is crucial.

- ✔ **To be part of the conversation:** Being part of the cultural conversation is no small thing. Most political and social issues end up with religious opinions mixed into the debate. The more you know about where those opinions come from, what they're based on, and what they mean, the better you can respond. It keeps you in the game. And if someone makes a reference to the road to Damascus or the prodigal son, you can avoid being discounted by knowing what they mean.

- ✔ **To make an informed decision:** When you have all the information, it's amazing how much better your decisions are. That's why I dress with the light on — so I don't discover at lunchtime that I'm wearing two different shoes. The same applies when dressing your mind in opinions, including your choice of religion or worldview. People who make a conscious choice about their worldview are more likely to end up in a positive one, while those who simply take what they're born into without examining it get the luck of the draw. A strong religious literacy helps a person choose well, which is better for everyone.

Doing religious literacy the wrong way

Many of the most obvious ways to get more information about religion aren't the best. So how does an atheist — or anyone, for that matter — discover more about religion?

Going to church seems like an obvious answer. But whatever its other benefits may be, churchgoing has little to do with religious literacy. Sitting in a pew of a single denomination week after week will teach me about a single sliver of a single piece of the religious pie — *if that.* As shown by some of the answers to the Pew survey I mentioned earlier, a person can sit in church 52 times a year and still know very little about even their own religion.

Worse still, with very few exceptions, attending church (or Sunday school or Bible study) in one denomination or religion will teach you almost zilch about other religions. And that's an essential part of real literacy. Experiencing just one denomination is like reading a few limericks and thinking you know poetry.

It also doesn't require attending long lectures or reading volumes of religious history or scripture. Good thing, too, because most people won't do that. Gaining religious literacy is easier and more interesting and fun than any of these.

Doing religious literacy the right way

Want to be as religiously literate as your average atheist? Try this:

1. **Notice religion in your everyday life.**

   Religion is everywhere, and noticing this saturation is a first step in doing religious literacy right. It's in the news, from the stem cell debate to climate change to terrorism to nonviolent action. It's in movies, in books, and on television. Politicians lace their speeches with it. In some parts of the United States — never mind which parts — the second question asked of any newcomer is, "What church do y'all go to?" Norse gods are represented in the days of the week, Roman gods in the months and planets, and the seven-day week itself is rooted in Jewish and Babylonian creation stories. Holidays were originally holy days. Countless figures of speech — a drop in the bucket, a fly in the ointment, a wolf in sheep's clothing — have biblical origins. Nike shoes, Midas Mufflers, a road atlas, the Olympics, and the first US space programs all borrow names from Greek mythology. All of this is religious influence.

2. **Cultivate your curiosity about it.**

   Doing so is easier when no one is making any demands on you, like insisting that you must accept it to be a good person. It's just knowledge, and it helps our understanding of who and what we are.

   Be sure to include the whole picture — good, bad, and ugly. You can't talk about Martin Luther King, Jr. without noting that he was a Baptist minister and that his religion was an important part of his inspiration. You can't grasp the terrorist attacks of September 11, 2001, without understanding Islamic afterlife beliefs. And the founding of the United States is reframed by noting that many of the US Founders were religious skeptics of one stripe or another.

3. **Follow that curiosity into knowledge.**

    Keep moving outward as far from your own culture as you can. Read myths and stories from many traditions. Watch movies with religious themes. No, not some crashing biblical epic. I'm talking about *Little Buddha, Kirikou and the Sorceress, Fiddler on the Roof, Jason and the Argonauts, Gandhi, Seven Years in Tibet, Schindler's List,* and *The Ledge.* This list alone touches six different belief systems, including atheism. That's five more than you'll get in a typical Sunday school. And don't forget comedies, like *Bruce Almighty, Dogma,* and the *Invention of Lying.* No reason to not have fun while you explore beliefs.

    Read the works of Karen Armstrong, Alan Dundes, and Joseph Campbell. And be sure to see religion firsthand by attending services in a few different religions. Not every week — I know you're a busy person, and most churchgoers don't even do that. Just once in a while. And chat with believers. Ask what they believe and why, then share your own thoughts.

4. **Connect your observations to create a web of understanding.**

    As you do all this, bit by bit, thread by thread, a more complete picture of religion as a human creation begins to form. It's really fascinating. You may not be an atheist when you're done, but you'll do better on surveys. And you'll never see the world in quite the same way again.

Becoming religiously literate doesn't happen in long lectures or sermons. Religious literacy is about thousands of small, everyday moments, and caring enough to weave them together.

Living as an Atheist in a Religious Extended Family

Most atheists and agnostics in the United States and Canada have extended families that are religious to some extent. Sometimes this presents no problem at all. But often the difference in worldviews can produce some real friction.

Some people, atheists and theists alike, wonder what the big deal is: *We have different opinions, so what? You like anchovies on your pizza, but they make me sick. So we order anchovies on half and get on with life! Religion is the same thing.*

Whether that conclusion is true depends on what religion means to people. For many, religion isn't just an opinion or a set of answers — it's an identity. It doesn't just describe what they think, it defines who they *are*. So when a family member rejects the family religion, it can feel to others in the family like a rejection of the family itself. I don't think some atheists recognize the way religion is tied up in identity, and how that complicates family dynamics when one person steps away from that religion.

These sections explore a few of the issues that commonly arise when a member of a religious family becomes an atheist and some ways to reduce the friction around those issues.

Drawing out family religious diversity

"I'm a secular island in a sea of religiosity." That's the single most common metaphor I hear from atheists in religious families. The atheist feels completely alone, completely "other" because everyone else seems exactly the same in his or her beliefs. Although the image is a very lonely one, it's also rarely quite true.

Oh it certainly feels like that as the family gathers around the table at Thanksgiving or Christmas and all heads bow. But even in the most orthodox and extreme religious communities, complete conformity of belief is an illusion. A spectrum of belief and a range of intensity in every group and every family exists, no matter how it appears on the surface.

Suppose my extended family is religious and typical. We're gathered at the annual family reunion. There's a lot of praising Jesus and thanking God. Every conversation about society or politics seems to include some reference to religion. There's a cross on the wall in every room. And why not? It's my uncle's house, not mine. I know that everyone but me goes to church once or even twice a week. I am "a secular island in a sea of religiosity."

Or am I? Yes, Grandma and Grandpa are traditional, Bible reading, God-fearing, grace-saying Southern Baptists, Aunt Gloria pumps her palms to the ceiling and yells "Hallelujah!" ten times a day, and Cousin Dave has the *Left Behind* series in audio and can't wait until two-thirds of humanity is plunged into the Lake of Fire. But when I scratch that hyper-religious surface a bit, a family spectrum begins to appear:

- ✔ Gloria's husband Mike is a deacon at the church, but wasn't especially religious until they were married.
- ✔ Uncle Rick hasn't ever really thought about it, but he goes to church and bows his head at the table, so he looks just as committed as anyone.
- ✔ Uncle Tim learned about Buddhism in college and thinks that would be cool, but thinks "no way in this family am I gonna be a Buddhist."

✔ Cousin Hannah has one best friend who is Jewish and another who is Mormon. She considers herself completely Baptist, but she just can't believe God would send them to hell.

✔ Cousin Kelly has read Sam Harris and thinks he's on to something.

✔ And good old Aunt Susan is wearing a T-shirt that says, "May the God of Your Choice Bless You" — hardly a Southern Baptist sentiment.

That's quite a mix. But when the family comes together, they naturally take on the religious intensity and color of the most religious members, so it seems like everyone is on the same page. But even though they're all lined up in the first pew on Sunday morning, a diversity of opinion and intensity is there. So an atheist is part of a *spectrum* of belief, not an island in a sea of religious sameness. And drawing out that spectrum is one of the healthiest things any family can do to make the full spectrum feel welcome.

Most families *do* religion, but they don't often talk *about* religion itself. I suggest that any family member wanting to relax the family climate around religious difference should try to make beliefs a more normal topic of discussion. Not pitched debate, just conversation. Bring up an interesting article. Mention that local Hindu temple that's going up. Or my personal favorite, have everyone take the Belief-o-Matic Quiz (see the nearby sidebar).

Creating a safe space for doubt and difference

When religious people discover they have an atheist among them, they don't all suffer fainting spells or throw tirades. Many are perfectly secure in their beliefs and happy to make room for diversity among their family and friends.

But knowing quite how to accommodate diverse beliefs is sometimes hard for those accustomed to thinking all of those around them believe as they do. I've had well-meaning religious friends say "bless you" when I sneeze, then go wide-eyed and apologize if they offended me! Honestly, if my skin is *that* thin, I'd better not get caught in the rain. Others ask if it's okay to say grace or to keep me on their Christmas card list. It's a very nice attempt to accommodate me, and I appreciate that, but there's no need to worry.

That's *my* reaction, you understand. As I say in Chapter 8, atheists vary in their allergies to religion. I don't mind in the least having someone express their religion around me. There's no need for somebody else to climb into a box so I can climb out. But someone with a more painful history regarding religion may have different sensitivities.

Recognizing what we share: The Belief-o-Matic Quiz

One guaranteed conversation starter is the Belief-O-Matic Quiz at `http://www.beliefnet.com/Entertainment/Quizzes/BeliefOMatic_OLD.aspx`. The quiz asks 20 multiple choice worldview questions, then spits out a list of belief systems and your *percentage of overlap with each*. It's a powerful and fun way to show that everyone has more in common than they previously thought.

I take it every year. Last time I came out 100 percent Secular Humanist and 92 percent Unitarian Universalist. But I was also pretty darn Buddhist (73 percent) and shared 60 percent with the beliefs of mainline Protestants. There's some nice common ground with my family! For some reason I'm less Jewish than I was three years ago, but a little more Catholic (up from 16 to 18 percent).

No matter what your own perspective, e-mail the link to all family members before your next gathering. The conversation it generates is wonderful. (Of course, some family members will enjoy learning about their overlap with other religions more than others. Be ready to catch evangelical Grandma when she learns that she's 70 percent Islamic.)

That said, I could do without a few of the more aggressive gestures. The grace at dinner that includes a request that the Lord "open the hearts of some members of this family" isn't respectful coexistence. And I don't see the statement "I'll be praying for you" as something benign when it's directed at an atheist. Praying for me is fine, even thoughtful. Announcing to me that you're doing so often has a very different purpose — expressing judgment and disapproval rather than care and concern.

Many secular families adopt mealtime rituals that serve the same emotional purpose as grace — slowing down, reflecting, acknowledging — without the religious overtones. Inviting a secular family member to offer a meditation instead of grace at a family gathering is a nice inclusive gesture. Give him or her a heads-up in advance, of course. And when an event is at the home of a nontheistic branch of the family, it's respectful to ask first before launching into a religious grace.

In general, creating a safe space for difference and doubt isn't about tiptoeing. What's needed is the opposite of tiptoeing, a willingness to allow discussions to go where they will, respecting people but letting ideas fend for themselves, and making sure no one is shutting down the honest expressions of anyone else. It takes a bit of getting used to, especially if a family is accustomed to thinking of itself as one big happy point of view. But being aware of the presence of difference and valuing that diversity is really half the battle.

Defusing family pressure

Even if everybody has good intentions, religious differences can cause real tension in a family. And if intentions aren't so good, it can tear a family apart.

If tensions are high in your family, direct communication is crucial, and it can start from either side of the religious divide. The key is to frame the conversation not in terms of winning and losing, but *détente.*

Many people think *détente* is the same as a ceasefire. It actually means *a reduction of tension and building of mutual confidence.* If I'm approaching my Baptist mother-in-law with the intention to "win," I might tell her why her religion doesn't hold water and demand that she show me the proper respect, adding that I won't let her see the grandkids until she agrees. That's hardly a tension-reducing approach. Whether I "win" or "lose," the tension just went up to 11.

If instead I approach with the goal of reducing family tension, I can start by honestly telling her that our relationship is important to me, which is why I wanted to have this talk. I can empathize with her concerns, showing that I understand how she feels, and that I know it must feel like I'm rejecting the family itself. Then I do what I can to reassure her that I'm still the same person, I still value honesty and feel love and compassion, and I still love my family and want what's best for them. Instead of building tension, this approach can drain tension away, replacing it with confidence and a strengthened relationship.

These things may sound obvious to some, but for others they can be an eye-opener. Family conflicts like these aren't mostly about ideas or beliefs. They are about people and relationships. Honoring, empathizing, and reassuring is exactly what's needed in that moment, and countless families have found this approach to be incredibly effective at cutting through the tension around these issues. It isn't the end of the process, of course — it's just an excellent beginning.

Connecting with others

Before the turn of the 21st century, atheists, agnostics, and humanists had difficulty finding each other, which led to even greater isolation. In the past ten years, thanks mostly to the Internet, the ability to connect with other nontheists has been revolutionized.

National organizations like the American Humanist Association and American Atheists have grown in numbers; social networking sites like Atheist Nexus and Meetup have made it easier for atheists to connect locally and in areas of shared interest; and blogs and discussion forums have allowed for an exchange of ideas and stories that was unthinkable a decade ago. To explore these resources in greater depth, turn to Chapters 13 and 14.

Feeling included for the first time

A few years ago, in January 2009, nonbelievers in the United States suddenly appeared, shivering and blinking, in a place they'd never been before — a major presidential address. Twenty minutes after being sworn in as the 44th president of the United States on that bitterly cold morning, Barack Obama described the diversity of worldviews in the country: "We know that our patchwork heritage is a strength, not a weakness," he said. "We are a nation of Christians and Muslims, Jews, and Hindus — and nonbelievers."

I'm not sure how long I remained frozen in front of my television. I may have missed a birthday or two.

If you've never been part of an excluded minority, I highly recommend it. For most of the country's history, if you weren't a white male Christian, the US presidency seemed to be a private club for somebody else — and just one symbol of a larger, deeper exclusion in the culture. Obama's election was an enormous breakthrough for African Americans. It wasn't the end of their exclusion, but it was an earthquake.

The president's willingness — in the inaugural address, no less — to include nonbelievers as part of the nation may not have been quite as revolutionary as his race. But for those of us hearing our name called for the first time — believe me, it was huge. In the eyes of our own government, we were no longer invisible.

Trying not to disappear

As I say in the "Coming out" section earlier, atheists differ quite a bit in their desire to make their atheism visible to those around them. Some are happy to go along for years with everyone assuming they're part of the religious majority. But at some point, many begin to feel it's dishonest. Others become uncomfortable with people thinking they hold beliefs that they actually find harmful, or they start to feel resentful about having to hide like a second-class citizen. Still others want to come out so they can help change the public image of nonbelievers, even if just in the minds of their own family and friends.

This last one's especially important. Being out makes it easier for others to be out, which makes it harder to stereotype nonbelievers, which causes attitudes to evolve. It has worked precisely this way for gays and lesbians, and it has the same effect for atheists.

Some atheists respond by shouting from the rooftops, framing every gesture and message in terms of atheism. Some choose more subtle ways, like

- ✔ Wearing a T-shirt or jewelry from a freethought organization or event
- ✔ Posting comments or sharing videos or other links on social media that gradually reveal a nontheistic perspective

✔ Offering a nontheistic "grace" at a family gathering

✔ Finding opportunities to express a nontheistic opinion in conversation

✔ Respectfully refraining from some religious practices or events, or modifying their participation

And nothing is as powerful as simply being out and normal. If all the stigma and fear were set aside for a single day, and every nonbeliever revealed his or her atheism to friends and family, it would change the public perception overnight. Atheism would no longer be some unthinkable opinion held by ill-defined "others" somewhere out there, but a normal part of the diversity of belief in families and communities everywhere.

Chapter 18

Getting the Best of Religion . . . and Leaving the Rest

. . . .

In This Chapter

▶ Understanding why people (really) go to church

▶ Making human communities

▶ Commemorating life

▶ Doing good together

. . . .

Mention "church" to ten different atheists and you may get ten different reactions. Some turn red with anger at the very word, seeing a place of manipulation, ignorance, and fear. Some are indifferent to it. Others are fascinated by the window it gives into the human mind and heart. Many atheists feel a sense of loss when they think of church, even a little envy, whereas others feel nothing but pure relief at leaving church and religion behind.

The difference has a lot to do with a person's past history. If I feel I was lied to and abused or frightened into belief as a child, resentment is an understandable reaction and can last a lifetime. If I never darkened the door of a church in my life, the whole thing may just be mystifying to me. But a large and possibly growing number of atheists see the benefits people get from belonging to a church community and want those same human benefits without having to park their own beliefs and convictions at the door.

So what are those benefits? Among others, religion offers the following:

✔ An established community that connects people to each other

✔ A pre-defined set of values and beliefs

✔ Common language and symbols that capture complex ideas

✔ Rituals to mark life transitions

- ✔ A sense of wonder, a way to transcend the mundane
- ✔ Comforting answers to big questions
- ✔ Consoling explanations to ease hardship and loss
- ✔ A way to join with others in doing good, such as volunteering and charitable giving, as a direct expression of what a person believes

I can happily do without some of these benefits. For all the time and effort it saves, I don't want my values and beliefs defined for me, and I'd rather not have comforting answers at the expense of actual ones. But other benefits on this list address real human needs that don't go away when a person stops believing in God. Some needs, like the desire to be part of a supportive community, can even increase after a person no longer thinks a caring God can offer that support.

This chapter looks at the benefits of theistic religion and church, and the many ways nontheists are finding those same benefits without God.

Realizing Why People (Really) Go to Church

Nothing is as obnoxious as having someone outside your head say he knows what you think and believe better than you do. If you want to exasperate an atheist, for example, just say that you know he or she really does believe in God, *deep inside*. I don't want to do the same thing in reverse by telling religious people why they *really* go to church.

But if I'm going to talk about how atheists can get the benefits of church without the church, I need to know what people are actually getting out of the experience — even if it's different from what they think. If going to church really is all about God, this section will be short. But if something else is going on, something that's not God-dependent, then I have something to talk about.

And guess what: When good research scratches the surface of churchgoing, it turns out that all sorts of human needs are being met. Those needs are placed in the frame of God and religion, but it's the picture inside the frame, the met needs of real people, that's really important.

A recent Gallup poll asked churchgoers to give the main reason — just one — why they go to church. You'd think most people would say "God." But only 27 percent of the respondents mentioned God or worship as their primary reason for going. Most said they go to be a part of a caring, supportive community, or for inspiration or personal growth, or to stay grounded — or just out of habit.

A secular humanist friend of mine has a lousy, stressful job dealing with grumpy people. She told me she goes to church just to be surrounded by friendly people once a week. Simple as that.

Community, inspiration, personal growth — these *can* all happen in the context of religious belief. But not one of them relies on the idea of a God.

A 2010 Harvard/Wisconsin study came to the same conclusions through a different door. They were looking at the connection between churchgoing and life satisfaction. A lot of other studies had shown that churchgoers are happier and more satisfied with their lives than nonchurchgoers. This team wanted to find out why. Is it belief in God — or is something else going on?

They found that churchgoers are happier than nonchurchgoers *only* if they have close friends in the congregation. Regular churchgoers who have no close friends in the congregation actually scored lower in life satisfaction than nonchurchgoers. The researchers said the high life satisfaction scores are almost entirely about the social aspect of religion — not theology, not worship, not God. People are more satisfied when they go to church because they build a social network in the congregation. They get that sense of belonging and acceptance that everybody wants to some degree. Take away the connection to other people, and you take away the satisfaction. And the worst thing of all would be going every Sunday, watching others connect, and not connecting yourself. It all makes sense.

Discovering that the smiles on the faces of churchgoers have more to do with people than with God is good news for those of us who don't believe. Most of us still feel that same need for social connection and community, but we can satisfy them very well outside of the church doors.

Creating Communities without Church (. . . or at Least without God)

The question remains how best to achieve the benefits of churchgoing, including a sense of community, for those people who would rather not sit through the supernatural stuff. This section looks at some creative and effective experiments in communities built around other, entirely human things.

Experimenting with humanist community

One experiment in this direction is religion that's built around something other than belief in God. At first, church without God may seem as silly as a restaurant without food. Isn't God the point? But if you've read the last few paragraphs, you know that God isn't the main point after all. Sure, God's name is on the shingle, and he's the one who is sung to and prayed to. But that's just one possible focus for a welcoming community that inspires its members to be better people.

Fostering community: Ethical Culture and the UUs

You can also build a community around that very desire to be better people and create a better world. That's a good nutshell description of Ethical Culture, a God-optional religion I discuss in Chapter 7. It also describes Unitarian Universalism (UUs), a denomination that comes together not around beliefs but around principles and values, including

- ✔ The inherent worth and dignity of every person
- ✔ Justice, equity, and compassion in human relations
- ✔ A free and responsible search for truth and meaning

Ninety-one percent of UUs choose "humanist" as one of the labels that describes them, and more than half are nontheistic. The UU principles show one way nonbelievers can and do gather in meaningful communities — by putting shared values and principles at the center instead of shared beliefs.

Understanding what former churchgoers really miss about church

Atheists who don't feel that social need so much (see Chapter 14) don't see any problem to solve — Sunday just got easier! Many express an overwhelming sense of freedom and relief after they walk out those church doors for the last time. But many other nonbelievers feel a genuine loss when they stop going to church (if they ever did go).

Most aren't missing the idea of God — which makes sense, because according to that Harvard/Wisconsin study among others, they probably weren't in church for God in the first place. Maybe they are missing the very same things that current churchgoers are actually getting out of church, like social connection, inspiration, and community.

To test this idea, you can search the Internet for phrases like "what I miss about church." Sure enough, a pattern emerges:

- ✔ "What I miss about church is the feeling of community."
- ✔ "The only thing about church I miss is the instant community support."
- ✔ "I miss joining with others to do good."
- ✔ "I miss the feeling of belonging that I had."
- ✔ "I miss the feeling of connection and common purpose."
- ✔ "I miss feeling a part of something greater than myself."
- ✔ "The fellowship and feeling of community is about the only thing I miss about church."

Taking some of the church out of churches

Sometimes humanism flows the other way as well. In addition to humanist groups moving toward some of the better aspects of church, some churches are becoming more humanistic. One of the most fascinating of these is the former Christ Community Church in Spring Lake, Michigan. The church's pastor is Ian Lawton, a soft-spoken guy recently relocated from Australia. Lawton realized that his new congregation was much more diverse in identity and belief than the church's name and symbols, and that the symbols, including the cross, were actually driving some people away.

After a lot of discussion with members, Lawton decided to take down the cross and rename

the church *C3 Exchange* — *C3* from its former name, and *Exchange* from its location on Exchange Street and the exchange of ideas — and to promote it as an inclusive spiritual community without a central creed, welcoming people of "all faiths and no faith."

The outcry from the Religious Right was predictable and intense. As Chris Stedman (refer to Chapter 13) and others know all too well, when it comes to culture war, the middle is the hardest place to stand. I have boundless admiration for people like Ian and Chris who stand there anyway.

Fellowship, community, joining, belonging — why, it's the same list of reasons people actually go to church!

There's no end to the fascinating experiments in humanist community going on right now. A group called the Fellowship of Freethought unites more than 700 humanists and atheists in the Dallas, Texas area around a busy calendar of volunteering, improving their community, learning, and connecting with others. Texas is a particular proving ground for these unique communities, including the North Texas Church of Freethought, the Houston Church of Freethought, Atheists Helping the Homeless in Austin and Dallas, and many more. Scores of other nontheist groups across the United States are discovering the satisfaction of these other aspects of community, from the Humanist Community at Harvard in Cambridge, Massachusetts, to the Fellowship of Humanity in Oakland, California.

Finding other tribes

Many atheists and humanists talk about being "citizens of the world." It's a beautiful, positive way of getting past the us-versus-them mentality that causes so much grief between people. But I also have an undeniable human desire to find a tribe, a smaller group of people who are like me in some meaningful way. I need a community I can wrap my head around, one that gives me a sense of belonging.

I felt this in a big way during my first few weeks as a freshman in college. I was one of 32,000 undergraduates, and I felt lost. (Think of the way the word "lost" is used in religious terms, and you can start to see the human needs under the surface.)

But I wasn't just one of 32,000. I was also part of the college marching band, an organization of 160 students with more than a century of traditions, a common purpose, even its own values and principles, one that met on a regular basis and accomplished things together. It was my tribe. Sometimes when I'd walk across campus, I'd start to feel lost in the sea of humanity — then I'd see another bandsman and *boom!* I had an identity, a tribal connection.

You've probably experienced the same thing. Though different people feel the pull of community to different degrees, people are social, tribal animals, and belonging to some special, graspable corner of the human community can be really helpful. Sometimes I don't need it. When I'm feeling confident and successful, I can wade out into the world on my own with no problem. But when I'm feeling less confident, when things aren't going as well and the world's treating me like something sticky on the bottom of its shoe, that's when I seek out that special corner of people who care about and are connected to me.

For many people, church community provides this special corner, a tribe connected by shared beliefs. For others, including atheists, the glue of community can be a shared interest, such as hiking or volunteering or making music. Community can be a matter of geography, like neighbors in a neighborhood, or fans of the home football team. It can revolve around stated values, like the UU principles I mention earlier in this chapter ("Experimenting with humanist community"). Or it can simply be the connection and support of a close, caring family.

There's a downside to tribalism, of course. It can divide people — by beliefs, language, culture, nationality, whatever — and set them against each other. One of the biggest complaints many atheists have about religion is its strong tendency to do exactly that, dividing Catholics from Protestants, believers from nonbelievers, the saved from the damned. The best expressions of religion and irreligion alike work hard to widen the tribal circle to include all of humanity, even as individuals continue to define their own little comfortable corners of the tribe. Striking that balance, with or without religion, is one of the challenges of modern human life.

Celebrating Special Days

Like most people, nonbelievers enjoy the way celebrations of all kinds — birthdays, holidays, rites of passage — shape the curve of the year, mark life's most meaningful moments, and connect people to other people, other years, and other times in their lives. There's no end to the variety of ways nonreligious people can and do celebrate these special days without a hint of religion. I discuss a few of these ways in the following sections.

Enjoying the holidays

Holidays are a perfect opportunity to take the best of a religious concept and leave the theistic parts behind.

Many holidays were originally holy days. But any holy day that relates to natural human needs and emotions eventually develops a secular version as well, while the more specialized or weird holy days stay in an obscure corner of the church calendar. So the Feast of St. Polycarp, patron saint against earaches and dysentery, is a holy day but not a holiday, while the feast of St. Valentine, patron saint of love and marriage, makes the crossing to a secular celebration. And why not? Good things are worth borrowing. (Valentine was also patron saint of the plague, but very few chocolates are exchanged on that theme.)

Consider these holidays and perspectives:

- **Thanksgiving:** It's a particular favorite of mine. You may have heard that the hardest moment for an atheist is when he feels grateful but has no one to thank? Honestly, this isn't a problem. I'm a very lucky and deeply grateful guy, and I've never had any trouble finding real live people to thank. Even when the thing I'm grateful for doesn't have a human origin — a sunrise, my health, a quiet forest — there's no problem saying, "Wow, I'm so grateful" without having to point that gratitude *at* someone. And I love having a whole holiday to focus and express the unending gratitude I feel for this wonderful, astonishing life.

- **Christmas:** I'm also a big fan of Christmas, as are most of the atheists I know. Not all, of course — search online for *Tom Flynn Christmas* for the best atheist arguments against the holiday. But those atheists who enjoy it have no trouble doing so without a hint of religion. Honestly, I was about ten years old before I even found out there was a religious version.

The idea of a festival on or around the winter solstice predates Christianity by millennia. It's always made sense to gather with those you love and celebrate friends, family, generosity, and compassion in the depths of winter, and I delight in doing exactly that.

And oh, for the record — although an atheist or two may grumble or howl when someone wishes him or her Merry Christmas, most atheists don't mind in the least. In fact, some say they really celebrate "Krismas," the spirit of generous giving embodied by Kris Kringle. So when they say, "Merry Krismas," they're celebrating a different myth entirely! (I kind of love that a lot.) "Happy Holidays" is also lovely — a very nice attempt to include those who aren't Christians. Inclusiveness isn't an attack, folks. The "War on Christmas," like many other culture wars, is a fabrication — useful to some agendas and annoying to everyone else.

Then there are holidays with entirely natural roots. Because the Earth spins on a tilted axis, the days grow longer and the nights shorter for half of the year, then reverse for the other half. Deep poetry exists in feeling the swing of that planetary pendulum. On just two days a year, in the middle of those two cycles, day and night are balanced at 12 hours each — the spring and fall equinoxes. One is the beginning of the long sleep; the other signals the coming resurrection of life each year. I seem to recall that some religion somewhere has borrowed that idea for its own story. And why not? Good things are worth borrowing.

The list goes on — Earth Day, Halloween, the Mexican Day of the Dead, Hanukkah, Chinese New Year, even satirical holidays like Festivus. Nonbelievers and believers alike are free to celebrate what they want and skip what they don't.

Celebrating birth

Stopping to mark meaningful life transitions has been a part of human culture for as long as culture has been around — and I can't think of anything more meaningful and inspiring than the birth of a child. Some of the most moving ceremonies I've ever seen have welcomed a child into the world and into a caring family and community. Sometimes the child is held high as family and friends raise their hands high around her, symbolizing their support. Sometimes water is sprinkled, solemn or joyful words are spoken, and a rose or a book or a candle focus attention on the promise of a new life. It's powerful stuff.

Many of these rituals included reference to God and religion, but not all — and the religious element is never essential to create something meaningful. Family, community, and the wonder of an interconnected world all give every life context and meaning, regardless of a person's opinions about gods.

Unitarian Universalist fellowships and Ethical Culture societies are just two examples of communities with warm and meaningful dedication ceremonies full of emotion and symbolism — and reliably free of the supernatural.

There's also a growing tradition of humanist naming ceremonies. Held anywhere from birth to age two, these ceremonies often include readings — anything from Marcus Aurelius to Dr. Seuss — songs, and family stories. The centerpiece is often a description by one or both parents of the origin, meaning, and family significance of the child's name. My favorite part is the naming of one or two special adults — usually called "mentors" instead of godparents — who promise to be a source of support and guidance for the child.

Although christenings or baptisms declare a specific religious identity for the child, humanist-naming ceremonies don't declare the child to be an atheist or a humanist — at least none that I've seen. Autonomy is a very big deal in the freethought community, and the idea of calling a child a "Christian" or an "atheist" flies in the face of that value. Instead, humanist parents will often underline the importance of letting their children work out their beliefs for themselves. (Chapter 19 discusses more on parental approach.)

Coming of age

When I was about 13, I went through a serious bout of bar mitzvah envy. A Jewish friend had his, and I was hooked. Not with memorizing a chunk of the Torah or having to follow the 613 Commandments in the Law of Moses. (Eating raisins is one of the things forbidden, I kid you not.) What attracted me was the idea of going through this formal passage from childhood to adulthood. Sure, I was going through that transition myself already, but gradually. Having a *moment* is different; it's a time when your community says, "Okay, you're not a little kid any more. You have more privileges, but we also expect more from you. Now have some raisin-free cake."

The *quinceañera,* the celebration of a girls' fifteenth birthday in Latin American culture, is another such coming-of-age tradition. Once linked to Catholic ritual, it's more and more often celebrated secularly in recent years.

Unless you count a particular birthday — 16 maybe, or 18, or 21 — the transition into adulthood usually goes unmarked today. The main exceptions are religious denominations, where there's obviously a big religious component. The child isn't just becoming an adult, but also taking on a religious identity.

Some humanist groups around the world have created meaningful, human coming-of-age rituals. The trick as always is to keep the things religion has done well without the belief-pledging and raisin-banning bits. One of the most successful in the world is the Humanist Confirmation program in Norway. Each spring, more than 10,000 15-year-old Norwegians take a course about life philosophies and world religions, ethics and human sexuality, human rights and civic duties. At the end they receive a diploma at a moving ceremony with music, poetry, and inspirational speeches. They're confirmed not into atheism, but into an adulthood grounded in the human values that underlie civil society.

UUs and Ethical Culture have similar coming-of-age programs, focused on the things most important in that transition — ethics, civic responsibility, sexuality — without stepping on the young person's autonomy about worldview and other allegiances. It's a beautiful thing.

Getting hitched

Religious church weddings have been the default for centuries. But the last few generations have seen the growth of alternatives to the standard clergy in front, Pachelbel's Canon, What-God-has-joined-together, Love-is-patient-love-is-kind wedding. Beach weddings, Klingon weddings, heavy metal weddings . . . I once heard the actual vows delivered Green Eggs and Ham style ("And I will love you in the rain, and on a boat, and on a train"). And you know what? There wasn't a dry eye. It was a perfect reflection of the couple's funny and casual approach to life.

For many years, most nonbelievers still ended up getting married in front of a clergyman in a church, myself included. If I had it to do over, I might go for a humanist wedding led by a humanist celebrant — an officiant trained by a humanist organization to perform meaningful and memorable nontheistic ceremonies of all kinds.

Like naming ceremonies and other adapted rituals, humanist weddings allow a couple to create an event that's meaningful and appropriate for them without invoking religious traditions or a God they don't believe exists. Though still somewhat uncommon in North America, humanist weddings have recently become enormously popular in Europe. In Scotland, just to take a single example, more humanist weddings are now performed than Catholic weddings. And they're projected to pass weddings in the Church of Scotland, the largest church in the country, by 2015.

Until recently, marriages solemnized by humanist celebrants weren't considered legal in most US states. Even Elvis impersonators marrying people in Vegas had to get themselves church-ordained first. In case you're wondering if it has something to do with the strong glue religion is said to provide a marriage, consider the fact that in the United States:

- ✔ Twenty-seven percent of born-again Christians have been divorced, compared to
- ✔ Twenty-four percent of other Christians, and
- ✔ Only twenty-one percent of atheists and agnostics

Fortunately in recent years, humanist celebrants credentialed by such US-national organizations as the Humanist Society have received the green light to conduct marriages in all 50 US states.

Humanist weddings aren't always dramatically different from religious ones. They usually have readings and music, an exchange of vows and rings, and a gathering of witnesses. In some cases it's possible for Aunt Mildred to get all the way to the reception before she wrinkles her forehead and says, "Hey, wait a minute . . . " On the other hand, creating an event that doesn't look one bit like a traditional wedding is possible. That's one of the benefits of any step away from tradition — people can shape something new that fits the individuals involved better than the received tradition ever could.

And what better way to start a life together than by affirming only the things in which you actually believe?

Remembering the dead

You'd think nonreligious funerals would be sad events, and they most often are sad — just like religious funerals, but no more so. I've been to dozens of religious funerals, and despite the implication that the departed has now become a glorified being in the very Presence of the Creator, people cry — kind of a lot. That's because no matter what you think happens next, death is sad. One way or another, a loved person is no longer here.

A religious funeral is a mix of remembering a life and anticipating an afterlife. The funeral of an atheist doesn't have to pretend that death is just a doorway into the next room, so there's a greater focus on celebrating and reflecting on a life and how very much it matters that the person whose life has ended was here in the first place. The act of taking stock of the extraordinary ripples that one life leaves behind is a powerful reminder to the survivors of how much their own lives matter to those around them.

Like their religious counterparts, humanist funerals usually include music — John Lennon's "Imagine" is a favorite — readings, rituals, and remembrances by close friends and family.

Humanist funerals can tap a very different set of inspirations and reflections. Many include readings that touch on the human connection to the physical universe, the fact that every atom in the person's body has existed since the beginning of the universe, passing through and being transformed by countless stars, then ending up on Earth, in stones, rivers, plants, animals and people, before coming together, momentarily, to form this unique person and this unique life. Now that this life is over, those atoms go back into the Earth to build other plants and animals, other people, and eventually other planets and stars, until the end of time. It's one kind of eternal life — perhaps not what religious minds imagine, but in its way no less poetic or powerful.

Everyone should make their wishes known before they die to spare the uncertainty and guilt of loved ones about the choices they make for the funeral. This is especially important for anyone who isn't traditionally religious. I can hear my atheist friends now — "Hey, what do I care, I'll be dead and gone!" News flash to them: *Your funeral is not about you.* You'll be dead. And it's not even about sending a "message to the world" about dying without illusions. It's about the loved ones you'll leave behind.

When a person with a fairly conventional religious identity dies, the family has to make plenty of decisions, but those decisions mostly involve coloring within existing lines — *which* hymns will be sung, *which* Bible verses will be said, *which* church cemetery will receive the remains. If you aren't part of that defined tradition, your death can leave your family utterly without lines and uncertain even of which colors to reach for. They want to honor your wishes, but they don't know how, and you'll have thrown them into this time-sensitive situation in the midst of their grief. Guilt and confusion aren't helpful additives to grief. So I always encourage atheists to make their intentions crystal clear — even if it just means saying, "I really, truly don't care what you do. Whatever seems right to you is fine."

As with other ceremonies, humanist celebrants are available to help plan and carry out humanist funerals in every North American state and province and in several European countries. Just search online for "humanist celebrant."

Counseling and Support without Religion

Religious institutions have long undertaken the task of counseling people in desperate need, rarely allowing a lack of qualification or credentials to dissuade them from the adventure. Sometimes the results are effective; sometimes (celibate priests as marriage counselors, for example) not. Treatment of addiction and grief counseling are two areas that have been dominated by religious language and approaches. Both are arguably effective for believers. This section introduces attempts to treat addiction and counsel grief and loss without appeals to a higher power.

Kicking bad habits without a "higher power"

Many alcohol and drug addiction recovery programs start with a nonnegotiable requirement — to enter the program and get well, you must recognize a higher power. Six of the Twelve Steps of recovery published by Alcoholics Anonymous (AA) refer to God — "turn our will and our lives over to God," "admit to God," "humbly ask God," "pray for knowledge of God's will," and so on.

If God (or a "higher power") is essential for recovery, what's an addicted atheist to do?

Even though AA works for many people, there's been a strong backlash against the Twelve-Step method in recent years, including its claims that an alcoholic is "never cured, always recovering" and the language of religious submission, which many say replaces one kind of dependency with another. Organizations like Rational Recovery, SMART Recovery, and Secular Organizations for Sobriety have pioneered effective treatments for alcohol and substance abuse that don't require one to claim belief in a higher power.

A service called the Secular Therapist Project (www.seculartherapy.org) was recently launched to help nontheistic people find therapists of all kinds who share their secular worldview.

Consoling those who grieve

When consoling survivors after the death of a loved one, religion has a definite advantage — assuming the survivors have bought the idea of an afterlife. Nonbelievers feel that the most mature, honest, and respectful way to encounter death is by acknowledging that it really is the end of their individual existence, as much they might prefer otherwise, and by consoling those who grieve with love and human compassion.

You don't have to be an atheist to console an atheist. But if you believe in an afterlife, know that it's *extremely* disrespectful to try to nudge him or her toward belief as a way of coping, or to say a loss was part of God's plan, or to suggest that someone who died is "in a better place." No matter how kind the intentions, it ends up saying, "Your beliefs are hopelessly inadequate, so here are mine." You'll only add anger and resentment to the grief, which is unkind. In fact, many atheists point to the intrusion of religious beliefs into their grieving process as one of the most challenging and painful parts of the loss of a loved one.

Most important, it's simply not true that belief in an afterlife is necessary to navigate grief. You can draw entirely on these natural resources and techniques:

- ✔ Be compassionate toward others.
- ✔ Validate the person's sadness, and don't try to push them through it too quickly.
- ✔ Be present and supportive without intruding.
- ✔ Ask what you can do, or better yet, just do it.

✔ Make a meal, send a card, or give a hug.

✔ Share memories of the loved one who is gone and talk about the impact he or she had.

✔ If there was a painful illness, mention that the pain is over.

None of this is rocket science. It's the time-tested way all people endure what seems unendurable — by turning to each other.

A mutual support group called Grief Beyond Belief was formed in 2011 to provide a safe place for nonbelievers to discuss and express grief — one of the few resources of its kind. The well-moderated Facebook group currently has more than 6,000 likes and provides an atmosphere free of the supernatural consolations that dominate most grief forums.

Doing Good Together

That Harvard/Wisconsin study I mention at the beginning of the chapter (the one that found churchgoing has more to do with social connection than a God connection) also found another big benefit: People get a huge boost from doing good together, and their communities grow stronger as a result.

Obviously doing good has a benefit for whoever you're doing good *for*. If you volunteer at a food pantry, people get to eat. But it turns out that the community that's doing the good also receives a big benefit. Meeting a group of friends on a regular basis to do meaningful, positive things together acts as glue for the group and boosts the well-being of its members.

Volunteering through a church certainly qualifies — but so does volunteering through your local community group, service club, or humanist group. And sure enough, atheist and humanist groups around the country are making community service and volunteering an ever-larger part of what they do. And in the process, many are finding that their members are more likely to keep coming and to be active when doing good together is a bigger part of the group's identity. It's yet another example of taking the best of the church experience and leaving the rest behind.

Asking Whether Anything is Sacred

Reframing traditionally religious rituals and practices in secular terms can be pretty disorienting for someone who sees church and religion as being about God first and foremost. It might seem that the nonbelievers have stripped out everything sacred. What could possibly be left of any value?

I'd humbly suggest that all the things that I've tried to separate from God in this chapter are all still "sacred" things:

- ✔ Community
- ✔ Connection
- ✔ Common purpose
- ✔ Belonging
- ✔ Inspiration
- ✔ Coming together to do good

Not sacred in that untouchable, unquestionable way, of course. Question them all you want — they can take it. These things are sacred in a fully natural and human way, meaning special, awe-inspiring, and deserving of respect.

And that list goes on and on, including things that all humans regardless of beliefs can hold sacred by this definition. God and religion work just fine as frames, and they've done so for many centuries. But when they put themselves in place of things that are genuinely sacred, like life, integrity, knowledge, love, a sense of purpose, freedom of conscience, and more, and make themselves sacred in that inflexible, thought-stopping, "hands off" meaning of the word — well, that's when you've started loving frames more than pictures. That's the kind of sacred I'd say everyone can all do without.

When every idea is open to discussion and nothing is trapped in the amber of an ancient age, "sacred" becomes a matter of human consensus. Suddenly believers and nonbelievers can talk to one another on common ground, even as they go their separate ways on the question of God. That's the future, and it's looking bright.

Part V
The Part of Tens

The 5th Wave   By Rich Tennant

"I suppose it's just my way of finding meaning in an absurd and meaningless world."

In this part . . .

Every *For Dummies* book has this part with fun and short chapters with zippy lists of ten of this or ten of that. In this part, you can read about ten interesting facts about atheists you may not know, ten famous people who you probably didn't know were atheists, and ten easy and fun ways you can look further into atheism.

Chapter 19

Ten Surprising Things about Atheists and Other Nonbelievers

. . . .

In This Chapter

▶ Finding atheists in your own backyard . . . and in foxholes

▶ Getting beyond stereotypes

▶ Raising freethinkers, not atheists

▶ Cooperating with religious people

. . . .

*T*his chapter focuses on ten things that you may not know about atheists, agnostics, and other nonbelievers.

They're All Around You

Even without some visible clue, you may assume that everyone around you — every neighbor on the block, everyone cheering in the stands at the soccer game, even everyone in our own families — is part of the religious majority. After all, most people assume that all the atheists are somewhere "out there," massed together in New York and Hollywood, while all of the people around them hold conventional religious beliefs.

In fact, every country, every state or province, and every community in the world has nonbelievers, just as they all have people who are gay, dyslexic, or left-handed. Recent research reports that more than 50 million nonreligious people live in the United States. For every person wearing unbelief on his or her sleeve or Facebook page, many more choose to keep it to themselves. You can even find many of them bowing their heads at the dinner table or sitting in a church pew every Sunday. I should know — I was an atheist attending church out of family obligation for more than 20 years.

They're Growing in Number

The fastest growing "religious identity" in the developed world is people who have no religion. They're sometimes referred to as "Nones."

In fact, traditional religious belief has been rapidly declining in Europe. Since the 1950s, 19 European countries have gone from majority belief in God to majority nonbelief. In the United Kingdom, just 38 percent of the population still holds belief in God. France is at 34 percent, Sweden is 23 percent, and Estonia brings up the rear in traditional religious belief at 16 percent.

Irreligion is growing more slowly in North America, but it's still the fastest growing worldview. It's harder to measure in Canada, because 33 percent of Canadian Catholics and 28 percent of Canadian Protestants also say they don't believe in God. The most recent Pew Forum study in the United States shows that "no religion" grew from 1 in 12 in 1990 to 1 in 5 in 2012.

Even in Latin and South America, nonbelievers are growing rapidly in number. Five percent of Mexico, 8 percent of Brazil and Ecuador, 11 percent of Argentina, and 17 percent of Uruguay consists of nonbelievers.

They Know an Awful Lot about Religion

The more a person knows about religion, the less likely he or she is to be religious. This isn't always true, but as a general observation, it holds up.

The United States is extremely faithful but mostly uninformed. People *do* religion, but they don't know much *about* religion. Europeans are the opposite — they know a lot about religion and tend not to believe it. The more a person learns about religion in detail, the less religion seems to hold up.

The US Religious Knowledge Survey asked 32 questions to assess the religious knowledge of respondents. Protestants on average correctly answered 16, which was also the average for Americans overall. Catholics brought up the rear with 14.7 — below the US average.

Top honors went to atheists and agnostics, with an average of 20.9 correct. Not surprising, really. Most atheists would say that they didn't decide to learn about religion after they were atheists; it was the learning that led them to *become* atheists.

They Tend to Behave Themselves

You may assume that atheists, being free of the watchful eye of God, are fixtures on the Naughty List. This assumption is especially insulting to believers, because it implies they'd be racking up felonies if only God weren't so darn attentive.

Atheists are the ironic proof that this insult to believers isn't true. As I note in Chapter 15, nonbelievers tend to behave ethically by almost ever measure you can think of. The fact that those who specifically identify as atheists are 3 to 5 percent of the US population but only 0.09 percent of the federal prison population seems to support my claim. And as I note in Chapter 15, the least religious countries on Earth also have the lowest rates of violent crime and the highest rates of international aid to poor countries.

The real breakthrough comes when a religious believer discovers which of the many moral, ethical people in his or her life are atheists. Just like finding out someone you know and love is gay, personal experience trumps all the stats in the world.

They Have a Lot in Common with Everyone Else

Picking an atheist out of a lineup is harder than you'd think. And as "Nones" continue to grow and diversify, they resemble the general population even more in race, education, income, and politics. In the United States:

- Seventy-two percent of nonreligious Americans are white (69 percent of the US population overall is white).

- Eight percent of nonreligious Americans are black (compared to 11 percent of the United States overall).

- Twelve percent of nonreligious Americans are Hispanic (compared to 13 percent of the United States overall).

- In 1990, the nonreligious were a little more likely to have gone to college than the general population (51 to 41 percent). By 2008, that gap had almost disappeared (55 to 52 percent).

- They're on the national average for income — 52 percent of Nones have household incomes under $50,000. The national average is 53 percent.

- Thirty-four percent of American Nones are Democrats; the same as the US average. The nonreligious were the single largest belief bloc supporting Barack Obama's re-election in 2012.

✔ Only 13 percent of Nones are Republicans compared to 24 percent over-all in the United States. That's a huge drop since 1990, when 24 percent of the nonreligious were Republicans.

✔ Independents are the largest category of the nonreligious at 42 percent compared to 31 percent overall in the United States.

They Can Be Nice, Normal, and Funny

Picture an atheist. My bet is that you're picturing someone grumpy, humor-less, and above all, *weird.* You may be surprised to know that 73.2 percent of atheists are actually nice — 8 percent above the national average.

Okay fine, I don't really have stats on niceness per capita. But ever since I've been writing books about atheism and humanism, I've met hundreds if not thousands of atheists and humanists. Some of them have admittedly been grumpy, humorless, and/or weird, but no more than the average. I've also met atheists and humanists who are decent, thoughtful, generous, and kind people, though again, no more than the average. Because atheists are most often in the news when they're angry, people naturally think of them as angry. That's a bit like thinking of most planes as crashing, or most children as missing.

The best way to discover just how nice and normal nonbelievers can be is to discover how many of the nice, normal people you currently know are non-believers. If your circle of friends and relations is on the national average, that's about one in five of the people you know. (Check out Chapter 12 for how funny atheists can be.)

They're in Foxholes, Too

"There are no atheists in foxholes" is an expression that doesn't have much to do with reality. It implies that no matter what his or her actual convic-tions, everyone will grab at belief in God when a serious-enough crisis looms.

The deathbed is one kind of foxhole, and myths about deathbed conversions of atheists and agnostics have long been created to prop up the concept. Most end up being fabrications by a few unscrupulous believers. (See one famous example in Chapter 7.)

As for literal foxholes, the (US) Military Association of Atheists and Freethinkers — also known as the Foxhole Atheists — is living proof that this *aphorism* (concise proverb or saying) is false. More than 11,000 current US military personnel identify as atheists, including thousands of combat veter-ans, and more than 300,000 indicate "no religious preference."

Many military atheists endure a very high level of anti-atheist discrimination, including harassment and even death threats from peers and commanding officers. (For a sobering example of the harassment, or to discover more about atheists in foxholes, search online for "Jeremy Hall atheist" or visit www.militaryatheists.org.)

They Don't Usually Raise Their Kids to Be Atheists

Most atheists don't raise their kids as atheists. The vast majority create space around their kids so they can sort these things out for themselves.

Protecting my kids' autonomy is important to me. We teach values in our home — good stuff like honesty, openness, tolerance, curiosity, and empathy — but my kids get to decide in the long run what social and political and religious labels those add up to, if any.

The best way to preserve that autonomy is to keep labels off of kids entirely as they grow up. Calling a child an "atheist child" or a "Christian child" is as silly as calling him or her a "Marxist child" or a "Republican child." Even as strong an atheist as the biologist Richard Dawkins agrees with this. Complex worldview labels require a lot of thought and experience to mean anything. So I give my kids space and opportunities to talk to people of many beliefs, visit churches, and stay in control of their choices.

Most atheist parents seem to agree with me. In fact, two recent studies of parents in North America found that more than 90 percent of very religious parents said they raise their children specifically to believe as they believed, but less than 10 percent of the atheist parents said they raise their children as atheists. The rest said they wanted their children to decide for themselves.

They're Not More Worried about Death than the Religious

Death is certainly the hardest reality of human life. Entire worldviews have been constructed to deny that it even happens. Although atheists don't like the idea of dying, they don't tend to be any more upset about it than religious folks. And despite their afterlife ideas, all the religious people I know are plenty unhappy about the idea of dying. So I meet them in the middle, in the honest place where mortals confront mortality.

Nonexistence is hard for an existing person to grasp. But if you didn't exist before your conception, why should your nonexistence after death worry you? It's just the same. Nonexistence means no heaven, but it also means no hell. It's the total absence of troubles of worries, of pain. As Epicurus put it, "While I'm here, Death is not, and when Death is here, I will not be. Why be afraid of something I will never experience?"

Thinking about death in this and other ways can actually lead to a calm acceptance. That's why atheists are no more worried about it than believers.

They Often Seek to Coexist and Cooperate with Religious People

You've probably seen the bumper sticker that combines symbols of several religions to create the word *COEXIST*. Many of the people driving those cars are believers, but many others are atheists.

Many different kinds of atheists exist, and they have many different attitudes toward religion and the religious. Some are antitheists who want to see an end to all religion. They write most of the books and get most of the press. But most atheists and humanists recognize both the positive and negative expressions of religion, just as they recognize positive and negative expressions of politics, patriotism, even science. These atheists and humanists feel that religion will always be here in some form, and the best approach is to encourage it toward its more positive and productive forms, even while strongly protesting the negative ones. That's why many atheists participate in the interfaith movement and support nonproselytizing religious charities. That's why Unitarian Universalists and many others provide a space for believers and nonbelievers alike to gather around values they share instead of being divided by what they don't.

So the next time you hear an atheist protesting against a religious idea or practice, ask yourself what's really being said. Is he or she really trying to destroy religion, or asking that religious people not unfairly push others out of the culture? If you disagree, engage the conversation with all of your passion and intelligence, and know that the odds are pretty good that the atheist on the other side of the table is willing to coexist and cooperate with religion, so long as you can both talk about how best to do that.

Chapter 20

Ten (Plus One) Famous People You May Not Know are Nonbelievers

In This Chapter

▶ Finding out who doesn't believe

▶ Nailing down the evidence of their positions

*F*amous people aren't always free to be honest about their religious opinions, especially if those opinions have wandered off the apple-pie average. But as Cicero said in Chapter 4, admitting to religious doubt out loud can be hard, although it's easy to do so in a private conversation.

An important step in putting negative stereotypes of religious disbelief to rest is making it known that people who are already known and loved — whether famous, or friend, or family — is a nonbeliever. This chapter lists ten (plus one bonus) famous atheists or agnostics who have revealed their opinions, one way or another, and tells how they've revealed them. Most haven't been mentioned in earlier chapters in this book.

If you want to see a longer list of confirmed celebrity atheists and agnostics, check out www.celebatheists.com.

The Guy Who Wrote Slaughterhouse-Five

The great American novelist Kurt Vonnegut, Jr. (1922–2007), author of *Slaughterhouse-Five,* 13 other novels, and more than 120 short stories, once said in an interview that "for at least four generations my family has been proudly skeptical of organized religion."

He wore his disbelief lightly — not an unusual thing for those individuals who were raised without religion — but it was an important part of his identity. Vonnegut served as honorary president of the American Humanist Association and was named Humanist of the Year in 1992.

He defined his humanism in a letter to AHA members: "I am a humanist, which means, in part, that I have tried to behave decently without expectations of rewards or punishments after I am dead."

Vonnegut liked to invoke religion once in a while, especially if it was good for a laugh. At the funeral of science fiction writer Isaac Asimov, another famous atheist, Vonnegut said, "Isaac's in heaven now" — which he said brought down the humanist house — and he once referred to himself as a "Christ-worshipping agnostic."

His statement that "The only proof I need of the existence of God is music" was meant as an ironic tribute to music, not as a statement of belief in God — but when he died, multiple commentators leapt on that quote as proof that he had become a believer.

He hadn't, and in his later works he made that plenty clear. "I am an atheist (or at best a Unitarian who winds up in churches quite a lot)," he wrote in 1991's *Fates Worse than Death,* and said that religious doctrines were "so much arbitrary, clearly invented balderdash."

When asked how his study of anthropology had affected him, Vonnegut said, "It confirmed my atheism, which was the religion of my fathers anyway."

The First Female Prime Minister of Australia

When she first met Barack Obama, Australian Prime Minister Julia Gillard joked, "You think it's tough being the first African-American President? Try being the first atheist, childless, single woman prime minister."

Gillard came out as an atheist in 2010 during an interview in her first week in office. She said she didn't intend to go through religious rituals for the sake of appearances. "I am, of course, a great respecter of religious beliefs," she said, "but they are not my beliefs. For people of faith, I think the greatest compliment I could pay them is to respect their genuinely held beliefs and not to engage in some pretense about mine." The United States should be so lucky.

When several religious groups said they would not support her in the next election, opposition leader Tony Abbott, a Catholic, said personal religious convictions shouldn't be part of the decision to support a candidate. And once again, the United States should be so lucky.

The First Atheist Over the Rainbow

Yip Harburg, the man who wrote the screenplay for *The Wizard of Oz* and the lyrics for its songs including "Somewhere Over the Rainbow," was a complete nonbeliever.

"The House of God never had much appeal for me," he said. "Anyhow, I found a substitute temple — the theater."

Harburg's contributions go well beyond the yellow brick road. He became known as "Broadway's social conscience" for his Broadway lyrics, which delivered messages about inequality and suffering under cover of song. "Brother, Can You Spare a Dime?" became an anthem of the Great Depression, while *Hooray for What!* (1937) was a musical protest against war and *Bloomer Girl* (1944) explored anti-racist and pro-feminist themes that were way ahead of the times.

In the 1950s, the House Un-American Activities Committee blacklisted Harburg for his political views — a badge of honor if ever there was one.

Harburg wasn't the only religious skeptic tied to *The Wizard of Oz*. Novelist Frank Baum, who wrote the book on which the movie was based, was of the same opinions. And (as I mention in Chapter 21) the story itself can be seen as a tale about turning away from dependence on a God (the Wizard) to realize that humanity can and does provide all the brains, courage, heart, and home it needs.

The First Woman on US Currency

Like most freethinkers, the religious opinions of women's rights pioneer Susan B. Anthony (1820–1906) changed over the course of her lifetime. Born into an orthodox Quaker family, she eventually joined a Unitarian church.

As her involvement in women's rights issues increased, she came to see all organized religion as an impediment to those rights. By the 1880s, she identified as an agnostic.

Her friend and collaborator Elizabeth Cady Stanton confirmed this in 1896, writing, "To-day, Miss Anthony is an agnostic."

Though several of the feminist leaders around her were more open about their atheist or agnostic views, Anthony had reason to keep her own cards close to the vest. Ernestine Rose (refer to Chapter 7) was open about her atheism and was constantly attacked for it, including having halls refuse to allow her to speak. Anthony's main goal was securing the vote for women, and she didn't want her religious doubt to distract from that, so she learned from the experience of others and mostly kept mum.

But she did speak up in their defense as needed. When an angry crowd at a women's rights convention called Stanton an atheist and claimed that God wanted her removed from leadership, Anthony took the floor. "I distrust those people who know so well what God wants them to do to their fellows," she said, "because it always coincides with their own desires." Boy, that's a good line.

The American public was momentarily made aware of Susan B. Anthony in 1979 when her face ended up on an odd little dollar coin that went out of circulation 20 years later. It's just as well — seeing Susan with "In God We Trust" etched beneath her nose was a bit hard to take.

Ten Points for Gryffindor!

Actor Daniel Radcliffe, who played Harry Potter in the films of the same name, was raised by a Jewish mother and a Protestant Christian father. But he says his upbringing wasn't very religious, and by age 12, he identified as an atheist, having decided that his only motivation for belief was fear — and that that wasn't a good reason to believe.

It was in a 2009 interview with *Esquire* magazine that Radcliffe confirmed his beliefs clearly. "I'm an atheist," he said, "but I'm very relaxed about it. I don't preach my atheism, but I have a huge amount of respect for people like Richard Dawkins who do."

"My dad believes in God, I think," he said in another interview. "I'm not sure if my mom does. I don't. I have a problem with religion or anything that says, 'We have all the answers,' because there's no such thing as 'the answers.' We're complex. We change our minds on issues all the time. Religion leaves no room for human complexity."

This of course played right into the accusations of the Religious Right in the United States, which had long pegged the *Harry Potter* films as anti-Christian. As a result of the backlash, the *Potter* films had to settle for being the most successful film franchise in movie history.

An A-List Actor and Philanthropist

Brad Pitt, who has made his name both as an A-list actor and as a compassionate philanthropist, is also an agnostic atheist.

When asked in an interview with the German magazine *Bild* if he believes in God, Pitt smiled and said, "No, no, no!"

"But is your soul spiritual?" the interviewer persisted.

"No, no, no!" said Pitt. "I'm probably 20 percent atheist and 80 percent agnostic. I don't think anyone really knows. You'll either find out or not when you get there, until then there's no point thinking about it."

He elaborated in a *Parade* magazine interview: "I don't mind a world with religion in it. There are some beautiful tenets within all religions. I grew up Baptist, and then the family switched over to more of an evangelical movement, probably right around the time I was in late high school. There's a point where you're untethered from the beliefs of your childhood. That point came for me when it was finally clear my religion didn't work for me. I had questions about Christianity that I could not get answered to my satisfaction, questions that I'd been asking since I was in kindergarten. I realized it didn't feel right to me, that one question just led to another. It was like going down a rabbit hole, each answer provoking another question. There were things I didn't agree with."

Pitt has made an enormous impact in the world of philanthropy. He founded the Make It Right Foundation in 2006 to finance the construction of 150 affordable houses in New Orleans's Ninth Ward after Hurricane Katrina and donated $5 million to support the project.

The same year, he and Angelina Jolie established the Jolie-Pitt Foundation to support humanitarian work globally, donating more than $8 million through the foundation in its first year.

The Founder of Ms. Magazine

Feminist political activist Gloria Steinem (b. 1934) rose to prominence as the face of feminism in the late 1960s and 1970s, founding *Ms.* magazine and articulating a clear and powerful message of gender equality. And like so many feminist pioneers before her, Steinem is nontheistic.

Like Susan B. Anthony, Steinem has always been careful not to let her personal religious view distract from women's issues. But when asked directly, she's always been clear.

"By the year 2000 we will, I hope, raise our children to believe in human potential, not God," she said in one interview. Though humanity didn't quite make the deadline, there's always hope for the future.

She expressed particular scorn for the whole idea of pleasing God to secure a seat in the afterlife. "It's an incredible con job when you think about it, to believe something now in exchange for something after death," she said. "Even corporations with their reward systems don't try to make it posthumous."

An Actual No-Kidding Bishop

One of the most puzzling characters in the nontheistic parade is John Shelby Spong (b.1930), a liberal theologian and retired Episcopal Bishop of Newark, New Jersey. Because he's a man of the cloth who doesn't believe in the existence of a supernatural God, he's a modern-day version of Jean Meslier, the atheist priest I discuss in Chapter 10.

There is one big difference between Meslier and Spong: Bishop Spong made his beliefs known while he was still in the active clergy, then continued to preach and teach despite the fact that he found most of the major Christian beliefs unbelievable.

For example:

- ✔ He doesn't believe in miracles.
- ✔ He doesn't believe there is an afterlife.
- ✔ He doesn't believe that Jesus was God or that he was resurrected.
- ✔ He doesn't believe in God as a supernatural being, period.

Despite that last one, he insists he's not an atheist but a nontheist. Even after reading much of his work, I'm not sure what he means. You can safely say that he isn't a believer in any conventional idea of God. Some have suggested he's best described as a believer in religion.

Spong has written several books including *Rescuing the Bible From Fundamentalism* and *Why Christianity Must Change or Die,* all devoted to keeping Christianity but freeing it from the idea of a supernatural god. In its place, Spong proposes the idea of God as the impulse that calls us to love one another.

"Theism, as a way of conceiving God, has become demonstrably inadequate," he said in that last book, "and the God of theism not only is dying but is probably not revivable. If the religion of the future depends on keeping alive the definitions of theism, then the human phenomenon that we call religion will have come to an end. If Christianity depends on a theistic definition of God, then we must face the fact that we are watching this noble religious system enter the rigor mortis of its own death throes."

Like Chris Stedman and Greg Epstein and Unitarian Universalism (check out Chapter 9 and 13 for more information), Spong is standing in the middle, which is a very difficult place to be. I have tremendous admiration for people who can manage it, even when I disagree with them or (in the case of Spong) when I can't figure out quite what they're trying to say.

The World's Coolest Astronomer

One of the most popular and influential communicators of science today is astrophysicist Neil deGrasse Tyson (b. 1958). Considered by many to be the heir to the mantle of the great science popularizer Carl Sagan, Tyson walks that tricky tightrope between academic science and popular science, and does so beautifully.

Tyson has been careful not to allow his religious skepticism to define him or to dominate his message about the wonder and importance of science. But when religious ideas step on scientific ones, as with "intelligent design theory," he's quick to respond.

When an interviewer asked Tyson if he believed in a higher power, he answered with typical thoughtfulness: "Every account of a higher power that I've seen described, of all religions that I've seen, include many statements with regard to the benevolence of that power. When I look at the universe and all the ways the universe wants to kill us, I find it hard to reconcile that with statements of beneficence."

Asked about early accounts of astronomy, he said, "A careful reading of older texts, particularly those concerned with the universe itself, shows that the authors invoke divinity only when they reach the boundaries of their under-standing. They appeal to a higher power only when staring into the ocean of their own ignorance. They call on God only from the lonely and precarious edge of incomprehension. Where they feel certain about their explanations, however, God gets hardly a mention."

In an interview on the *Point of Inquiry* podcast, Tyson described himself as an agnostic.

One of the World's Richest (and Most Generous) People

Billionaire investor and philanthropist Warren Buffett (b. 1930) is the first, second, or third richest person on Earth, depending on what day it is. He's also one of the most generous, having pledged to give at least 85 percent of his wealth away to charity, mostly through the Bill and Melinda Gates Foundation.

Buffett's attitude toward religion was revealed in the 1995 biography *Buffett: The Making of an American Capitalist:* "He did not subscribe to his family's religion. Even at a young age he was too mathematical, too logical, to make the leap of faith. He adopted his father's ethical underpinnings, but not his belief in an unseen divinity."

Several years later, the humanist activist Warren Allen Smith wrote to Buffett, asking him to confirm his beliefs. Buffett returned a postcard with a single word on it: "Agnostic."

An Actress, Activist of the First Rank, and another Harry Potter Alum

Academy Award-winning British actress and screenwriter Emma Thompson (b. 1959) is well-known for acting in or writing screenplays for such notable films as *Howard's End, Sense and Sensibility, Love Actually, Nanny McPhee,* and the *Harry Potter* series.

Less commonly known is her political and environmental activism, including her service as a patron of the Refugee Council and her ambassadorship with ActionAid, for whom she travels internationally to draw attention to poverty in the developing world.

Thompson has made her religious disbelief refreshingly clear. In a 2008 interview with *The Australian,* she said, "I'm an atheist; I suppose you can call me a sort of libertarian anarchist. I regard religion with fear and suspicion. It's not enough to say that I don't believe in God. I actually regard the system as distressing: I am offended by some of the things said in the Bible and the Koran, and I refute them."

Chapter 21

Ten Fun and Easy Ways to Explore Atheism

. . . .

. . . .

*W*ant to explore the world of religious doubt and disbelief even further? This chapter is a short guide to doing just that.

Read the Books

Atheists may not believe in God, but they certainly believe in books — and they spend a ridiculous amount of time between their covers. In fact, it's one of the two places most of them learned to be atheists. (The other place is church.)

I introduce many great works related to religious disbelief in Part III of this book and elsewhere, and you can search online for countless more. Here are a few more of my personal favorites:

- ✔ *The Demon-Haunted World: Science as a Candle in the Dark* **(Random House/Ballantine):** Carl Sagan wrote this passionate cry against superstition and in favor of reason.

- ✔ *Against All Gods: Six Polemics on Religion, and an Essay on Kindness* **(Oberon):** A.C. Grayling drafted these 64 pages of solid gold.

- *The Portable Atheist: Essential Readings for the Nonbeliever* (Da Capo): Christopher Hitchens authored this collection of short, brilliant writings by nonbelievers.

- *Infidel* (Free Press): It's a gripping retelling of Ayaan Hirsi Ali's escape from an arranged marriage, leaving Islam, and becoming one of the world's most prominent atheists.

- *Religion Explained* (Basic Books): Anthropologist Pascal Boyer explains just what religion is and why we have it.

- *Holy Writ as Oral Lit: The Bible as Folklore* (Rowman & Littlefield): My favorite folklorist, Alan Dundes, shows how the Bible evolved from oral to written tradition.

- *Unweaving the Rainbow: Science, Delusion, and the Appetite for Wonder* (Houghton Mifflin Harcourt): Not Richard Dawkins's most-often-read book, but it's one of my very favorites. It challenges the wrongheaded idea that understanding something diminishes the wonder of it.

- *The Magic of Reality: How We Know What's Really True* (Free Press): Also by Richard Dawkins, he wrote it for young adults, but it's entirely worthwhile for old adults as well.

Follow Blogs, Pods, and Vlogs

Blogs, podcasts, and video logs online are the real way to keep up with the current goings-on in the freethought community. Some are happy to offend and spoiling for a fight; others want to give peace a chance. And of course there's everything in between. Search these names for today's voices of unbelief:

- **Chewing on the big issues:** Daylight Atheism, Atheist Ethicist, Greta Christina's Blog, New Humanism, Skepchick, Rationally Speaking, Black Agenda Report, American Freethought podcast

- **Responding to the news of the day:** Friendly Atheist, Butterflies and Wheels, Blag Hag, Pharyngula, What Would JT Do?

- **Talking doubt to the camera:** Cristina Rad, Pat Condell, the Atheist Experience

- **The former Muslim perspective:** Maryam Namazie, AHA Foundation

- **In categories all their own:** Epiphenom — the science of religion and nonbelief, Symphony of Science videos, Why Won't God Cure Amputees?, NonProphet Status

As always, this list is abbreviated. But go to almost any atheist or humanist blog and you can find a blogroll in the sidebar listing other recommended voices.

Listen to the Music

The British-Australian musician/comedian/atheist Tim Minchin got a shout in Chapter 12, but I really can't talk about music and unbelief without mentioning Minchin one more time.

To hear a beautiful anthem for the humanist heart, go to YouTube and find Minchin's song "White Wine in the Sun." For some funny, fairly mild parodies of religious belief, find the songs "WoodyAllenJesus," "The Good Book," and "Peace Anthem for Palestine." Need a little more spice? Listen to "My Neighbor's Ass" (relax, it's about the Tenth Commandment). And if you're entirely unoffendable, check out "The Pope Song."

For more laughs, find and enjoy the music of Roy Zimmerman. And for songs of hope, anger, and joy from the atheist perspective, there's Shelley Segal's *An Atheist Album*.

Finally there's the one song so simple, so beautiful, and with such universal appeal that people all around the world can't stop singing it, even though it's a dream of a world without religion: John Lennon's "Imagine."

Think about Thinking

Nothing has a greater potential to change the way you see yourself and the world than a good self-taught course in how people think. Discovering how the human brain has evolved, how ancient fears drive their behaviors and beliefs, and how confirmation bias affects people's decision making and changes the way people see the world is fascinating (and a little scary).

Over the course of centuries, some great thinkers have developed the principles and tools of critical thinking so people can get past obstacles and see the world clearly when so inclined. These principles aren't hard to understand, and they empower individuals — as consumers, as citizens, as parents, and as human beings.

How We Know What Isn't So by Thomas Gilovich (Free Press) and *Don't Believe Everything You Think: The 6 Basic Mistakes We Make in Thinking* by Thomas Kida (Prometheus Books) are great introductions to the topic. Neither is written from an atheist perspective, but the principles they describe are the principles by which many atheists thought their way out of religion.

The books of Michael Shermer, including *Why People Believe Weird Things* (Holt) and *The Believing Brain* (Times Books), are more specifically related to religious belief and disbelief — and come down on the side of the latter.

Be Touched by His Noodly Appendage

There's no better peek you can get inside the head of atheism than the Church of the Flying Spaghetti Monster. This fun and clever "belief system" was created in 2005 by a 20-something wiseacre named Bobby Henderson in response to the decision by the Kansas Board of Education to allow creationism to be taught alongside evolution in Kansas science classrooms. So glad to hear you're teaching the controversy, said Henderson. But why stop there? You'll also want to include my belief that a Flying Spaghetti Monster created the world.

Originally intended as a one-shot parody with a point, FSMism (or Pastafarianism) is now its own full-blown religion, neither more nor less strange than any other, with its own scripture, founding myth, rituals, obsessions, loves and hates, and loopy logic. Chapters of the church have sprung up around the world, especially on college campuses. (For more on Pastafarianism, flip to Chapter 12.)

Read the Bible

Science fiction novelist and atheist Isaac Asimov once said that the Bible, properly read, is the most potent force for atheism ever conceived. "Properly read" means you read it yourself — don't take cherry-picked verses from Reverend Lovejoy *or* from Christopher Hitchens. If the whole thing is too daunting, get a good start by reading just Genesis and Matthew, perhaps the two most influential books, then go from there. Read with an open mind, as if you're encountering it for the first time. You won't believe what you find. And you'll get an unbeatable insight into the minds of those who've set it all aside.

To take it to the next level with dueling commentary, read the New International Version, with lots of explanatory footnotes from the Christian perspective, and consult the Skeptic's Annotated Bible online for an entirely different slant.

Watch Letting Go of God

When I'm asked for the best intro to atheism, especially for non-atheists, I highly recommend Julia Sweeney's funny, personal, brilliant monologue *Letting Go of God.* Available on DVD, this astonishing one-woman show begins as the actress/comedian describes her Catholic childhood. Far from hating and resenting it, Sweeney loved being Catholic. But many years later, a doorstep visit from two nice Mormon boys with an incredibly strange and upsetting theology gets her wondering whether her own belief system is really any better. She decides she wants more than anything to know the truth about the world and starts with a close look at her own church.

The bright, honest light doesn't flatter the church she's identified with all her life, and she starts circling out into other religions — first the usual suspects, then some less familiar Eastern faiths. And once again, the closer she looks, the worse it all appears.

Finally she begins a crash course in science — biology, astronomy, geology, and more — and the contrast is incredible. She eventually shows God the door, with tenderness but no regrets.

The two-hour masterpiece is never preachy or pushy. It's one very human person's process — moving, self-deprecating, hilarious — of letting go of God. You aren't likely to find a better first glimpse of atheism (except the one you're holding, of course).

Watch Other Movies That Challenge Beliefs or Explore a Natural Worldview

You can pop some other films into the queue that open a different, challenging window on religion. A few favorites include the following:

- ✔ *The Wizard of Oz:* You heard me. Frank Baum (who wrote the book) was a religious skeptic and Ethical Culturist. Yip Harburg (who wrote the screenplay and songs) was an atheist. It's not hard to see the whole story as a parable about turning away from dependence on a god (the Wizard) and realizing all the brains, courage, heart, and home humanity seeks from God has always been right in their own hands. Atheism is all about paying attention to the man behind the curtain. (For much more, search online for *Wizard of Oz atheism*.)

- ✔ *Inherit the Wind:* A fictionalized treatment of the 1925 Scopes "Monkey Trial." Not to be missed.

- ✔ *Jesus Camp:* A 2006 documentary about a Christian evangelical summer camp near Devil's Lake, North Dakota where children learn to "take back America for Christ."

- ✔ *Contact:* Written by scientist Carl Sagan (agnostic) and starring Jodie Foster (atheist), this 1997 film depicts the first contact with alien life and the philosophical and religious implications for those involved.

- ✔ *Dogma:* Two angels kicked out of heaven find a loophole to get back in, but walking through that loophole just may end the universe. Adult language (and just about everything else).

✔ *The Invention of Lying:* Directed by British atheist Ricky Gervais, this movie imagines a world in which no one ever lies. When one man learns how to lie, he bends it to his advantage, including the fib that death isn't the end.

✔ *Life of Brian:* One of the best religious satires of all time. It sends up not Jesus but the Messiah fever that was rampant in first century Judea, and the fallible humans who simply can't help mucking up the message.

Talk to an Atheist

The best way to find out more about atheism is to talk to an atheist. Nothing cuts through the misunderstandings and assumptions like a face-to-face chat.

Many religious people who know they have atheists in their families aren't sure if they should bring it up in conversation. Sometimes they just don't want to make the person uncomfortable. But trust me — whenever a religious friend or relative asks me about my point of view, I'm delighted. It almost always ends up being a wonderful, door-opening conversation. Just prepare to see your own beliefs from an entirely new perspective.

Join the Club

If you're an atheist, agnostic, humanist, skeptic, freethinker, what have you — you may consider joining the club!

A number of national and international organizations exist with different missions, flavors, and emphases. Some examples from countries around the world are as follows:

✔ **British Humanist Association** (www.humanism.org.uk): "Working on behalf of non-religious people who seek to live ethical and fulfilling lives on the basis of reason and humanity."

✔ **National Secular Society** (www.secularism.org.uk): Charles Bradlaugh (see Chapter 7) founded this organization in 1866. It campaigns for the separation of religion and state in the United Kingdom and "promote[s] secularism as the best means to create a society in which people of all religions or none can live together fairly and cohesively."

✔ **American Atheists** (www.atheists.org): Madalyn Murray O'Hair (see Chapter 8) founded this US organization, which is "dedicated to defending the civil liberties of atheists while advocating for the complete separation of church and state."

✔ **American Humanist Association** (www.americanhumanist.org): This association serves as "a voice for Humanism in the United States; to increase public awareness and acceptance of Humanism; to establish, protect, and promote the position of humanists in our society; and to develop and advance humanist thought and action."

✔ **Atheist Alliance International** (www.atheistalliance.org): "A global federation of atheist and freethought groups and individuals, committed to educating its members and the public about atheism, secularism and related issues." See also its sister organization, Atheist Alliance of America (www.atheistallianceamerica.org).

✔ **Center for Inquiry** (www.centerforinquiry.net): Philosopher Paul Kurtz (see Chapter 8) founded this center "to foster a secular society based on science, reason, freedom of inquiry, and humanist values."

✔ **Foundation Beyond Belief** (www.foundationbeyondbelief.org): This membership organization comprises compassionate humanists supporting charities and volunteering in their communities.

✔ **Humanist Canada** (www.humanists.ca): This Canadian national organization founded in 1968, "promotes the separation of religion from public policy and fosters the development of reason, compassion, and critical thinking for all Canadians through secular education and community support."

✔ **International Humanist and Ethical Union** (www.iheu.org): This umbrella organization was founded in 1952 in Amsterdam to represent humanist, atheist, rationalist, secular, skeptic, freethought, and Ethical Culture organizations around the world and to promote humanist values.

✔ **Society for Humanistic Judaism** (www.shj.org): This group was founded by Rabbi Sherwin Wine (see Chapter 8) "to mobilize people to celebrate Jewish identity and culture consistent with a humanistic philosophy of life, independent of supernatural authority."

✔ **Freedom from Religion Foundation** (www.ffrf.org): Anne Gaylor and Annie Laurie Gaylor founded this organization "to promote the separation of church and state and to educate the public on matters relating to atheism, agnosticism and nontheism." This group often serves as the legal arm of the freethought movement.

✔ **United Coalition of Reason** (www.unitedcor.org): This US-national organization works to raise the visibility of local nontheistic groups by promoting the fact that nontheists live in every community and by facilitating communication and cooperation among local nontheistic groups.

✔ **American Ethical Union** (www.aeu.org): Social reformer Felix Adler (see Chapter 7) founded this ethical religious movement without creed to promote the idea that living in accordance with ethical principles is central to living a meaningful and fulfilling life and dedicated to creating a world that is good for all.

✔ **Atheist Centre** (www.atheistcentre.in): Ramachandra Rao (better known as Gora, see Chapter 8) and his wife Saraswathi Gora founded this institution founded in 1940 to promote positive social change in India.

Of course the community and connectedness I describe in several chapters of this book happen not at the national and international level, but right there in your local community. Most large cities and many small ones have local freethought organizations. It's a terrific opportunity to meet others who share your worldview, exchange ideas, socialize, and work together to improve your community as an expression of what you believe, which makes sense because no one is up there to do it. To find these local groups, just search online for your city and the words "atheist," "humanist," or "freethought."

If you don't live in a city (or even if you do), meetup.com is a great way for people with shared interests to find each other. Many of the largest groups on Meetup are atheist and humanist groups.

Index

• *N* •